KENYA I

(1902–1

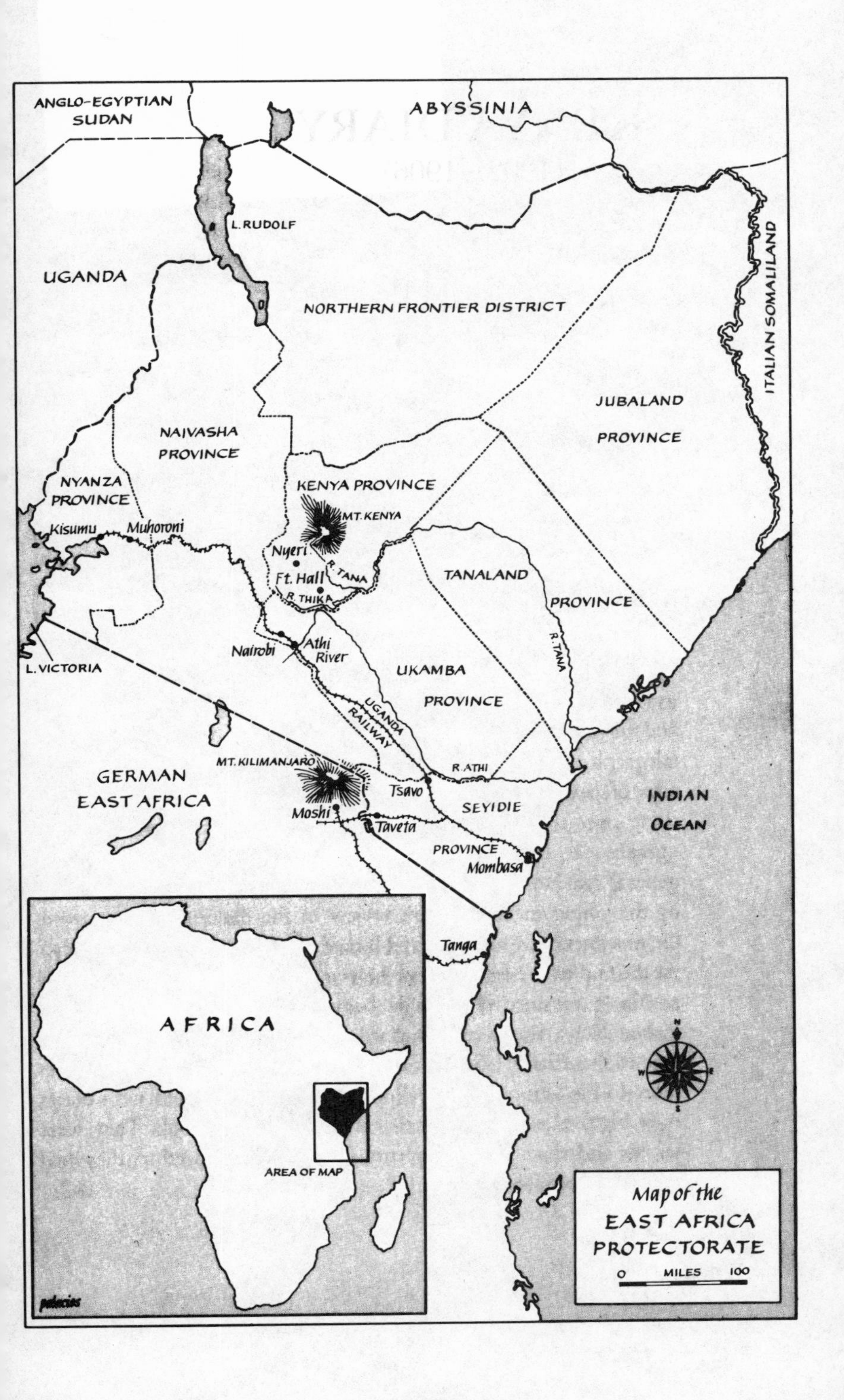

ANGLO-EGYPTIAN SUDAN
ABYSSINIA
L. RUDOLF
UGANDA
NORTHERN FRONTIER DISTRICT
ITALIAN SOMALILAND
JUBALAND PROVINCE
NAIVASHA PROVINCE
NYANZA PROVINCE
KENYA PROVINCE
MT. KENYA
Kisumu
Muhoroni
Nyeri
Ft. Hall
R. TANA
R. THIKA
TANALAND PROVINCE
Nairobi
Athi River
L. VICTORIA
UKAMBA PROVINCE
UGANDA RAILWAY
MT. KILIMANJARO
R. ATHI
GERMAN EAST AFRICA
Tsavo
SEYIDIE PROVINCE
Moshi
Taveta
Mombasa
INDIAN OCEAN
Tanga
AFRICA
AREA OF MAP
N
W
E
S
Map of the
EAST AFRICA
PROTECTORATE
0 MILES 100
palacios

KENYA DIARY
(1902–1906)

RICHARD MEINERTZHAGEN

With a new preface by Elspeth Huxley

ELAND BOOKS, LONDON
&
HIPPOCRENE BOOKS, INC., NEW YORK

Published by
ELAND BOOKS
53 Eland Road London SW11 5JX
&
HIPPOCRENE BOOKS, INC.,
171 Madison Avenue, New York, NY 10016

First published in 1957 by
Oliver and Boyd, Edinburgh

ISBN 0 907871 10 0
First published in this paperback edition 1983
Reprinted 1984

Printed and bound in Great Britain
by Redwood Burn Ltd, Trowbridge, Wiltshire.

PREFACE TO 1983 EDITION

IT WOULD be useless to pretend that this is a pleasing book or that its author emerges from it as a sympathetic character. Richard Meinertzhagen was a killer. He killed abundantly and killed for pleasure. The diary of the five years he spent in the East Africa Protectorate, as the present Kenya was then called, when a young officer attached to the King's African Rifles, is filled with records of the animals he killed for sport and the tribesmen he killed for duty. These extracts from his diaries were not published until fifty years after their composition. Meinertzhagen himself admits to feeling shocked when, in his old age, he re-read the record. But he did not excuse it. "I have no belief in the sanctity of human life or in the dignity of the human race," he wrote. "In Kenya fifty years ago, when stationed with a hundred soldiers amid an African population of some three hundred thousand, in cases of emergency where local government was threatened we had to act, and act quickly. To do nothing in an emergency is to do something definitely wrong, and talking comes under the category of 'nothing.' Thank God there was no time or opportunity for talks, conferences and discussions."

It is hard to imagine a sentiment more out of keeping with the notions of today. One has only to dip into these diaries to apprehend how profound has been the revolution in our attitudes within the lifetime of many still alive. "When I arrived in the country I was obsessed by an unashamed bloodlust," he writes. "Hunting is man's primitive instinct and I indulged it to the full." Today the tally of slaughtered animals, then present in such astonishing abundance, seems nauseating. Most of the wild animals he shot, it is true, went to provide meat for soldiers and porters, but by no means all. He had only to see an animal, provided he was reasonably sure it was a male, to shoot it. Yet – and this is a recurrent paradox – he was an excellent naturalist, and in later life became an ornithologist of world repute.

But it is when he comes to killing people that his attitude seems most out of keeping with current views. He was, of course, a soldier trained to kill when necessity arose. Today we feel that soldiers, although killing is their trade, ought not actively to enjoy it. Meinertzhagen generally did. He was a bold and fearless young man who relished danger, excitement and the exercise of lethal skills. The record of tribal warriors shot or bayoneted – and even of his own men, when they disobeyed his orders – makes gruesome reading. Here, in its nakedness, is an aspect of what would nowadays be called the unacceptable face of colonialism.

Unacceptable or not, it happened, and therefore must be accepted as a fact of history. The merit of this book, I think, lies in its honesty. Here is a day-to-day account of what it was like to be a young British officer commanding native troops, living in lonely stations among tribesmen still following patterns of life set by their ancestors and almost unchanged for centuries. Tribe was continually at war with tribe, or with other sections of the same tribe; warriors went forth with spear and bow-and-arrow to carry off their neighbours' livestock and women; literacy was unknown, superstition rife, and almost all those aids to be a more civilised way of life were lacking. A great gulf then separated the pale and dark skinned races. Now it has been bridged by education.

There is much in this book that will give offence to the one race, and cause pain to the other. When Meinertzhagen went to East Africa in 1902, the European nations were proud of, not penitent about, their empires. The imperial heyday might be drawing to its close, but few people as yet knew it. Much has since been written about the exploitation, greed, oppression and general wickedness inherent in colonialism, but most white people at the time believed that the men they sent out to administer and police these distant lands were bringing gifts, not snatching prizes, and in particular the gift of law and order, to people who had hitherto got on without it, but had not got on very far. Although Meinertzhagen found plenty to criticise in the way the Protectorate was being run, he never doubted that the *Pax Britannica* would be better than the existing state of affairs for everyone, including the Africans – the Africans most of all. You can't make an omelette, he might have said, without breaking eggs. And you might as well enjoy, if you can, smashing the eggshells.

If, today, the white man's burden has become a burden of guilt, there is little here of comfort for the black man either. No one likes to be told that his ancestors were savages with certain nasty habits and uncivilised ways. I have little doubt but that a Romanized Briton, living in luxury in a villa equipped with hypocausts, baths and tesselated floors, fluent in the Roman tongue, clothed in the Roman toga and given, perhaps, to quoting from the odes of Horace, did not care to be reminded that his early British ancestors were clothed in skins and woad, lived in miserable huts and were generally ignorant of the refinements of life in Rome. So may today's African Minister, senior civil servant, banker, academic or whatever, living in luxury in a Nairobi villa and with a chauffeur-driven limousine, resent Meinertzhagen's unadorned descriptions of the life-style of his tribal ancestors. Time, I feel sure, will mellow this resentment; might it even bring about a reversal of attitudes? Just as the self-made man will boast of his rise from humble origins, so may the Westernized African come to take pride in the speed and wit with which so many of his people have crossed the cultural gulf to which I have already referred.

If Meinertzhagen never doubted the need to impose and enforce the rule of law, he by no means despised the African tribesmen. For one thing, their warriors were brave. For another, he came to hold views opposed to those of his masters on the policy of inviting white settlers to take up apparently unoccupied land in order, by introducing efficient methods of farming, to develop the country. With a prescience remarkable in a young subaltern writing some eighty years ago, he told the Commissioner, Sir Charles Eliot, that "the country belongs to Africans and their interests must prevail over those of strangers." One day, he added, Africans would be educated and then there would be trouble, especially among the Kikuyu. When "medicine men are replaced by political agitators there will be a general rising." The fact that fifty years elapsed before the publication of these diaries, by which time the Mau Mau revolt had taken place, has awakened questions in some people's minds. Could he really have been so wise so long before the event? The whereabouts, if any, of the original diaries is unknown; those preserved in the Rhodes House Library in Oxford are typescript copies. But he was an intelligent man, and a knowledge of history need not be profound to suggest that conquered peoples, if not all but exterminated (like the Red Indians in North America) or eventually absorbed (like the Normans in Britain), will sooner or later get rid of their conquerors. Meinertzhagen's presence lay in his belief that this change would come sooner rather than later, and that the ownership of land would be the crux.

He took part in several punitive forays against the Kikuyu, and in a major campaign against the Nandi. As with matrimony, these operations were not taken in hand unadvisedly, lightly or wantonly. Their object was to punish crimes. In one case, a party carrying mail was cut to pieces by marauding warriors; in another, a white farmer peaceably engaged in buying sheep was tortured to death in a manner that revoltingly anticipated the worst of subsequent Mau Mau atrocities; in a third, a party of Indian traders was murdered, disembowelled and left to the hyenas. In the case of the Nandi their warriors, incited by their *laibon* (chief witchdoctor), having speared to death an American missionary, were ambushing and murdering African soldiers and porters and stealing telegraph wire and railway lines on such a scale as to make retribution inevitable. So, those who fell to the guns of the King's African Rifles were not innocent victims of colonial brutality; they had committed what were crimes in anyone's book. The penalty was a heavy communal fine in the shape of livestock. If the tribesmen paid the fine and surrendered the actual murderers, when these were known, that was the end of the matter, but when their warriors attacked the patrols, inflicting casualties in their turn, then they were in trouble.

It was during these operations against the Nandi that an incident, fully described in these pages, caused Meinertzhagen's downfall. The *laibon*, who was at the bottom of the trouble, was shot, either by Meinertzhagen himself or by his native officer, while the two men were shaking hands during a pre-arranged truce which was broken, in Meinertzhagen's version, by the *laibon's* followers intent on turning the truce into an ambush. By his outspokenness and sometimes arrogance, Meinertzhagen had made enemies among older men in the administration, one of whom he had accused of dishonesty as well as incompetence. Rumours were circulated that Meinertzhagen, not the *laibon*, had broken the truce. These rumours have, over the years, become part of the Nandi historical canon. Three successive military courts of enquiry exonerated him, and a recommendation went forward for the award of a medal, possibly even the Victoria Cross. But the civil power was not satisfied and the Commissioner, who had the last word, ordered his recall.

So his military service in East Africa ended for the time being. During the Nandi campaign he had evolved methods of intelligence-gathering which, in the first World War, he developed and perfected to a pitch where he became, in the words of the *Times* obituary, "one of the best and most colourful intelligence officers the Army ever had." First in the East African campaign against von Lettow-Vorbeck, then on Allenby's staff in Egypt and Palestine, his exploits grew into legends of audacity and cunning. He never fought with kid gloves, or indeed with any gloves at all. Later, he became chief political officer in Palestine (he was an ardent Zionist) and filled several peace-time politico-military posts before resigning from the Army to devote himself to ornithology and travel.

If candour, conciseness and exactitude are virtues in a diarist, he was a virtuous writer. While lists of slaughtered animals do not make compulsive reading, there are also shrewd judgements of his fellow-men, careful observations of animal behaviour, touches of sardonic humour. In *The Seven Pillars of Wisdom* T.E. Lawrence described him as "an idealist of the deepest, a strategist, a geographer and a silent, laughing, masterful man with an immensely powerful body and a savage brain, which chose the best way to its purpose, unhampered by doubt or habit." Mr A.T. Matson, historian of the Nandi people, in less ornate language considered him to be "the most exceptional man I have known, and the only one who gave me some sort of inkling of the effect that Livingstone, Gordon, Lugard and Lawrence had upon the people they met." He could be irritating, too self-confident, self-righteous at times: cast in bronze, yet with a curious streak of deviousness and now and then an endearing quirk, as when he exempted elephants from his blood-lusting obsession: "They are such wise animals . . . and to kill them for the fun of killing, or for the momentary gain of their ivory, is to my mind immoral. It is a pity that an intelligent animal like an elephant should be shot in order that creatures not much more intelligent may play billards with balls made from its teeth."

Meinertzhagen remained nearly all his life hooked on action as on a drug. In 1918, by then a senior staff officer, he hitched a ride in a Canadian armoured car, took possession of a Hotchkiss gun in the turret and slew twenty-three Germans, ending up by chasing a staff officer on foot, armed with a knobkerrie he had seized from an African the moment before it had cracked down upon his skull. It is strange that so blood-thirsty a man should have come from so civilised and peaceable a background. His father was a gentle, prosperous merchant banker with a large family and a large estate in Hampshire, his mother a sister of Beatrice Webb. After leaving Harrow, he wanted to read zoology at Cambridge, but his father put him into the City and proposed a stock-broking career. His family had labelled him a black sheep, an accusation that was to rankle for the rest of his life.

An unhappy relationship with his mother seems to have lain at the root of much of his prickliness and aggression. They never got on well and, according to his biographer John Lord, he craved a love she was never able to give, or at least openly to express. Where he sought affection, she responded with criticism. A need to prove that he was not a black sheep perhaps fuelled his craving for action; a bitter response to rejection may have lain behind his addiction to the bush and the society of primitive people. "I have had a good leave in England," he wrote on his return to Africa in 1905, "but I feel that my ties with my family and my home are even looser than before. I prefer Africa and the savage to England and the over-civilised society which lives there."

Richard Meinertzhagen's first marriage was very short-lived, and his second ended in tragedy when his wife died in a shooting accident in Scotland. She left him with a small daughter and two sons. The elder of these, whom he dearly loved, was killed in the second World War at the age of nineteen. His old age was devoted to birds and to editing his diaries for publication. The most successful of these was titled, significantly, *The Diary of a Black Sheep*. He also published several books on ornithology, the best known of which, *The Birds of Arabia*, has become the standard work on the topic. He died in 1967, at the ripe age of 89.

PREFACE

INSIGNIFICANT EVENTS may have important results. My five years in Kenya resulted from a snipe shoot in Burma. Our Commanding Officer in Mandalay was a man who was liverish and ill-tempered in the morning, hilarious and vulgar in the evening. But one day I was flattered by his asking me to take him out snipe shooting near Mandalay on a Sunday. I knew most of the best ground in the district; I doubt if he had ever shot a snipe in his life. On the Saturday he said casually, "You bring the lunch and the cartridges." So on the Sunday morning off we went. It was a hot day, with masses of snipe and lots of shooting, but my Commanding Officer scarcely hit a bird. At lunchtime he slept in a wet paddy field for two hours, drank vast quantities of beer at my expense and had fired off well over a hundred cartridges, also at my expense.

On the Monday morning I was arraigned to the Orderly Room and received a severe dressing down for having been absent from Church Parade. As I had gone shooting at the request of my Commanding Officer and had supplied both lunch and cartridges I thought that a particularly mean trick and decided I must leave the battalion; I took the first opportunity.

If it had not been for that snipe shoot I might have stagnated in the narrow groove of regimental soldiering. As it turned out I learned responsibility and self-reliance, I learned bush-craft, I learned to shoot straight, and incidentally I saved sufficient money to make myself independent of my father.

The following pages from my diary are exactly as I wrote them at the time, including bad grammar and split infinitives. The only deletions are references to matters other than Kenya, a few rather unkind remarks about people, and about a dozen deletions at the request of my publishers, who were nervous of proceedings for libel. The main object of this book is to show the type of life young subalterns led fifty years ago in a colony which now oozes respectability.

Two criticisms may occur to the reader: one, the excessive taking of human life; the other, the slaughter of game.

As regards the first, a soldier enters a fight to come out on top in the shortest possible time and lose the fewest possible casualties. In my view, any means to achieve those ends are justified. In the long run, inflicting heavy casualties on an enemy will shorten the duration of a conflict, it will teach a lesson and will result in a more enduring peace than less violent measures. War cannot be carried out without some degree of cruelty and suffering; these curses of war are inevitable, and nobody knows this better than the soldier; but they can to a large extent be reduced by an iron discipline. Cruelty, unnecessary slaughter and suffering after victory are almost always the outcome of bad discipline. The strain of war on the individual will lead to acts of unnecessary suffering if discipline is relaxed.

As regards the second criticism, the fighting and hunting activities of man require an outlet; if suppressed, hatred and malice occur. There are outlets which are not harmful. Active sport and competitive games are substitutes; hunting, the joy of adventure and facing danger, discovery and creation are other outlets. We should neither ignore nor regret them.

To Gerald Lathbury I tender my very best thanks for a most generous foreword which is quite undeserved. All the sketches and photographs are my own, though several were reproduced in Routledge's *With a Prehistoric People* as his own work.

I apologise most humbly if I have hurt the relatives or friends of anyone mentioned in these pages; a diary records the opinions of the moment and does not pretend to represent considered criticism. How often have I misjudged people who on better acquaintance have become fast friends!

There is no index; the marginal headings with dating and place-names should be sufficient to discover names or events.

R. MEINERTZHAGEN

17 KENSINGTON PARK GARDENS
LONDON, W.11

FOREWORD

BY LIEUT.-GENERAL SIR GERALD LATHBURY

K.C.B., D.S.O., M.B.E.

commanding troops in East Africa

THE AUTHOR, Colonel Richard Meinertzhagen, is best known as an ornithologist of international reputation, but he was also a fine soldier, brave and resolute in the field, as is apparent from reading between the lines of these diaries, and with a distinguished record on the intelligence staff in the First World War.

I am pleased to have been asked to contribute a foreword to the diaries, although I fear that with my limited knowledge of Kenya and the fact that the events described in these pages took place before I was born I shall be able to do them scant justice. I found the book fascinating and spent New Year's Day reading it from cover to cover. True, some readers will recoil at the extent of the bloodshed described, and the author himself comments on this aspect; but life, human and animal, was held cheap in those days, and the white man was a small minority in a country peopled by warlike and potentially hostile tribes. I wonder too whether we are always very honest or logical in our approach to the problems of the use of force. It is often kinder to take strong measures in the beginning and so avoid subsequent loss of life: it should not be forgotten that fatal casualties in the Mau Mau rebellion between 1952 and 1956 reached five figures.

The diaries—and they are really written as such, without any embellishment—are packed with incident and excitement, and are enlivened throughout by the author's sense of humour and the pungent criticism in which he excels. Many of the descriptions of the country in the early days and its people and wild life would alone make good reading. Although the author—Captain

Meinertzhagen as he was then—deals firmly and even ruthlessly with the many difficult situations with which he is faced, there is at the back of it all a real understanding of the African point of view and rights and an affection for the people themselves. In fact one of the most remarkable aspects of the book is the prescience displayed by this young army officer of twenty-four who argued with the High Commissioner against white settlement, foreseeing the problems it would raise, who foretold that German East Africa would become part of the British Commonwealth ten years before the First World War, and who was one of the first to realise the need for game reserves even in those early days. The latter part of the diaries covers the Nandi rebellion and the killing of the Laibon, for which Meinertzhagen was sent home, despite the fact that he had been exonerated by three courts of enquiry and recommended for a high award. It is good that the facts of this incident are to be published, for they have been distorted by malicious propaganda.

I would like to end by telling a little story about Colonel Meinertzhagen which happened while he was staying with us in Nairobi last year, visiting his old haunts and collecting a few birds. He returned before dinner one evening, and a lady who was present and who hates collecting said: "I suppose you have been shooting birds again, Colonel Meinertzhagen." The Colonel, who is slightly deaf and is suspected of using it on occasions to his advantage, appeared not to have heard. The question was repeated, with no result. They then leaned towards one another and the lady shouted the question, adding by way of explanation: "You know—bang bang!" "No—bang," he replied very politely; and that was the end of the conversation. Colonel Meinertzhagen has seldom found it necessary to use a second shot, whether killing an enemy, stopping a charging lion or expressing an opinion or contrary point of view.

NAIROBI
January 1957

PART I

NAIROBI, FORT HALL, NYERI

I was stationed in Burma with my regiment, the 1st Battalion Royal Fusiliers, when a request came in for officers to volunteer for service in Africa with local forces. I applied at once and was accepted. That was in April 1902 and I was aged 24, a full-fledged Lieutenant. From Rangoon I travelled to Bombay by ship and embarked for Africa.

28 . IV . 1902. *Indian Ocean*

I embark for East Africa

I embarked on the German East African ship *Safari*, bound for Mombasa, and am heartily glad to get off at last on my introductory trip to the Dark Continent.

29 . IV . 1902. *Goa*

We call at Goa

We put in at Goa this afternoon but remained only a few hours. I landed and shot a few birds for skinning. It is a miserable Portuguese settlement of tumbledown white buildings. The few Portuguese officials whom I saw looked both physical and moral wrecks.

10 . V . 1902. *Indian Ocean*

We run into the South-West Monsoon

On 3 May we ran into the full blast of the south-west monsoon, which has turned the calm sea into a choppy squally ocean and has made the ship most uncomfortable. The *Safari* is a slow tub, dirty and badly found. The food is good so long as one does not mind the rather greasy cooking of the Germans.

Cross the Equator

I crossed the Equator for the first time on 7 May.

Flying fish

While I was walking on deck this evening a flying fish hit me on the leg and fell on the deck. I picked it up and placed it in a bath of sea water, where it quickly recovered, and I was able to observe it closely. They are not unlike a herring. The wings of this one extended from just behind the gills to the root of the tail, and it used them in the water as fins. It was most active in the bath, and I threw it back into the sea before turning in.

German cruelty towards a monkey

The German captain of this ship has a monkey, which is the victim of all sorts of practical jokes by the German officers and crew. I hold no brief for monkeys, but I strongly resent any form of cruelty to any animal. This monkey is frequently tied to a cord and hoisted up into a mast, where he is kept in mid-air uttering screams of terror. This rejoices the hearts of the German officers, who revel in such cruelty. They also apply burning cigarette ends to his posterior and roar with laughter at the poor creature's discomfiture. They make him touch live electric wires and collapse with laughter when the monkey pulls his hand away. They make him drunk with spirits and jeer at him as he reels about the deck. If the monkey shows signs of rebellion he is severely beaten. It is obvious from the monkey's behaviour that his existence is one everlasting terror of his tormentors. This afternoon they made the poor creature almost comatose with drink, and to cure him they decided to tie a line round his waist and let him dangle in the sea for a bit. I protested but was politely told to mind my own business. So the monkey was thrown overboard lashed to a line. He gave out a piteous yell as he was being thrown. I could stand it no longer, and taking out a knife, I cut the line. I trust that he quickly drowned: he was so drunk that he cannot have lived long in the water. The Germans all jabbered with rage, gesticulated, and were, I thought, at one time about to lay hands on me. But they decided not to. I told them they were a lot of cowardly savages and left them livid with rage on deck. I should dearly have loved to throw them all after the monkey, and I told them so. In consequence I am by no means popular on board.

12 . V . 1902. *Mombasa*

We arrived off the African coast this morning in a driving rain. Land was dimly visible, and it was not till the afternoon that we made the entrance to Mombasa Harbour. The weather cleared as we entered the harbour, and I was much struck by its beauty. The spick and span town, the vivid green and freshness of the country, the palm trees and the old Arab buildings formed a picture which was not only quite new to me but of extreme natural beauty. I shall never forget my first introduction to East Africa.

Arrive at Mombasa

It was dark before I could land, and with darkness came heavy rain. The customs officials were particularly troublesome and only allowed me to take bare necessities with me, leaving the rest of my kit in the customs shed. Not knowing a soul in East Africa or speaking a word of the language, I really did not know what to do with myself. But a coolie, speaking something I could not understand, seized my one package and marched off with it. The street up which we went was dark and narrow, it was pouring with rain, I was drenched to the skin and the place seemed deserted. At last the coolie turned in at a building where I saw a lot of Europeans drinking at a bar. It was the Mombasa Club, the pride of East Africa. I marched up to one of the members and told him my predicament, and he at once took me in charge and introduced me to Lieut. C. L. Barlow and Lieut. E. V. L. Wardle, both of the East African Rifles and both recently arrived in the country from South Africa. I secured a room in the Club, my new friends insisted on my dining with them, and all is now serene. I am full of hopes for the future in this new country and shall dream of the adventures of Harris and Gordon Cumming in South Africa. I am already in touch with the romance of Africa, and the Dark Continent has me firmly in her grip.

Mombasa Club

Barlow and Wardle

13 . V . 1902. *Mombasa*

Immediately after breakfast I walked down to the customs, insisted on seeing a European and had no difficulty in getting my things through. I then moved into the

Mombasa

house in which Barlow and Wardle were living, and reported myself to the battalion headquarters.

It is pleasantly cool here and rained most of the day. Mombasa is an old Arab town built on a coral island. It is separated from the mainland by a narrow strip of sea, now spanned by the Uganda Railway bridge. The narrow streets and the old fort, over which flies the red standard of the Sultan of Zanzibar, give the place an old-world appearance. Except for the town the island is covered with dense bush, infested with pig and small gazelle. At the southern end of the island is the port of Kilindini, not yet developed, and near here is an attractive banyan forest with the ruins of old Portuguese forts.

The trolley line in Mombasa

The method of getting about in Mombasa is unique. In the days of the late East African Company a light railway was started from Mombasa with the intention of getting railway communication with the interior. It did no more than start, and when the project of the metre-gauge Uganda Railway materialised, these light railway lines were laid along every road in Mombasa with small sidings at every office or private house. The trolleys are pushed by two coolies and rattle along at a good rate. Most resident Europeans have their private cars, but others can be hired.

Birds

I have not yet seen many birds. I saw a large crow (*Corvultur*), a kite (*Milvus*), lots of weaver birds, a few babblers and an odd quail. Hemprich's gull is common in the harbour, and I caught a glimpse of an oriole with a black head. Swallows and swifts are abundant everywhere but were both tropical species unknown to me.

Butterflies

Butterflies are very abundant, there being many kinds familiar to me, including *Junonia*, *Atella*, *Papilio*, *Idmais* and the inevitable *Hypolimnas*. There are many varieties of *Danais*.

Snails

There is a huge land snail on the island, which shows itself in profusion in wet weather. It is called *Achatina fulva* and is the size of a cricket ball and handsomely coloured. There appear to be many varieties of it. I have also seen many lizards.

Mrs. Anderson

I met a lady this afternoon when wandering among the baobab trees looking for snails; she was accompanied by a native nurse and two small boys, one in a ramshackle perambulator. She told me she was a Mrs. Anderson, and we sat talking for a long time in the shade of a baobab tree; I liked her, and she told me a lot about the country. She came up here from South Africa in 1900.

[This was Maia Anderson, who later married Meyer during the First World War, when I got to know her well. The child in the perambulator must have been Claude Anderson of the *East African Standard*.]

18 . v . 1902. *Nairobi*

I left Mombasa by rail yesterday for Nairobi, arriving this morning. The headquarters of the East African Rifles have been recently transferred from Mombasa to Nairobi; they are henceforth to be called the 3rd Battalion of the King's African Rifles.

Leave Mombasa for Nairobi

On waking up in the train this morning I found we were near a station called Simba. The country was fairly open, with a few scattered thorn trees. I could scarcely believe my eyes on seeing 7 cock ostriches feeding quietly within 100 yards of the railway and many herds of zebra and haartebeeste grazing all over the plains. But more wonderful than this was the dome of Kilimanjaro Mountain, the morning sun shining on the perpetual snow-cap. It stood out clear-cut in the crisp morning air and was a wonderful sight.

Kilimanjaro and big game

Game was plentiful throughout the journey, the train not frightening them in the least. The main game reserve is on the south of the railway, but herds of zebra and antelope were equally plentiful on both sides of the line. Many herds of zebra, one of which must have contained thousands of individuals, were roaming over the open plains, accompanied by a large percentage of foals. Haartebeeste and Grant's and Thomson's gazelle were equally numerous. I saw lots of ostrich, also quite a number of both great and lesser bustard.

I counted the game on the south side of the railway between Athi River Station and Nairobi. It amounted to 5 rhinoceros, 18 giraffe, 760 wildebeeste, 4006 zebra, 845 Coke's haartebeeste, 324 Grant's gazelle, 142 Thomson's

Game census

gazelle, 46 impala, 24 ostrich, 7 great bustard and 16 baboon.

Falcons following the train

While the train was in motion I noticed two falcons flying with it. They kept on stooping at doves and rollers which the train disturbed from the telegraph wires. They followed us for about 4 miles, when they knocked over a dove. I was told by my fellow passenger that this is a not uncommon practice of falcons in East Africa, and that they follow not only trains but also caravans, in the hope of killing flushed birds.

Arrive Nairobi

I arrived at Nairobi soon after noon. Capt. J. D. Mackay met me at the station and drove me up to our quarters. He is the adjutant and seems a nice fellow. As there have been cases of plague, all troops are under canvas. We should have six companies here, but most of them are up the line protecting the railway coolies from a tribe called the Nandi.

Nairobi is about 5500 feet above sea-level and is delightfully cool and fresh today.

The only officers here now are Bailey, Swire and Mackay. I am just off to bed and a hyaena is howling outside.

19 . V . 1902. *Nairobi*

The King's African Rifles

I am posted to No. 8 Company. The personnel is mostly Swahili, but there are a good many Sudanese and Masai in the ranks. The recruiting of the two latter has been stopped for political reasons. We are all living under canvas, but barracks are being built for us on the hill south of the railway station.

At orderly room today there were two men up, one for "severely frightening a British officer." The officer was Bailey. Apparently he was on his pony, and coming round a corner met a soldier who saluted so smartly that the pony shied and off came Bailey. The soldier was punished by being awarded ten on the bare bottom with a strip of rhino hide, which I thought most unjust. The other man's crime was "being found in bed with the sergeant-major's wife." He got 25 lashes.

My company is in a shocking state; the men are dirty and ill-disciplined. When inspecting them this morning I lifted the tarboosh off a man's head; his hair was a seething, crawling mass of lice.

I was out on the plains this afternoon and tried to stalk a Thomson's gazelle, but the ground was so flat and devoid of cover that I could not get nearer than 200 yards, when I fired and missed.

My first shoot in East Africa

20 . V . 1902. *Nairobi*

I was out again today in a different direction and soon came across a herd of Thomson's gazelle. I had to take my shot at 200 yards and hit one. After running about a quarter of a mile I managed to get close to him again and killed him. He proved excellent eating this evening.

I shoot my first Thomson's gazelle

I came across a large number of human skeletons this afternoon. They originate from a bad famine among the Masai last year. I brought home two or three good specimens.

Human skulls

[These, with several other skulls from other tribes, were taken home and given to the Royal College of Surgeons.]

27 . V . 1902. *Nairobi*

Three days ago Swire and Bailey shot 50 great snipe in an afternoon. I was out over the same ground today and saw only one, which I shot. These are the European great snipe and only occur here during the rains. They must be late breeders in northern Europe if they are still in the tropics now. The one I killed today had a slow and even flight, not at all like the flight of the common snipe.

Snipe

A fellow called Roberts, who is out here big-game shooting, has been brought into Nairobi having been badly mauled by a lion. He came up with the animal in the open and took his shot at 150 yards with a Mauser rifle, hitting him in the stomach. He then gave him a second shot with a ·450 cordite rifle, on which the lion charged and knocked down the native gun-bearer. Roberts then gave him a right and left with his ·450 cordite rifle, hitting him in the lower jaw and shoulder. The lion then left the gun-bearer and went for Roberts,

Roberts is mauled by a lion

who gave him another right and left, hitting him again in the jaw, and another shot in the chest. The lion flinched but came straight on and knocked him down and sat on him. Roberts, with great presence of mind, gave him his arm to maul while he got another cartridge into his rifle and blew the lion's brains out. Meanwhile one arm was badly mauled. But the lion made little or no use of his claws.

That is just the type of real good game lion I want to meet. Blane, who was shooting with Roberts at the time, gave me this description. It certainly does not testify to the killing powers of these new cordite rifles. I cannot help thinking that if Roberts had had a 12 bore Paradox the accident need not have occurred.

Frederick Jackson on rifles

I first met Frederick Jackson when I was a boy. He was introduced to me in the Bird Room of the Natural History Museum by Bowdler Sharpe about 1894. He is now Deputy Commissioner out here, and I renewed our acquaintance today. After discussing birds we passed on to Roberts' accident. Jackson has done a deal of big-game shooting and wrote the African section of the Badminton *Big Game Shooting*. He does not believe in small bores for any game, on the principle of the skewer and a man's fist. If a man hits another in the chest with sufficient force to knock him down, and then hits him with a skewer using the same force, the second blow will penetrate but will not knock down; in fact, Jackson argues, the harder a blow from a skewer the less would it be felt, though the eventual result of the blow might be fatal. This theory may be all right for charging lions, etc., but I am a great advocate of small bore rifles, as they are more accurate and easier to shoot with. If one shoots straight, all I require the rifle to do is to penetrate. If one's first shot at a dangerous beast is well placed—and one should not shoot, without a reasonable chance of placing it well —the beast should not be in a position to charge. I rely on my first shot at dangerous game to place them completely *hors de combat*.

[This was Sir Frederick Jackson, a keen ornithologist and a man of great charm. He later became Governor of Uganda.]

I . VI . 1902. *Nairobi*

B. G. Alan

I have made friends with a local lawyer in Nairobi called B. G. Alan. He has only just come out and his practice is not yet built up. We went out shooting today and stalked to within 30 yards of a herd of zebra. There was a blue wildebeeste among them, but I never got a shot at him.

[I got to know Alan well later on. He started life in Nairobi with £300 and died about 1920 worth £150,000. He started in partnership with another solicitor called Tonks, but they soon separated. I renewed my friendship with Alan in 1914. He never married and died soon after the First World War.]

The Stewart brothers

The only shop in Nairobi is a small tin hut which sells everything from cartridges at eightpence each and beer at five shillings a bottle to sardines, jam, tinned food, paraffin, etc. It is run by two bearded brothers called Stewart. The poor fellows say they are doing a roaring trade but that none of their customers will pay their bills and they may have to close down.

The only hotel here is a wood and tin shanty sometimes known as Wood's Hotel and sometimes as the Victoria Hotel; it stands in the only "street," known as Victoria Street. Mr. Jeevanjee has a soda water factory; he also owns several bungalows, including the K.A.R. lines, for which we pay him rent. Then there is also a firm called Boustead and Ridley, General Merchants; they built Nairobi Club.

7 . VI . 1902. *Nairobi*

East African Rifles

Hatch is our colonel and resides in Mombasa; he is not much good. Harrison [Col. E. G. Harrison, D.S.O., who later distinguished himself in the First World War] is second-in-command and is in charge of a large detachment in Jubaland. J. D. Mackay is adjutant. Capt. Bailey commands the Nairobi Detachment; he has no practical knowledge of soldiering. Mackay is a ranker, keen, of the sergeant-major type, but most anxious to get efficiency; I like him. He won his commission at Omdurman; he is both helpful and considerate. My brother officers are mainly regimental rejects and heavily in debt; one drinks

Brother officers

like a fish, one prefers boys to women and is not ashamed. On arrival here I was amazed and shocked to find that they all brought their native women into mess; the talk centres round sex and money and is always connected with some type of pornography. Being very junior I cannot do much about it, but I objected not only to the tone in mess but also to native women being brought into mess; they told me that if I did not like it I could return whence I came, so I wrote out a complaint and asked them to read it and said that if they did not reform at once I should send it in officially. They were furious but complied. Row No. 1.

> They say I'm a quarrelsome fellow.
> God rot it, how can that be?
> For I never quarrel with any,
> The whole world quarrels with me.

My company

My company is composed of 125 Swahilis with a few Sudanese and 4 Masai, the latter being useless. The Swahilis are excellent material, very willing and cheerful but quite undisciplined and untrained; they have the mentality of children; my first duty is to learn their language, and then I shall have no difficulty in bringing the company up to my standard, that is, an efficient fighting machine and perfect discipline. The native officers are not much good and the N.C.O.s have little control, but I shall soon alter that.

My company is armed with single-loading Martini-Henry ·450 rifles with old-fashioned bayonets, and each man has a machete, an excellent weapon for cutting bush and incidentally ideal for close fighting. Every man has two pairs of boots, which they always take off on the slightest excuse. I examined the rifles this morning and found every one rusted up and corroded; in one case the breech mechanism would not work owing to rust and in another case the barrel was completely blocked by rag. All this is going to take some time to get right, but in six months' time I am going to have the best company in the battalion. I have already asked for 24 new rifles but am told there are none and that we shall be re-armed with the ·303 service rifle shortly. I enquired about musketry and a rifle range. Apparently we have not yet reached that stage; I was told I could have 10 rounds a man for practice, Bailey adding, "There is plenty of game, practise on that." I shall do no such thing; I am getting to despise Bailey.

Flogging

Last week I brought up a man to orderly room for insubordination; he told his sergeant that his mother was a crocodile and his father a hyaena. Bailey sentenced him to 25 lashes. As his company officer I had to witness the flogging. The culprit was lashed to a triangle, his breeches were removed, and he was then flogged by a hefty Sudanese with a strip of hippopotamus hide; he was bleeding horribly when it was over and I was nearly sick. I hated and resented the punishment so furiously that I went off to the orderly room and expressed my thorough disgust at such brutal punishment, which I thought should be ordered only in cases of violence or cruelty; and said that a flogging should always be automatically followed by discharge, for how can a man have any self-respect left after a brutal public flogging? Bailey and Mackay gaped in astonishment, told me I was squeamish, that I did not understand the African and that it was gross impertinence questioning an orderly room punishment. I rejoined that never again would I have any of my men flogged unless they were discharged; I was then told by Bailey that if I did not like flogging and that if I made any further complaints I could revert to my regiment; I said I certainly should. I fear I was very angry, but never again does a man in my company get flogged so long as I command. Row No. 2.

This is all a shocking start with a new regiment. After tea I went for a long walk on the Athi Plains to recover my temper and consider my position. I hope I shall be sent to an out-station as a nuisance. When I came into the mess this evening Bailey refused to speak to me and the others looked down their noses at me. But Mackay went out of his way to be pleasant, which gave me much pleasure. I feel I have won both rows.

Oxpeckers taking refuge on an eland when chased by a hawk

I saw a small herd of eland this afternoon, grazing near a herd of Masai cattle. On the eland was a small party of yellow-billed oxpeckers or tick birds. When I approached the eland the birds flew off screaming loudly and went off towards the cattle. In mid-flight a lanner falcon stooped at them; they at once turned and flew back to the eland, screaming loudly, and took refuge under the belly of the bull eland; the lanner hovered above, but he failed to dislodge them.

The game on the Athi Plains is astounding. There are countless herds of zebra, wildebeeste, haartebeeste, and Grant's and Thomson's gazelle, and today I saw no fewer than 8 great bustard. As one moves about these vast herds just walk off, usually within easy shot, all rather suspicious and curious but not frightened. I also saw many ostriches, the cocks running off with flapping wings and zigzag run, looking like a lot of ballet girls with their naked pink legs. I also saw hyaena and jackal, and some small quail were very common in the grass. Warthog, some with large litters, kept jumping up out of the grass and running off with their tails in the air, a most comic sight, and this evening as I sat out after dinner I heard lion roaring. This is certainly a wonderful place and exceeds my wildest dreams of Africa's big game; I fear I am developing a blood lust, but I must improve my rifle shooting if I am going to do any good.

8 . VI . 1902. *Nairobi*

The Masai form of greeting

I was out on the plains to the south of Nairobi today and shot a bull wildebeeste. On my returning home I saw a Masai shepherd running towards me with a spear. On approaching me he spat in the palm of his hand and displayed it before me with a smile on his face. I thought he wished to shake hands with me but could not bring myself to do it. It appears I also should have spat in his hand. If I had done so he would have esteemed it a great honour, and the harder and more voluminous my spit, the better would he have been pleased.

Concubines

Nearly every man in Nairobi is a railway official. Every one of them keeps a native girl, usually a Masai, and there is a regular trade in these girls with the local Masai villages. If a man tires of his girl he goes to the village (*minyatta*) and gets a new one, or in several cases as many as three girls. And my brother officers are no exception.

I counted the game on the Athi Plains this afternoon in an area of about 10 square miles south of Nairobi. It amounted to 2430 zebra, 967 wildebeeste, 846 Coke's haartebeeste, 932 Grant's gazelle, 546 Thomson's gazelle, 146 impala, 8 steinbock, 2 duiker, 46 eland, 19 giraffe, 1 rhinoceros, 86 ostriches, 1 cheetah, 5 hyaena, and a pack of 7 hunting dogs. As though that were not enough, there were 1467 head of Masai cattle in the area.

Game census

9 . VI . 1902. *Nairobi*

Sir John Kirk dined in our mess, having come up here from Mombasa yesterday. He was our consul in Zanzibar and was keenly interested in the suppression of the slave trade. He seemed to me rather bitter about Stanley but was interested when I told him I had met him on more than one occasion. It seemed to me that he claimed to be the hero of the suppression of the slave trade and rather resented both Livingstone's and Stanley's activities in that direction. Kirk was not an inspiring personality, small, with a little beard, poor physique, dour and without personality. Doubtless he was a first-class consul, but it struck me he was jealous of Stanley.

Sir John Kirk

11 . VI . 1902. *Nairobi—Fort Hall Road*

To go on "safari" is to travel with a caravan of porters. Today I started off on safari, as I have been ordered to take charge of our detachment at Fort Hall, or Mberri, which is not far from Kenya Mountain. I am accompanied by an escort of 3 N.C.O.s and 9 men, and 23 porters. Each porter carries a load of about 50 pounds, besides his food for 4 days.

I start off on "safari"

I had not gone more than 3 miles out of Nairobi when I spied two small gazelle slightly larger than "tommies." Their horns were slender, and in one the tips were inclined to curl back. Both had an indistinct flank stripe. I do not know what they are. [These were female Grant's gazelle.]

Two strange gazelle

Nairobi River

I saw lots of ostrich, haartebeeste and warthog. After having travelled 11 miles I halted and camped on the Nairobi River, a pleasant stream with pools, on which were lots of spur-winged geese.

I see my first lion

At dusk, as I was sitting outside my tent ruminating over the pleasure it gave me to be once again away from civilisation, my escort yelled out "simba!", which means a lion. I just caught sight of him trotting along a low rise some 500 yards off. He stopped and had a look at us, then moved on at a trot and disappeared over the brow. If it had not been so dark I should have gone after him.

12. VI. 1902. *Ruiru River*

Game on the march

We continued our march at daybreak in a northerly direction over the vast rolling plains, seeing plenty of ostrich and other game on the way. After 16 miles we halted near the Ruiru River. In the afternoon I took a walk round camp and found fresh spoor of rhinoceros. At one time I must have been close to an ostrich nest, as an old hen was most restive and anxious. I made a good search for the eggs but could not find them. We waded across a large papyrus swamp today, getting wet up to our middles. In the middle of the swamp I saw buffalo tracks.

13. VI. 1902. *Thika River*

Camp on the River Thika

An uneventful march of 14 miles to the River Thika, which is here a slow muddy stream about 150 feet wide. We camped on the right bank, where I saw plenty of hippopotamus spoor. Just before we reached camp I shot a small bustard with a grey throat and ferruginous on the back of the neck. In the evening I saw a herd of about 12 waterbuck which contained two fair-sized heads, but as they were on the left bank of the river I was unable to follow them up.

I am badly handicapped by having no book on the birds of East Africa. The result is that I have no idea of the names of the many birds I see, or of which are interesting and which are common.

14 . VI . 1902. *Punde Milia Camp*

Giraffe

Made a long march today of about 23 miles over rough country. I saw a small party of impala soon after dawn, and soon afterwards I saw a herd of 14 giraffe at close quarters. I first spied them about half a mile off, when I saw 4 feeding off some thorn trees on the skyline. As I walked towards them I was concealed by a dip in the ground, and when I again came into view the whole 14 were only 100 yards from me. Advancing with my camera I easily got within 70 yards, but even from that distance they looked minute in the finder of my camera. I took several exposures of them before they quietly walked off. The bull of the herd, a very dark beast, stood out from all the rest by his size. Giraffe have an ungainly stride and seem to be lame in all four legs, besides having their shoulders dislocated. When they moved off they did so in a single line like a string of camels, the old bull bringing up the rear. They all, even the youngest cows, had horns. I observed some of them feeding off low bushes, when they looked absurd, having to splay out their forelegs to enable their heads to reach so low.

Punde Milia Camp

I camped at a spot where I found good water. I am told it is called Punde Milia, or Zebra Camp. I saw large herds of zebra in the neighbourhood. In the evening an old Kikuyu chief paid me a visit, bringing me a fowl as a present, which proved most acceptable. He also explained to me that in a recent fight he had had all the fingers of his right hand chopped off, which he insisted on proving by producing the fingers from a small tobacco tin. This did not improve my appetite for my dinner off his chicken.

[The old gentleman paid me a second visit a few days later, when he presented me with a fine serval skin, for which I made him a present of 5 rupees.]

Game census

Game seen today over 23 miles on both sides of the road were 14 giraffe, 3 rhinoceros, 18 warthog, 276 zebra, 18 wildebeeste, 186 Coke's haartebeeste, 18 impala, 138 Grant's gazelle, 168 Thomson's gazelle, 3 steinbock, 18 waterbuck and 48 ostriches.

15 . VI . 1902. *Fort Hall*

H. R. Tate

I continued my march to Fort Hall at dawn. Soon after starting I met Tate on the road. He is the District Officer at Fort Hall and is on tour through the district. Immediately after leaving Punde Milia the country becomes more undulating and covered with low bush, with a little native (Kikuyu) cultivation.

I arrive at Fort Hall

We arrived about 10 a.m. at Fort Hall, where I found Hemsted, the District Officer and only white man in the station. Fort Hall consists of two grass huts, in one of which live Tate and Hemsted, and in the other of which the work of the district is conducted. A stone house is being constructed for S. L. Hinde, the Sub-commissioner, who is now on leave. All these buildings are enclosed within a stone wall and ditch. Outside the wall are the grass-roofed police lines and the grass huts of my men. Then there is a small bazaar consisting of two Indian traders, who rob the unfortunate Kikuyu with cheap beads and cloth.

Welcome from the local Wakikuyu

Several local Wakikuyu chiefs, having been told that I was arriving today, came in to greet me. They arranged a dance in my honour, performed by 20 young men and 20 young girls, all dressed up in everything but clothes. The girls alone wore small pieces of greasy cloth about their middles, but the men had nothing on but beads, wire, and small strips of white fur round their legs. The dance interested me a great deal and consisted mainly in swaying the body backwards and forwards. It was essentially barbaric and lacked all sense of grace or decency.

Mongoose

In the evening a chief presented me with a live mongoose, which I believe is called *Zorilla*. It has a striped black and white fur, but has been hurt and does not look like living. Hemsted has two young serval cats alive.

17 . VI . 1902. *Fort Hall*

Guinea-fowl

This evening, after I had finished my work, I was out shooting with Hemsted. We bagged 6 guinea-fowl and 4 yellow-throated spur fowl. A chief called Kenuthia presented me with the skin of a colobus monkey this evening.

Kenuthia, a minor chief living at Fort Hall; his large finger rings can be seen

Kikuyu warrior in fighting kit. Fort Hall

A Kikuyu warrior. Fort Hall

Kikuyu warrior

19 . VI . 1902. *Fort Hall*

Kenuthia's drunken joke

Apparently the Kikuyu occasionally have parties which include dances and much native beer. Last night Kenuthia had a party, and about 11 p.m. he and his guests started shouting rude remarks at us and firing arrows into the station, but they all had balls on the points. Nobody was hurt. Today Kenuthia and some of his men came in and apologised to Hemsted and me, hoping nobody had been hurt. Hemsted told him that any repetition of drunken orgies would be met with a very heavy fine.

20 . VI . 1902. *Meragua River*

A shoot on the Meragua River

I have come down to the junction of the Meragua and Tana River for a shoot. My camp is some 8 miles from Fort Hall. I saw plenty of haartebeeste, oribi, waterbuck and impala, some of which I killed. The oribi are a horrible (no pun intended) nuisance. They are very abundant, and as soon as they see anything suspicious they start barking; when they make off they run in all directions, jumping in the air in a ridiculous fashion and whistling all the time. They go about in parties of from two to four, and it is difficult to spot the buck, as the ears usually hide the small straight horns. For dinner I enjoyed some haartebeeste soup and an oribi steak.

Precautions against natives

As soon as I reached camp I built a thorn fence or *zariba* round the tents. The local natives have a reputation for treachery, and it is as well to be on one's guard. As it was getting dark we heard a party of Wakikuyu near the camp, and I have little doubt they have inspected the camp with an idea of loot. But I have taken the precaution of having sentries on all night.

This is all Kikuyu country and there are a few villages and cultivation, but it is mainly used as grazing ground.

Apes and a red lynx

I saw a large party of apes or baboons near camp this evening. I chased them for some distance, but they went too fast for me. But I ran into a red lynx or caracal, which I shot. He is a beautiful creature with nice tufts of hair on his ears.

21 . VI . 1902. *Meragua River*

Shooting

It was drizzling this morning at dawn, which made it cooler than usual. The large ground hornbills and monkeys were very noisy round camp. I was away at 7 a.m. and soon ran on to 8 waterbuck, one of which I killed. After sending the head and meat back to camp I went on in search of more game. I saw plenty of oribi but could not get a shot for a long time. At last three stood about 150 yards from me, and killing the largest I was disgusted to find it was a female. I noticed today that single oribi are usually males, and parties of three are usually all females. In the afternoon I killed another waterbuck and 3 guinea-fowl.

22 . VI . 1902. *Meragua River*

Native capacity for eating meat

During the last 36 hours my camp, consisting of 18 niggers, has completely consumed a waterbuck, a hartebeeste and an oribi. That means that each man must have eaten at least 10 solid pounds of meat. No wonder that most of them are today suffering from general lassitude.

A wounded impala

In the afternoon I stalked a buck impala who was feeding in company with some doe waterbuck. I had to take a long shot and hit him in the stomach. He galloped off and then stood looking very sick. He finally lay down, but the country was too open to attempt a closer approach. Meanwhile some oribi had spotted me and commenced to make a great fuss by jumping and whistling, and they played so on the feelings of the wounded impala that he got up again and made off into thick bush, where I lost sight of him. Rain then coming on, and darkness approaching, I returned to camp, but I hope to recover him tomorrow morning.

23 . VI . 1902. *Meragua River*

Eight lion

I was out at dawn after the wounded impala and on the way killed another waterbuck. No sooner had I got on to last night's blood spoor of the impala than I saw 8 lion trotting across a piece of open grass towards a large reed bed. They were some 300 yards distant. I only had time to spot one maned lion among them when they got into the reeds. At the spot where they entered the reeds I saw several heads looking at me, so I walked slowly in their direction and at 150 yards took a shot at one of their heads but missed. There were several snarls and roars, but they all disappeared. I was now at a loss to know what to do. The reed bed was some 5 acres in extent and dense. It was bounded on one side by the Tana River and on the other by about 300 yards of short grass. I only had two nervous niggers with me, so I sent one up to Fort Hall for Hemsted, while I and the other watched the reed bed to see that the lion did not break out. At 2.39 p.m. Hemsted arrived and we proceeded to walk through the reeds. Of course we never saw one, but we frequently heard them as they dashed through the reeds. One of our niggers saw one close to him and fled. So at dark we had to abandon the attempt.

[I did not realise at the time how foolhardy we were. To try to walk up 8 lion in dense reeds is asking for trouble; we should have left them alone and waited outside at dusk, when no doubt we should have got a shot as they started off on their evening hunt.]

When I saw the lion first in the open, they appeared more like fat, sleek sheep and not a bit like the King of Beasts. But the sight of 8 lion all in a bunch made my mouth water a bit. I noticed that lion spoor is much smaller than that of the tiger.

I left the waterbuck's carcass out tonight and shall visit it tomorrow at dawn in the hope of finding some lion eating it.

24 . VI . 1902. *Meragua River*

Rhinoceros

I was out before dawn to watch the waterbuck carcass but saw nothing; the lion must have polished him off in the middle of the night, for the carcass was picked dry and numerous fresh lion tracks were in the neighbourhood. I saw some impala about 400 yards away and was just going to stalk them when a couple of rhinoceros trotted out of the bush within 30 yards of me, heading for the reed bed. I quickly slipped a solid bullet into my

Mannlicher and fired at the largest beast at 75 yards. Both animals turned and ran back across me towards some scrub. The smaller of the two held its tail erect while the larger one did not, so I presumed my bullet had had effect. I followed them and found them standing together among some thorn scrub in which they were almost invisible. Creeping to within 40 yards I put a second bullet into the beast's shoulder, at which she headed again for the reed patch. I knew she was badly hit by the way she ran, so I gave her another two shots, both of which hit her in the ribs. I rushed after them, and just before entering the reeds the large beast turned and faced me in the open. I sat down and fired at her chest, whereat she turned towards the reeds, and walked slowly into them, so that I lost sight of her. As I did not fancy walking up wounded rhinoceroses with a Mannlicher, I sent to camp for my 8 bore cannon. When this arrived I followed the spoor cautiously into the reeds and soon caught sight of the smaller beast standing watching me. As this beast was only three-quarters grown I did not wish to kill him, so tried to frighten him away. I threw stones and cartridges and shouted but he merely snorted at me, though he stood but 20 yards from me. Eventually I fired off the 8 bore, at which he crashed into the reeds and I saw him no more. The larger beast, an old female, was lying dead a few yards further on. I photographed her and then commenced to cut her up. Her dorsal skin was nearly two inches thick. I was sorry to find her in an advanced state of pregnancy, for I cut from her a perfect young rhino, just ready to be born. It had hair round the eyes and on the face, back and rump. In adult rhino there is only hair on the eyelashes, tail and ears. I skinned the young one complete and shall have it set up.

The horns of the cow are poor and much worn, which denotes an old beast. We had some difficulty in removing them, but by working under them with a knife for nearly two hours we eventually removed them from the skull. The horns of a rhino are not attached to the skull but grow on the skin, being really congealed hair. The whole camp having come to the scene, and a hunting party of Wakikuyu having also turned up, all the meat was taken

A Kikuyu warrior

Kikuyu warriors

away. The beast was so heavy that it took 10 of us to turn her over.

In the afternoon I killed a buck oribi at 40 yards with my Mannlicher. *Oribi*

[I described these oribi as a new race in the *Proceedings of the Zoological Society* some years later, naming them *kenyae*. They are closely allied to Haggard's oribi.]

25 . VI . 1902. *Fort Hall*

Tomorrow being Coronation Day, Tate asked me to shoot some haartebeeste for meat for the natives at the festivities at Fort Hall. He sent down 20 porters to carry meat and I shot 2 haartebeeste for them. *Coronation Day*

I walked back to Fort Hall in the evening, having shot 3 waterbuck, 2 impala, 3 haartebeeste, a rhino, a red lynx and an oribi, and having seen 8 lion. I killed everything with my Mannlicher, with which I am well pleased. I used nothing but hollow-pointed bullets, except for the solids I used on the rhino. *Return to Fort Hall*

Tate has returned from his tour, and he, Hemsted and I all feed together. I like both Tate and Hemsted.

My pay in India was exactly £108 a year, and now I find myself with £400 a year under cheaper conditions, for outside luxuries such as cartridges, alcohol, etc., living is absurdly cheap. Eggs three a penny, sheep 3 rupees, a chicken half a rupee, and we grow our own vegetables. My daily expenditure on food is only about the equivalent of 2s. a day. So, with the small allowance Father gives me, I am rapidly becoming a capitalist. *Untold wealth*

[On joining the K.A.R. my capital value was £0. On leaving the K.A.R. after nearly 5 years I found myself possessed of over £3000.]

26 . VI . 1902. *Fort Hall*

Today being the Coronation Day of King Edward, we decided to have a general holiday and a military review, and give the local savages a treat. All the local chiefs were invited to come in, and the haartebeeste meat, supplemented by an ox and a goat, was distributed among them. We had a little ceremonial drill in the *boma*, which *Coronation festivities* consisted of a sort of amateur trooping of the colour. I marched my detachment of 22 men about the station, firing an occasional *feu de joie* with ball ammunition, and frequently presenting arms to a Union Jack on a pole. I could not help smiling at the rather Gilbertian touch to the whole proceedings, but our hearts were in the right place.

Tate gave the savages a speech in Swahili, but he might as well have spoken in English for aught the Wakikuyu understood. The natives, of course, thought we had all gone mad and understood nothing of the proceedings. Hemsted, in as ragged clothes as his 30 police, stood to attention for 35 minutes, not daring to give a word of command, which he knew no man of his would either understand or obey.

Native dancing

In the afternoon the natives gave us a treat. A large party of young men and girls danced together for many a hot hour. To my mind the dance was most suggestive and immoral, but that did not make it any the less interesting. I imagine the origin of all dancing is to incite or play on the sexual senses. In the dances I witnessed this afternoon the last phase is the bolting of the lady into the bush, hotly pursued by the young man. As both are almost nude, and as the girl is invariably caught and tripped up, the climax of a Kikuyu dance can best be imagined. It certainly could not be introduced into Belgravia, though modern dancing in England is sometimes little better than these savage displays in tropical Africa.

The men dancers had their heads smeared with red earth saturated with sheep's fat, and were bedecked with beads and copper wire, which gave them the look of veritable little demons. The grimaces they make as they dance made me roar with laughter, and the efforts of the men to finish up the final dance with the girl they fancy were too ludicrous. They, of course, take the whole proceeding most seriously. Most dancing is done with the heads and shoulders, the legs having but one step, which is continually repeated. The women wriggle at the hips.

Sports

We also tried some sports, which were not a success, as the winner always had to fight the rest afterwards. I noted that the winner of a race $2\frac{1}{4}$ miles long did the course in exactly 14 minutes. There was also a tug-of-war between my men and the police, which my men won. That again led to a free fight later on.

The symbol of the red feather

I found out a curious custom among the Wakikuyu. There is a bird here which lives in the forest called a plantain-eater. It is about the size of a cuckoo, has a crest, and is dull green in colour with brilliant crimson on the webs of the primary feathers. It is apparently a custom among the Wakikuyu that once a year every unmarried girl who has reached the age of puberty—that is to say, over about 11 or 12 years—must wear one of these crimson wing feathers in her head ornaments, and that while she so wears it she is not allowed to say No to any man, but can dispense with it as soon as the man has satisfied himself. She need only wear the feather on one day in the year, and on that day must travel at least once to the nearest village by daylight. Of course in most instances the appointed day for wearing the feather is arranged with the girl's favourite young man. The custom is aimed at making it uncomfortable for young girls who refuse to marry.

I discovered this custom by accident. I passed a girl on the road wearing such a feather. She smiled at me in a rather awkward manner, and was at once seized round the waist by a young man who was walking near me and carried off into the bush, where after a brief struggle all was silent. As I was unable to understand such impetuous behaviour on the part of the young Kikuyu and the lack of resistance on the part of the girl, I enquired of the Government interpreter, who told me the above detail. He added that any girl misusing the scarlet feather, or using it more than once a year, was subjected to a severe beating by the whole of her village as a loose character.

6. VII. 1902. *Thika River*

The Government mail party are cut up by Wakikuyu

At 9.30 yesterday morning a native youth came into the *boma* (Fort Hall) with the story that the mail party had been cut up and destroyed by Wakikuyu on the Thika River while on its way into Nairobi. We at first thought it was a lie or another outrage by a well-known man-eating lion on the Thika River. But at noon our worst fears were realised, when a message from Hemsted, who is working on the road about 15 miles from here, brought definite information that the mail had been cut up on the Thika and 29 miles from here. Three porters and a policeman had been murdered, and some others travelling with the mail had been wounded.

[See also 7 . IX . 1902; the culprits turned out to be the Kihimbuini people, a section of the Merouka Kikuyu. They got well punished.]

I leave Fort Hall for the Thika

On hearing this I collected 20 of my men and started off at once for the scene of the outrage, with food for 5 days. When we reached Punda Milia camp, some 15 miles on the road, it began to get dark and 5 of my 8 porters ran away, so I commandeered another 5 from the road working party. As some of my men and porters could not keep up with the 5 miles an hour at which I was travelling, I went ahead with but 4 of my men. Hemsted had meanwhile also proceeded to the scene, but as he had but 2 rather unreliable policemen with him I was anxious to reach him as soon as possible. We had a long and weary march, with occasional showers. We reached the Thika River at 2.40 a.m., where I was relieved to find Hemsted safe. I think he was mighty glad to see me. The last few miles of my night march were far from pleasant, for we were passing through a district doubly dangerous. There was the risk of having my small party rushed by the Wakikuyu, or attacked by the famous man-eating lion of these parts. The night was pitch dark, and when about a mile from the Thika we heard a lion roaring not far from us; soon afterwards a lion kept parallel with us and only a few yards away, as was clear from the low grunts which were continually made. This induced us to fix our bayonets and proceed with great caution.

The massacre

Hemsted had arrived here yesterday evening and found a dreadful scene. The 3 dead porters had not been buried and were smelling. The wounded, comprising 9 men and 2 women, were lying about groaning, and were a mass of flies and maggots. Several unwounded survivors had not attempted to get them water or to assist in any way.

One of the survivors gave me the following account.

The party had built for themselves a small thorn *zariba* in which they were all asleep, when about 10 p.m. a large party of Wakikuyu rushed them, spearing and shooting arrows in all directions. The one policeman fired a shot, at which all the Wakikuyu fled. The mail bag was untouched, so also was a piece of rhino skin and some trophies which I was sending into Nairobi. I fancy the whole business was done by the Merouka tribe, who live in the neighbourhood, and was prompted by the sheer love of killing. They are notorious for their lust for blood. In their hurry to decamp they have left several spears, bows and arrows in the grass, some of which I have collected.

The wounded

Some of the wounded are in a bad condition. I have sent Hemsted back to Fort Hall for medical stores, and have sent a runner to Nairobi for a doctor, but I fear both will be some time in reaching me. Two of the most seriously wounded are women. One has a spear thrust under the right arm, and as it comes out under her left arm, I wonder she is alive. The spear had not been extracted, Hemsted not having been able to face it. After a severe tug I managed to pull it out and stuffed the hole with permanganate. The other woman has a bad wound in the stomach and from the wound protruded some part of her inside which might have been anything. It was a mass of maggots, so I cut it off with a pair of scissors and sewed up the hole, having stuffed it with permanganate. Both are in bad pain and I doubt if they can live. A Masai with a spear wound in his lungs may die at any moment. Dressing the wounds of these poor wounded is quite the worst job I have ever undertaken, for my only medical stores are permanganate, cotton-wool and lanoline. I have also administered large doses of tea and whisky, and I can do no more. The flies are a great nuisance, so I have rigged up some shelters for the wounded and have detailed natives to continually fan them with brushwood fans.

But my main work today has been the construction of a stiff thorn *zariba* which cannot be rushed by natives. The rest of my men having arrived here this afternoon,

I forwarded the mail bags to Nairobi. The garrison of my post is now 15 rifles and myself.

Just before dark I took a stroll round camp to see if there were any signs of lion. I shot a waterbuck within 150 yards of camp and got all the meat into the *zariba* before nightfall. I have set all hands on to make soup for the wounded.

Precautions

Immediately after dark we heard natives calling on the other side of the river, doubtless a scouting party of the Wakikuyu, to see what was happening. A few fire signals were made, so we all stood to arms for an hour. But as a precaution I have 4 double sentries round the camp this evening.

7 . VII . 1902. *Thika River*

A man-eating lion breaks into my camp

In spite of all my precautions, last night proved that my defences were inadequate against lion. About 10 p.m. a small party with stores and an escort of 15 police arrived from Fort Hall. We let them into the *zariba*, and I again dressed the wounds with the carbolic which had been sent out, and gave the two women a good injection of morphia. I then lay down on my bed. The night was stuffy and I was sleeping out. Suddenly a piercing cry rang out from a man who was sitting round a camp fire with his comrades. I jumped up with my revolver, thinking the natives had got in, and just had time to see by the failing light of the camp fires the image of a lion jumping over my *zariba* with a man in his mouth. We fired in his direction in the hope of making him drop his victim, but we failed. It appears that the lion leaped into the *zariba* and seized a porter by the buttocks, but, on this man yelling, let go his hold and seized the next man by the throat, probably killing him instantly, and decamped over the thorn *zariba*. I rushed out of the *zariba* into the dark with a lamp and my rifle, but we could neither hear nor see anything, so returned.

I then attended to the porter's buttocks. The lion had gripped him firmly and had punctured his skin with the four canine teeth. I washed these wounds out with strong carbolic and dressed them. No sooner had I completed this than two lion began to roar and grunt quite close to the *zariba*. Whenever they roared we fired a few cartridges in their direction, and this went on for two hours before they finally made off. But as I was still nervous about a second attack by perhaps more than one lion I sat up all night to encourage the sentries, whose nerves were on the verge of collapse.

I track the man-eater

As soon as it was light enough to see this morning I tracked the man-eating lion. The trail was not difficult to follow, owing to the broken bead necklaces, small pieces of cloth, a certain amount of blood and the claw marks of the galloping lion as he tore across the soft mud near camp. Though his victim had been silent it was clear that a struggle had taken place, for there were marks on the ground where the man had dug his fingers in to try to stop himself. He had also pulled out a handful from the lion's mane. The fact that he had been seized by the neck would account for his inability to shout. Some 300 yards from camp we came to the site of the last struggle. The grass was drenched with blood, and covered with small pieces of bone and human skin and the man's skull. It was obvious that more than one lion had partaken of this ghastly feast. The ground was now rocky and tracking became impossible, so we abandoned the idea of going further. Doubtless the party of lion are at this moment not far distant and probably lying up in the thick fringe of bush along the Thika River. I have several men out watching for any signs of them.

[On 26 . XII . 1903 I killed both the man-eating lion and the lioness.]

The wounded

The porter suffering from the lion's teeth is doing well, but the carbolic I stuffed into his wounds this morning hurts more than the wounds themselves. The other wounded are in a bad condition. The Masai has developed pneumonia and is unconscious. He will die before tomorrow. The woman with the stomach wound is much worse and is exuding a sort of green fluid from the wound. She is suffering terrible pain, so I have given her a real good dose of morphia. My carbolic is almost exhausted and I am using my shirts and pyjamas as bandages.

A party of Wakikuyu near camp

I had patrols out all day. One of them sighted a party of armed savages, and, acting under my orders, opened fire, killing one of their number, whose arms they brought back to camp. So that's good. I have turned all available hands on to increase the thorn *zariba*, and we are now impregnable against natives. A lion might jump over it, but he could never get back with a man in his mouth, for it is now 7 feet high and 4 feet thick.

Meat for camp

I retrieved the rest of the waterbuck which I shot yesterday, and also killed a buck Thomson's gazelle, and the camp is now busy making soup. There seems to be plenty of game about here, for this evening I saw lots of zebra, waterbuck, impala, gazelle, ostrich, wildebeeste, haartebeeste and steinbock.

8 . VII . 1902. *Thika River*

The doctor arrives

Last night passed without incident. I was out at dawn with a patrol and saw a fine warthog, but was unable to get near enough for a shot. At 9.30 a.m. Dr. Corke arrived from Nairobi with plenty of medical stores and with an escort of 10 police and 30 Masai spearmen. He has brought few provisions with him, so he and I must economise. It is a burden off my mind to transfer the wounded to his care and to know that they will be properly dressed in the future. The Masai who was wounded in the lung and the woman with the abdominal wound died early this morning, and I buried them before Corke arrived.

Warthog

In the afternoon I scoured the country for lion, but saw no signs. During my walk I spied a warthog feeding towards me. I remained still until he was no more than 30 yards from me, when I put a bullet into his heart. He ran nearly 200 yards before he fell dead. They really are the ugliest animals I have ever seen. I am always much amused by the way they hold their tails erect when they run, the small tuft of hair at the tip bending over backwards. They also amuse me when they go to ground, for they enter their earths backwards. On this account it is unwise to stand in front of an occupied earth, for he comes out like a rocket.

In the evening I ran across two small hornless antelope, one of which I wounded. I persuaded one of the Masai to try to run him down. It was a fine sight to see the man running with spear and shield over rough ground, till eventually he overtook and caught the beast. I have not seen this antelope before, but suspect they are a kind of reedbuck. [These antelope proved to be Chanler's reedbuck.]

Two unknown antelope

9 . VII . 1902. *Thika River*

The lion were roaring near camp again last night but did not molest us. Tate arrived from Fort Hall this morning, and we shall all proceed to Nairobi tomorrow.

Tate arrives

I was out on patrol all the afternoon, but saw nothing. I returned about dark, and about 9 p.m. a rifle shot rang out not far from camp. We all got to our alarm stations at once and put out all the fires.

A false alarm

Soon after the shot rang out we discerned figures about 100 yards from the *zariba*, so I scrambled out with the Masai, hoping they were Wakikuyu, but they turned out to be the Nairobi mail party with a trader's caravan. The trader had fired off his rifle at a lion which came quite close to him. It was fortunate for him that I went out with the Masai, else he would most certainly have been speared. I had the greatest difficulty in holding these warriors back and preventing them spearing the whole party. The slightest encouragement or signal from me would have entailed a wholesale slaughter. They became most excited and uttered their peculiar war-cry, a sort of grunt.

10 . VII . 1902. *Ruiru River*

We packed up this morning and marched to the Ruiru River, where we are now camped. Corke shot a magnificent warthog near camp in the evening.

We commence ou[r] march to Nairobi

Just at dawn I noticed a little smoke coming from the bush bordering the Thika River and about a mile from camp. I sent 20 Masai to investigate, with orders to attack any armed party of natives. They apparently surprised a

A hunt

scouting party of Wakikuyu, for with yells and whoops we saw about 15 Wakikuyu fleeing up the opposite bank of the Thika with the 20 Masai after them, but the former had a long start and I do not think any were caught. But it was a fine sight, the Wakikuyu firing arrows back as they fled, and the Masai running with their shields in front of them.

11 . VII . 1902. *Nairobi*

To Nairobi

Soon after leaving camp this morning we met Lieut. Swire and 20 men of the King's African Rifles on their way to establish a permanent post at the Thika Crossing. He took my Masai back with him. We reached Nairobi in the late afternoon, having come 23 miles. Tate rode his grey mule, but I walked the entire distance. After refitting we hope to get back to Fort Hall in a day or so.

13 . VII . 1902. *Nairobi*

A visit to Lenana, the head of all the Masai

Tate and I rode out to pay a visit to Lenana, the chief of all the Masai, whose kraal is about 5 miles from Nairobi towards Ingong. Sendeyo, his brother, who has been hostile towards him for many years past, has had a bad quarrel with the Germans near Kilimanjaro which led to fighting and the discomfiture of Sendeyo. He has therefore fled from German East Africa and has thrown himself on the mercy of his brother, who has received him in a friendly manner. I saw both Lenana and Sendeyo. The former is Jacob, the latter Esau. Lenana has the brains, but did not impress me. Sendeyo is a magnificent specimen of the Masai warrior, with an open face and a cheerful disposition.

I thanked Lenana for having sent out 20 of his warriors to me on the Thika. He promised always to help me whenever I wanted help. Sendeyo afterwards begged me, if I wanted Masai warriors to fight the Wakikuyu, to let him know, as he knew better than Lenana what was wanted and would come himself. I doubt whether Sendeyo and Lenana will remain friends for long.

Lenana; paramount chief of the Masai

A minor chief at Fort Hall in monkey-skin cloak

Kikuyu dancing boy

Apparently some years ago the East African Government presented all paramount chiefs with a handsome malacca cane staff surmounted with a brass head on which the royal arms were embossed. Lenana had one of these, and I admired it and was asked to handle it, and was so much impressed by it that he had to give it to me. I had forgotten that if one admires any article too much the owner must give it to the admirer. Tate told me I must not accept it, so I refused, but after I left a runner overtook us and insisted that I take the staff; so I have it. [I subsequently gave this staff to Sir Evelyn Baring in Nairobi in January 1956.]

Lenana gives me his staff

Apparently Charles Eliot, the High Commissioner, learned that Beatrice Webb is my aunt, so he asked me to dine with him this evening. My only clothes were a dirty old shirt and shorts. I explained my predicament and refused, but he insisted on my coming. He is not my idea of a High Commissioner; he looks more like a university don or a priest. He is a scholar, a philosopher, and a very able man with great vision. He amazed me with his views on the future of East Africa. He envisaged a thriving colony of thousands of Europeans with their families, the whole of the country from the Aberdares and Mount Kenya to the German border divided up into farms; the whole of the Rift Valley cultivated or grazed, and the whole country of Lumbwa, Nandi to Elgon and almost to Baringo under white settlement. He intends to confine the natives to reserves and use them as cheap labour on farms. I suggested that the country belonged to Africans and that their interests must prevail over the interests of strangers. He would not have it; he kept on using the word "paramount" with reference to the claims of Europeans. I said that some day the African would be educated and armed; that would lead to a clash. Eliot thought that that day was so far distant as not to matter and that by that time the European element would be strong enough to look after themselves; but I am convinced that in the end the Africans will win and that Eliot's policy can lead only to trouble and disappointment.

Sir Charles Eliot

14 . VII . 1902. *Nairobi—Fort Hall Road*

Leave Nairobi for Fort Hall

Tate and I left Nairobi on our return journey to Fort Hall. It rained incessantly all day. We camped on the Nairobi River.

17 . VII . 1902. *Fort Hall*

Arrive at Fort Hall

We marched into Fort Hall this afternoon, having completed the 68 miles in 4 days. On the 15th Tate shot a good rhinoceros on the Mekindu River. On the 16th we passed through my old camp on the Thika, which is now occupied by Swire and a detachment of the King's African Rifles. He has seen nothing of either lion or Wakikuyu. I saw a giraffe near the Thika River.

Native arrogance at Fort Hall

During our absence Kenuthia and two other smaller chiefs have been giving trouble. They got very drunk one evening and told Hemsted that now that there were so few soldiers in Fort Hall they intended to attack the station. Hemsted merely laughed at them but fined them 5 goats each, which they paid today. But it was most impertinent of Kenuthia and is significant. What a man says when he is drunk he thinks when he is sober. Dear old Tate takes a most serious view of the occurrence and talks about sending for more troops, etc. I told him I would, in the event of a Kikuyu attack on Fort Hall, guarantee not only to defend the station but to burn every village within 5 miles in 24 hours, but that on the first shot being fired I should shut him up in the guardroom, as his sad face would be likely to discourage my men. Tate is beginning to see jokes and to appreciate the humour of the situation. Here are we, three white men in the heart of Africa, with 20 nigger soldiers and 50 nigger police, 68 miles from doctors or reinforcements, administering and policing a district inhabited by half a million well-armed savages who have only quite recently come into touch with the white man, and we are responsible for the security in an area the size of Yorkshire. The position is most humorous to my mind, but we seem to be handling it quite well. A small chief gets drunk, threatens to stamp out our authority, and is fined

Kikuyu dancing boys

Kikuyu dancing boys

Kikuyu dancing boys

The three dancing girls who visited me. The centre one became a great friend and used to bring me honey and milk once a week

5 goats. The humour of that alone is sufficient to allow us to drown our fears.

20 . VII . 1902. *Fort Hall*

Hemsted and I had a Sunday shoot on the Tana River, where we saw plenty of game. We bagged 2 oribi and 2 impala.

A Sunday shoot

22 . VII . 1902. *Fort Hall*

Tate wants me to build a bridge over the Tana, so we rode down to have a look for a suitable spot. The river is as broad as the Test at Mottisfont, or some 40 yards across, deep and with a strong current. The bed is rocky but rough. I found a suitable spot for the bridge, which I shall come down and build in a week or so. I promised Tate I should call it Tate's Bridge.

A bridge reconnaissance on the Tana River

I caught sight of two hippopotami just above the site of my bridge, their noses, eyes and ears projecting from the water. They are the first I have seen.

Hippopotami

25 . VII . 1902. *Near Fort Hall*

When I was in Nairobi I collected some survey instruments and a plane table. I started off today to survey the road towards the Aberdare Mountains, camping about 9 miles west of Fort Hall. The country is thickly cultivated and has never been mapped before, so I am doing good work. In the evening the Wakikuyu brought me in some sheep, bananas, milk and sweet potatoes.

Survey work

26 . VII . 1902. *Tusu*

I came on to Tusu, at the eastern base of the Aberdare Mountains. This is the home of Karurie, the paramount chief of all the Wakikuyu. I took 8 hours to cover the 16 miles. I had only time to map in the actual route and a few hundred yards on either side, as the country is so hilly and enclosed.

Survey work

Karurie

Yesterday I paid a visit to Karurie, a major chief of the Wakikuyu and an old man who has proved himself loyal to the administration. He has 40 huts in his village, 39 wives, over 60 children, and many cattle, sheep and goats. He used to have a large store of ivory, but was robbed of this by a white trader called Boyes. This adventurer offered to take the ivory to the coast and sell it. Karurie allowed him to do this, but never saw Boyes again. Boyes is now living in England on the proceeds, and calls himself the King of the Wakikuyu. His kingship would cease very suddenly if he ever put his nose into Karurie's village again.

"White Fathers"

Poor Karurie is afflicted by three Italian missionaries who have recently arrived at his village. They belong to the White Fathers. I lunched with these three men yesterday in a grass hut. They are doing a roaring trade with the innocent natives, and are living a most immoral life. They have enticed young boys and girls into their mission, and under the pretence of teaching them religion and administering remedies for diseases from which the children are not suffering are introducing a code of immorality which is completely foreign to the Wakikuyu. They are certainly not "white," but doubtless will soon be fathers.

Smith, the immoral missionary

With them was an Englishman called Smith, a carpenter by trade. Kibarra-barra, the Fort Hall interpreter who is with me, told me that Karurie is furious with Smith, as he tells the converted girls that they cannot be true Christians until they have slept with a Christian. He sleeps with one or two of these young ladies every week. I asked Karurie if it were true and he produced seven girls who had been dealt with by Smith; they all testified to the truth of the story. So I paid a visit to Smith and told him he would have to come into Fort Hall with me and that I should recommend that he be deported. Smith was very indignant but is now packing up.

Return to Fort Hall

I left Tusu yesterday afternoon and walked back 8 miles towards Fort Hall. It rained and blew hard all last night. Today I marched into Fort Hall, having covered the last 17 miles in 4 hours. I have put in an official report to Tate about the missionaries at Tusu, and they are going to be removed, having completely shocked Tate's sense of decency.

29 . VII . 1902. *Fort Hall*

East African Syndicate

A party of the East African Syndicate arrived here today for the purpose of prospecting in the district. A Mr. Barchard, one of the party, is a cousin of Miss Jenkins, who married Ashton Radcliffe of Fonthill.

Hemsted and I think we find untold wealth

Hemsted and I thought the other day we had found alluvial gold in the Meragua River. We had carefully washed many basins of sand and there remained a residue of a yellow powder. We showed this to Barchard, who pronounced it to be mica of a worthless character. So our hopes of untold wealth are dashed to the ground.

Dancing girls

Three dancing girls paid me a call this afternoon; I did not quite understand their motive, but they were well behaved and pleasant, and brought me honey and sweet potatoes. One of them asked if she might be my servant. I thought that a bit forward, and refused; she said that she would bring me honey once a week, as she heard I had been very kind to her family. When and where? However, we shall see what is behind this courtesy.

30 . VII . 1902. *Fort Hall*

Tate ordered to the Rendile Country

Yesterday Tate received a letter from the Commissioner, Sir Charles Eliot, ordering him to the Rendile country south-east of Lake Rudolph, to investigate and collect evidence to enable the Government to prosecute three European traders who are now in custody in Nairobi, charged with murder, raiding, and the wholesale slaughter of elephants. The names of these three are Smith, Vincent and Atkinson. I hope Tate manages to get what is wanted, as human wolves of this sort do such infinite harm to the prestige of the white man among savages.

Tate left here for Nairobi today. We shall all miss him, in spite of his dismal looks and cheerless disposition.

Tate takes Smith into Nairobi with a strong recommendation for deportation. Smith is quite open about his immorality and can see no harm in it.

3 . VIII . 1902. *Fort Hall*

Shooting

On 1 August Hemsted and I went down to the junction of the Tana and Mathyoia Rivers, where we shot some impala and oribi. We turned the cook on to catch fish and he secured a fine basket of eels, which proved excellent eating. I saw an otter in the Tana.

Eels and otters

The Chaplin brothers

Two brothers called Chaplin, who have come out on a big-game shoot, arrived here today. I was at Harrow with both of them.

Mount Kenya

Mount Kenya is but 40-odd miles from here, and this evening it stood out very clear, which enabled me to get some good bearings on to the summit. My results show that the War Office map of East Africa is incorrect as regards this mountain.

8 . VIII . 1902. *Fort Hall*

A leopard

I was down at the junction of the Tana and Mathyoia Rivers today and shot a leopard. I was sitting down by the bank of the Tana contemplating the wonderful outline of the snow-capped Kenya when I saw the leopard emerge from the bush some 500 yards from me. I crept into the bush, and keeping along near the river, approached to within 80 yards of him. He was sitting up like some huge cat, licking his flanks. My first shot hit him in the ribs, when he came bounding towards me, though he did not see me. I killed him at 20 yards with a shot through the spine. He was not charging me but merely rushing for shelter.

10 . VIII . 1902. *Tana River*

Bridge-building

I came down here yesterday to build Tate's Bridge. I was busy all yesterday cutting spars, shaping them and lashing them together. I have made four good trestles, bound with copper wire, so they should last for some time. I have not yet got them into position, and this is going to cause some trouble, as the current of the river and its depth prevent us working in the water. But I hope to complete it tomorrow.

In the afternoon I shot an Egyptian goose and in the evening I went to a pool just above the bridge where I had previously seen hippopotami. It was not long before I heard grunts and snorts quite close to me in the reeds, and soon 4 hippo appeared in midstream, puffing and blowing, yawning, and showing to advantage their capacious mouths and the curiously complicated dentition. As they yawned they gave a curious coughing bark, best imitated by drawing in one's breath and making a noise at the back of one's throat. I noticed that they have the power, presumably by standing on their hind legs on the bed of the stream, of raising their whole head and shoulders out of the water, and it was in this position that I shot the largest bull of the four. He sank at once to my shot. He was only 60 yards from me, and I should have hit him through the brain with a solid bullet from my Mannlicher. I am certain to recover him tomorrow when he floats, as some rapids below him prevent him being carried too far down stream.

Hippopotami

11 . VIII . 1902. *Tana River*

I was out at dawn and soon located the dead hippo, who had floated downstream nearly to my bridge, and was grounded on some rocks in midstream. I waded out and tied a rope round one of his hind legs, which enabled us to pull him into shallow water near the bank. We then commenced to cut him up in the water. I cut a strip of skin from his nose to his tail, and then tried to sever his head from his body—no easy job. His head, without any neck, weighed 250 pounds. He proves to be a large bull with excellent teeth. My men and porters are desperately keen about the meat and have managed to get it all into camp. They consider hippo meat a great delicacy.

I recover the hippopotamus

All my men pretend they are Mohammedans, though none of them ever say their prayers. The only Mohammedan habit they practise is that no animal may be eaten unless it has had its throat cut before death. It is, of course, impossible to cut a hippo's throat; that difficulty is surmounted by saying the hippo is a fish, as it lives in water. And I have often noted that they will cut a dead animal's throat when I am not looking.

Fish

Some of my porters caught several large fish which had been attracted by the blood in the water, also some fine eels. They were pulling them out as fast as they could throw the bait in and landed over 200 pounds of fish and eels in an hour. I return to Fort Hall tomorrow, and shall have completed the bridge.

16 . VIII . 1902. *Tana River*

Shoot on the Tana River, combined with survey work

I am down surveying the country on the right bank of the Tana River and am not neglecting my opportunities for a shoot. I arrived in camp in the afternoon, having surveyed all the morning. I killed an oribi and a waterbuck near camp, the former giving me a good stalk. During the day I saw a great deal of fresh lion and rhinoceros spoor.

17 . VIII . 1902. *Tana River*

Tana River

I surveyed all the morning, travelling some 6 miles down the Tana River. It is a grand river and quite beautiful with the tropical vegetation and huge forest trees which border its banks. It runs in a deep ravine where the Meragua joins it, and just before the latter river makes its junction it tumbles over some falls whose height I have been unable to estimate, but they must approach some 300 feet sheer drop.

In the evening I killed a waterbuck and an oribi as meat for the men. I had been frequently told that the Kikuyu would not eat wild game meat. This is wrong; they love it and eat masses of it if they can get it. When I return from a shooting holiday I always found men, old women, boys and girls, sometimes as many as 50 people, awaiting me, when I would distribute my meat. This often resulted in a scramble, but when they learned that shouting and greed meant no meat, they soon learned to control and behave themselves. They particularly like the flesh of the hippopotamus, but will not touch waterbuck; neither do I.

18 . VIII . 1902. *Fort Hall*

Return to Fort Hall

I returned to Fort Hall this evening. During my absence from the station a new officer has arrived to replace Tate, a man called McClean, whose past life has also been spent as a schoolmaster.

19 . VIII . 1902. *Fort Hall*

The Wakikuyu murder a policeman

News came in this evening that a policeman had been murdered by a village only a mile or so from the station, as a protest against the white men. McClean, Hemsted and I at once held a council of war, at which I strongly advocated either immediate and drastic action in the shape of surprising the village this very night and arresting the murderers, or the weaker policy of dealing with the matter through the chiefs and relying on them to bring the culprits to justice. I favoured the former course as being the stronger. Hemsted agreed with me but McClean demurred; so I pointed out the evil effect on the native mind of allowing such a crime to go unpunished, and told him that if he did not act at once the natives would take it as weakness on our part and might attack the station, in which case military operations would be involved. After a short argument McClean agreed to go out tonight and punish the village. If they offered resistance, we should use force.

Our primary object is therefore to surround the village before dawn and await results. Not a soul in the station knows our intentions. I shall take 22 rifles and McClean is taking 20 police, who will not be much use, as they do not yet know how to fire their guns.

20 . VIII . 1902. *Fort Hall*

We surprise the Wakikuyu

At midnight I sent a reliable native to the offending village to ascertain what was happening. He returned at 3 a.m. this morning, saying all the neighbouring villages had joined forces with the offending village and were at the moment conducting an orgy round the dead policeman's body, which had been badly mutilated. A council of war had been held by the natives and they had decided to march on Fort Hall at dawn. So we marched out of the station at 3.30 a.m., crossed the Mathyoia and reached our destination half an hour before dawn. The village had bonfires burning and the Wakikuyu were dancing round them in all their war-paint. It was really rather a weird sight. The alarm was given by a native who tried to break through our rather thin cordon. He refused to stop when challenged and was shot down. There was then a rush from the village into the surrounding bush, and we killed about 17 niggers. Two policemen and one of my men were killed. I narrowly escaped a spear which whizzed past my head. Then the fun began. We at once burned the village and captured the sheep and goats. After that we systematically cleared the valley in which the village was situated, burned all the huts, and killed a few more niggers, who finally gave up the fight and cleared off, but not till 3 more of our men had been killed.

The result of salutary action

At 3 p.m. we returned to Fort Hall and told the chiefs who had assembled to meet us that they were to go out to the village at once, get into touch with the local chief, bring him in, and generally spread the news that our anger was by no means appeased. They returned just before dark with a deputation from the village, saying their chief was killed and they begged for mercy. McClean fined them 50 head of cattle, at the same time intimating that half would be remitted if the murderers of the policeman were produced. This they promised to do tomorrow. We have told them that we are quite prepared to continue tomorrow what we began today, and I think they are impressed. Such nonsense as attacking the station is completely driven from their stupid heads. So order once more reigns in Kenya District.

27 . VIII . 1902. *Fort Hall*

Repentance

This morning there came a deputation from the offending village, bringing presents of milk, honey and goats to all of us, and dragging two of the murderers with them. They owned to the murder and regretted it, stating they had been misled by their medicine men. The medicine men were also produced, and each received one year's imprisonment this afternoon. The actual murderers were condemned to 6 months' hard labour.

This little episode was merely a trial of strength between the medicine men's regime and ours. These men are, of course, opposed to our rule, as they are unable to retain their power, which is of an iniquitous nature. They play on the superstitions of the ignorant and have complete control over them. This we are determined to break, and we went a long way yesterday and today in destroying the cruel and unjust power of medicine men.

The wrong way

I blame McClean for causing this trouble. The headman of the offending village was asked a week ago to come into Fort Hall to explain some thefts in which it was believed he was implicated. He did not come, so McClean sent out a Swahili policeman, who could not speak Kikuyu, to bring the man in. That was asking for trouble. The Government interpreter, for whom the Kikuyu have a great respect, should have been sent. What happened was this. The policeman, on reaching the village, found an orgy going on. He shouted at the headman in a language he did not understand, threatened to shoot, loaded his rifle, seized the headman and tried to drag him along. All the guests then fell upon the policeman and killed him. Two medicine men were among the party and they apparently encouraged the villagers to kill the man, saying the government at Fort Hall was too weak to do anything about it.

[In October 1902 these same villages revolted and troops were sent out to punish them. The trouble was attributed to medicine men, so two of them were publicly hanged in Fort Hall, which stopped the trouble temporarily; but the Kikuyu are ripe for trouble, and when they get educated and medicine men are replaced by political agitators there will be a general rising. (Note written in October 1902.)]

23 . VIII . 1902. *Fort Hall*

Survey on the River Tana

I came down to the Tana yesterday and continued the survey downstream and along the Kitui path. I saw some antelope I had not seen before, and I fancy they must be female lesser kudu.

Malaria fever

Last night I had a touch of fever, so crawled back to Fort Hall this afternoon and went to bed with a large dose of quinine in me.

Colobus monkeys

While on my way in I saw a troupe of the black and white colobus monkeys on the Tana. I bagged 4 adults with my shotgun and skinned them in bed this evening.

Introduction of hut tax and its result

Word went forth from Nairobi that a hut tax of 3 rupees a hut is to be imposed on the Kikuyu. This has been explained to the Kikuyu, and as they have very little coin they were told that one sheep in lieu of 3 rupees would be accepted. The result is that sheep have been dribbling in with no arrangements to keep them; many have been stolen and many are suffering from foot rot. There is no market for them, and so they have become a burden to the administration—the first time in history when a tax has become a burden to the collector of taxes. It shows a great lack of forethought. Today we have 746 sheep, all penned up and largely lame from foot rot. So Hemsted today called in the Kikuyu chiefs and told them to take their sheep back. Of course, first come, first served, but all the sheep are gone. But what a muddle and lack of organisation!

26 . VIII . 1902. *Fort Hall*

Karurie's account of the origin of the Wakikuyu

I am out of bed and all right today. Karurie came to Fort Hall this afternoon and told me a curious myth regarding the origin of the Wakikuyu. He says their ancestors came from near Lake Rudolph and the founder of their race had three sons. One was told to go into the plains and tend the cattle. This one became the ancestor of the Masai. Another was told to cultivate, and he gave rise to the Wakikuyu and Wakamba. The third was told to hunt wild animals and live in the forests, and he gave rise to the Wandorobo. When the Wakikuyu or Wakamba wanted sheep, cattle or goats, they used to beg them from the Masai and were killed for their trouble, which originated the feud between these races which exists to this day.

The myth is, of course, contrary to fact, because the Masai are of Nilotic origin and the Wakikuyu are not.

The local chief Kenuthia, on hearing I would be leaving Fort Hall soon, gave a large dance on my parade ground this afternoon. The people erected a huge shelter of wild banana leaves in which I sat like a king. McClean and Hemsted were not invited and there was no room for them in my banana throne, so they had to sit outside. Hemsted was amused; McClean, much on his dignity, was annoyed. The dances were excellent, young men and girls going through all sorts of sexual antics. The final dance was done by 7 young ladies—a direct assault on my morals. I gave them each a bunch of beads, and I gave Kenuthia a magnificent sheep which cost me 4 rupees.

I am fêted by Kenuthia

29 . VIII . 1902. *Fort Hall*

Barlow arrived here today with the relieving detachment which returns on Sunday next. I am remaining on for a few weeks to finish the survey work I have commenced and to try to map the route over the Aberdare Mountains.

My detachment is relieved

31 . VIII . 1902. *Fort Hall*

Hemsted, Barlow and I visited the Tana. Hemsted bagged 2 rhinoceros, 2 waterbuck, a reedbuck and an oribi in less than 2 hours. The rhino charged him together or he would not have killed them. They both lay dead touching each other. We wanted the other game for the station.

Shooting

We had a great dance this evening in honour of the arrival of Barlow and to bid me farewell. The men dancers all arrived on this occasion painted with white earth and bedecked with bustard feathers in their heads. Women did not take part in the dancing.

I . IX . 1902. *Near Fort Hall*

McClean and I left Fort Hall this morning for the Aberdare Mountains, which lie between Fort Hall and Lake Naivasha. Our idea is to pass over Kinangop Peak or as near to it as we can get, to locate the headwaters of the Thika and Chania Rivers, and then follow down the Chania to see if it enters the Thika River or not. We are now camped about 10 miles west of Fort Hall.

We start off for the Aberdare Mountains

3 . IX . 1902. *Aberdare Mountains*

Tusu

Yesterday we reached Tusu, where Karurie lives. Karurie himself is ill, but we saw his mother, a wizened-up old woman, toothless and hideous.

Kinangop

Today we marched into the hills at the base of Kinangop. The track was scarcely discernible, being overgrown and tangled with fallen trees and creepers. We were in thick forest through the day with dense thickets of tall bamboo. The vegetation was luxuriant and dripping with moisture. On the lower slopes we found begonias in profusion, both red and white, both small plants and creeping varieties. There were also dock plants, stinging nettles, violets, pansies and wild roses. All sorts of ferns and mosses were in profusion and in clusters of thousands of varieties. As we approached 7000 feet we came across thistles.

Flora

We camped at 2.45 p.m., having done about 8 miles in as many hours. The hills are shrouded in cloud and the temperature is low, about 46° Fahrenheit. I found surveying difficult and was only able to take a few observations when clouds lifted. We have not seen the top ridge of Kinangop, some 13,000 feet up, owing to the cloud not having lifted. Our camp is near the headwaters of the Meragua River, a mere trickle through a bed of moss and fern. There are signs of elephant near the camp. It is now pouring with rain, and we are shivering with cold. I suspect some of our porters will desert in the night, as they do not fancy ascending the hill tomorrow, considering it haunted.

4 . IX . 1902. *Aberdare Mountains*

The ascent

We were not sorry to get on the move again at dawn and stretch our stiff and rain-sodden limbs. Only one porter deserted in the night, so we can proceed with all our loads. Soon after dawn the clouds cleared off the serrated ridge of Kinangop and the sun shone brightly, giving us a gorgeous view and enabling me to take some useful observations. The track became worse and worse, almost disappearing soon after leaving last night's camp. We climbed up and up, the temperature fell lower and lower, and our breath came quicker and quicker as we got into the alpine zone of tropical Africa. The porters behaved well and stuck to their work like veritable niggers.

Kinangop Peak

After 5 hours' stiff climb we reached the summit of the main ridge, and there was Kinangop Peak about half a mile to the north. I made a rapid rush to get to the top, and succeeded after an hour's scramble over wet rocks in getting a magnificent view of the whole Kikuyu country to the east, with Mount Kenya in the distance, while to the west lay the deep Rift Valley with the huge lake of Naivasha gleaming in the sun. To the south lay expanses of forest with the vast Athi Plains stretching towards Kilimanjaro, which was just visible. To the north lay the continuation of the Aberdare Mountains and the open plains known as the Markham Downs. The country on the top was open but very rough. Huge boulders lay about in confusion, clothed in moss and fern; stunted bushes grew between the boulders, often festooned with fantastic lichen. On the very top of Kinangop, under a huge boulder, grew a flower very like cyclamen, and clusters of maidenhair fern. I had been well rewarded. After stopping there an hour and taking numerous observations, I began the descent on to the Naivasha or western foot of the range.

On the summit of Kinangop I built a cairn 6 feet high, and in it I placed a small bottle of beer with a request that should it be unearthed by anyone at some future date he should drink my health and drop me a line to 25 Rutland Gate.

Fauna and flora

In my descent, and in the open country above the forest, I noted juniper, violets, wild roses, crocuses, blackberries, lichen of infinite variety on both rock and tree, gladioli (red and yellow), "red-hot pokers," everlasting flowers, clover, and many other familiar European plants and shrubs. At that elevation there was no sign of tropical life. The only bird I saw was a small brown pipit, which I failed to secure, and on a small stream was a common sandpiper. I saw no insect or animal life above the forest.

Headwaters of the Thika River

In this open moorland country rises the Thika River, which I crossed frequently as a small mountain torrent, whose crystal waters I drank. I could trace the stream right down to the plains, which has proved invaluable for my survey. The porters and McClean having got well ahead, I made a rapid descent and caught them up just as they were pitching camp in a glade of the forest at about 6000 feet. Our camp is at the sources of the Chania. It was bitterly cold and rained hard all night. At dusk quantities of some variety of wood ibis flew over the camp.

Sources of the Chania River

I am delighted with my day's work. I have located the headwaters of the Thika and Chania Rivers, I have been the first white man to ascend Kinangop Peak, and I have seen the tropical alpine zone in all its glory. It now remains to be seen whether the Chania and Thika join waters or whether the Chania flows into some other river.

5 . IX . 1902. *Aberdare Mountains*

Difficulties of survey in the forest

It rained all last night and was still pouring when we struck camp this morning. We now turned south along a forest track leading through dense bamboo with occasional marshy glades. Survey was almost impossible, and I had to rely on pacing for distance and general compass bearings, frequently taken on sound. But I was able to check my bearings by theodolite readings both this morning and this afternoon. After 6½ hours in the forest we were glad to camp at noon, having covered barely 9 miles.

A large party of armed natives passed us this afternoon. They would give us no satisfactory explanation of where they were going. Found several ferns new to me and 3 distinct varieties of maidenhair fern.

Game

We passed several "salt licks" in the bamboo forest. At one of these there were fresh tracks of buffalo and elephant. In fact elephant tracks are everywhere, and they seem to be abundant in these thick jungles. Within a few yards of our camp is a large patch of freshly turned earth, evidently the work of some old tusker last night.

Two unidentified forest animals

While wandering in the forest at dusk I saw two animals I have never seen before. Unfortunately I caught only a fleeting glimpse of them. The larger was a huge red antelope of sorts with white stripes. I could not see

Waterfall on the Kemakia River near our camp, with our two guides standing in the foreground

A Kikuyu boy at Fort Hall

the head, only the rump. It seemed even larger than a haartebeeste. The other was an enormous black pig, probably a forest variety of the warthog. Here again I only just saw the beast for a moment. [These were no doubt the bongo and the forest hog.]

Waterfall on the Kemakia River

Our camp is near a magnificent waterfall on the Kemakia River, the roar of the falling water being a most soothing sound. Both wood ibis and parrots are common round the camp, but otherwise both bird and animal life is scarce.

6 . IX . 1902. *Aberdare Mountains*

A night disturbed by elephant

We did not pass an altogether pleasant night. Soon after dark the camp was alarmed by a single elephant tearing down bamboos close to the camp. It was too wet to light fires, so we had to content ourselves with standing to with arms. Our Wakikuyu made matters worse by recounting to us the habits of the Aberdare elephants who delight in playing havoc among camps, and how they resent the presence of white men in their jungles. They kept on trying to impress me with the great weight and strength of an elephant and what little chance we stood against such leviathans. However, there was nothing to be done. It was pitch dark, raining hard, and very cold, and we were standing about waiting to be rushed by 4 tons of elephant. We, of course, could see nothing. The elephant was not more than 30 or 40 yards from camp, and whenever he moved we heard him. After a time we heard no noise, and thinking he had gone away we retired to our tents. But about midnight the sentry rushed into my tent, telling me the elephant was upon us and tearing down the tents. There was a loud tearing and cracking noise in camp. McClean and I rushed out and found the brute playing havoc with a tent. We could not see him but fired in his direction, when he made off with a trumpeting squeal, and we heard him crashing through the forest as he forced his way through the bamboos. After that we were left in peace, but we were too scared for further sleep. At dawn I was on to the spoor, which I followed for some distance, but the elephant had evidently gone some way, and as there was no trace of blood, presumably we had not touched him, for which I was thankful.

More elephant

Soon after leaving camp we saw a party of 7 elephant some 150 yards from us in a glade. One of them was a fine old tusker. Now, much as I might desire to shoot an elephant in self-defence, I have never had any desire to kill them for sport. They are such wise animals, and might be so useful to humanity. Domesticated elephants are delightful characters, and to kill them for the fun of killing, or for the monetary gain of the value of their ivory, is to my mind immoral. It is a pity that an intelligent creature like the elephant should be shot in order that creatures not much more intelligent may play billiards with balls made from its teeth.

This party of elephant watched us for a minute or so and then slowly walked over the open grass into the forest. I was much impressed by the deliberation of their movements. It would have been an easy matter to intercept them and to kill the old bull, whose ivory must have been worth £100, and I congratulate myself that I, an impecunious subaltern with a modern rifle in my hands, should have resisted the temptation.

We afterwards again saw two elephant, and it was obvious from the frequency of the spoor that we were travelling through one of their strongholds.

We emerge from the forest into cultivated areas

About noon we got out of the bamboo forest and entered cultivated country. We camped at a place called Kadiarra. Several rather surly Wakikuyu came to have a look at us and refused to bring in or sell us food for porters. They are obviously most unfriendly, so I have double sentries on the camp tonight.

Painted lady butterflies

I saw several painted lady butterflies today, both near camp and in the bamboo forest. This ubiquitous insect seems as common in the tropics of Asia and Africa as it is throughout palaearctic Europe and Asia. Neither altitude nor latitude seems to check its distribution.

7 . IX . 1902. *Kihimbuini, Kikuyu Country*

We had no alarms last night. Our route took us through hilly country with dense bush frequently cleared in patches for cultivation. We saw few villages or even natives.

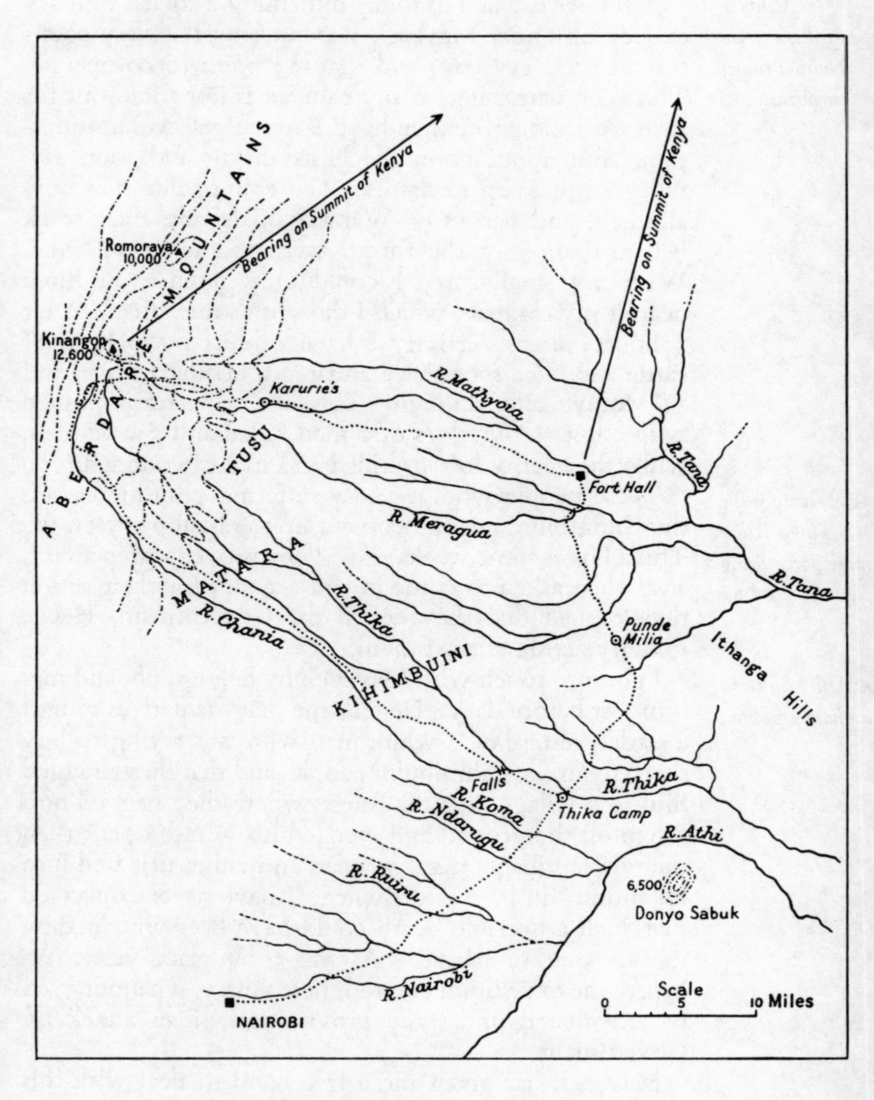

Sketch map of the main results of my survey work in the Fort Hall district, none of which had been previously accurately mapped

Military expedition from Nairobi rather embarrasses us

A runner reached us today informing us that a military expedition under Maycock was entering this very country on this very day, and that we were to co-operate. This is embarrassing, as my caravan is not fitted out for field operations; neither have I much reserve ammunition. But about noon we heard firing and soon saw villages going up in flames. The countryside was now alarmed, and parties of Wakikuyu, driving their stock before them into the forest, were visible on all sides. With my small force I could only pounce on those nearest my caravan, which I did with some effect. After 3 hours' intense activity I have captured 170 head of cattle and over 1000 sheep and goats, besides 17 men and 34 women and children. This has been accomplished with a loss to ourselves of 2 men killed and 3 wounded, while the enemy lost 17 killed and many wounded.

Revenge for the Thika River mail party being cut up

These people who are now suffering punishment are the Kihimbuini people who cut up the mail party on the Thika River some weeks ago. They proved unrepentant, and when asked to come in and account for their action they replied that they defied the Government. Hence military action against them.

A settler killed in a ghastly fashion

I got into touch with Maycock by heliograph, and met him just before dark. He tells me that the natives caught a settler yesterday, a white man who was trying to buy sheep from the Kihimbuini people, and that they dragged him to a village near the forest, where they pegged him down on the ground and wedged his mouth open; then the whole village, man, woman and child, urinated into his mouth till he was drowned. I have never conceived that such a horrible death could have been invented by the savagest of natives. As this took place yesterday, before the expedition entered the country, it cannot even be extenuated under the provocation of an attack by Government.

Maycock has given me a free hand to deal with this village, which I shall do at dawn tomorrow morning.

Camp

We camped between the Thika and Tana Rivers, and had some difficulty in finding a suitable spot for defence and for housing our captured stock and prisoners. The men prisoners are sleeping in the open, but I have given a tent for the women and children. They are in a state of great nervousness, but I have told them that they will be liberated as soon as operations cease. I gave them a bucket of milk, plenty of meat and vegetables, and firewood, so they spent a more or less contented night.

This evening, after dark, the country was lit up by the smouldering villages, and the stillness of the night was often broken by the war-cries of these poor misguided savages. The horrible death they meted out to one of my own countrymen fills me with anger, and I shudder when I imagine what the poor fellow's last moments must have been. It does not incline me to feel too mercifully towards the Kihimbuini, and I shall teach the offending village such a lesson at dawn tomorrow as will be long remembered among the Wakikuyu.

I blame the authorities in Nairobi for sending an expedition into this country without warning us and without closing the district to trading settlers. They did neither. Our little camp is by no means safe tonight, as we only have 40 rounds per rifle left, no machine gun, and a large perimeter. We can but hope for the best and trust that the Kihimbuini are as apprehensive as we are tonight.

8 . IX . 1902. *Kihimbuini, Kikuyu*

Drastic punishment for the village which murdered a white man

I have performed a most unpleasant duty today. I made a night march to the village at the edge of forest where the white settler had been so brutally murdered the day before yesterday. Though the war drums were sounding throughout the night we reached the village without incident and surrounded it. By the light of fires we could see savages dancing in the village, and our guides assured me that they were dancing round the mutilated body of the white man.

I gave orders that every living thing except children should be killed without mercy. I hated the work and was anxious to get through with it. So soon as we could see to shoot we closed in. Several of the men tried to break out but were immediately shot. I then assaulted the place before any defence could be prepared. Every soul was either shot or bayoneted, and I am happy to say that no children were in the village. They, with the younger women, had already been removed by the villagers to the forest. We burned all the huts and razed the banana plantations to the ground.

In the open space in the centre of the village was a sight which horrified me—a naked white man pegged out on his back, mutilated and disembowelled, his body used as a latrine by all and sundry who passed by. We washed his corpse in a stream and buried him just outside the village. The whole of this affair took so short a time that the sun was barely up before we beat a retreat to our main camp.

[My drastic action on this occasion haunted me for many years, and even now I am not sure whether I was right. My reason for killing all adults, including women, was that the latter had been the main instigators of not only the murder but the method of death, and it was the women who had befouled the corpse after death. McClean, who was with me as Political Officer, was naturally consulted; though he refused to give his consent to my action, he told me he would not interfere if I thought it was a just punishment, so the responsibility is entirely mine.]

Close of operations

As operations ceased this evening I gave orders for the camp to be struck, and we marched for the open plains on the south of the Thika River. We soon crossed the Chania River, which we now followed, as it became apparent that it did in reality flow into the Thika. We soon reached the junction of the two rivers, and immediately above the junction the Chania tumbles over some beautiful falls, where we lunched. These falls must be at least 150 feet high. We named them the Chania Falls. The Chania here is a larger river than the Thika.

A haul of sheep

While we were lunching we suddenly heard the bleating of sheep. Off rushed Kebarabara, our interpreter, to secure them. They turned out to be a flock of Kihimbuini sheep which had been driven down here for safety, and were under the charge of children, the men having fled at our approach. After cajoling the children with sugared almonds they were released, and went back into the bush —minus their sheep.

We reached my old camp on the Thika River at 4.30 p.m. and camped. My old *zariba* still stands, so we made use of it. It was here that the mail party were cut up some weeks ago, and it was here that the man-eating lion stole one of my porters. We killed 12 sheep, so that my men, the porters and prisoners should all have a good meal. And as we have but one sentry on tonight there is general rejoicing.

Thika River Camp

10 . IX . 1902. *Fort Hall*

We camped at Punde Milia last night and marched into Fort Hall this afternoon, releasing all our prisoners before entering the station.

Return to Fort Hall

13 . IX . 1902. *Punde Milia Camp*

Started off for Nairobi and camped at Punde Milia. There I met the mail party, so I opened the bag and extracted my letters.

Commence my return journey to Nairobi

I am sorry to have left Fort Hall, as I had a real good time there. My time was full of adventure, and I appear to have had my full share of excitement. I am not looking forward to the comparative civilisation of Nairobi and shall again try to get out on detachment as soon as possible.

15 . IX . 1902. *Ruiru River*

Yesterday I camped on the old spot on the Thika River. Soon after starting from Punde Milia I saw 3 cow eland.

Thika Camp

When I crossed the famous patch of reeds some 7 miles north of the Thika, which always holds lion, I saw 2 of them, both males, walking in the open and about 800 yards distant. They had not seen me, so I halted my caravan and stalked them. They moved slowly, and I made for a small rise which they would pass. My tactics were successful and they passed within 30 yards of me, walking slowly; but alas, my Mannlicher would not work and the magazine jammed. So I had to rest content with watching these 2 superb lion, and as soon as they were out of sight I rejoined the caravan, cursing my luck.

Lion. A missed opportunity

Today I camped on the Ruiru River.

Ruiru River

16 . IX . 1902. *Nairobi*

Return to Nairobi

I arrived back in Nairobi today. On my way in I saw rhino, eland and plenty of the commoner game. I shot several sandgrouse (*Pterocles senegalensis*).

I meet Hinde

This evening I met S. L. Hinde, the Sub-commissioner of Fort Hall, who has just returned from leave and goes to Fort Hall tomorrow. I did not see him long enough to form much opinion of his ability, but should not say it was exceedingly great, though he appears to be pleasant enough and to have plenty of energy. He started life as a doctor in the Congo, then married and came to East Africa, where he has been till recently, at Machako's.

26 . IX . 1902. *Nairobi*

Refitting

I have been busy lately refitting my company and getting them into a better state of discipline. They are sorely in need of a month or two of solid barrack square drill. And they will have to shoot a great deal better than they do at present before I am satisfied with them. But they are good material, being mainly from the Manyema tribe of the Congo and the Wanyamwezi from German East Africa.

Simba Manyema

I have a splendid fellow in my company, as large and as strong as an ox. I have made him my gun-bearer. He cares naught for man or beast, seldom speaks, and is always at my heels. I suspect he is a cannibal, thus following the custom of his tribe.

Shooting

I was shooting on the 21st when I bagged a spur-winged goose and great bustard with my Mannlicher, which is again in serviceable order.

Ostrich

Today I killed a fine old cock ostrich. An ostrich is a curious bird. They strike me as being also most indecent, having naked pink legs. When they run with their wings outstretched they look every bit like ballet girls. I hit this bird in the body and he fell at once, but was struggling on the ground when I approached him. I eventually killed him with an axe, which was no easy matter, for his strong legs were going like a windmill and one blow from them would have broken a bone.

I had never before examined the anatomy of an ostrich. The sternum has no keel, and the heart and liver lie immediately below it. The gizzard contained a great deal of gravel and grit, while in the stomach were green food, some small gourds about the size of golf balls, and some seeds of a wild bean. His wing feathers were freshly moulted and perfect. I brought home a leg, which we ate this evening. It tasted like good beef.

28 . IX . 1902. *Nairobi*

Major Burnham

Met a distinguished scout from South Africa, a Major Burnham, who is up here on behalf of a new enterprise, the East African Syndicate; he is trying to negotiate the purchase of many thousands of acres of land, but as there is no survey it is difficult to allocate any given area except where bounded by rivers. Burnham is camped just outside Nairobi, not far from Ainsworth's house.

16 . X . 1902. *Lake Nakuru*

A trip to Nakuru

I have been out shooting from Nairobi on most Sundays since I returned from Fort Hall, and during weekdays I have had all my time taken up with improving my company. They are shaping well. I have been given 10 days' leave and came by rail to Nakuru today, where I arrived just before dark. The Rift Valley, through which we passed in the afternoon, was teeming with game of all sorts, mostly zebra, Grant's and Thomson's gazelle and haartebeeste. I am stopping the night at the dak bungalow near the station, where Blane and Roberts are also stopping. They are out here on a big-game shooting trip. The dak bungalow and the station are the only buildings in the place.

17 . X . 1902. *Nakuru*

Neumann's haartebeeste

I was out all the morning chasing Neumann's haartebeeste, of which I bagged 4 bulls. They interest me a great deal, as I suspect they are really hybrids. I shall try to get a series for the British Museum.

The lake

In the evening I strolled down to the lake shores, shooting a hare on the way. The lake is salt and fringed by a belt of bush. In this bush I found large flocks of guinea-fowl, and round the lake I saw myriads of flamingo, geese, duck and waders. I recognised many European migrants, including shoveller, marsh sandpiper, little stint and greenshank.

18 . x . 1902. *Nakuru*

Another visit to Lake Nakuru

I spent the day by the shores of the lake, watching the hippopotami, duck and waders. About 12 hippo were close in to the shore, and by lying concealed in the bush I was able to get a good view of them at close quarters. The young calves were sporting about, one coming on to land within a few yards of me and gambolling about in the mud. Its gigantic mass of a mother got concerned about it, and coming out of the water pushed it back again. The youngster rode on its mother's back for a considerable distance.

Flamingo

I stalked a flock of flamingo and with one solid bullet from my Mannlicher killed 7. I also killed 3 guinea-fowl and a pigeon (*Columba guinea*).

When I returned to the bungalow near the station I developed a bad attack of malaria, and also heard the news that we are to send a detachment to Somaliland to take part in the coming operations. This decided me to return to Nairobi this evening. A goods train leaves here at 10 p.m. tonight, landing me in Nairobi early tomorrow morning.

27 . x . 1902. *Nairobi*

A company leaves for Somaliland

Much to my grief, my company has not been selected for service in Somaliland. Capt. Breading and Lieut. Swire are going with the Sudanese Company. They are lucky fellows, and I expect they will have some good fighting. I wish them both good luck and a safe return.

31 . x . 1902. *Nairobi*

Tate and Barrett return from the Rendile country

I understand Tate had great difficulty in persuading either Rendile or Samburu people to come to Nairobi to give evidence against Smith, Vincent and Dr. Atkinson, who had been raiding around Marsabit. These three ruffians had brought a huge herd of sheep and goats to Naivasha and then to Nakuru. The District Officer at Naivasha, Howard Macallister, failed to report the raid, and the truth only leaked out when some of the raiders' porters complained about their wages. Frederick Jackson, then acting for Charles Eliot, got Tate and Barrett to go north from Nairobi to try to get witnesses for a prosecution, and with the greatest reluctance three witnesses were brought back. Donald, the Town Magistrate in Nairobi, heard the case, and Arthur Neumann also gave evidence for the prosecution. The accused were committed to the High Court, where they were tried before a panel of settlers, but no white jury would ever find a white man guilty on coloured evidence.

Tate had been away 85 days and during that period had covered 1050 miles.

2 . XI . 1902. *Nairobi*

Lion in camp

Last night as Barrett and I were going to bed a terrific noise suddenly broke out from the cattle kraal, only 100 yards off. A lion grunted and roared, cattle were snorting and stampeding, hyaenas were yelling blue murder, and jackals and foxes took up the strains with a high-pitched chorus of barking. I seized a lamp and my revolver, Barrett took the sentry's rifle, and Maycock ran out of his tent with a spear. We ran towards the kraal, from which all the cattle had stampeded. It appears that the lion had had the impertinence to try to force an entrance into the kraal, had alarmed the cattle, who stampeded, and had then begun to roar. The lion was still grunting and growling near the kraal when we arrived on the scene and we followed him by his noise for some distance, but of course could not see him. The hyaenas were mobbing him, which made it easy for us to follow. I never heard such a din as was running in front of us. Though we were within a few yards of him on several occasions we never saw him, and we eventually lost him just below the club. One does not expect such incursions in places like Nairobi.

Game in Nairobi

But to show how much in the wilds we are, an elephant walked through the Sub-commissioner's garden in Nairobi last month and tore up several newly planted croton bushes. The last race meeting we held was broken up by an angry rhinoceros, who held the course for over an hour. And only last August a zebra dropped a foal on our parade ground, and the following night a lion actually killed a zebra within 100 yards of the mess building. Buffalo occur in a swamp only two miles from Nairobi, and leopard are frequently seen within the cantonments.

6 . XI . 1902. *Nairobi*

John Boyes

Met a man called John Boyes, a cheerful rogue who some years ago impersonated the Government at Karurie's in Kikuyu. The Government foolishly brought all sorts of charges against him, but Boyes was acquitted. But I believe he got away with a lot of Karurie's ivory, which he sold at the coast, and never refunded Karurie. I sold Boyes a rifle, but he has never paid me for it; he says he cannot do so, as he is broke—a slippery customer.

8 . XI . 1902. *Nairobi*

Eastwood's accident with a rhino

About a fortnight ago news came into Nairobi that Eastwood, a Uganda Railway official, had been charged and smashed up by a rhino near Baringo. We have just had the details. Eastwood had shot a rhino, and as he was skinning it another rhino approached. He went after it, wounded it with a ·577 cordite rifle and followed it into long grass. He eventually came upon him lying down. The rhino rose to its feet, and Eastwood, firing again, again knocked him down. But the rhino rose a second time and charged. Eastwood hit him twice in the chest but failed to stop him. The beast came on, and Eastwood had no time to load again, so he turned and ran. The rhinoceros followed him like a terrier, caught him up and knocked him down. The rhino then knelt on Eastwood's left arm, breaking it in two places, and proceeded to gore him with his horns. Eastwood's chest is crushed and bruised, many ribs are broken, and he has a nasty gash on the hip. Luckily the rhino soon left him, and Eastwood, being unable to move, lay for two hours in the scorching sun, when his boys found him and carried him into Baringo. But during those two hours Eastwood must have suffered torture, for it was by no means certain whether his boys would find him or not, and to add to his troubles vultures began to collect round him. It was this which really saved him, for their presence brought the boys to where he was lying.

Medical assistance was at once sent for from Baringo. Dr. Falkener started off from Nakuru and completed the 85 miles in two days, amputating Eastwood's left arm half an hour after his arrival.

The latest news is that Eastwood is still in a critical condition.

23 . XI . 1902. *Nairobi*

Sir Charles Elio

The Commissioner, Sir Charles Eliot, arrived here today from Mombasa, and we all had to troop down to the station to meet him. I have seen a little of this man since I have been in the country and have heard a great deal about him. He is not attractive, though no one denies his very marked ability. He openly dislikes soldiers, which is not encouraging. I should say he is a man completely wrapped up in his work, with little time for aught else. He is out of touch and harmony with the world in general. His pet hobby is the study of Nudibranchs or sea slugs. Never did a man more closely resemble the objects of his hobby. He is invertebrate, with an icy cold nature, unsympathetic, but a scholar of the first rank. His enemies refer to him as a Levantine, judging purely on his outer appearance. I should like to get to know him better, as I feel there must be a great deal behind that cold, untidy and unprepossessing countenance.

When I met him last July I liked him. Today he said I must come and dine with him again. I certainly shall if he remembers. I understand he is tremendously shocked by the nakedness of Africans. I like it; but I fear the day is fast approaching when flannel suits and pretty frocks will give a cloak to political upheaval and all the evils of embryonic nationalism.

Barton Wright

Meanwhile a Land Office under my friend Barton Wright has been started with a view to parcelling out land to settlers. Eliot thinks there is a great future for East Africa, transforming it into a huge white farming and stock area. Perhaps that is correct, but sooner or later it must lead to a clash between black and white. I cannot see millions of educated Africans—as there will be in a hundred years' time—submitting tamely to white domination. After all, it is an African country, and they will demand domination. Then blood will be spilled, and I have little doubt about the eventual outcome.

McQueen

I met a settler called McQueen in the club and had a long talk with him about security in the future. He takes the view that the white man is the master race and thas the black men must forever remain cheap labour and slaves—a most dangerous prospect. McQueen is one of the very few white settlers here: he farms at Ngong.

24 . XI . 1902. *Naivasha*

An expedition to the Tetu country

A short time ago the Wakikuyu of the Tetu country, which lies between the Aberdare Mountains and Mount Kenya, cut up an Indian caravan which was passing through their country. They murdered the whole party and looted their goods. They have refused to pay a fine and have sent most insolent messages in to Government. It has therefore been decided to send a small military expedition against them. Hinde has applied for me to command it, at which I am much flattered. I shall enter their country from the west, crossing the Aberdare Mountains from Naivasha, while Barlow from Fort Hall will enter their country simultaneously from the south.

Today I left Nairobi by rail for Naivasha, where I shall wait for the guides Hinde has promised to send.

Protectorate officers at Naivasha

I found a fellow called Wise in charge of Naivasha with Collyer as his assistant. Dr. Mann was in medical charge. Collyer is a huge fellow and has only recently left the university to join this administration. The poor fellow is suffering from consumption and I fear has not long to live. Mann is a curious little man with one eye. He is quiet and full of humour; I like him.

I heard an amusing story from Mann. Three years ago he was serving in Jubaland with Jenner the Civil Officer, who was afterwards murdered by the Somali, and the soldier was St. John Wake. Now Jenner had a complete set of false teeth, Wake had a wooden leg, and Mann has but one eye. They were all three presiding at a big and important native meeting at Kismayu on a particularly hot day. The proceedings got tedious, so Jenner, feeling uncomfortable about the mouth, removed his teeth and placed them with a rattle on the table. The Somalis stared but said not a word. Soon afterwards Wake unscrewed his wooden leg and laid it beside Jenner's teeth on the table. As time went on, Mann found his false eye causing him discomfort, and removed it, tossed it in the air and put it in his pocket. This was too much for the savage Somalis, who rose to a man and fled from the presence of white men who could thus play about with their teeth, legs and eyes.

A story about Dr. Mann

My party is camped not far from the railway station, which is some three hundred yards from the lake. Collyer and I took a stroll to the lake this evening and I shot an Egyptian goose. We saw thousands of duck, teal, gulls and waders on the lake, and a good many snipe.

Lake Naivasha

25 . XI . 1902. *Naivasha*

Dr. Mann and I visited an island in the lake. We passed close to a school of hippo, which we did not molest. We found several waterbuck on the island, but they were all hornless or very young males. I think the females swim there to give birth to their young, as when we were about to leave the island we spied a waterbuck swimming towards the island. We rowed out to it, and fastening a rope round her head brought her to land. She was heavy in calf. We had some trouble releasing her.

A trip on the lake

I heard from Hinde today. He expects to get guides to me by the 28th. If so I shall start on the 29th.

News from Hinde

26 . XI . 1902. *Naivasha*

Collyer and I bagged some guinea-fowl and a dik-dik this evening. Dik-dik are antelope no larger than hares,

Shooting

and these are the first I have seen. It turns out to be the variety known as Cavendish's dik-dik. They are not uncommon in the scrub at the back of Naivasha.

27 . XI . 1902. *Naivasha*

Cheetah and wildebeeste

Collyer and I were out again on the flats east of the lake and witnessed an interesting sight. There was a small herd of wildebeeste with several calves, many quite small. As this is the first occasion on which I have seen calves we sat down and watched them. Then, to our surprise, about 400 yards from the herd we saw a cheetah with a half-grown cub; she was watching the wildebeeste, the cub beside her, and the end of her tail was slowly wagging. Then she began to stalk the herd, no doubt hoping to get a calf, several of which were gambolling about some 20 yards from their mothers. When some 150 yards from the calves the old cheetah suddenly flattened out in full stride. The wildebeeste spotted her at once, took fright and made off, the calves rather behind. Suddenly, when the cheetah was but 20 yards from the nearest calf, the whole herd turned in their wrath and charged the cheetah, who turned and fled; but the wildebeeste continued their charge to where the cub was, and using their horns and feet killed it. The old cheetah made herself scarce and made no attempt to rescue her offspring. I was glad to see that the cheetah does not always have it all her own way. Collyer collected the cub and is now skinning it, but it is in a terrible mess.

29 . XI . 1902. *Aberdare Mountains*

We leave Naivasha for Tetu

We left Naivasha today, the guides having arrived last night. In addition to my company I have 150 Masai spearmen. Today we camped about 7 miles out of Naivasha and on the edge of the plains at the foot of the Aberdare Mountains. We were compelled to stop here, as for the next 17 miles there is no firewood.

Masai habits

I noticed a curious habit of the Masai today. Whenever they passed a tree which had fallen across the path they placed on it a small bunch of grass or foliage. They also heap up small piles of stones at certain places, especially where two paths branch. Some of these heaps are of considerable size. I asked both my men and the Masai why it was done, but all they could say was that it is an old custom.

30 . XI . 1902. *Aberdare Mountains*

We cross Laikipia

Today we crossed the rolling downs known as Laikipia, and we are now camped on the lower slopes of the western edge of the Aberdare Mountains. It was a gorgeous day, and we had a good view of the whole range from Nandarua (Kinangop) to Sattima and the Markham Downs further north. We are now at the edge of the bamboo forest, and there are masses of elephant tracks in the neighbourhood.

I am hoping that our entry into the Tetu country will come as a complete surprise. None of my party know what we are going there for, or even what is our destination. My only fear is that the guides have been told by Hinde and that they have given us away during their journey here.

I . XII . 1902. *Aberdare Mountains*

We ascend the Aberdare Mountains

We broke up camp at dawn and at once entered the bamboo forest, taking all precautions against an ambush. The track was narrow and tortuous and the ascent was steep, so we went slow. We reached the summit and open country about noon after a 6 hours' march. We continued down a gentle slope for another 4 miles and camped on the eastern edge of the range, still in open country, but in a slight hollow and out of sight from the surrounding country. We are now midway between Sattima and Nandarua. I developed another dose of malaria this morning and tried to walk it off today, without much success. But with the help of 50 grains of quinine I should be all right tomorrow.

There were two rhino near camp this evening, feeding in the open. I would not let anyone disturb them. They must have been at about 9000 feet, which is a high altitude for pachyderms.

What is the plural of rhinoceros? If one uses "rhino" it suffices for both singular and plural. One cannot say rhinoceroses or rhinocerotes or rhinoceri!

2 . XII . 1902. *Tetu. Kikuyu Country*

We enter Tetu and commence operations

We descended into the Tetu country early this morning, passing through dense forest and bamboos. Our coming must have been known to the natives, for we found the path blocked at several places by trees, and numerous pitfalls, with sharp stakes therein, were dug on the path and cunningly covered over with loose earth. Only one man fell in, and he got badly spiked in the sides and hips. After that we went very carefully, which delayed our advance. I had timed myself to reach cultivation about 8 a.m. but actually never debouched from the forest till noon.

These pitfalls are a most effective method of defence, for they are easily dug and well concealed; even the smallest track may have many. If the Kikuyu had suspected an invading force through the Aberdare forest we should have had much more trouble with these pits. As it was I had two men marching in front of the column with probing sticks, which made progress slow. One stretch of path was very heavily "pitted," as many as 14 being dug over a distance of a hundred yards. If we had been suspected there would have been a poisoned arrow ambush at each group of pits. The Masai are very afraid of them and walked with great apprehension.

Just before we left the forest I formed the column up in a glade, dividing them up into raiding parties of 25 Masai spearmen and 15 rifles. We were not altogether unsuccessful in surprising the enemy, and burst on the cultivated area, meeting with little organised resistance. I remained with a central reserve and rapidly built a camp and *zariba*, clearing the ground for 100 yards round camp. One of our parties got into difficulties at a village, so I went to their assistance, rushed the enemy's defence, which was arrows and spears, killed some 20 of them and returned to camp. It was a busy day. By evening all our parties got safely into camp, having suffered only 2 killed

Section of a pitfall with sharpened stakes which the enemy had dug across our path. They were usually about 5 ft. deep and 3 ft. in diameter

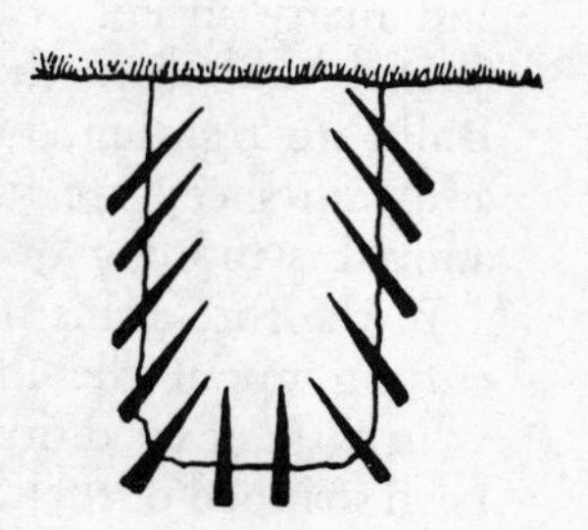

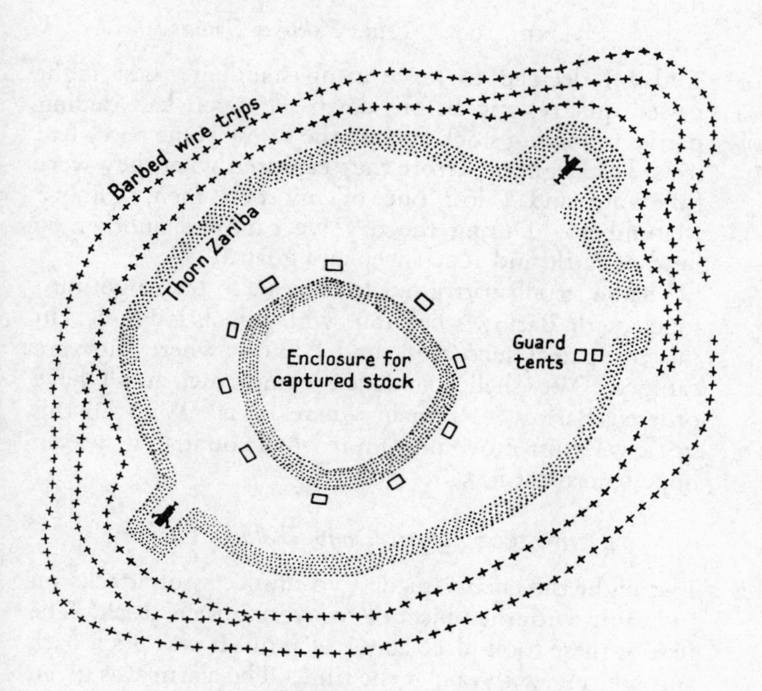

Plan of our camp on 2 December

and 5 slightly wounded. We captured 665 head of cattle and many sheep, which are at the moment creating a fearful hubbub in the kraal in the centre of our camp. Bulls are fighting, billy goats are incessantly amorous, and ram sheep are furiously butting each other. Every animal is mooing or bleating as loud as God will let it.

In the forest this morning we passed the scene of the cutting up of the Indian traders, as a punishment for which this expedition is taking place. The bodies had been stripped of their clothing and mutilated. The stench was awful. We made a heap of the bodies and burned them.

3 . XII . 1902. *Tetu. Kikuyu Country*

We continue operations from a standing camp

Today I decided to leave camp standing. Last night passed quietly, and before dawn we again had raiding parties following stock far into the forest. One party had some hard fighting before they captured what they were following and I lost one of my best men, Laiboro Matumbato. During the day we captured another 60 head of cattle and 1000 sheep and goats.

I had a strong patrol out to the east to try to get into touch with Barlow's column, with which is Hinde. In this the patrol succeeded, and I know where they are camped. We shall join forces tomorrow, and I have ordered Barlow to remain where he is. With all this stock we must move into more open country, if we can hope to protect it.

4 . XII . 1902. *Nyeri Camp. Kikuyu Country*

Night attacks

Last night the enemy made two unsuccessful attacks on my camp with the object of recovering their stock. The first of these took place about 11 p.m. It was pitch dark and pouring with rain at the time. The alarm was given by a volley of arrows being fired into the camp. Two of the carriers were hit. The sentries at once raised the alarm and the men got to their places at once, but not a minute too soon. The rush came only from one quarter, and was not pushed home. It was mainly yelling and firing of arrows from a distance. We lost two killed and several wounded. I had some difficulty in stopping the firing of my men, which continued long after the enemy had withdrawn.

The second attack was more determined and took place about 1.30 a.m. It came without any warning and from two sides. A shower of arrows and spears accompanied the rush, which put 7 of my men out of action. The yelling which took place with the attack, the rattle of our two machine guns and the noise of our rifles stampeded some of the cattle, who broke through the *zariba* and caused a gap. The enemy at once took advantage of this and tried to effect an entrance into the camp. I rushed to the spot with the small reserve of mine, killing the two leading enemy, who were actually inside the *zariba*. I now called on the Masai to make a counter-attack through the gap, to which they responded bravely, rushing out with their war-cries and finally disposing of the attack. I stopped the firing at once, so as to give the Masai a free hand outside, and in an hour we were comfortably settled down for the rest of the night, which was now perfect starlight, warm and still. Mann was busy with the wounded, but I turned in to sleep, quite happy that we should not be troubled again.

Our casualties during the night were 4 soldiers and 5 Masai killed, and 11 soldiers and 14 Masai wounded. Our carriers had one killed and 7 wounded. We found the dead bodies of 38 enemy outside our defences in the morning. I must own I never expected the Wakikuyu to fight like this.

We join forces

Owing to the number of wounded our march was considerably delayed. Moreover, I had to retain my whole force as escort to the stock and the wounded. We left camp at 10 a.m. and reached Barlow's camp on the Chania River and just under Nyeri Hill at 3 p.m. Here I found Barlow with only 60 rifles, Hinde with 40 useless police, my friend Hemsted, Collyer, Mr. Scoresby Routledge, a friend of Hinde's who is globe-trotting and out to see the fun, and, to my great disgust, Mrs. Hinde.

Women and civilians accompanying military expeditions

I was determined that Mrs. Hinde and Routledge should return to Fort Hall at once. I protested to Hinde and told him I strongly resented their presence in camp. He told me it was no business of mine, so I replied that

I was sending the wounded back to Fort Hall tomorrow under a strong escort, and that if his wife and Routledge did not accompany them I should withdraw the whole force, including Barlow's company, for I had no intention of continuing operations with women and civilians present who are only here "to see the fun." Hinde reluctantly gave way this evening, and both his wife and Routledge return to Fort Hall tomorrow. We shall have quite enough to do protecting camp and our captured stock without the extra responsibility of looking after a woman and a civilian, neither of whom is performing any duty connected with the expedition. I am sorry that Hinde has forced me into the position of appearing disagreeable to his wife and Routledge, both of whom are quite nice people. [Scoresby Routledge came out to study the Kikuyu tribe and later wrote *With a Prehistoric People*, 1910. He and his wife visited Easter Island and wrote another book on the former civilisation of that place.]

5 . XII . 1902. *Nyeri*

Future operations

Just to keep the enemy busy and screen the party which I am returning to Fort Hall with the wounded and captured stock, I sent Barlow and Hemsted out to the Gura River on a raid. I got all the wounded and captured stock off to Fort Hall under a strong escort.

We send for reinforcements

Hinde, Barlow and I had a council of war this evening. We decided we cannot continue operations, after our rather heavy casualties, unless we receive another 200 Masai spearmen and until my company is made up to strength. So I have sent in a letter to this effect to Nairobi. Reinforcements cannot be here for at least 8 days, so in the meantime I intend to make this present camp impregnable so that I can in future leave but a small garrison in it.

The naming of Nyeri

I had further words with Hinde regarding the site of his camp. It has no field of fire, is too far from water, and has too many hollows in which the enemy might concentrate. I told Hinde I had selected a spot closer to Nyeri Hill and only 2 miles from our present camp. He did not like it but had to give in. Moreover, he told me he had decided to call the place Fort Hinde after his wife.

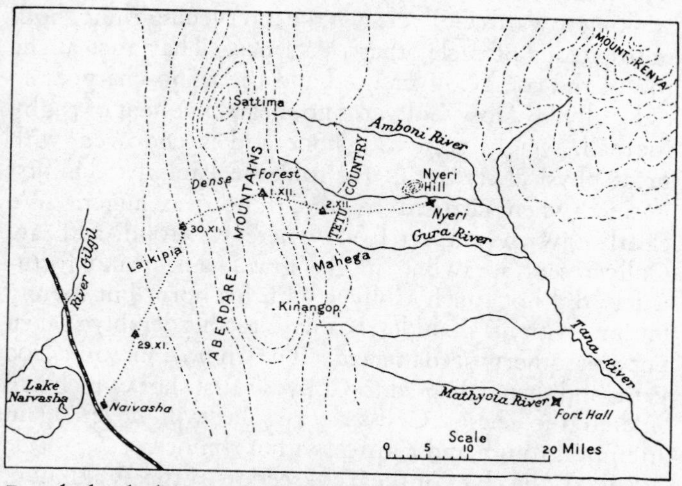

Rough sketch showing the country in which we operated against the people of Tetu, and which culminated in the establishment of a Government station near Nyeri Hill

I told him that the spot to which I intended to move would be called Nyeri after the prominent feature close by.

6 . XII . 1902. *Nyeri*

Moved camp to the position I chose, Hinde grumbling not only because his wife and Routledge are returning to Fort Hall but because I refuse to call the place Fort Hinde.

Spent the day turning all hands on to make the place impregnable—a large ditch, thorn *zariba* and barbed wire.

7 . XII . 1902. *Nyeri*

Rhinoceros

Rhinoceros are in great abundance round here. This evening we counted 16 from the camp. I sent Collyer out to get some meat for the porters, and we watched him stalk a rhino about half a mile off. But he had not noticed that between him and the rhino which he was after stood another rhino. Collyer was too far off for us to apprise him of this fact. There was a slight rise; on one side was Collyer walking up it, and on the other side, walking towards Collyer, was the intervening rhino, both unsuspicious of each other's presence. They met at the top of the rise. Collyer fired and the rhino charged; so did Collyer. Now Collyer is no mean exponent of rugby football, weighs some 15 stone and is endowed with great physical strength. He told me later that his first instinct when charged by the rhino was anger. We clearly saw the impact from where we stood, and saw Collyer sent sprawling in the grass. The rhino fortunately did not touch Collyer with his horn, but merely hit him with his shoulder. Collyer is considerably shaken but not otherwise damaged. The rhino ran some 200 yards and then collapsed to Collyer's first shot, which had entered the chest. Collyer vows he will never again attempt a rough and tumble with a rhinoceros.

We capture the chief of the Tetu Wakikuyu

Kekeri, the chief of the Tetu section of the Wakikuyu, together with his son, were captured yesterday by some friendlies, hiding in the bamboo forest, and surrendered to me today. Both he and his son have repulsively cruel faces. I shall send him as a political prisoner to Nairobi, to be dealt with by the Commissioner.

Political action

Now arises the question as to whether political action cannot end this military expedition. I have approached Hinde, who is in political charge, and he thinks they require still more punishment. To this I am compelled to agree, but I cannot help thinking that he could bring the Tetu people to terms during the next week if he so desired. I suspect that he wants more captured stock to give him sufficient revenue to build his new station here. If that is the case, it is most immoral. So as matters stand the operations are to continue.

10 . XII . 1902. *Nyeri*

Nyeri

Things have been peaceful here. The fortified camp is finished and impregnable against savages. It has an ideal field of fire for 600 yards in all directions, a complete barbed wire entanglement, and a ditch and parapet which would defy the most ardent savage. It could be easily defended by 50 rifles.

Rhinoceros

I took a stroll round camp this evening after work and coming round a corner met a rhinoceros face to face walking in my direction. There was no cover, so I fired point blank at his chest at but 20 yards. He staggered and nearly fell, but recovering himself made off. I gave him another shot as he ran but failed to stop him. He bolted towards the camp, when all my men and about 100 Masai spearmen gave chase. I yelled to them to let him be, but it had no effect and the hunt continued. The rhino could neither go fast nor far with his wounds, and was soon brought to bay and charged the whole crowd of us. We scattered and he stood. I fired again and the Masai encircled him and tried to spear him, which prevented me firing again for fear of hitting a man. He soon charged again, and singling out a Masai hunted him as a terrier does a rat. Nobody could fire for fear of hitting a man, so we yelled and tried to divert his attention. But he stuck to his victim, caught him up and tossed him some 10 feet into the air. The man fell clear of the rhino, who did not turn but went a short distance and stood. I quickly got the men out of the way and dropped the rhino dead with a shot in the neck. The Masai who had been tossed suffered a bad rip up the right thigh, but no artery or bone has been damaged. Dr. Mann has him in hand and thinks he should be about again in a month or so.

Wounded rhino chasing and tossing a Masai

On cutting up the rhino we found 15 Martini bullets in him which had been fired by my men, three Mannlicher bullets of mine and two ·303 bullets. These latter rather puzzled me, as none of us had been using such a rifle. There were also 37 Masai spears sticking in his hide when he fell dead. He looked like a Christmas tree.

When we were finishing the cutting up, Collyer, puffing and blowing, arrived on the scene and claimed the rhino. The ·303 bullets had been fired by him some little time before I had met the rhino face to face. So, as he could prove first blood, he took the horns, which were quite good, measuring over 24 inches each. Hemsted, Barlow, Hinde and I each took a foot. I shall have mine made into an inkstand.

14 . XII . 1902. *Nyeri*

Shooting rhino The number of rhino here is incredible. We and our men have in the last few days been compelled to kill 17, and yet the country is teeming with them. Barlow and I yesterday evening found 3 across our path when we were returning home. We shouted at them, but they only got excited and refused to budge. I had an 8 bore rifle with me and at 30 yards bombarded the nearest beast. I missed him, but the roar of the cannon sent him flying for miles with all his companions. We saw 21 different rhino today.

Arrival of reinforcements from Nairobi 200 Masai spearmen, and 40 rifles of the King's African Rifles arrived here this evening from Nairobi, having covered the distance of 150 miles in 5 days, each man carrying his own food for that period—not bad going! We shall restart operations on the day after tomorrow.

16 . XII . 1902. *Tetu. Kikuyu Country*

We restart operations Leaving Hinde and Collyer in Nyeri, I sent Barlow and Hemsted with 25 rifles, 10 police and 180 Masai to Mahega's country. Mahega is a neighbouring chief and has thrown in his lot with the people of Tetu, harbouring their cattle, etc. Barlow left camp before dawn and made a night march to Mahega's village, which he has destroyed, capturing many head of cattle. He works up to the bamboos tomorrow. I am in heliographic communication with him.

I left camp with Dr. Mann and 40 rifles, 4 police and 200 Masai spearmen. We followed up the Chania River, searching Nyeri Hill on the way, and camped at 4 p.m. about 2 miles from the bamboos, encountering no resistance.

17 . XII . 1902. *Tetu. Kikuyu Country*

Operations in the bamboo forest There was a certain amount of aggressive shouting round our camp last night, but no attack materialised. I have decided to stop where I am today and send strong patrols into the bamboos to try to get some more stock which I know is hiding there. I sent out another patrol towards Barlow which reached his camp and returned this evening.

It is now 11 p.m. and the patrol I sent into the bamboos has not yet returned, though we can hear them firing on the opposite side of the Chania River, which is much too swollen for them to cross at night. I have got into heliographic communication with them and have told them to stop where they are, but said that if they are heavily attacked I will come across somehow and get them out of it. The reply has just come in that they are quite comfortable and are only being sniped. They have 12 head of cattle and 450 sheep and goats with them.

18 . XII . 1902. *Tetu. Kikuyu Country*

Good work in the bamboo forest

Yesterday's patrol came into camp soon after dawn with their stock, having had some hard fighting. They had a 4 hours' running fight in the bamboos, losing 3 of their number and being hampered by 11 wounded. They then had to guard their captured stock throughout a pitch-dark night. The patrol commander was my Masai corporal, whom I publicly complimented on his work this morning, to his gratification.

Native concentration near my camp

Before dawn this morning it was evident that a considerable body of savages were in the vicinity of my camp. Now the Wakikuyu have the habit of entering our old camps as soon as we leave, digging up the dead, and mutilating them. So I decided to teach them a lesson. I arranged that we should break up camp, and that I and 15 Masai spearmen should remain in ambush within the *zariba* and pounce on the savages as soon as they entered the place. We were successful beyond our wildest dreams.

A successful ambush

The column marched out as usual under Dr. Mann, with orders to halt 2 miles distant and return to our old camp the moment they heard a rifle shot. I and the 15 Masai secreted ourselves in and about heaps of brushwood within the *zariba*. When the column got out of sight, savages came from all directions, flocking towards our camp. A shot from my rifle was to be the signal for attack. As soon as I had counted 50 inside the *zariba*, I fired at the nearest man, who dropped. We all broke from our ambushes with a yell, I rushed to the entrance, and there we had entrapped 49 fully armed warriors of the Tetu people. The Masai were out like lightning and began to kill at once. The whole affair was quick and quiet, and as it all occurred in the open and within a few yards of me I had an excellent view when I was not myself kept busy. I held the entrance with my bayonet, being shielded on either side by two Masai with their massive shields of buffalo hide. A good number of the enemy bolted for the door, but none got past me. I was surprised at the ease with which a bayonet goes into a man's body. One scarcely feels it unless it goes in to the hilt. But one frequently has to make a desperate tug to get it out. In the end not a single one of the enemy escaped, all being killed. I had my shirt ripped up by a spear, 3 Masai were killed, and most of them had been cut about. One could hardly avoid it in a pure hand-to-hand encounter.

Masai methods of fighting

The Masai fought with their shields in front of them and used their spears as stabbing weapons throughout. I never saw one use the knobkerrie or short sword (*seme*). Once their man is down they use their short sword, inserting it on the shoulder near the collar bone and thrusting it down, parallel to the longer axis of the body, through the heart and down to the bladder. The length of the sword is such that it does not protrude.

I doubt if the people of Tetu will worry us again for some time.

Return to Nyeri

I now joined the column which was fast approaching us and we marched for Nyeri. I heliographed to Barlow also to return with all captured stock. There is little doubt that this stubborn tribe will now come in and listen to reason.

Both my and Barlow's columns reached Nyeri at dusk, having captured in all 184 head of cattle and over 1200 head of sheep and goats.

Close of operations

At a conference this evening we unanimously agreed that there was no further use for military operations and that the people of Tetu would surrender.

The birth of Nyeri

It was also decided that the Government station should be sited on our actual camp and that it should be called Nyeri.

20 . XII . 1902. *Nyeri–Fort Hall Road*

While out near camp yesterday I woke two sleeping rhino. They both proved most aggressive and came blundering to where I was standing. I killed them both with a right and left from my little Mannlicher. When they rolled over they were touching each other within ten paces of me. One of them required a *coup de grace* as he lay struggling to get up.

Rhino

Late last night one of my patrols reported large lots of stock to our east on the Tana River. I at once sent out a strong patrol, who got back this morning with 62 cattle and over 6000 sheep and goats—a great haul. At dawn this morning the elders of Tetu, some 60 persons, came in and sued for mercy. After photographing them I left them arguing with Hemsted and Hinde. Barlow and I marched to the Gura River and camped on its right bank.

A final raid

The elders of Tetu sue for terms

21 . XII . 1902. *Fort Hall*

We did a long march into Fort Hall. There I found Neligan, a new officer recently out from home. Barlow had a touch of fever last night and had to be carried the whole distance.

Arrive at Fort Hall

25 . XII . 1902. *Fort Hall*

Yesterday I paid a hurried visit to my old haunts down by the Tana River. The grass was so long and the heat so oppressive that I was glad to get back again yesterday evening.

Christmas Day

We all dined together this evening and tried to make the best of a Christmas in Central Africa. Our effort to be jovial fell very flat. The fact is we are all completely worn out with the excitement of the last few weeks. I personally feel more like bed for a month than Christmas festivities.

31 . XII . 1902. *Nairobi River*

On the 28th I left Fort Hall with my company for Nairobi, camping at Punde Milia. On the 29th I marched

I leave Fort Hall for Nairobi

to the Thika, which was very swollen by the recent heavy rain, which made crossing difficult. While supervising the crossing of my company I met Mr. R. Weeks, a new District Officer, en route for Fort Hall. We camped together. He had my English mail, also my plum pudding from home. At the Thika there were a good many lion about. They roared incessantly throughout the night, and early next morning I just caught a fleeting glimpse of an old male as he disappeared into the bush which fringes the river.

I meet Weeks at the Thika River

At dawn on the 30th there were several lion roaring in the vicinity. It was a foggy morning, and I tried to follow them up by the noise they were making but did not come up with them. I came on a brace of whistling teal on a puddle, both of which I shot. On the evening of the 30th I camped on the Ruiru River.

To the Nairobi River

This morning I marched on to the Nairobi River, where I am now camped. During a stroll round camp in the evening I bagged a cheetah. When I first spied her I thought she was a lioness, as she lay on an ant-heap surveying the country. I made quite a good stalk to within easy range and killed her with one bullet. She had cubs in her which were just ready for birth.

Hunting leopard

Tomorrow I shall march into Nairobi, where both I and my company will be glad of a few days' rest.

1 . 1 . 1903. *Nairobi*

Arrive Nairobi

Marched into Nairobi, where I met Radford, the K.A.R. doctor, a man of extreme indolence but a nice fellow, also the immaculate Brancker, Mackay, my old friend Maycock, and the pugnacious but attractive red-haired Barrett. Our mess and bungalows are now completed on the hill south of the railway station, and tonight I shall enjoy the luxury of dining off a white tablecloth and sleeping under a roof, things I have not experienced for 8 months.

Joseph Chamberlain

While I have been away from Nairobi, Joseph Chamberlain, the Colonial Secretary, has paid the colony a visit. He lunched in our mess and made an excellent speech. I am so sorry I missed it all.

18 . 1 . 1903. *Nairobi*

Ainsworth

I have seen a good deal of Ainsworth, the District Commissioner in Nairobi. He lives on the Kikuyu side of the Nairobi River, where the stepping stones are. He is a first-class fellow and I like him. He tells me the Nairobi River is the recognised boundary between the Masai and the Kikuyu and that his house was built where it is as it controls the crossing of the Nairobi swamp, which used to be used by both tribes for raiding. There is a Kikuyu village within 400 yards of his house. [Ainsworth's house was on the site of the present Coryndon Museum.]

Sandbach Baker

At Ainsworth's this afternoon I met a settler called Sandbach Baker who was given 5000 acres of Kikuyu land by Eliot in 1901, provided he supplied Nairobi with meat. This he does. I asked if the Kikuyu were compensated, and he said the land was unoccupied owing to a decrease in the population a few years ago due to famine and disease. He tells me that if I care to ride out any morning he will sell me fresh butter; I shall certainly do so whenever I can, for I dislike tinned butter. [Sandbach Baker was the original owner of the Muthaiga estate, which was subsequently sold to Morrison, who developed the garden city; it was originally all Kikuyu land.]

19 . 1 . 1903. *Nairobi*

Manning and Sykes

Manning was out here a little time back; he is our Inspector-General. A story from Uganda relates that when he inspected the company of Captain Sykes he said: "Now, Captain Sykes, I should like to see your company do the bayonet exercise." Sykes replied: "So should I, sir."

Rhino, ostrich and giraffe

I was out on the Athi River today and came across 2 rhino, 5 giraffe and a hen ostrich. The latter was sitting on eggs, and whenever the giraffe or rhino came near her she jumped up, ran towards them and made them clear off; she actually struck the rhino with her foot when he was very close to her eggs, and the rhino gave a snort, lifted his tail and went off in a trot. I imagine a kick from an ostrich is most painful.

Race meeting

Today was a great day for Nairobi, for the local race meeting was held. The rank and fashion of the whole colony assembled. The motley collection of so-called racehorses was equalled only by the class of the owners and jockeys. Barrett rode in the hurdle race and got one of his spurs mixed up with the horse's bridle. I rode in a flat race, coming in third, but as there were only five starters it was not much of a success. The whole entertainment afforded me great amusement, because it required such a deal of imagination to take it seriously.

We drove down to the course in a four-wheeled conveyance hired from the bazaar, drawn by four horses which subsequently ran in the races. None of the horses had previously been introduced to four-in-hand harness, and one of them had actually never before had a vehicle behind him. The driving of this outfit was allotted to me, and it proved most exciting. It was half an hour before we got started, and then we made a good pace, cantering the whole 2 miles. Barrett had a horn which he blew at intervals. Our arrival on the course was magnificent, and fortunately the horses pulled up decently in front of the "grandstand." But we decided to walk home, my brother officers declining a second drive.

An interfering rhinoceros

As the second race was finishing a silly rhinoceros was seen trotting towards the galloping horses. We all shouted to the riders to look out, and they returned at a pace which seemed to exceed that of the race; the rhino could not make head or tail of the flags, the horses, and the general noise of shouting and laughter, and with his tail in the air he kept making little charges here and there. Nobody had a gun to scare him away, and we just had to wait for at least half an hour before he took himself off.

Delamere

Met Lord Delamere at the race meeting. He has just returned from England. He is an enthusiast about the future of East Africa and remarked: "I am going to prove to you all that this is a white man's country." "But," I humbly said, "it is a black man's country; how are you going to superimpose the white over black?" Delamere is a quick-tempered man; he said, rather impatiently, "The black man will benefit and co-operate."

30.I.1903. *Zanzibar*

Zanzibar

Leaving Nairobi on the 27th, I arrived in Zanzibar this afternoon to recoup after breaking three ribs from a fall off my pony. Am staying with Sinclair, who took me round this afternoon to see the famous slave raider Tippoo Tib, a very old man. He is not allowed to leave Zanzibar, nor does he want to. I tried to get him to talk of slave raiding days, but he clearly did not like it. He gave us coffee from a gorgeous silver pot which I admired, so he had to give it to me. Sinclair told me afterwards that I must never admire anything in an Arab house, as they are under an obligation to present it to the admirer. I offered to take it back, but Sinclair says that would be an insult, so I shall keep it.

Tippoo Tib

Sinclair tells me that Tippoo is a very wealthy man and that all his servants are slaves. The old man spoke very little and was clearly embarrassed by his past activities, and I think he was rather glad to be rid of us. I am sorry about the coffee pot.

22.II.1903. *Nairobi*

Company training

On the 19th Barlow's and my companies came out to a spot towards Ingong for company training. During off-moments we got some good shooting, bagging two great bustard, a crane, a rhino, an impala and a Grant's gazelle. The largest bustard weighed just over 26 pounds.

Having completed our outdoor training, we marched into Nairobi this afternoon, Barlow's company acting as an enemy to mine in bush fighting. Some of my men got very excited and nearly came to blows with some of Barlow's men. They do not understand sham fighting.

E. G. Harrison

During our absence Major E. G. Harrison has arrived from Jubaland. He takes over from Col. Hatch in April next, the latter's time being up. Hatch has not impressed us much. Harrison seems a different type of man, with energy, common sense and humour. I like the look of him.

23 . II . 1903. *Nairobi*

I apply for land

Land is going cheap—a halfpenny an acre plus survey fees. There is a particularly attractive plot close to our lines which is full of guinea-fowl, duiker and steinbock. I applied for it some time ago, but the Land Office is so congested that they move slowly. Government officials are only allowed to take up 10 acres, and this I have done. I have also got an option for 6 months on about 45,000 acres, an area between the Ithanga Hills and the Tana. I have asked Father to lend me £5000 to develop it and build a cottage. It is a wonderful estate, full of game, and I should make it a sanctuary. But I expect Father will just laugh. I shall then go to the bank and ask them.

28 . II . 1903. *Nairobi*

Game census

There is a bigger concentration of game on the Athi Plains than I have ever seen before. I counted the numbers today over an area of about 12 square miles south of Nairobi. It amounted to:

1247 wildebeeste	946 Coke's haartebeeste
832 Grant's gazelle	134 eland
621 Thomson's gazelle	68 ostrich
887 impala	1465 zebra
8 rhino	32 giraffe
2 hyaena	17 great bustard

3 . III . 1903. *Nairobi*

My birthday

I have today completed my 25th year. I presented myself with a pony called Natalie which I have bought for 800 rupees. She is 14 hands, well up to my weight, and is said to have been "salted," that is to say has had and recovered from horse sickness.

Mrs. Donald presented me with a fox terrier puppy which I have christened Baby.

Tomorrow Barrett and I are giving a dance at the Club to which we have invited the whole of Nairobi. I cannot think why we have broken out into such festivities, for neither of us cares a scrap about dancing. I think the real reason is that we are both rather perverse by nature and instinctively do the thing which we are least expected to do.

16 . III . 1903. *Muhoroni*

I left Nairobi yesterday on 10 days' leave. Travelling all last night on the Uganda Railway, I reached Muhoroni this morning. Here is the railhead, some 30 miles from Kisumu on the Victoria Nyanza. I met a railway engineer called Gailey, who kindly gave me lunch and gave me all the information I wanted about the country from a shooting point of view. This afternoon I killed an Abyssinian oribi, and on my way home was drenched by one of the habitual thunderstorms of these parts.

A trip towards the Victoria Nyanza

Gailey

17 . III . 1903. *Near Muhoroni*

I marched to Mile 554 on the Uganda Railway, where I camped on the line. This was the only dry spot, the whole of the surrounding country being under water. In the afternoon I killed a Jackson's haartebeeste and two topi antelope, both of which are new to me.

Mile 554

In the evening a construction train passed by and cut all the ropes of my tent, which I had tied to the line. I had not been expecting trains, and the collapse of my tent came as a sudden and unpleasant surprise.

My tent collapses

19 . III . 1903. *Nakuru*

On the 18th I returned to Muhoroni and took train to Njoro on the eastern slopes of the Mau escarpment and on the western edge of the Great Rift Valley. From Njoro I walked to Nakuru, seeing a great number of the little red steinbock on the way. I must have seen nearly 50 of them lying out in the short crisp grass. If they see one they are off at once, but if they merely smell or hear one they crouch down with neck outstretched on the ground and can be easily walked up.

I take train to Njoro

Steinbock

Dined with Sidney Couper, an engineer of the Uganda Railway, who is also kindly putting me up.

20 . III . 1903. *Nakuru*

I marched round the eastern shores of Lake Nakuru and camped on the Enderet River, which enters the lake at its southern extremity. I shall never attempt such a march

I camp at the south end of Lake Nakuru

again, for it is entirely waterless. The lake water is brackish and gives one violent diarrhoea. In fact today I was compelled to halt the caravan half-way round and allow the porters to come on empty, so distressed were they from the heat and lack of water. They returned in the evening for their loads, some not reaching camp till after dark.

I found game numerous here, comprising mainly Neumann's haartebeeste and Grant's gazelle. Guinea-fowl abound and form a welcome addition to my larder.

This evening as the sun was setting I had great delight in watching at barely 50 paces the frolics of a whole litter of foxes, who came out of their earth and played about in front of me for over an hour. I never saw their mother.

21 . II . 1903. *Lake Nakuru*

Hippopotami

Last night every hippopotamus in the lake seemed to be near my tent, grumbling and grunting. There is a large patch of reeds near the mouth of the Enderet, and they had come out to feed in this patch. I was out at dawn and killed some good buck, and on getting back for breakfast I found another white man in my tent. He was the naval doctor of H.M.S. *Forte*, also on a shooting trip. He stopped and had breakfast with me.

The doctor of H.M.S. "Forte"

Ducks, waders and hippo by the lake

I sat by the lake most of the day watching the hippo, duck and flamingo. There are still a few northern waders about, notably greenshank, marsh sandpiper and little stint. One single sanderling attracted my attention for being so far inland. To consort with hippo in winter and polar bears in summer must be a delightful experience, and yet that is what this small bird must do every year.

I move camp

At 4 p.m. I moved camp about 5 miles further inland, primarily to get away from these noisy and frivolous hippopotami, but also to get clear of the hosts of mosquitoes which make life after dusk unbearable.

22 . III . 1903. *Elmentaita*

I move to Elmentaita Station

As I looked out of my tent this morning at dawn there were two bull Neumann's haartebeeste within 50 yards. From my bed I slew the largest, which turns out to be a most interesting specimen, more closely resembling Coke's haartebeeste than any other I have shot. I am more than ever convinced that the Nakuru haartebeeste is no valid species, but a hybrid between Jackson's and Coke's. The fact that it is not constant within a given area precludes its being given even subspecific value. Neumann's haartebeeste was described from much further north and has nothing to do with the Nakuru animal.

The validity of the Nakuru haartebeeste

I moved camp today to Elmentaita Station, seeing on the way a herd of 8 eland. At Elmentaita I met Neumann, whose name was given to the haartebeeste. He is a professional ivory hunter, conducting his work somewhere around Lake Rudolph. He is a quiet, unassuming little man, with a faraway and rather sad outlook on life. We had a long chat together about game and the glories of the simple wild life in Africa. Neumann's native name is Bwana Nyama, or the Lord of Meat. This was given to him on account of his fussiness in always insisting on his meat having a fly-proof cloth tied round it, a precaution the natives could not understand. Neumann is just off back to Rudolph.

Neumann the elephant hunter

23 . III . 1903. *Eburu*

I marched to Eburu, shooting on the way a cock ostrich and three more hybrid haartebeeste. Round Eburu I found quantities of the rock rabbit, *Hyrax* or dassie. I believe their nearest relative in dentition is the hippopotamus. Their peculiar whistle when alarmed and the extreme activity which they display over rocks make them attractive little beasts. They have beautiful skins, which are much prized by the Masai for the manufacture of cloaks. In the evening I saw both klipspringer and reedbuck.

I move to Eburu

Hyrax or Dassies

[This hybrid haartebeeste was later described by Heller as *nakuruensis*. My series, now in the British Museum, proves that the animal is a hybrid and should not have been given a name.]

24 . III . 1903. *Eburu*

This morning I had a long and fruitless walk in the hills north of Eburu, seeing only one lot of female reedbuck.

Chanler's reedbuck

In the afternoon I was out in a different direction and bagged 2 nice reedbuck. One could not wish for a more sporting kind of shooting than is afforded by these small antelope. They are wide awake, they live in country as rough as the highland crags of Scotland, and being of the same colour as the rocks they are extremely difficult to spot, as they stand motionless on the slightest alarm. When they make off they bound over rock and boulder with the agility of a goat, uttering all the time their characteristic whistle.

I also saw klipspringer today.

Hot springs

These hills contain a number of hot springs and fissures in the rocks out of which exudes hot steam. I examined several such places and found all the surrounding rocks quite warm. The natives assert that all the game come round these hot springs at night in order to keep warm, but I found no signs of this being the case.

25 . III . 1903. *Eburu*

Klipspringer and reedbuck

I had a jolly day in the hills, killing my first klipspringer and another reedbuck. On my way home I killed a buck impala. From the top of the hills at the back of Eburu I had an excellent panoramic view of the whole of the Aberdare Mountains, Lakes Nakuru and Elmentaita and the Rift Valley. It really is a weird part of the earth.

Return to Nairobi

I return to Nairobi tomorrow.

7 . IV . 1903. *Nairobi*

Pig-sticking

Last January we started pig-sticking seriously. Our previous efforts were rather hampered by the lack of proper spears (our improvised weapons were bayonets lashed to bamboo poles), but we imported some proper hog spears from India and then began serious business. De Crespigny and I hunted together.

The African warthog is a very different beast from the wild pig of India. His home is underground, and if chased he makes straight for his hole, from which nothing will turn him. If one gets between him and his hole he

R.M. Nairobi. March 1903

My Masai orderly and my pony Natalie, with a haartebeeste which I speared from her back

charges at once. Neither does he jink like the Indian pig but makes a straight run, which makes spearing easier; but on the other hand, if one is anywhere but directly behind him he has a nasty habit of suddenly turning into one's pony's forelegs, which entails a crash if not worse. Since we started in January we have killed 27 pig without mishap and must have chased over a hundred; our best ground is just north of Nairobi, but the country is riddled with holes and traps, which makes slow going; also, if the pig is not far from his hole, he reaches it and disappears backside first in a flash. These holes are usually those of the ant bear and sometimes not very deep. On one occasion we could just reach the pig by inserting a spear; we pricked him and out he came with a grunt, sent us both flying on our backs and scampered off to another nearby hole. My pony Natalie bolted and I had to walk home.

On one occasion we chased a cheetah to a standstill after about 2 miles fast going. When completely done he lay down and we could easily have killed him, but let him off as he looked so pathetic. He was so cooked that he allowed us to stroke his tail. On another occasion we ran into 4 lions. De Crespigny was all for tackling them, but I was more cautious. Our ponies would never have faced them, and we were not sure about a lion's reactions to a pony and a hog spear.

Our best run was after 3 wild dogs; it took us 2 miles hard going to fetch up with them. I speared one and De Crespigny secured a second. They twisted and turned better than any Indian pig and set up a sort of whining bark at the last moment; when they realised they were beat they hunched their backs rather like a pariah dog when chased, and slowed down.

Our most amusing hunt was after a troop of baboon; they screamed and scolded, scattering in all directions, but we soon caught them up. Their grimaces were so human that we spared them. One old man, when I was within spearing distance, was full of fight and made an attempt to catch hold of Natalie's legs, which nearly unseated me, for the horse swerved as I was leaning over shouting at the ape.

8 . iv . 1903. *Nairobi*

Col. Hatch and Sir George Whitehouse leave Nairobi

On the 5th Col. and Mrs. Hatch left Nairobi and Major Harrison assumed command of the 3rd Battalion. Thank God we have a first-class man. Harrison distinguished himself in the Uganda Mutiny and is the right type of soldier for these parts. He delegates responsibility, is very firm yet considerate, and stands no nonsense from anyone. And I flatter myself that he likes me, which is more than most people do.

Tomorrow Sir George and Lady Whitehouse also leave for home, he having terminated his appointment as Manager of the Uganda Railway. The railway gave them a big dinner at the Club this evening, which I attended. There were eulogistic speeches and much bad champagne.

10 . iv . 1903. *Voi*

I leave Nairobi for Taveta

We have a small detachment of troops at Taveta on the German frontier near Kilimanjaro. They have had no officer with them and in consequence have been giving trouble, being inclined to become insubordinate. I have been detailed to go to Taveta with a relieving detachment and enquire into the causes of the old detachment's conduct. I consequently left Nairobi last night by train for Voi, where I arrived this morning. Sir George Whitehouse kindly allowed me the free use of his carriage, so I travelled in comfort. Near Simba Station I saw a fine leopard crouching by the side of the line.

Arrival at Voi

I arrived at Voi soon after dawn and found only 30 porters had been engaged for me, so I sent round to the bazaar for another 50. After some delay I got these, but they are mainly Wataita and not capable of carrying heavy loads. After a 15-mile march I reached the Government station of Mwataate in the Taita Hills and found Mr. Reddie in charge. I dined with him and was compelled to listen to a most inferior gramophone after dinner.

Mwataate Station

Our road today was through thick bush. After 12 miles from Voi we crossed the Voi River, a shallow fordable stream. This is the only water in this dry area.

Voi is not much above sea-level and consequently very hot and sultry. The bird life is quite different from what I have seen elsewhere, being much more tropical.

11 . IV . 1903. *Maktau. Serengeti Plains*

I march to Maktau

After leaving Mwataate we reached the Bura marsh in one and a half hours. Thence I came on to a spot called Nikomeni, where I found water and filled up all my water cans. A kerosene oil tin filled with water weighs 40 pounds and will suffice 8 men per diem. We then passed up a slight incline to the waterless Serengeti Plains and reached Maktau Rock just before dark. Here we camped, having covered about 22 miles during the day. Just north of the road at Maktau is a small rock pool, dependent on rain-water. This was dry, so we used the water we were carrying.

Birds and butterflies

The bush about Maktau is not so thick as it was near Bura. Birds were numerous, including bustard, rollers, small hornbills, flycatchers, doves and francolin. I also saw for the first time the handsome vulturine guinea-fowl, with its gorgeous sky-blue back. Butterflies were abundant and in infinite variety, reminding me of the insect life at the base of the Nilgiri Hills in the hot weather.

12 . IV . 1903. *Mbuyuni. Serengeti Plains*

To Mbuyuni

Marched about 12 miles to a spot called Mbuyuni, where the waterhole had completely dried up. The bush here is not so thick and I came across numerous clear spaces, mostly in slight depressions. Game was abundant, including ostrich, Grant's and Thomson's gazelle, steinbock, Coke's haartebeeste and zebra. I also saw for the first time the gerenuk or Waller's gazelle, with its long giraffe-like neck.

I camped under the huge baobab tree which gives to this spot the name of Mbuyuni, *mbuyu* being Swahili for the baobab tree. In the evening I had a good view to the south of the snows of Kilimanjaro and the peak of Meru Mountain, which lies immediately over Arusha.

Game census

Game seen between Maktau and Mbuyuni today includes 17 ostrich, 34 giraffe, 4 rhinoceros, 8 gerenuk, 67 oryx, 94 Grant's gazelle, 59 Thomson's gazelle, 146 eland, 264 Coke's haartebeeste, 426 zebra and 8 steinbock, also 5 great bustard.

13 . IV . 1903. *Taveta*

To Taveta

I marched 15 miles into Taveta, passing the Njoro watercourse (now dry) about 8 miles this side of Taveta. Close to Njoro is the small hill of Salaita, which constitutes an important military position to any force defending Kilimanjaro. I was much struck by the natural strength of the Salaita position.

There are no Europeans in Taveta, so I stopped at the mud house known as the Civil Bungalow. It had been raining hard just before I entered Taveta, and rain was still dripping from the ceiling to the floor in all the rooms of this shanty when I arrived. It is intensely hot here, and mosquitoes are a great nuisance.

15 . IV . 1903. *Mbuyuni. Serengeti Plains*

Kilimanjaro

I had a splendid view of Kilimanjaro early this morning. The huge snowfields were clearly visible through my glasses. It does seem a shame that this wonderful mountain should have been given to Germany. But I do not doubt we shall eventually get it. We seem to get most of what we want—eventually.

I stopped in Taveta yesterday, enquiring into the troubles of the detachment and installing the new men.

I leave Taveta

This morning I marched out with the old detachment and camped at Mbuyuni. Saw a small herd of eland and many impala. I killed a female steinbock which appears to differ from others I have shot. The crescentic forehead mark is more clearly defined, and there is a dark stripe running from the nostrils up the face for 3 inches or so. The general colour is not so red as usual.

Eland

While I was lunching in camp I saw some eland about a mile distant. There were about a hundred altogether. They were in an open space and unapproachable, so I decided to wait until they fed into more stalkable country. About 4 p.m. they had fed into bush country, and by making a long detour to get the wind right I got to within 200 yards of them and lay down in a slight hollow. Meanwhile the wind had dropped. After waiting for them to feed still nearer a puff of wind blew from behind me, and up went all their heads in great alarm. The whole herd moved and trotted past me at only 50 yards—a magnificent sight. The last to come were 3 old bulls. I fired at the largest and broke his shoulder. He stumbled, galloped for some 200 yards and then stood. I again stalked him and at 30 yards broke his hind leg. He fell at once. While I was trying to cut his massive throat he managed to get on to his knees and with one toss of his head sent me sprawling, hurting my ankle, so I had to kill him with another shot in the neck. He proved to be a huge beast, measuring 15 hands 2 inches at the shoulder.

17 . IV . 1903. *Mwataate*

Yesterday I walked to Maktau, but my ankle had swollen to such an extent that I could walk no further and reluctantly had to send in to Reddie for a hammock to carry me in here. It arrived at 2 p.m. and I reached Mwataate at 11 p.m. The porters who carried me the 20-odd miles did extremely well, and I paid them liberally for their services.

To Maktau

I am carried

19 . IV . 1903. *Nairobi*

Yesterday I was carried into Voi, caught the evening train to Nairobi and arrived here today. I think there must be a small bone broken in my ankle, and I shall probably be laid up for a fortnight.

Am carried to Voi and reach Nairobi

10 . V . 1903. *Nairobi*

Called on Delamere and his wife; they are now living in huts on the south side of Nairobi Swamp, not far from Ainsworth's house. Delamere is still enthusiastic about the future of Kenya. I take the view, with which Delamere has no patience, that in a hundred years' time there may be 50,000 white settlers with flourishing farms and 5,000,000 discontented and envious natives; can the white

Lord Delamere

man hold out against numbers without terrific slaughter?

I liked Lady Delamere—very lovely, graceful and charming, and quite out of place in this savage country. Delamere asked me to come to breakfast some morning.

12 . v . 1903. *Nairobi*

Game census

I made a game census today of animals between Nairobi and the Athi River south of Nairobi over an area of about 24 square miles; I was assisted by Harrison. We counted:

18 giraffe	894 wildebeeste
4 rhino	276 Coke's haartebeeste
11 wild dogs	46 eland
22 warthog	326 Grant's gazelle
7 great bustard	184 impala
684 zebra	426 Thomson's gazelle
2 common duiker	7 steinbock

Over 4000 head of Masai cattle

13 . v . 1903. *Nairobi*

Mrs. Anderson

I met Mrs. Anderson, whom I had previously seen in Mombasa last year; she is up for a visit. She tells me she has bought from the Parsee Jeevanjee a local newspaper called the *East African Standard*, which was founded in 1901 under the name *African Standard*. Good luck to her! I liked her more than ever; she is a Belgian with a strong foreign accent, and we lunched together at the Victoria Hotel, a miserable dirty place—tinned salmon, rancid butter, high meat and maggoty cheese, the whole garbage costing me 8 rupees.

17 . v . 1903. *Nairobi*

Shooting on the Limoru Marsh

On the 15th Rawson, Harrison, Bailey, Allen, Powell and I came to Escarpment Station for a duck and snipe shoot in the Limoru Marsh, but it was not much of a success. There was too much water to enable us to get near the duck. Yesterday we got very little shooting, so we moved to Limoru Station, where we got a few duck.

In one marsh near the station we found abundant tracks of hippopotami. Harrison made a brilliant shot at a duck with his rifle at 200 yards. We returned to Nairobi this evening.

8 . VI . 1903. *Nairobi*

Flamingo on Elmenteita and Nakuru

I visited Lakes Elmenteita and Nakuru for survey purposes. [The trip formed the subject of a paper for the R.G.S., with map, but the whole packet never reached London and no copy was kept.] I was busy with plane table and theodolite the whole time and did no shooting. The level of water at Nakuru had sunk very low, and the west end was largely mud-flat with about two inches of water in many places. Both flamingos (*ruber* and *minor*) were breeding there, the former in preponderance. Egg-laying had just started, and I took several for eating. The small flamingo colony was separated by about 200 yards from that of *ruber*. Elmenteita was also very low, and there was a much smaller breeding colony of both flamingos there, the lesser one numbering only about 50 nests. Here again egg-laying had just commenced and I took several for food. At Elmenteita the nests were in much deeper water—about 8 inches.

12 . VI . 1903. *Nairobi*

Black Barnes and Eastwood

The traffic manager of the railway is Eastwood, a quiet unassuming man. The auditor of the railway is a man called Barnes—known as Black Barnes, as he has a thick crop of black hair and is usually unshaved. I went down to the station today to meet Eastwood, as I wished to see him about transport for some men going up country. Barnes was on the platform and in a furious temper with Eastwood about something. He said to me: "Just you watch me meet the swine—he's not going to like it!" So I watched. On Eastwood alighting, Barnes went up to him and said: "Eastwood, you're a bastard, and if you don't know what that means it implies that your mother was a whore!" Barnes, having delivered himself, marched off. Eastwood said nothing.

18 . VI . 1903. *Nairobi*

Accidents on manœuvres

We conducted some manœuvres today within the battalion, using only blank ammunition. The dummy enemy was represented by Maycock's Masai company. Their position was assaulted by Barrett's Sudanese company, who in the excitement of the moment fixed their bayonets and charged. The Masai also lost their heads and fixed their bayonets; a few men produced ball ammunition, which was fired at the Sudanese, wounding two men. The position became most realistic, the Sudanese freely bayoneting the Masai and killing three of them. The Masai eventually fled, with the Sudanese in pursuit. I doubled my company to the scene, and with the help of all the British officers present we separated the excited Masai and Sudanese. Harrison vows he will never have these two companies out again on manœuvres. I do not agree that this is a remedy at all. These two companies require a deal more discipline, especially fire control and fire discipline. I would guarantee to have both companies under complete control in two months after concentrated barrack square drill.

24 . VII . 1903. *Nairobi*

Rhino and lion

On 7 July I bagged a brace of rhinoceros and today I shot a lion under rather peculiar circumstances. I first saw him feeding on a zebra which he had killed. He was then some 800 yards from me. I stalked unseen to within about 350 yards, and as concealment was no longer possible I crawled towards him in the open. He was lying down as he fed. He soon spotted me and stood up. I also rose to my feet, at which the lion, after a momentary stare, bolted, but soon wheeled round and bounded to his kill again with a roar. This was no doubt to impress me, and I was bound to say it did make me think. He stood with his forepaws on the zebra, snarling and growling at me, looking the picture of rage. He was still too far for a certain shot, so I began to walk round him in a circle, edging nearer and nearer as I walked. He moved round so as continually to face me. When I was not more than 150 yards from him I stopped. He at once lay down by his kill in about 12 inches of grass, looking extremely threatening. As I wished to get still closer before I fired, I again started off and walked straight for him. When 120 yards from him he ceased growling and I got on to a small ant-heap, where I could see the ominous twitching of the tip of his tail. His teeth were bared, and I expected him to charge at any moment. But I was now too far committed to retire, so advanced another 25 yards to another ant-heap, whence I could get a clear view. The moment I halted he stood up, his tail up, his teeth gleaming in the sun. Taking as steady an aim as I could, I fired, and to my intense relief he collapsed in the initial bound of his charge. I had fired not a moment too soon. I do not like lion when I have to face them single-handed in the open. He was a fine old beast, and on cutting him up I found my bullet had raked him from the chest to the stern.

Calling my porters up, we skinned him and returned to Nairobi this evening.

I . VIII . 1903. *Nairobi*

Race meetings and gymkhanas at Nairobi

The day before yesterday we had one of the usual race meetings here. The same old horses ran, the same old jockeys rode. Every horse in the colony was entered, and owners rode their own beasts. Brancker won the Machakos Cup with Aladin, and I came in second in the Lilliput Handicap on Natalie.

We held a gymkhana today. I easily won the trotting race on Natalie and a threading-the-needle race. In the latter we worked in partners. I galloped to the lady with needle and thread, she threaded it, and I had to gallop back to the starting point with the threaded needle. My lady was Miss Elliot (Mark II), the daughter of the local forest officer.

Mr. Block

I met Mr. Block this morning, recently arrived from South Africa and exploring possibilities of making his fortune in this country. Being a Jew I think it more than likely he will succeed, as he seems to be full of ideas. He asked my advice, and I told him I thought that most money could be made from land speculation; to this he replied that he had little cash—£20—a pony, and a sack of seed potatoes. I advised him to borrow from the bank and apply for land. I liked him, for he was full of enthusiasm.

3 . VIII . 1903. *Nairobi*

My views on religion

I was today asked to fill in an official form asking to what religion I belonged. I wrote: "To all religions which recognise the Unknown God." I have been told that my answer is insufficient and will not do. But I have refused to alter it and it must stand.

I should like here briefly to state the history of the evolution of my religion. As a boy at Fonthill I used to think a great deal about religion. I practised all the usual rites and formulas of the Church of England. I said my prayers every night, I followed church services, meaning every word I said, and I accepted without question the doctrines of the Church of England. When I went to Harrow I began to realise that a great deal of what I was asked to believe was humbug and could not possibly be true. The subject caused me a great deal of uneasiness and worry, but I continually dwelt on the subject, reading as much as I could and probing as deeply as my boyish intellect would allow.

I was soon convinced that so long as one acted as a good Christian such matters as devotional worship, ritual and ceremony were of little consequence and in fact were matters of detail. Such detail might be necessary for those whose confidence in themselves is not too strong, but I had full confidence in my ability to conduct myself as a good Christian, and I held an immovable faith that there was a God. As God I represented to myself an unknown influence for good, endowed with a power both omniscient and omnipotent. It could punish and reward. It could be appealed to for consolation and could grant it. But beyond this I was not prepared to go. I regarded the Holy Ghost as a mere phrase which I was unable to appreciate. I looked on Christ as one of the best men who ever lived, as one who has done untold good to the world in construing the meaning of God better than had ever been done before or since. But I shrank from the idea that Christ was the actual son of God. I believed him to be a mortal man of a calibre which inspired respect, gratitude and attention, not reverence or adoration.

I accepted the Bible as a book which teaches the difference between good and bad, between righteousness and sin, and which better than any other book exemplifies to the world the presence of God and what that power is. It is a priceless book, and of great educational value to modern society in all its strata.

I believed prayer to be the sole communion between man and God, and to me it gave great consolation and comfort. It gave me strength to do what I knew was right. It gave me as a boy the correct intellectual and spiritual stimulus.

But I have never been able to see that this Unknown God differs in any respect from the God of the Jews, the Roman Catholics or Mohammedans. It must be the same identical God. The detail of worship is real detail. Ritual, ceremony, the form of prayers, church worship and all pertaining thereto must be matters of detail. To suppose that such a force as God can be so narrow-minded as to care about such detail is unthinkable.

I have therefore practised extreme tolerance towards all religions which worship the Unknown God. I should be equally at home in a Mohammedan mosque, in St. Mark's Church, in a Baptist chapel or Canterbury Cathedral. Such places of worship are no more to me than my own bedroom. And yet I regard such places of worship essential as reminders of religion to the mass of humanity who require such reminders. Even to the idolatrous Brahmin or Hindu I extend sympathy. The votaries of these religions are unable, through lack of imagination and education, to extend their perception to beyond what they can see. They must see an image which to them represents God. But it is the same God.

The longer I live, the firmer am I convinced of these ideas. I do not style myself as irreligious or agnostic. I agree with the baptism of children as a symbol that their sponsors accept on the child's behalf that the child will be brought up to acknowledge God. I agree with all religious ceremonies which introduce a spiritual element into a mere civic entertainment or society function. I agree to the celebration of marriages in church, though I do not regard it as indispensable. But I cannot agree to confirmation and the taking of the Sacrament except as an outward and ostentatious form of confirming one's conscience and reinforcing a tottering faith in God.

But I have never been able to make up my mind about resurrection and an afterlife. I cannot imagine that my spirit or intellect or whatever one is pleased to call it ceases entirely at the death of the body. I believe something goes on, and I have hazy views of something in me being conscious after death and exercising an influence over those I leave behind. Such powers may only be retained by some of us. But of this I have no concise idea. I have, however, sufficient faith to realise that I do not entirely stop at death. This gives me great consolation and leaves me with little fear of dying.

4 . VIII . 1903. *Nairobi*

De Crespigny and I go lion-sticking

An exciting day which I do not wish to repeat. De Crespigny and I went out on our ponies with hog spears to try to get warthog. We were on the Athi Plains south of Nairobi, and about 4 miles out we spied a lion, a solitary beast. He was about 800 yards off on a small mound and lying down. De Crespigny was all for attacking at once, but I thought the risk too great, as our hog spears were only bayonets lashed to bamboo poles and we had no idea of a lion's reaction to being ridden. He might run or crouch and spring, or he might even attack. I advocated leaving the brute alone; I did not like the idea at all and thought it would end in disaster. But de Crespigny got more and more excited and finally said: "I'm off—come on!" So I reluctantly followed, thinking him quite mad; but then the de Crespignys are a foolhardy lot. De Crespigny was better mounted than I and rapidly drew ahead. When the lion saw us coming he stood up, looked rather worried and finally galloped off, with de Crespigny only 50 yards behind him and gaining fast. When he got within 20 yards of the lion the beast crouched, facing the charging horse, but de Crespigny's horse made a violent swerve within a few feet of the lion and off came de Crespigny, sprawling on the ground within 10 feet of the lion, who was now alternately watching de Crespigny on the ground and me coming up at a gallop with lowered spear. It was really a most ridiculous situation. There was de Crespigny fumbling for a pistol which was caught up in a holster, sitting within spitting distance of an unwounded and angry lion. But as I got almost to spearing distance, the lion, watching me intently and obviously preparing for a spring, I heard de Crespigny's pistol go off and the lion rolled over, my spear entering a dead lion. I must admit I was scared stiff. I went and caught de Crespigny's horse. We then skinned the lion and returned home in silence. I thought it a mad enterprise, but de Crespigny pretends he enjoyed it thoroughly. No more lion-sticking for me. The risk is not justified.

We celebrated with champagne at dinner. I asked de Crespigny if he had experienced any sense of fear. He replied: "Of course I did! I was terrified of being afraid —I was afraid of myself, not the lion." That was the triumph of a family tradition.

Colonel Harrison, who heard of our exploit, has forbidden us ever to ride a lion. He says it is not fair on the horses or on ourselves and that we have not been sent out here to run such stupid risks. But he added, "My God, I should like to have been there!"

6 . VIII . 1903. *Ruiru River*

Yesterday I left Nairobi en route for Fort Hall, where I am to relieve the present garrison with my own company. Last night I camped on the Nairobi River and today I came on to the Ruiru. Game was scarce, and I was unable to get meat for my men.

I leave Nairobi for Fort Hall

7 . VIII . 1903. *Thika River*

I came on to the Thika River today, and though my old *zariba* has been burned I pitched camp on the old spot.

Camp at the Thika Crossing

Just before reaching camp I suddenly came on 6 giraffe —an old bull, 4 cows and a calf. They were not more than 40 yards from me when I surprised them in a fold in the

Giraffe

ground. As they made off I was much struck by their awkward ambling gallop. When on the move they hold their head and neck so that the top profile of their upper parts is one straight line from the tip of the tail to the crown of the head. When they canter, the hind legs are placed on the ground far in advance of the forelegs and outside them. The calf which accompanied this party was not much larger than a donkey and its mother was most concerned about it, as it could not keep up with the rest. The old bull also took a fatherly interest in the calf, keeping behind it all the time.

Rhinoceros

This evening I took a stroll round camp and shot a fine rhinoceros. I had a fairly easy stalk to about 30 yards, and on peeping over an ant-hill found a large warthog, also feeding close to the rhino. The pig was such a fine specimen that I was in two minds as to which I should fire at. I decided to take the rhino. She fell to my shot, which passed through her neck. It was not till after she fell that another rhino ran out of some long grass. Though not full grown, this second beast was by no means to be disregarded. He stood so close to me that I tried to take a photo of him, and to my dismay I saw through the finder of my camera that he was coming in my direction. I snapped the camera and jumped to one side as he passed me with a snort and lay down near the ant-hill. After snorting for a while he made off. Without her intestines my first rhino weighed 1495 pounds.

On my way back to camp I killed two sandgrouse and a guinea-fowl for the pot.

Kaninge and Tumbes

I have two excellent Masai boys as servants, Kaninge and Tumbes, aged about 14. They are clean and intelligent; I got them from Lenana, and I pay them 20 rupees a month. Tumbes looks after my clothes and cooks. Kaninge is a good skinner after a fortnight's training, and he carries my camera and shotgun when I am out. I am slowly teaching Tumbes to cook. I am thankful to say both are scrupulously clean and honest.

9 . VIII . 1903. *Punde Milia*

I stop a day on the Thika

I stopped yesterday on the Thika River in order to skin the head of the rhino I shot. I saw lots of game, including the giraffe I saw yesterday. I saw a great many warthog, all sows or small boars. Old boars are usually solitary, bad-tempered old gentlemen, who remain underground all day and only appear in the evening or early morning.

I shoot a lioness

Soon after leaving camp this morning I halted the caravan and had breakfast. As soon as I began to sip my cocoa I heard shouts of "*Simba!*" from my men, and looking up saw 4 lion, 2 males and 2 females, stealing away out of a small reed-bed and making for a neighbouring hill some 500 yards away. I at once set off in pursuit, and passing up a fold in the ground to intercept them I found myself suddenly within 100 yards of a lioness. She saw me at once and went bounding off to my right. I took a snap shot and bowled her over in her tracks with a shot through the heart. We afterwards saw the remainder of the party making off at a canter over the next ridge. Leaving a party to skin her and bring her into camp, I rejoined the caravan and proceeded to Punde Milia, where we camped for the night.

To Punde Milia

Man-eating lion

Man-eating lion have been worrying this neighbourhood. I was shown the tree whence a native had recently been dragged by a lion. The lion took him off a branch 10 feet from the ground. From the claw marks on the trunk it was clear that the lion had had difficulty in reaching his victim.

10 . VIII . 1903. *Fort Hall*

I reach Fort Hall

Marched into Fort Hall, where I again met Maycock, whose company I relieve, Mr. and Mrs. Hinde, and an official of the Administration called Lawson.

11 . VIII . 1903. *Fort Hall*

Hinde and his large lion

Hinde is a humbug. Lawson shot a lion yesterday, and not wanting it gave the skin to Hinde. Hinde pegged out the skin and employed two natives to keep on stretching it while it was still fresh. It now looks like a crocodile. This evening at tea Hinde came rushing in, and not seeing me in the room shouted excitedly to his wife, "It's now over ten feet, darling!" And they are still stretching it. No doubt in a few months it will have been Hinde who shot the lion.

12 . VIII . 1903. *Fort Hall—Nyeri Road*

To Nyeri

As half my company is to be at Nyeri, I left Fort Hall today for that place, camping at Wambogo's village. Wambogo is the paramount chief of these parts, and as his people have been giving trouble lately my old friend Tate, taking advantage of my troops, came out to join me from Nyeri this evening with a view to having a big *shaurie* or conference with the local elders tomorrow. I shot a partridge near camp in the evening—a poor effort for the glorious twelfth. These local partridges are really francolin. They have puzzled me by their infinite variety, and when I get settled down I must collect some specimens.

13 . VIII . 1903. *Wambogo's*

A "shaurie"

Today we held a big *shaurie* with the local chiefs of the Wakikuyu. Karurie came in to attend. After hearing all that had to be said, Tate said that he was far from satisfied with the behaviour of certain of the lesser chiefs, who had been inciting the people to rebellion. He asked me if I thought it was safe to arrest these men at once, and I told him I would arrest the lot if he wished it. So he gave me the names of 7 unfortunates and I arrested them. We are marching them into Nyeri tomorrow, where they will remain for a week or so, just to quiet their ardour.

Witch doctors and leopards

Kibarrabarra, the Masai interpreter at Fort Hall, told me two horrible stories about Kikuyu witch doctors. When an old person becomes a burden on a village, his or her body is sewn up in a leopard skin, taken out of the village and placed beside a path. A young fellow is then told by the witch doctor that there is a leopard by a certain path and that he must go out and spear it. The young fellow, knowing the game, goes out and spears the old burden, and the witch doctor then explains that the old person had turned into a leopard.

Again, if the witch doctor has a down on anyone he gathers a certain bulb which stinks like carrion and runs a trail from the bush to the person's hut, even soaking the person's blankets in the stench, which the intended victim does not notice. A leopard gets on to the trail, follows it

Wambogo

Nyeri Station with Nyeri Hill in the distance

up and kills the man. The leopard finds it so easy that he later becomes a man-eater.

14 . VIII . 1903. *Nyeri*

To Nyeri, where I find Neligan and McClure

Marched into Nyeri today, where I found Neligan, who leaves tomorrow for Fort Hall, and a youngster called H. R. McClure, who has just left the Navy. He is quite a boy and a friend of Tate. He is not yet in the Administration but hopes to get appointed shortly.

15 . VIII . 1903. *Nyeri*

McClure and a couple of rhino

This afternoon McClure and I took a stroll towards Nyeri Hill. McClure has a great Dane—a dog of great size. During our walk we surprised a couple of rhinoceros, who, getting our wind, ran towards us. We scattered to get out of their way. McClure's dog naturally went bounding after his master, and McClure, seeing a monster following him, thought it was the rhino and yelled with fright, much to our amusement. McClure is a mere boy and thoroughly enjoyed the joke when it was all over.

McClure's dog is a huge overgrown puppy and most friendly. McClure lives with me in my grass hut, and this evening an old Kikuyu on his way to my house was spotted by the dog, who went bounding towards him, wishing to play and be petted. The old gentleman, never having seen a dog of such dimensions, gave one shriek and fled, but on being overtaken by the dog he knelt down and spat in his hand as a token of friendship. He was shivering with fright when the dog came up to him and, having been taught to "give paw," placed his huge foot in the old gentleman's hand, much to the latter's delight.

We saw 17 rhino today.

16 . VIII . 1903. *Nyeri*

I kill a lion

All last night there was a lion roaring near my camp, so two hours before daylight I dressed and went out towards the roaring, getting quite close to him in the dark. As dawn approached I saw him walk slowly into a small patch of reeds by the river. There was a small pond on the other side of the patch. As he had not seen me, I posted myself above and close to the reeds, and then fired my shotgun into the patch. At my second shot out he came with a roar and bounded up the opposite slope. At my third shot he fell over and was dead by the time I came up with him.

As I was skinning the lion a small flock of teal settled on the pond. I bagged two on the water and another as they rose. With my third shot I killed a peregrine falcon who stooped at the teal. I shall make him into a skin.

20 . VIII . 1903. *Nyeri*

Major Harrison pays me a visit of inspection

On the 18th Major Harrison arrived to inspect my company and the station. He was accompanied by a globe-trotter called Broun, late of the Army Medical Corps. Yesterday we were busy with work. Today I marked a good rhino down for Harrison and took him out to shoot it. He took his shot at 40 yards and stunned the animal. Harrison's gun-bearer rushed in and jumped on to the prostrate animal. But as soon as the rhino had recovered consciousness he struggled to his feet, upsetting the audacious fellow. Both Harrison and I fired together at the rhino's brain and killed him instantly.

Broun also shot a rhino today.

23 . VIII . 1903. *Fort Hall*

We move to Fort Hall

Harrison and I moved into Fort Hall yesterday. He returns to Nyeri and back to Nairobi through Naivasha tomorrow. Hinde accompanies him to Nyeri. I remain in Fort Hall for a while with Neligan and Lawson, two civil officials.

Lawson and a porter

Lawson fancies himself as a walker, so I betted him that a porter carrying 60 pounds would beat him over a distance of 18 miles; Lawson carrying nothing beyond his huge bulk. This morning the event took place. I promised the porter the amount of the bet—10 rupees—if he beat Lawson, which he did, arriving over a mile ahead. These hefty Swahili porters are indeed wonderful.

My house at Fort Hall with pied crows in foreground

Weighing an Oryx

Heard from Father today; he will have nothing to do with my scheme for buying the land between Ithanga and Tana, so I shall lose it unless a Nairobi bank will lend the money.

I lose the Ithanga Hills

5 . IX . 1903. *Fort Hall*

I have been setting a lot of traps for small mammals lately. A hyaena got caught last night but released himself by biting off his own foot. So I have now fixed all my traps to a log weighing some 50 pounds, which is just heavy enough for a large animal to drag and yet too heavy for him to get away completely. It also leaves a good track when dragged. I have also trapped many mongoose of three varieties. They are savage little devils to get hold of when trapped.

I try to trap mammals

I have been making a rough survey of a typical bit of Kikuyu country to show areas under cultivation (see map). The millet suffers serious depredations from flocks of weaver birds, which descend in thousands when the seed is ripe. To guard against this a small platform is erected in the middle of the crop, and at various places in the crop are tin cans filled with pebbles. Each can is connected to the platform by native cord, and when the birds descend a small boy in the platform pulls a string and scares the birds off. It appears to be most effective, but as often as not the small boy falls asleep.

3 . X . 1903. *Fort Hall*

We have been having a series of mishaps here of late which have been most disconcerting. About three weeks ago Neligan developed fever. Lawson and I were the only Europeans in the station, and as Neligan got worse and worse it became clear that his attack was not ordinary malaria. Lawson and I diagnosed it as rheumatic fever. We took it in turn to sit up all night with him, which was most wearing. After the tenth day we decided to send into Nairobi for a doctor, telling the authorities that Neligan was to our minds suffering from rheumatic fever. After six days an answer came from Nairobi telling us to give him salicyclic acid. Was there ever such a stupid

A series of mishaps

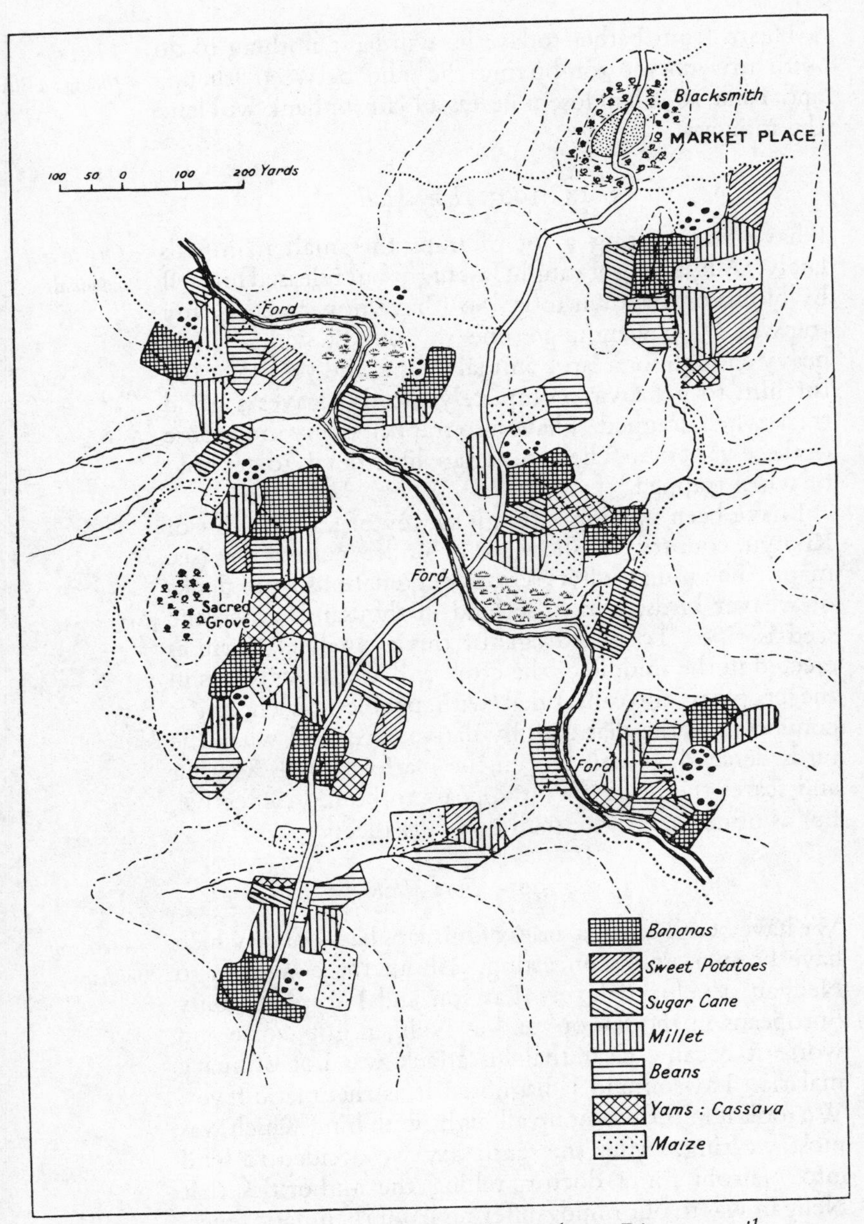

Type of Kikuyu country at a spot on the Mathyoia River two miles west of Fort Hall

message? Of course none of us had salicyclic acid; nor, if we had had, did we know how much to give him. So I sat down and wrote the following to the principal medical officer of the Protectorate at Nairobi:

> Your message regarding salicylic acid has been received. We have none, and if we had we should not know in what doses to administer it. Neligan's condition is worse, his heart is weak, and we cannot take any further responsibility for his recovery or death unless you can make some more sensible suggestion than to suggest an obscure drug to persons who do not dabble in drugs. In our opinion a medical officer of sense should be sent here at once, and I beg of you to take immediate action. If you select a man who can ride, he can take my pony Natalie and if necessary do the whole trip in twenty-four hours. I take all risk on the pony's account. Show this letter to Major Harrison and it will be sufficient authority to allow you to have the pony.

This was sent off on 28 September, and on 1 October a doctor, Drake-Brockman, arrived on my pony Natalie. But this only added to our troubles, for Drake-Brockman arrived with a bad attack of blackwater fever on him. We at once bundled him into bed, but not before we had got from him the salicylic acid and its correct doses. So here we were with two dangerous cases. I now sent the following message into Nairobi by poor Natalie, who will have covered 120 miles in 48 hours:

> Drake-Brockman has arrived with an acute attack of blackwater fever. But we have received from him the salicylic acid and directions for its use. We now have two patients, both suffering from dangerous diseases of which we know nothing. At all costs you must send out another medical officer with all speed, as both Lawson and I are completely tired out. You must not use my pony again, as she also is on the point of collapsing.

5 . x . 1903. *Fort Hall*

A second doctor arrives, so I leave for Nyeri

The second doctor arrives here this evening, and as both Hinde and Routledge also came in from Nyeri I started off for that place, where my absence is causing much delay in the construction of the new huts for my men. I leave this afternoon.

Hinde is a doctor by profession but takes no interest in our patients, though one of them is his own officer.

Arrive Nyeri

Early this morning I reached Wambogo's village, where I slept for an hour or so and came on to the Gura River for breakfast, which I had with McClure, who now has a camp there for the purpose of building a permanent bridge. He accompanied me into Nyeri, where I arrived soon after noon. I found my men flourishing and their huts well advanced. But my few Masai are not standing the climate at all well, and I shall have to send them back to Nairobi. When a Masai gets ill he gets sulky, and they soon become useless as soldiers.

[In 1949 I again met Wambogo, on 6 April, at Nyeri. I wrote at the time: He was delighted to see me and held my hand for some ten minutes, which touched me deeply. He invited me to his village, offering me a house all to myself and lots of women to wait on me; then he suddenly burst out with political worries which he had clearly been bottling up. "Give us back our old times," he said. "Give us back our land. Remove the Indians with whom we cannot compete; remove our grievances; you have put yourselves in the wrong by creating grievances. You have given us better health and security, which has increased the population, and we can no longer grow sufficient food in our restricted reserves." I asked him if he would prefer to return to paganism, Masai raids, epidemics and insecurity. "Yes," he replied at once. "Willingly. We were better off and much happier; sooner or later there is bound to be a clash, an armed clash, between black and white in Kenya; I want to avoid that."]

The China Ornament

About 6 months ago I picked up a small tortoiseshell kitten, which has since grown into a cat. She follows me about everywhere and has been christened the China Ornament. When I travel she is carried in a basket, and is released on arrival in camp. Last night I let her out as usual at Wambogo's, and when we came to move on she was nowhere to be found, so we had to go on without her. I shall be sorry to lose her altogether, but cannot help feeling she will turn up somehow. Cats are such sagacious little animals.

8 . x . 1903. *Nyeri*

One of my men, Juma bin Suleiman, came to me today saying he had caught me a fine snake. He then proceeded to produce from his hat a huge puff adder which he had captured in the grass close to my hut. He handled it with complete lack of fear. After photographing it I placed the venomous beast in spirits.

A puff adder

McClure and I saw 5 rhino within a mile of my hut this evening.

9 . x . 1903. *Nyeri*

I witnessed a marvellous migration of elephant this morning travelling from Mount Kenya to the Aberdares. When it was barely light and the sun not yet risen, one of my men hammered at the door of my hut shouting "*Tembo, bwana, tembo nyingi sana!*—Elephant, sir, many elephant!" I tumbled out of bed, and there was the black mass of Mount Kenya in sharp outline with the sun scarce risen behind it; the light was poor, but my man soon pointed out a long black streak of moving animals not a quarter of a mile off and on the north of the river, all slowly moving west from Kenya to the Aberdares. I quickly put on a pair of long boots and dashed out in pyjamas, ran down to the river and got swamped crossing it—a good cold bath; I had no gun with me. Creeping up a small gully, I found myself but 60–80 yards off this huge stream of moving elephant, going very slowly, sometimes in small groups of eight or ten, sometimes two or three together and an occasional solitary beast; lots of calves; and to right and left I could see no end to the moving mass, each following in the other's trail. I tried in vain to count them, for the head of the column was in the far distance and the tail was approaching me, but I should say there must have been about 700 animals. They were moving at a steady walk, not feeding; the last beasts to pass me were a cow and a very small calf, and the rear of the column was level with Nyeri Hill as the sun rose behind Mount Kenya. I shall never again see anything like that.

Mass migration of elephant

This movement of elephant had seriously disturbed the many rhino in the neighbourhood; I counted 11 of them all trotting about with their tails in the air and resenting this encroachment on their privacy.

Several Kikuyu whom I saw this afternoon tell me that this movement of elephant does not take place every year but perhaps every third or fourth year.

Now how does this mass of elephant manage to assemble before migration? That stumps me!

10 . x . 1903. *Nyeri*

The China Ornament is recovered

The China Ornament turned up at my hut in Fort Hall on the evening of the 8th in an emaciated condition and was sent on to me by a special porter today. The reunion was happy. It is extraordinary that this small cat should have walked back some 16 miles from Wambogo's to Fort Hall, entirely ignorant of the road. From the box in which she was carried she could never have even seen the road. It is an excellent example of pure homing instinct.

10 . x . 1903. *Nyeri*

A shoot

Tate and I went for a shoot along the Mazeras track. I got a sing-sing waterbuck. During the hunt we were worried by three rhino who repeatedly threatened to charge down on us. After weighing the buck we left him out for the night, as it was getting too late to cut him up and bring the meat back to camp.

12 . x . 1903. *Mazeras Country*

A tour into the Mazeras country

Tate and I left Nyeri today for a tour in the Mazeras country, which lies on the left bank of the Tana and among the foothills of Mount Kenya. The chiefs of Mazeras are of doubtful loyalty, and our trip is designed to put them in the right frame of mind and to "show the flag."

We crossed the Chania by a flimsy faggot bridge, and on reaching the Tana we found it so low that most of the porters waded across. There is, however, a tree or two felled across it, which form a good bridge.

In the afternoon I got into heliographic communication with Nyeri, some 12 miles distant.

I find surveying difficult in this country, as my main resection points are always disappearing. It is also difficult to recognise trees and other landmarks from points of view other than the one from which the original bearing was taken.

13 . x . 1903. *Mazeras Country*

Today we moved camp about 4 miles to Tumutumu Hill, where we had a big *shaurie* in the afternoon. We find the natives quite friendly, but the big chiefs are rather sulky. Our camp is just above where the Gura River joins the Tana.

We move to Tumutumu Hill and have a native conference

I killed a brace of francolin, and from my tent I shot a huge hornbill with my rifle as he squawked from the top of a forest tree. In the evening I shot a few doves (*Turtur senegalensis*) which proved excellent eating.

Soon after I got into bed I heard a pathetic little squeal close to my tent; I went out with my torch and found a huge python wrapped round a jackal, whose head only was visible. I fetched my shotgun and fired into the python's body, at which he unwrapped himself and threw himself about in contortions; so I blew his head off and killed him. The jackal was apparently lifeless, so I carried him away from my tent and deposited him in some grass. Meanwhile Tate had come out, asking what was the matter. I showed him the python and the jackal, but on visiting the latter we found him breathing, and in about 10 minutes he suddenly came to and went off into the night.

Python and jackal

14 . x . 1903. *Mazeras Country*

We moved camp today to a spot between the Tana and Gura Rivers and immediately west of their junction. In the evening I bagged 2 brace of guinea-fowl from a large flock. The 4 birds weighed 14 pounds. In the afternoon Tate had a satisfactory talk with the local chiefs, who seemed most friendly.

We camp between the Tana and Gura Rivers

15 . x . 1903. *Nyeri*

We made a long march back to Nyeri today. On our way we passed a large grove of trees which is sacred to

Return to Nyeri

the Wakikuyu. The grove contained a small troop of the black and white colobus monkeys, which are also considered sacred. The local people believe that if these monkeys are killed some great catastrophe will befall the whole tribe.

As we entered Nyeri we met Hinde and Drake-Brockman returning to Fort Hall. Drake-Brockman had almost recovered from his blackwater fever and had yesterday killed 3 rhino—2 adults and a young one. They had a long tale about them being charged, but some of my men who were out with him at the time tell me that these 3 rhino were deliberately stalked and shot, without any provocation. It was pure slaughter, as none of the 3 had a decent horn among them. Apart from the lie, it was an unsportsmanlike action and a breach of the game regulations.

19 . x . 1903. *Mboni River, North of Nyeri*

I start on a trip to the Pesi Swamp

I left Nyeri today on a trip north to the Pesi Swamp for the purpose of surveying the country. I took my dog Baby and my cat, the China Ornament, with me. One of my main objects was to define the watersheds between the Tana and Guaso Nyiro systems. I camped this afternoon on the Mboni stream. As soon as my tent was pitched it began to rain in torrents, which gave an opportunity to two of my porters to bolt back to Nyeri. Just as it was getting dark, a rhino came and drank at the stream about 200 yards from camp.

20 . x . 1903. *Northern Guaso Nyiro River*

The Northern Guaso Nyiro River

I marched 11 miles to the headwaters of the northern Guaso Nyiro River, crossing the Enaiboryik stream on the way. At the spot where I crossed the Guaso Nyiro I shot a duck (*Anas sparsa*) which rose from its nest. The bird also contained a fresh egg, so I had roast duck and five boiled eggs for dinner. My men also gathered some small damson-like fruit which made an excellent tart. One of my men, Lance-Corporal Killalisho, added to my comfort by bringing me some wild honey which he had found in a hollow tree. So I made a first-class meal on the products of the country. But when he gave me the honey he warned me not to eat too much of it, as it would act as a powerful emetic. To this I paid scant attention, as I am particularly fond of honey. I ate as much as I wanted. Sure enough, after an hour or so I was violently ill. What is it about wild bees' honey which renders it such a strong emetic?

The emetic properties of wild bees' honey

I saw today some rhino, and was surprised to see the same hybrid haartebeeste which are so common round Nakuru.

Game

My tent was pitched close to a deserted Dorobo encampment. These people live by hunting, and it was clear that they had had good sport in the neighbourhood. The ground was stewn with the heads of rhino, in all 25 skulls, impala, zebra and bushbuck. I saw no haartebeeste or smaller gazelle. It convinced me of the amount of harm these people must do to game, but they are fast dying out, which is a blessing. It will be a race between the game and the Wandorobo.

A Dorobo camp

But on the whole game was scarce in the neighbourhood. I saw one herd of zebra, a few Thomson's gazelle and a small herd of impala. I shot a female steinbock for meat. This latter I should never have recovered if my terrier Baby had not run it down and held it till I got up, for it was only wounded in the foreleg.

21 . x . 1903. *Ungobit River*

I made a long march to the Ungobit River, crossing on the way the Elkaju Lyuringen, Donyo Uasin and Loldama streams.

Ungobit River

Last night we had a lion close to the camp, which caused much alarm to my Goanese cook. But we kept large fires burning all night and were not disturbed.

The river Ungobit runs here in a deep gorge, which is densely wooded and with frequent grassy glades. I saw no game except for a few Grant's and Thomson's gazelle and steinbock.

22 . x . 1903. *Mutarra River*

Soon after leaving camp I spied a large bushbuck feeding in a glade, but my men disturbed him before I could

To the Mutarra River

approach him. After a long march through fairly open country we reached the Mutarra River, crossing several dry watercourses on the way. Game became more plentiful as we got further north.

A record impala

Near the dry watercourse called Misis I killed a record impala, and soon after blundered on to a cow rhino and her young one in thick thorn bush. My Goanese cook was seen slinking off through the bush in an opposite direction, but my men gave chase and brought him back. This was the first rhino he had seen: the apparition had reduced him to a state of mental collapse. After a few threatening grunts the rhino cleared off with her beloved offspring.

Oryx beisa

Soon after the rhino disappeared I spied the first *Oryx beisa* I have ever seen, feeding with a herd of zebra. I watched him through my glasses for some while until the whole party spotted my caravan and made off. I subsequently saw two more herds before reaching camp. Grant's gazelle, which have been described as Bright's variety, became more numerous as we advanced.

Amurra salt lick

Quite close to camp is a large salt lick. The local game must be in the habit of using it to a very large extent, as I saw abundant spoor of rhino, giraffe, oryx, zebra and smaller stuff. The place abounds with horned guinea-fowl, roving about in packs of 50 to 60.

23 . X . 1903. *Pesi Swamp*

Pesi Swamp

I reached the Pesi Swamp today. Soon after leaving camp this morning we crossed a stream called the Nairobi Leboi, and on crossing the next rise the whole Pesi Swamp was in view. No open water was visible. I pitched camp about a mile above the spot where the Pesi River enters the swamp, and close to a ford which from the innumerable rhino and other game tracks is regularly used by larger game when crossing the Pesi River. The river was here muddy and sluggish, though not broad. The actual swamp, along whose southern fringe I walked this afternoon, is only a few miles long. I was unable to estimate its breadth or gauge its density. The bottom was soft mud, overgrown with reeds and papyrus. It was

Weighing a Warthog. Christmas 1903

H. R. Tate and his grey mule. Nyeri

clear that after heavy rains the marsh extends far beyond its present limits. We are now at the end of the dry season.

I found survey work difficult in this country, where conspicuous features are almost non-existent and those which do exist are difficult to see in the thorn scrub.

Oryx

In the evening I got close to a herd of oryx and killed a couple of cows. Though I was but 30 yards from the herd I was unable to determine the sexes, so I killed the two largest beasts. Warthog, waterbuck, Grant's and Thomson's gazelle and guinea-fowl were numerous everywhere.

Game census

Big game seen today include 18 elephant, 34 giraffe, 17 rhinoceros, 198 zebra, 436 oryx, 66 waterbuck, 186 Grant's gazelle, 109 Thomson's gazelle, 5 bushbuck, 3 duiker, 88 impala, 46 eland, 18 warthog and 44 ostrich; also 88 haartebeeste.

24 . x . 1903. *Pesi River*

I march west from the Pesi Swamp

I marched up the south bank and slightly away from the Pesi River for about 5 miles. We then entered some dense thorn scrub and followed up a dry watercourse full of huge boulders. In this watercourse I found a lump of fossil ivory. Eventually we found a little water, and being uncertain of our next water we pitched camp. The neighbourhood is a mass of fresh elephant and buffalo spoor, but we saw practically no game all day.

Fossil ivory

My whole caravan found a certain wood in the bush from which native knobkerries (*rungus*) are made. They all turned out in the evening, and each man cut himself a suitable stick.

25 . x . 1903. *Markham Downs*

Markham Downs

This morning we ascended to the northern continuation of the Aberdare Mountains, which are usually called the Markham Downs. They comprise rolling grassland intersected by deep wooded ravines, in which there is often a small marsh or trickle of water. There are also large clumps of forest trees, and strips of wood running north from the main forests of Sattima.

On reaching the western limits of these downs we found ourselves on the edge of an escarpment overlooking the El Bor Lossat Swamp, which lay about a mile distant. The escarpment we were on is part of the eastern lip of the Great Rift Valley. The height of my camp is 7775 feet.

Birds on the swamp

In the evening I paid a short visit to the swamp. I was surprised to see a small bunch of pintail duck. I had no idea they came so far south in winter. There were also a large number of pochard (*brunnea*), teal and Egyptian geese. Marsh and pallid harriers were abundant, and there were a few ibis of three varieties, gulls and terns, herons and waders. Among the latter I recognised little stint, marsh sandpiper and one single avocet. The escarpment down which I went to the swamp is scored with elephant tracks, and they form the best path. Game is scarce. I saw two herds of zebra on the downs, a single cock ostrich, a few sing-sing, and a large herd of haartebeeste near the swamp.

Game

Survey work

I had to abandon plane table work when crossing the downs, as my tripod was damaged. This afternoon I mended the tripod and have taken the precaution of measuring a new base of 1040 yards. I shall work back to my original traverse from this base so as to check my previous work.

26 . x . 1903. *Markham Downs*

Return journey

On leaving camp this morning I struck south-east across the Markham Downs, passing just north of Satima Peak. I crossed on my way the upper waters of the Pesi River and camped on the Mutarra stream, but much higher up than my previous camp on that river.

Puff adder

I was nearly struck today by a puff adder. I was walking through long grass in trousers, and only just saw the brute coiled up when my foot was almost on him. I gave a desperate leap to keep clear of him, and he struck at me as I leaped. My dog Baby at once ran in to see what was the matter, and it was only by giving her a terrific kick, which sent her flying for yards, that I prevented the snake from striking her also. I soon despatched the snake with my shotgun, but it took me a long time to explain to Baby why I had kicked her so roughly.

A cheetah

In the afternoon, after pitching camp, I ascended a neighbouring knoll to take observations, and set my men to build a cairn of stones which will be useful to me tomorrow in my survey work. I was helping and was stooping down to pick up a rock when my eyes lit on the furry tail of a hunting leopard which had been lying right among us all the time. Of course he was up and away in an instant, and not having my rifle handy he escaped without a shot. It is wonderful how these animals can hide themselves in surroundings which give them practically no cover.

A leopard stalking gazelle

Very soon after this I spied a leopard some 500 yards off stalking a herd of Grant's gazelle in the open. He managed to get within some 50 yards or so and then lay down, slowly wagging the tip of his tail. I watched him in this attitude for some 20 minutes, but the gazelle were feeding away from him and he obviously could not approach nearer without being seen. The ground afforded practically no cover, but I made an attempt to stalk him. He saw me and made off into some bush.

The long-haired Thomson's gazelle of the Markham Downs

On my way back to camp I shot a Thomson's gazelle, but he was only wounded. Baby gave chase and pulled him down. These gazelle differ from those of the Athi Plains in having a much shaggier coat with longer hair. They should be separated as a distinct race if the difference proves constant in this region.

Woodpigeons

I found woodpigeons abundant in the woods near camp. They belong to that spotted race (*guinea*). I shot a brace, and the cook made me an excellent pigeon pie this evening.

27 . x . 1903. *Loldama River*

Eastern slopes of the Aberdare Mountains

I marched a long distance today, crossing the headwaters of the Ungobit and Loldama streams. The country through which I passed was fairly open and intersected by wooded ravines. I found survey work easy, owing to the numerous small rocky eminences.

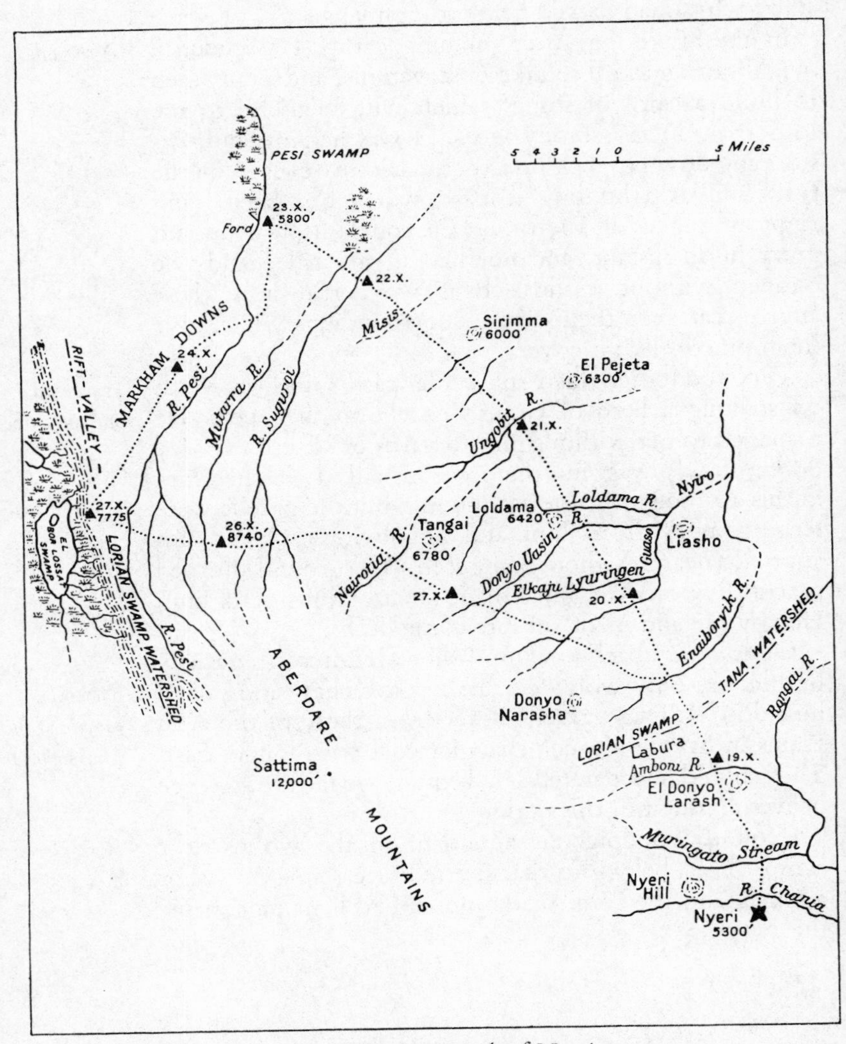

Map of country north of Nyeri

I was much struck by a small plant which covers the grasslands about here. It has leaves like a primula and a small deep blue flower about the size of a violet. I secured several roots, which I shall send to England.

A beautiful plant

During the whole of my trip I have not encountered a single native.

No natives

28 . x . 1903. *Nyeri*

I marched into Nyeri this afternoon, having been successful from a survey point of view.

Return to Nyeri

Tate tells me there is a plan on foot to offer the Jews a home on the Uasin Gishu Plateau. I hope they refuse it, for it is just asking for trouble. In the first place, the Jews' home is in Palestine, not in Africa. The scheme would only add to political confusion, and God knows there will be enough trouble here in 50 years when the natives get educated. Also, the Jews are not good mixers—never have been; they have their own religion, customs and habits and would constitute a most indigestible element in East Africa if they came in any numbers. Why not persuade the Turks to give them Palestine? The Arabs are doing nothing with it, and the Jews with their brains and dynamic force would be a tremendous asset to Turkey.

A home for Jews in East Africa

7 . xi . 1903. *Nyeri*

Last night my men caught a hyaena in a trap and called me out to shoot it, which gave me much pleasure. These brutes have been worrying me lately, and I have been sitting up by moonlight over a bait. But they were too suspicious to give me a shot, though I saw them on every occasion.

Hyaena

On these bright moonlight nights Mount Kenya shows up clearly, its snowfields glistening. I really must make an attempt to get to the top, but I never seem to have time. Just at the moment the country is too disturbed, and I should never get porters to accompany me.

Kenya by moonlight

8 . XI . 1903. *Nyeri*

My company is charged by two rhino

I was out this morning with my company carrying out a route march when two rhino became most threatening. After some snorting, I halted the company and made the men lie down. The rhino soon became very excited, raised their heads and tails, and trotted across our front. They suddenly halted some 50 yards from us and at once charged my rear section. I fired at the rump of the leading beast, and turning he halted and began to paw the ground. The other beast also pulled up, and they were both facing us at only a few yards. I could not take any further risks with my men, so fired at the neck of the nearest rhino. He dropped at once, and the other beast charged direct for the centre of the column. Shouting to the men to make a gap for him, I put two bullets into him. He, however, succeeded in passing through my company and collapsed about 150 yards on the other side. It spoke well for the discipline of my men that not a soul left the ranks during the whole proceedings, neither was there any talking.

9 . XI . 1903. *Nyeri*

King's birthday

Today being the King's birthday, I fell the company in and presented them with a small bullock and proclaimed a general holiday after three cheers for the King. I thought such an arrangement was better than a ceremonial parade.

Hyaena and bushbuck

In the afternoon I went along the Mazeras road for a shoot, accompanied by Tate on his grey mule. I had left the road to look into a small ravine when I saw a hyaena stalking a small sing-sing waterbuck. As I was watching the stalk a bushbuck walked out of a clump of reeds only 75 yards from me. I killed him with one shot. He weighed 157 pounds. I think bushbuck are one of the most attractive African antelope.

While we were returning home the dogs gave chase to a hyaena, and Tate on his mule accompanied them. They ran in a circle, and I managed to intercept the brute and kill him with one shot. He proved to be a large dog with very yellow fur and very distinct black spots. The strength of these hideous animals lies entirely in their head, neck and shoulders. He weighed 138 pounds. I left two men with him while Tate trotted back to the *boma* to send out 4 men with a pole and rope to bring him in.

13 . XI . 1903. *Fort Hall*

Move to Fort Hall

I left Nyeri yesterday and spent last night with McClure, who has a camp on the Gura River. I came into Fort Hall today, where I find Humphery and his wife have arrived. He is the new District Officer.

16 . XI . 1903. *Fort Hall*

I am sent to Eml to arrest Gibbon and bring him t Fort Hall

When I returned to Fort Hall on the 13th Hinde told me he was worried by information to the effect that a low-class man called Gibbons with some 30 armed Swahilis had installed himself in the Embu country south-east of Mount Kenya and was collecting hut tax and extorting ivory from the natives. He had hoisted the Union Jack to give Government protection to his nefarious actions. I volunteered to start at once for his camp, arrest him, and bring him back to Fort Hall to answer for his sins.

I accordingly left Fort Hall at 6 p.m. on the 13th and, crossing the Tana in the dark, travelled all night. At dawn we crept into some thick forest, where we remained throughout the 14th. I had two guides with me, who informed me we were now some 15 miles from Gibbons' camp. We had done about 20 miles during the night, and I do not think our presence was suspected by the local natives. These people are not directly administered by Fort Hall and have in the past resented Government control, so I am not over-anxious to advertise my presence.

As soon as it became dark on the 14th we started off again, my plan being to arrive at his camp at dawn, surround it, and if possible secure my man and disarm his retinue without bloodshed. Our march was uneventful, and we reached the vicinity of Gibbons' camp about two hours before daylight, which gave me plenty of time to reconnoitre the place and see what sentries he had on his *zariba*. The enclosure was large, surrounded by a stiff thorn *zariba* with three large tents inside, and with but one sentry on the door of the *zariba*.

I had 25 rifles with me, and I disposed them round the camp while I and two men stalked the sentry. The man was half asleep, and it was not until I covered him at close quarters with my rifle that he was aware of our presence. I at once told him to keep quiet and drop his rifle, which he did at once. We then closed in on the camp, and at the first streaks of dawn we all entered. I went direct for Gibbons' tent, which I rightly judged to be the largest. My men very quietly roused the armed retinue, advised them to keep still and not utter a sound, and then proceeded to collect their rifles. The Swahilis were completely taken by surprise and surrendered without any show of resistance. When I reached Gibbons' tent, I threw back the flap and said in a loud voice: "Gibbons, hold your hands up or I shall shoot!" He woke with a start, made an effort to produce a revolver from under his pillow, and swore a terrible oath. I was on the point of pulling the trigger when he put his hands up. I then told him that I arrested him on a charge of illegally collecting hut tax and despoiling the natives. He said it was not true, but I told him he would have to come to Fort Hall with me to answer to the Sub-commissioner. Telling my men to remove his revolver and rifles, I ordered him out of his tent, and setting a couple of men over him, with orders to shoot if he stirred, I proceeded to pack up his ivory and boxes, which were considerable. I also pulled down the Union Jack.

I now helped myself to breakfast off Gibbons' stores and gave Gibbons his portion. He was now very sulky, refused to answer questions, and used the most provoking language to me and my men. When I began to move his ivory he grew frantic, and I had to threaten to bind his hands if he went on with his threatening language. Our difficulties were now increased by the local natives arriving on the scene and adopting a menacing attitude. They were all armed, wanted to know why we were removing their "Government official," how they were going to be paid for the ivory they had given him, and a host of other awkward questions. I replied to them all that if they had any complaint they must make it at Fort Hall, to which they said they did not recognise Fort Hall or the British Government. Their attitude became so threatening that I ordered my men to clear the camp, which they did. But there were still crowds waiting outside the camp, yelling at us and obviously most displeased.

But I had some useful hostages. Within Gibbons' camp were some 14 young girls, all local inhabitants. Apparently Gibbons had compelled the local chiefs each to supply him with a concubine, and here they were. I now told the natives that these girls would accompany me to the Tana River, where I should release them, but that if I had any more fuss from armed natives all the girls should accompany me to Fort Hall, and in that case a pretty heavy price would have to be paid for their release. The local chiefs then volunteered to come with me as far as the Tana, so all was well.

After collecting Gibbons' rifles and those of his men, piling them in a heap and burning them, we started for home at 11 a.m. The order of march was as follows:

5 of my men and 1 guide;
Gibbons' 24 men, each carrying a load of ivory or a box;
10 of my men;
Gibbons;
myself and 1 guide;
2 of my men;
the local chiefs and the 14 young girls;
8 of my men.

Before starting I explained to every man that we should resist any attempt to escape by instant rifle fire. We marched the whole of yesterday, but our progress was slow. We camped some 12 miles from Fort Hall. I asked Gibbons to dine with me. This he refused to do and became most abusive, so I confined him to his tent, and placing 4 sentries on him told them that they must shoot if he attempted to escape. As I had a presentiment that Gibbons might try to escape or try to shoot me I kept awake till after midnight, and at about 1 a.m. I heard talking coming from his tent. I saw him standing in the door of his tent, speaking inaudibly to a sentry. I approached the spot at once, and on Gibbons seeing me he attempted to wrench the rifle from the sentry's hands. I at once struck him with the butt of my weapon full in the face, felling him to the ground. The men fell on him, and we soon had his arms and legs bound. I then lashed him to a tree trunk and, placing a man to watch him, went to bed, satisfied that I should have no further trouble from the man. I then found out that Gibbons was trying to persuade one of my men to lend him his rifle, promising him in return a large sum of money. My man was persuading him to return to his tent when I heard the conversation and interrupted them.

At dawn I released Gibbons and gave him his breakfast in my tent. He continually swore vengeance on my head. We left camp for Fort Hall soon after daylight, retaining the same order of march. On reaching the Tana River I released the 14 young girls, who returned to Embu with the chiefs. On reaching Fort Hall today I made a full report to Hinde and handed Gibbons over to him. He was formally charged with raiding the natives, with taking by force native women, with illegally collecting Government taxes for his own benefit, and with murder in having shot a native during one of his raids. He goes to Nairobi for trial tomorrow.

Hinde is delighted at the complete success of my mission and gave to each man who accompanied me a sheep and 5 rupees. We had covered 82 miles in 78 consecutive hours, carrying our own food, each man with a rifle, bayonet and 150 rounds of ammunition—not a bad performance.

19 . XI . 1903. *Tana River*

Shooting on the Tana River

I am down here for a couple of days' shooting, just north of the Mathyoia and close to the Tana River. There are some splendid waterfalls near camp which are a perpetual source of joy to me. Rushing water is a most restful force, and I can sit and watch it for hours on end.

I shot a solitary waterbuck near camp, a very heavy beast with a poor head. Among antelope solitary beasts are usually heavy and with poor heads. The best heads are usually to be shot from large herds. One very rarely sees good heads in herds of buck alone. The single buck of a herd would probably have a good pair of horns with which to eject other bucks from the herd, but a poor body, as he has a large harem to serve, and vice versa with a solitary buck. A herd containing nothing but bucks nearly always consists of young animals and is seldom worth following.

There are a large number of dog-faced apes near camp. One of them tried to chase my dog Baby and I was compelled to shoot him. He weighed 67 pounds.

20 . XI . 1903. *Tana River*

I move to the Meragua River

I crossed the Meragua River today in order to reach my favourite spot where it joins the Tana. Saw quantities of game, including many oribi, rhino and waterbuck.

21 . XI . 1903. *Tana River*

Oribi

I have never seen oribi so plentiful. The males never seem to be solitary, though females often are. One frequently sees 4 females together. When halted the buck usually lies down, and when alarmed the female is usually the first to jump up, whistle and run off, the male rising after her and following.

Crocodile

I sat for a long while by the Tana River near a huge pool, watching the heron, kingfishers and hippo. My perch was on the bank, near a small sandpit, and I had not been there long before a large crocodile emerged from the water not 6 feet from me and slowly crawled on to the sand, where he lay on his stomach, shut his eyes and prepared for his siesta. Very slowly I drew a bead on his head and fired. He lay perfectly still, so thinking he was dead I got hold of his tail and began to try to pull him up the bank. But he gave a twist with his tail which sent me sprawling on the sand and the brute leaped back into the stream before I could give him another shot. He must have been about 8 feet long, and his weight when I tried to move him seemed immense. I return to Fort

Return to Fort Hall

Hall tomorrow, having had a most restful time with nature.

29 . XI . 1903. *Tana River*

Lawson and I have a joint shoot on the Tana River

Yesterday Lawson and I came down to the junction of the Tana and Mathyoia Rivers. Today we crossed the Meragua, and I saw three roan antelope. They were very tame and allowed me to approach within 100 yards before they made off. I was much struck by the smallness of the horns of these huge beasts and by their ears, which seem much too big for their heads. When I was within 60 yards of them they trotted off with a high action, which made my first introduction to this splendid antelope a pleasant one. There are a good many roan in the Ithanga Hills but few people ever molest them, which probably accounts for their tameness.

Roan antelope

Lawson's lack of shooting etiquette

In the evening Lawson and I decided that I should follow the Tana up and that he should follow it down. I had left camp and had already shot a nice impala when I was surprised to see Lawson. He said he had changed his mind and would follow the Tana up. I let him have his way and said nothing, but after cutting up the impala worked away from the river. I had been going some 15 minutes when I spied a lioness some 400 yards off. She saw me at about the same time and retired into some dense bush by the river. I took up a position near where she had gone in, hoping she might reappear later on. Again Lawson turned up. I told him what I was doing, and he announced his intention of also waiting for the lioness and took up a position some 150 yards from me. After about 20 minutes a leopard emerged from the bush directly opposite me and but 50 yards from me. Lawson, though he could not fail to see that I had covered it with my rifle, at once fired at it, and missed. I immediately pulled my trigger and the beast dropped dead. Lawson now came up to the spot, and we measured and weighed the leopard. Meanwhile my annoyance with Lawson was becoming acute, but looking up towards the bush I saw the lioness standing not 40 yards from us and watching us. I said, "Keep quite still, for the lioness is out again." He at once gesticulated, and shouting, "Where?

Lioness and leopard

View from my tent of the falls on the Tana

R.M., Baby and Rhinoceros. Nyeri

Where?" seized his rifle, took a shot without aiming, and finally succeeded in scaring the beast into the bush again. Never again do I go shooting with Lawson.

We return to Fort Hall tomorrow. *To Fort Hall*

6 . XII . 1903. *Punde Milia*

I have been out here since the day before yesterday, *I bag two lion* seeing to the road and continuing my survey into the Ithanga Hills. There were lion roaring near camp before daylight this morning, so I got my porters to beat out several swampy bits on the Punde Milia stream. My fourth beat was a patch of about 3 acres, and from the way Baby barked I knew there was some large animal resting there. After turning the porters in I took up a position above the patch. By the movement of the reeds I could see there was more than one large animal inside, and very soon 2 lion emerged and looked around. They then, oblivious of my presence, walked along, keeping parallel to but outside the reeds. I fired at the leading animal, and he dropped in his tracks. The second wheeled round and faced me only some 40 paces from me. I fired at the second; he turned with a bound into the reeds, but I had heard the thud of my bullet. The porters were, of course, out of the reeds in no time and off back to camp, leaving me and my orderly. It now started to rain hard. Leaving my orderly to watch the patch of reeds from above, I went down to the dead lion and began to skin him. Having completed this, I returned to camp with the skin. I returned to the reeds in the afternoon, when my orderly reported having seen nothing come out of the reeds, so I decided to follow the wounded lion into the reeds, feeling confident he was too badly hit to offer much fight. There was a good blood spoor and after 30 yards I could see him, but to my horror his flanks were still heaving, with me but 6 feet from him. After parting the reeds carefully in order to get a better view I put a bullet into his neck which killed him. He was the finer of the two and had a blackish mane, with large tufts of dark hair at the elbow and on the chest, which is not common in wild lion.

8 . XII . 1903. *Punde Milia*

A fine bull giraffe

I now have nearly 400 men working on the road, and I am hard put to it to find food, especially meat. I find antelope go nowhere, so today I took advantage of a herd of giraffe which turned up near camp yesterday evening. Stalking was impossible. One might as well try to stalk the Eiffel Tower on a billiard table. I hid behind an ant-heap and tried to get my men to drive them to me, but it was of no avail. So I finally used stratagem. I had, some weeks ago, constructed a framework of wood and canvas to represent the body of an ostrich. Under this I could walk, carrying in my right hand my rifle and in my left a pole with a dummy head, to represent the ostrich's head and neck. By walking slowly and by manipulating the ostrich's neck so as to simulate feeding, I managed to get within 40 yards of the herd. They paid not the slightest attention to me. So I gradually sat down, took deliberate aim at the bull giraffe's lower neck and fired. He fell after staggering a few yards. I am delighted with the trick and must try to get some photographs by the same means.

An old trick

11 . XII . 1903. *Tana River*

More survey down the Tana River

I am making a trip down the Tana River to survey to its junction with the Thika. I am now camped 14 miles from Fort Hall, near where the Thara stream runs in. I shot an oribi and a warthog and saw three rhino. Two of them were within sight of my camp most of the afternoon. In the evening I was fortunate in witnessing at close quarters an old hippo with her calf, both on land. The youngster was gambolling about like a young pig. The old cow moved very slowly with her head held low, the nose almost touching the ground: she looked gigantic, and ever so much larger than a rhinoceros.

12 . XII . 1903. *Tana River*

I move down the right bank of the Tana

I moved further down the right bank of the Tana, surveying as I went. I camped near a spot known as the Old Swahili Ford, but there was not much of a ford. Game became more plentiful, and I had no difficulty in shooting a waterbuck and impala for the men.

Hippopotami

Hippopotami are very numerous near here. I watched a small herd of them in a pool, and just before dark killed the bull with one shot, as my men were most anxious for the hide and some of the meat. He sank to my shot, but I shall recover him tomorrow morning when he floats. I saw many crocodile on the sandbanks.

13 . XII . 1903. *Tana River*

I recover the hippopotamus

I found the hippo dead and stranded in some shallows some 400 yards below where I had killed him. He turns out to be a not very large bull. The bullet, a ·256 Mannlicher solid, had entered the brain and must have killed him at once. We had some difficulty in recovering him, as the Tana was rather swollen. But I swam out to him with a cord and then 7 of my men followed suit, and with their help we pulled him to shore, where we were able to cut him up in about 2 feet of water.

Snapping fishes

While cutting him up we were much worried by fishes who swarmed round the carcass to pick up any titbits. They nibbled our feet and actually took a piece out of one of my men's toes. We eventually caught several on hooks baited with a piece of hippo meat, the largest of which weighed 19 pounds. They were a sort of barbel, with evil-looking tentacles hanging from their jaws.

An inquisitive rhinoceros

In the afternoon I killed a waterbuck, and while cutting him up a rhino came and watched me from about 100 yards. He seemed intensely interested, and remained standing there for nearly an hour.

Tortoises and water tortoises

I found large numbers of land tortoises all over the country, some being as large as 18 inches across. I also saw a water tortoise in the Tana which must have been at least 2 feet across, but he was very shy.

Return to Fort Hall

I shall send my caravan into Fort Hall tomorrow, while I shall sketch down to the Tana–Thika Junction and then follow them up. That will complete my survey as far as I can do without making an extensive trip of many days' duration. At present, what with half the company at Nyeri and half at Fort Hall, I get little time for anything but purely military work.

24 . XII . 1903. *Punde Milia Camp*

A party of us have a Christmas shoot on the Thika River

Hinde, the Sub-commissioner at Fort Hall, has been rather ill of late. Dr. Pritchard, who arrived here the other day, decided to move him into Nairobi, and he started in today. We all thought it would be a good opportunity to accompany him part of the way and enjoy a Christmas shoot. Lawson (Asst. District Officer), McClure, Pritchard, Routledge and the Hindes all set out today, only myself with Lawson and McClure going for the shoot, the remainder going straight into Nairobi.

We camped this evening at Punde Milia, where I killed several green pigeon for dinner.

25 . XII . 1903. *Thika River*

To the Thika River

Christmas Day. This morning we all trekked to the Thika River, where we camped. In the afternoon I killed a warthog, a Thomson's gazelle and a blue wildebeeste. We had our Christmas dinner with the Hindes on the very spot where 18 months ago a lion took a man out of my camp. Our English mail arrived in camp this evening and was most welcome.

26 . XII . 1903. *Thika River*

I kill a lioness

Lawson, McClure and I went on to the Athi River near where it flows close to the Thika and there camped. The remainder of the party went on to Nairobi. It rained heavily soon after we started and we all got drenched to the skin.

In the afternoon I walked some distance down the Athi River and, not seeing much game, struck across to the Thika. As I was walking along the edge of a ravine I caught sight of an animal running through the bush some distance off but did not take much notice of it, thinking it to be a warthog or hyaena. I had walked a little beyond the spot where I had seen the animal when I saw a lion making off some 200 yards off. I quickly turned the safety catch over and was on the point of taking aim when on my flank I heard a roar and a growl. Turning at once, I found a lioness charging towards me through the grass. She was already almost on me when I fired from my hip and jumped out of the way. By a great bit of luck my bullet had hit her in the head, and she rolled over dead on to the spot where I had been standing. I quickly gave her another shot through the heart to make certain. The boy carrying my camera was some 200 yards behind, and I called to him to come up. After taking a hurried snapshot of the dead lioness I rushed forward to where I had seen the first lion. I soon came on him, now accompanied by a younger lion and only 150 yards from me. As they made off through the long grass I took a snap shot and hit the larger one. He fell over and roared, but picking himself up again he made off into some thick bush. I raced after him but there was no blood spoor, and I abandoned the chase—not too unwillingly, for the bush was much too thick to follow up a wounded lion successfully.

On returning to my dead lioness I measured her and found she was in milk. I searched everywhere for the cubs but found no trace.

[Though I did not realise it at the time, these lion were almost certainly the famous man-eaters of Thika, as depredations ceased with their death; they had accounted for over 50 Africans.]

28 . XII . 1903. *Thika River*

I find my lion

Both yesterday and today McClure and I searched for my lion, and this morning we found the carcass, badly eaten and torn by hyaenas. It was nearly 2 miles from where I had hit him, and it was only by watching the vultures that we discovered him. His skull showed him to be an old beast with very worn teeth.

Chanler's reedbuck

Yesterday afternoon I strolled up the Athi River, where I found lots of Chanler's reedbuck on the rocky edges of the river bed. I got quite close to a small combined herd of these delightful buck mixed with impala, which presented as pretty a scene as I have witnessed. I watched them for some time before I disturbed them.

Move to Thika Camp

Today I killed a fine warthog near camp. In the afternoon we moved camp back to the Thika crossing. Last night we were regaled by two lions roaring at each other on either side of the Athi River. It lasted some 2 hours before they relinquished the contest.

30 . XII . 1903. *Fort Hall*

Return to Fort Hall

Yesterday we camped at Punde Milia, and today we marched into Fort Hall, having had a most enjoyable Christmas holiday.

1 . I . 1904. *Fort Hall*

We see the New Year in

Last night we all dined with Mr. and Mrs. Humphery and later decided to see the New Year in sitting up for a hyaena. But no hyaena came. Instead we killed a fox which came nosing round our bait.

6 . I . 1904. *Nyeri*

To Nyeri

Yesterday I left Fort Hall for Nyeri, where I arrived today, having camped last night with McClure on the Gura River.

12 . I . 1904. *Nyeri*

The dummy ostrich

Some time ago I constructed a dummy ostrich by stretching the skin of a female ostrich over a bamboo frame the exact size of the ostrich's body. The head and neck were separate; I would place the body over my stooping body, carry the head and neck in my right hand and my rifle in my left hand. I found that if one approached game upwind the ruse was most effective, and with ease I could get near every kind of game—sometimes as close as 25 yards—but with a rhino I had to be careful, as with their bad tempers they dislike any animal approaching them too closely. Also I found that warthog resented my approach beyond 20 yards, when they would snort and grunt and show signs of charging. To shoot I had to sit down, discard the head and neck and tilt the body back, which rather disturbed animals. However, before they realised what was happening I usually managed to pull the trigger. My nearest approach was to a giraffe at but 10 feet and ground hornbill up to almost touching distance.

My one fear was lion and leopard, who might attempt to stalk me and jump on my back; but I was fortunate, and it never occurred.

On one occasion I tried the trick on a small flock of wild ostriches. The cock came out to investigate and was very suspicious, walking round me and lifting his feet very high; when about 10 yards from me he started to stamp the ground with one foot, and as I was afraid he might attempt to mount me I suddenly threw off the dummy, and he decamped at top speed, zigzagging and with flapping wings.

If game became a little restive I found that by lowering my head and neck to a feeding attitude it soon restored confidence; but many animals like oryx and roan, though never suspecting the ruse, would resent a near approach, and an old buck would often toss his head and show displeasure if I got closer than about 30 yards. I should have liked to try it on wild dog but never had the opportunity, nor did I ever come across any of the large cats when I had my dummy.

Oxpeckers

I have been studying the habits of the oxpeckers or tick birds (*Buphagus*) and have been able to get very near them, sit down and watch them only 25 yards away. They not only eat ticks but also sip up the blood from sores, and in several cases they will peck at sores and make them larger; they can move up and down and sideways. When nest-building they pick hairs off the animal and collect a bunch in their mouth, place it on the animal, and then collect more until they have a mouthful; then off they fly to their nest. I never saw an animal resent their attentions.

13.1.1904. *Chinga's. Near Nyeri*

Survey near Nyeri

I am out from Nyeri on a survey trip with my plane table. I had intended going to Tusu, but I find work is too slow and I have not much time at my disposal. I am camped at Chinga's, where McClure met me. I did not reach camp till 6 p.m., as I could not get the bearings I wanted to complete a resection. What makes this country so difficult to survey is the lack of satisfactory points. Trees have a wonderfully annoying habit of disappearing when wanted, and small knolls look so different when viewed from other points. If I erect small beacons they are as quickly removed by the Wakikuyu, who look on them as some work of the Devil. The work is most disheartening, and sometimes I feel inclined to give it up in disgust.

Bad class of administrative officers in British East Africa

The authorities give no help. The administrative officers, with few exceptions, seem to dislike their country being mapped by soldiers. In fact the soldier is not in favour in British East Africa. This is largely due to the low class of man who is appointed to administrative appointments. Few of them have had any education, and many of them do not pretend to be members of the educated class. One can neither read nor write. This is not surprising when one realises that no examination is required to enter the local Civil Service. Sir Clement Hill, who recently visited the colony on behalf of the Foreign Office, remarked that "so long as Civil Servants were enlisted from the gutter" we could not expect a high standard of administration. When such men are given unlimited power over uneducated and simple-minded natives it is not extraordinary that they should abuse their powers, suffer from megalomania and regard themselves as little tin gods.

17.1.1904. *Nyeri*

Gura River

Last night I returned with McClure to his camp on the Gura River, having completed my survey of Karima and Wambogo's areas. In the evening we enjoyed a bathe in the Gura, which was pleasant but mighty cold. We dined off some doves which I shot.

To Nyeri

I returned to Nyeri today.

21 . I . 1904. *Nyeri*

We are still worried by the numbers of rhino in the neighbourhood of the camp, and Tate is always trying to persuade me to kill a particularly bad-tempered beast which haunts the Fort Hall Road. So this evening I attacked him. He had not large horns, but I thought it would be a good opportunity to weigh and measure one. I stalked him to about 100 yards and let drive with my Mannlicher, aiming behind the shoulder. I heard the bullet strike. He made off over a small rise, up which I scrambled, and found him standing but very sick about 200 yards from me. I was just working round for a second shot when he tottered and fell. I then walked straight to him, Baby running in and yapping at him. This induced the monster to get on his legs again. I was now some 70 yards from him, so I gave him another shot behind the shoulder, at which he dropped his hind-quarters, which left him sitting on his rump. He looked every bit like a huge pig. But he soon rolled over on his side and kicked his legs in the air. I then got within 10 yards and put two shots from my 12 bore Paradox into him to see what effect they would have. Both bullets entered the skin but failed to go further. They were both fired at the flank. If I had fired at the neck perhaps they might have gone further in, as the skin on the neck is thinner. As he still had a kick in him I finished him off with a solid in the neck from my Mannlicher, when he expired with a shiver.

Rhinoceros

As it was now late and getting dark I left him, meaning to return tomorrow. There is really little risk in leaving a rhino out all night, as hyaenas and vultures cannot tackle his hide, and nothing could damage his horns. A troop of lion might tear him about, but just at present there are no lion round the station. Natives tell me that it is not till the third day after death that decomposition sets in and hyaenas can tear the skin.

22 . I . 1904. *Nyeri*

I returned to my rhinoceros early this morning and found him intact. I managed to weigh him all, except for the

I weigh and measure my rhinoceros

viscera. These I estimated at about 500 pounds. I weighed him in the following portions:

hind legs	330 lb.
forelegs	369 lb.
body skin	206 lb.
head and neck	248 lb.
carcass (in two pieces)	720 lb.
liver	48 lb.
heart	20 lb.
lungs	32 lb.
viscera	500 lb.
blood, offal, etc.	48 lb.
Total weight ..	2521 lb., or 1 ton 1 cwt.

Notes on rhino

This animal was an old bull and seemed a full-grown beast in good health. I should therefore doubt whether any rhino would exceed a ton and a half. Cows probably weigh slightly less.

I have noted the following facts about rhino. Males are usually solitary but sometimes wander about in couples. I have never seen more than two full-grown rhino together. Cows are accompanied by their offspring until the next calf is born, when the older youngster is driven off by the mother. By this time the older youngster is three-quarters grown. Bulls never consort with cows unless the latter are in season, when the pair keep company for some 8–10 days. At that time one can see the parents and a half-grown youngster. The calf stays with its mother during the whole period of gestation.

31.1.1904. *Nyeri–Naivasha Road*

In search of Jackson's francolin

I am camped in the bamboos at the foot of the Aberdare Mountains in order to try to secure some specimens of Jackson's francolin. I only killed the red-legged francolin and never saw a Jackson's. All the paths round here are spiked and studded with nasty pitfalls, which have been made by the Wakikuyu to keep intruders away. Like Agag, I walked delicately amid such surroundings.

It poured with rain all the evening, which made things rather miserable. Routledge was to have joined me, but never turned up on account of the rain. As he had arranged to bring food, I missed him. As it was I dined on roast francolin and nothing else. I return to Nyeri tomorrow.

5 . II . 1904. *Nyeri*

A visit from a big-game hunting party

Yesterday Count L. Hunyadi, an Austrian, and two Americans, Mr. and Mrs. Cordeza, arrived here on their way from the Tana River to the northern Guaso Nyiro. They have already killed lion, buffalo, giraffe and eland. They left for Laikipia today. They all dined with us last night. They were quite a cheery party, though Hunyadi appeared to be fonder of Mrs. Cordeza than was her husband.

8 . II . 1904. *Nyeri*

A fussy rhino pays the penalty

I was out this afternoon trying to get some meat for my men and was just going to stalk a fine waterbuck when I disturbed a sleeping rhino in some long grass. He got my wind and thundered past me at about 20 yards distance. I lay down and he never saw me. I hoped he would clear out, as I had no wish to kill him, but he was thoroughly excited and wheeling in all directions got my wind again. This time he judged my position too accurately, and charging towards me I fired at his chest when he was some 30 yards from me. It failed to stop him, and I had to jump aside to let him pass. I quickly gave him a couple more solids from my Mannlicher, and he collapsed.

On my way home I killed a fine serval cat.

11 . II . 1904. *Fort Hall*

To Fort Hall

I left Nyeri yesterday and arrived at Fort Hall today. Last night I camped with McClure on the Gura River.

The new bridge which McClure is building over the Gura River is almost complete; in fact I crossed it with my caravan, the first to do so.

I shall probably not see Nyeri again and am sorry to leave Tate, whom I like. He is a conscientious administrator and gets on well with the Kikuyu, who respect him. He is a well-educated man of the right type for an undeveloped country and undeveloped peoples. My only quarrel with him is his secretiveness. He tells me nothing about his work and seldom enlightens me regarding Kikuyu reactions to the administration. This is a pity, for I am more or less responsible for security and a closer liaison with me might have been helpful. But I like him, for he is always cheerful and has a welcome sense of humour.

Hinde and his wife are away on the Tana River to try to secure a roan antelope.

The coming expedition against the Irryeni

I had a letter from Col. Harrison today telling me that Dickinson is coming here to command Brancker's and my company during the forthcoming expedition against the Irryeni. His letter is in reply to one I wrote him telling him I did not intend to stand interference in military operations from civil officials. They could control the general policy but must not interfere with operations. I am glad to see he agrees with me.

14 . II . 1904. *Tana River*

A shoot on the Tana River

Adams, Lawson and I came down to the Tana River for a shoot at the junction of the Tana and Meragua Rivers. Adams is the first medical officer to reside at Fort Hall. This afternoon I crossed the Meragua River and searched in vain for roan antelope. Indeed, I saw very little game. I came across an old female rhinoceros with a newly born youngster lying beside her. I got to within about 30 yards of her, took a photo and cleared out. She was not in the least suspicious and stood broadside on the whole while, but the light was poor and I fear her picture will not be a success.

Adams' adventure with lion

Today Adams saw two lots of lion, one party of two and another of three. He was stalking a waterbuck when he came on the two lion only 40 yards from him. They had not noticed him. He had one cartridge in his ·450 cordite rifle but no more in his pockets—a most inexcusable state of affairs. With this one cartridge he fired at and missed the lion. The lioness at once bounded towards him, but Adams lay very low and she never spotted him. Adams' boys then coming up, both lions cleared off.

There is no excuse for walking about Africa after big game with only one cartridge, and still less for taking on a couple of lion under those conditions. If he did make up his mind to fire he should have shot the lioness, as they are always the most dangerous: it is well known that a lioness will often charge if her spouse is fired at. A lion seldom takes his wife's part if attacked. It was lucky for Adams that he missed the lion. If he had wounded him or killed him the lioness would have made a much more determined attack and would most certainly have got Adams.

Altogether it was a bad business, and it is through lack of knowledge that accidents happen. The only redeeming feature is that Adams kept his head throughout.

I killed rather a good Coke's haartebeeste in the morning and an oribi in the afternoon.

Bad ammunition

The last batch of Mannlicher ammunition I have received from Messrs. Holland and Holland is far from satisfactory. About one in five of the bullets drop short and strike the ground 20 to 30 yards in front of me and would, of course, have no effect on an animal. It has made me rather nervous of dangerous game, for with a small-bore rifle I rely entirely on penetration, and one cannot afford to make mistakes with rhino or lion. I never use anything else now but the Mannlicher and have had such success with it against dangerous game that I have complete confidence in it. I am sure the essence of killing dangerous game is to get as close as possible and make certain of placing one's first shot in such a manner as to completely knock the beast out. With a cool head and accurate shooting one can rely for the rest on penetration.

We return to Fort Hall tomorrow.

20 . II . 1904. *Fort Hall*

Preparations for the Irryeni Expedition

Brancker with his company arrived today from Nairobi. Dickinson of the D.C.L.I. also arrived to take charge and command Brancker's and my company. I am not much impressed by Dickinson. He seems lazy.

The Irryeni have in the meanwhile been surpassing themselves in the insulting messages they have sent in to Hinde. They have been stopping caravans from passing through their country and have murdered several policemen. They must learn their lesson.

Hyaena by moonlight

My dog Baby sleeps IN my bed and my cat the China Ornament sleeps ON my bed. Last night just after I had fallen asleep I felt the China Ornament dancing about on top of me. My bed faces the only window in my grass hut, and the window has no glass. When I woke up I was shocked to see almost the whole window blocked out by a huge hyaena with forepaws on the window sill. His enormous bulk was silhouetted against bright moonlight, and he looked terrific. The China Ornament had all her hackles up and back arched; I had visions of man-eating hyaenas and was scared. I slowly reached for my shotgun, which I always keep by my bedside, and had almost come to pulling the trigger when the beast removed himself. I ran out of the hut at once but saw no sign of him. I shall put out a bait for him tomorrow.

21 . II . 1904. *Fort Hall*

Assembly

I have now concentrated my company at Fort Hall, and Brancker left here for Nyeri, whence he will operate.

23 . II . 1904. *Fort Hall*

Orders from Dickinson

I got my orders today for the preliminary movement against the Irryeni. We operate from both Nyeri and Fort Hall. Humphery accompanies me as Political Officer. The orders are sketchy in the extreme, and

Dickinson obviously does not intend to be worried too much about them. As far as I can see he intends to sit in Mrs. Hinde's lap at Fort Hall most of the time and then adjourn for a shoot on the Tana—a pretty state of affairs for the commander of an expedition! But I foresee that I shall soon be in complete charge, as Dickinson understands not a bit of this form of warfare. That is obvious from his orders and has been confirmed by what he has told me. His last word to me this evening was, "Never mind my orders. Just you carry on and don't worry me too much. I'll back you up in anything you do."

See Appendix I 2a

24 . II . 1904. *Fort Hall*

Plan of operations

Our Masai Levies arrived here today from Nairobi and appear to be a pretty good lot. There are 500 of them. Our plan is roughly as follows. Tomorrow Brancker starts from Nyeri and marching in an easterly direction crosses the Tana. Tate accompanies him as Political Officer, and his column consists of 100 rifles and 200 Masai Levies. I also leave Fort Hall tomorrow with 60 rifles and 250 Masai Levies and march in a northerly direction. Adams has medical charge of my column. Brancker's column has no medical officer, at which I have loudly protested, but there does not appear to be one available. It is a downright scandal to send troops out on an expedition without a medical officer.

25 . II . 1904. *Irryeni Expedition*

We start operations agai[nst] the Irryeni

My column left Fort Hall with Humphery, Adams and Elder. The latter is an Australian who has taken up land near Fort Hall and has ingratiated himself with Hinde. He has been given the contract for the disposal of all captured stock on a commission basis.

We reached the Tana soon after 6 p.m. and halted on the left bank till it was dark enough to move on. My plan is to march all night and surprise the Irryeni at dawn.

We left the Tana at about 9.15 p.m. with a fair moon. We marched in a northerly direction till about 1 a.m., when the moon went down, and we had to continue in the pitch dark till 4 a.m., when we halted.

I assembled the column, as we were then on the edge of the enemy's country, and explained to them the situation and the work for the day. I split the column up into 4 patrols who were to raid rapidly all the nearest villages and capture cattle, while I stayed in a central position with a reserve to attack at once any serious opposition. The supply porters camped on the Ziba River and were busy for the rest of the day making a thorn *zariba*.

By the evening we had captured 325 cattle and 550 sheep and goats. The Irryeni were taken completely by surprise and fled in all directions into the Kenya forest. Fortunately they had had no time to organise resistance, and today I doubt if either side suffered any casualties.

27 . II . 1904. *Gutu. Irryeni Expedition*

Elder leaves for Fort Hall with captured stock

Elder left here at dawn with all our captured stock, which he is first taking to Meranga, where Hinde and Dickinson are. He then takes them on to Fort Hall, where they will be sold by public auction.

We are ambushed and Adams is almost killed

We marched to Gutu's village today and are now in the heart of the Irryeni country. What might have been a nasty incident occurred today. Adams and I joined a small flank party which was working through bush. He and I were about 50 yards ahead of my men when we came on a small stream with a patch of reeds some 2 acres in extent. We were suddenly fired at with arrows, about 7 or 8 falling quite close to us, but we could not see whence they were coming. I put a shot or two into the corner of the reed bed, thinking they were probably coming from there. No sooner did I fire than about 12 armed natives charged us from about 40 yards, and what was still more exciting a full-grown lion bolted from the reeds on the other side about 90 yards from us. Adams, like an ass, shot at the lion and wounded him, the beast slinking back into the reeds. I took the first 4 natives and bowled them over, killing the last as he was just going to spear Adams. My men rushed up, and between us we disposed of the rest, shooting them all. In the fracas one of my men was killed with a spear. I swore at Adams for shooting lion when we were being attacked by niggers, but he was incorrigible and wanted to go in after his lion.

Captured cattle being escorted over the Ziba River by a patrol

The Leguinan or Captain of my Masai Levies

This he and I did, and what followed persuaded me never to go shooting again with Adams.

A unique right and left

We had followed the lion in some 10 yards when another armed native jumped up and was just going to throw his spear at Adams when I shot him, and almost simultaneously there was a roar and the lion appeared within 5 yards of Adams. I fired at once and killed him with a bullet through the neck. All this happened in a few seconds, and Adams had not even fired his rifle off since entering the reeds. He is desperately slow with his rifle, and by now I was not only getting rather uncomfortable in this reed patch but had also completely lost confidence in Adams' ability to look after himself. So I took him by the shoulders and removed him hurriedly from the thick reeds. We then surrounded the patch and set fire to it. It burned well, and we recovered the charred remains of one nigger and one lion. Adams was loud in his protestations at my not allowing him to recover his lion before it was burnt. But I explained to him that he was lucky to have got off with his life. It was a bit too exciting for me.

[Adams was full of apologies and gratitude later on and gave me a silver tobacco holder. But the poor man was a drug addict and killed himself with morphia about 1906.]

Fired at from trees

But the excitement of the day was by no means over. As this flank party were moving under some thick trees, one of my men was wounded by an arrow. I soon joined them, but the foliage was so thick we could see nothing in the trees. I halted the column and got the two machine guns up, and we poured a hail of bullets into the trees. There was at once considerable movement among the branches, and as niggers showed themselves we picked them off with rifle fire. Five fell with sickening thuds. Thinking that there were no more in the tree, I went with Adams under the largest and had a good look up. Adams spotted another, so I told him to fire. He shot, and down came the fellow within a few feet of us; but he was not dead and had his short sword still in his hand. Adams, before I could stop him, blew the fellow's brains out, and so close to me was his head that a hot fid of human brain hit me in the eye as the head was split open. It was very disgusting.

A false alarm at night

As though we had not had enough for the day the following unpleasant incident occurred soon after dark. We were all settled down for the night in camp and behind a good thick thorn *zariba* when one of the sentries challenged and, receiving no answer, fired. It transpired that one of the Masai, against my orders, had left the camp and was strolling about outside. He was hit by my sentry in the forearm, which was badly shattered just above the wrist. Adams said he must amputate at once, so we placed him on a table and commenced work. Humphery looked after the instruments and dressings, while I administered chloroform. I soon became so engrossed in the operation that I forgot about the chloroform and was administering it in huge doses, dabbing it on freely to prevent the patient coming to. Never having done anything like this before, I thought the more he got the quieter he would keep. But I noticed that he stopped breathing suddenly, and Adams came to the rescue and pulled him round by artificial means. It gave me quite a fright. We then proceeded with the operation, and when the man came to he was quite happy. We rolled him up in some hot blankets and put his friends to watch him during the night.

Captured stock

The strength of my column being sadly reduced by the escort I had to give Elder for his stock, and by 4 casualties which I had today, the strength and number of patrols have had to be reduced. Though we inflicted considerable casualties on the enemy we did not succeed in capturing much stock, only 46 cattle and 79 sheep being brought in.

28 . II . 1904. *Gutu's. Irryeni Expedition*

Patrolling in the forest

We did not move camp today but sent out two strong patrols into the forest, both of which succeeded in capturing cattle and sheep. One patrol lost 3 killed and the other suffered no casualties. After the lesson we gave them yesterday they are demoralised, and there is little sign of them near camp. Last night was quiet, which is most unusual on these expeditions, when the natives keep up a chorus of yelling throughout the night.

29 . 11 . 1904. *Kavali. Irryeni Expedition*

Cattle raiding into the bamboo forest of Mount Kenya

Today we marched still further up the Ziba River to a place called Kavali, where we camped. As a result of a council of war with Humphery and the leader of the Masai Levies I shall stop here for a day or so and send raiding parties into the bamboo forest on the southern slopes of Mount Kenya. We are now as close to this mountain as we can conveniently get without entering forest. For the sake of security we cannot afford, with our small force, to camp anywhere except in an open space.

I am compelled to use drastic methods to maintain discipline

Before this expedition started I issued an order to my company and to the Masai Levies that if any man was guilty of killing women or children he would be shot. My men are mere savages in the laws and customs of war, and the Masai are bloodthirsty villains to whom the killing of women and children means nothing.

Today we had occasion to rush a small village in which some of the enemy were concealed and from which they were firing arrows at the column. I quickly formed up 10 of my men and 30 Masai and rushed the place. The enemy ran, and we killed 4 of them. I formed up this party some 150 yards on the other side of the village before moving on, and then heard a woman shriek from the village, which I had presumed empty. I ran back to the village, where I saw two of my men and three Masai in the act of dragging a woman from a hut, and the body of a small boy on the ground, one of the Levies being in the act of withdrawing his spear from the little body. Another levy was leading a small girl by the hand and was about to knock her on the head with his knobkerrie. I yelled to him to stay his hand, but I suppose his blood was up, for he paid no attention to me and killed the child. Meanwhile one of my own men bayoneted the woman within 30 yards of me. Putting up my rifle I shot the man dead and then his companion, who I think contemplated having a pot shot at me. The Levies bolted, but I bagged them all three before they were clear of the village.

I now returned to the column, fell in my men and what Levies there were and marched them all into the village. There I stood them to attention in front of the bodies of the woman and her two children. I explained matters and told the men that if any of them harboured any sympathy for these murderers he could step out in front and I would deal with him. Not a soul moved. I then ordered a party to bury the woman with her children but I particularly left my two men and the three levies unburied and at the mercy of hyaenas and vultures.

Such are the bare facts. Humphery was at first furious but later thought I had acted wisely but perhaps too harshly.

I have no intention of making a laboured defence of my action in this matter. In my own mind I did the only thing possible under the circumstances, and am satisfied that I acted rightly. What I did was contrary to military law and therefore illegal. For this reason and because I am aware of the temperament of our Commissioner, Sir Charles Eliot, who would most certainly take a serious view of my actions, I have not reported it.

The lesson to be taught was discipline, and my object was to stop once and for all such barbarous habits as the killing of women and children in cold blood and to enforce the carrying out of my orders.

Some may think I was too harsh, others may concur with what I did. I acted with a cool head, fully weighing the consequences, and would do it again under similar circumstances. War is necessarily brutal, but it need not be made too brutal. If black troops and undisciplined levies are allowed to get out of hand, as they most surely will if not ruled by iron discipline, disaster is the result.

The two men of my company whom I shot were Manyema and men whom I personally liked. The levies were Masai elmoran of the Kapiti tribe.

2 . III . 1904. *Kavali. Irryeni Expedition*

Orders from Dickinson

Early this morning I received a letter from Dickinson. He is quite wrong about enemy stock having moved towards the Tana River. We have ample proof that it is in front of us. The reason why Dickinson wants to follow the Tana down is that there is some of the best shooting in Africa in that direction. After showing the letter to Humphery, I persuaded him to write me a letter informing me that under orders from the Sub-commissioner, Kenya Province, the column must move further into the Irryeni country; so I have written to Dickinson to say we are going forward, not back. Moreover, it is just as important to punish the tribe as loot their cattle. I want a good fight in the forest, not to take part in a cattle- and goat-lifting competition.

Today we had several small brushes with the enemy, who have recovered from their first astonishment and are now showing more fight. We killed some 24 of them today, while I had four men hit. We also captured 29 prisoners.

3 . III . 1904. *Kavali. Irryeni Expedition*

More orders from Dickinson

My 26th birthday. Early this morning I received a further communication from Dickinson in which he again urges me to come back and join in a wild-goose chase down the Tana River. I now hear he has Mrs. Hinde in his camp and is looking forward to a good shoot on the Tana. I have told him I shall not be back at Fort Hall till 6 March, as I have information to prove that the bulk of the enemy and cattle are in the Kenya forest and not on the Tana. Moreover, the enemy are now in the mood for a good fight, and it would be a pity to miss the opportunity of teaching them a lesson.

We got a fine mob of cattle out of the bamboos today, but not without losing 5 men. I was out with the patrol, and for about 10 minutes we had a good stand-up fight with the enemy in the forest. Neither side could see the other well, and arrows are unpleasant things when flying about in thick undergrowth.

4 . III . 1904. *Irryeni Expedition*

Close of the first phase in the operations

We now have so much stock with us that I shall have to return. Casualties and sickness have also reduced my force to such an extent that it would not be wise to continue operations.

I left camp at daylight, and after marching till noon we got out of the enemy's country and camped.

5 . III . 1904. *Tana Ford*

Return to the Tana River

We struck camp at 5.30 a.m., but I stopped behind with a small party of men to ambush some of the enemy who had been howling round our camp last night and who I knew would come to our old camp as soon as we left. Sure enough they came, and we bagged 3 of them. I camped at the Tana ford, but Humphery and Adams went straight in to Fort Hall.

I am sleeping under a huge tree in which there are lots of green pigeon. Their pleasant cooing is most restful.

6 . III . 1904. *Tana Ford*

Refitting

I sent all our captured stock into Fort Hall and rode in myself, returning to my camp here in the evening. Our total captures were 782 cattle and 2150 sheep and goats. We killed 796 of the enemy. I met Brancker in Fort Hall. He tells me his column captured about 300 cattle and 6000 sheep and goats, while Dickinson's main camp raked in 602 cattle and 4500 sheep and goats without firing a shot. There seems to be some doubt whether the latter captures are enemy property.

As Humphery is still not clear in his mind regarding the division of responsibility between military and political officers when serving together on a column I got Dickinson to draft a letter for our guidance. Humphery is a bit inclined to interfere, and this should put things right.

7 . III . 1904. *Tana Ford*

Fresh operations against the people of Embo

All the chiefs of the Irryeni came into Fort Hall yesterday and submitted to Government. To show what curious creatures they are, they now say that as we are going to punish the people of Embo they will give us every assistance, as they also have a grudge against them. Tomorrow we start for the Embo country, which lies on the south-east slopes of Mount Kenya. To get there we have to pass through the Irryeni, our late enemies. Humphery and Adams joined me again this afternoon. Just before dusk I killed a nice warthog near camp.

McClure and his wounded boy reach my camp

McClure arrived in camp just after dark, having come through from Nyeri with a party. Just before reaching me he was attacked and his boy got a spear through his chest, the point protruding under the shoulder blade. We extracted it, washed the wound and sent him through to Fort Hall. By all the rules of surgery he should die, poor fellow.

I catch and execute a spy

My men caught a man from the Embo in my camp this evening disguised as a porter. He was on the point of clearing out to warn his people when he was arrested. This occurred at 9.15 p.m. At 9.20 we tried him by field general court-martial and found him guilty. He was shot at 9.45 p.m.

Orders from Dickinson

I received orders this evening. There is nothing much in them except that it seems to be all left to me.

8 . III . 1904. *Gutu's Village. Irryeni*

We start on the Embo Expedition

We started on the Embo Expedition at 5.45 this morning, my column comprising 66 King's African Rifles, 15 Police and 400 Masai levies. Though we marched with full military precautions through the Irryeni country we met with nothing but friendliness from our late enemies. In fact all the villages turned out with their women to cheer us on, and I raked in another 150 spearmen to help with stock.

We marched through Keggio to the Ziba River and camped at Gutu's village at 1 p.m. We shall burst in on the Embo tomorrow, but they know we are coming.

9 . III . 1904. *Embo Expedition*

We reach Embo and commence operations

The Irryeni country is separated from Embo by a strip of forest some 5 miles in extent. There are two paths through it, one to the south which would have been our more direct line of advance, and the other to the north. I had taken great pains to induce the enemy to believe we were coming by the south road, and sent a patrol along it yesterday just to divert the attention of the people of Embo. Today I also sent a strong force on the southern road, and so completely did they deceive the enemy that they nearly got overwhelmed in the forest and had to withdraw hurriedly, losing two men. That was just what I wished, and I rushed the main body along the northern path and we met not a soul but a few of the enemy scouts. We are now camped on the eastern fringe of the Embo country, but in open cultivated country.

By 4 p.m. the enemy commenced to gather in our vicinity and we had several little scraps, in all of which the enemy suffered badly. Like the Irryeni, they do a lot of ambushes from trees, which is disconcerting, but my men are beginning to understand it and are pulling them down like young rooks. One of my men got 7 from one tree.

We found a huge cave near camp whence we could hear the lowing of cattle and the bleating of goats. The cave adjoined the River Numindi. I did not care about assaulting it, for two reasons. I should have suffered heavy casualties if there were warriors in it, and also if, as I suspected, there were only women and children with the stock we should have undoubtedly killed some of them in the dark. So we dammed the river and turned it into the cave. That brought them all out, and we captured 15 women and children, 47 cattle and 9 goats. I released the women and children, but they refused to go, preferring to stop in our camp, so I allowed them to do so. They help in cooking my men's food.

10 . III . 1904. *River Ruppingazi. Embo*

Move to the Ruppingazi River

I moved camp today further into the heart of the Embo country and built a strong *zariba* on the left bank of the River Ruppingazi. From our camp we get a fine view of Mount Kenya. My men said they always thought that snow came out of the ground and must be very hot—in fact "white hot."

I remained in camp this afternoon, sending out strong patrols in every direction. The people of Embo are showing a considerable amount of fight and in two cases have

My bugler boy, Ali Wadi Songoro, a boy who never grew up: he was with me for five years and was the cause of the suicide of an administrative officer who forced him to commit an act of indecency

A Nandi family

charged right up to our bayonets. They must have lost heavily. We lost 3 soldiers and 11 levies, all killed except 4 levies. We captured only 7 head of cattle and 22 goats the whole day.

A note on the Waembo

The Waembo are a branch of the Wakikuyu, whom they closely resemble, but they speak a different language and have different customs. Their huts are mostly made of banana leaves and not of grass. They have two types of knobkerrie, one being long (about 2 feet 6 inches) with a ribbed head, and the other a much deadlier weapon, having a round stone lashed to the end, the whole being bound with leather. Their dancing shields are also unique, being very thin and narrow. Their spears are mostly of the bay-leaf type, but smaller and more elegant than those of the Wakikuyu.

Wicker jars for storing food

The Waembo have curious wicker jars for storing food which remind me of the famous oil jars of Crete which gave rise to the story of the hiding of the thieves of Ali Baba. They are astonishingly heavy, and one which we rolled down a slope went crashing into a banana grove and demolished several trees before it was checked.

11 . III . 1904. *Embo Expedition*

Patrolling in the bamboo forest

I accompanied a patrol after cattle into the bamboo forests of Mount Kenya. The people of Embo did not put up much of a fight today, and on two occasions they abandoned their stock without showing a sign of resistance.

A pig new to science

Just as we were emerging from the forest the leading man of my patrol fired a shot at something which I could not see, and on coming up I found he had killed a huge pig with long black hair, unlike anything I ever heard of. I put a piece of the skin into my haversack but left the carcass. I shall send to bring it in tomorrow. As we had several of the enemy in the vicinity I could not remain and examine her, for she was a sow, but I now wish I had brought home the skull, which was unlike that of any pig I know.

A benighted patrol

One of my patrols never returned last night, and as it did not turn up this morning I was beginning to feel anxious, but at 10 a.m. they rolled in, dead beat and with no cattle. Yesterday they had followed stock far up on to Mount Kenya but never came up with it. They then lost their way, got benighted, and slept out in the bamboos. I was mighty glad to see them back.

We move south

At 11 a.m. we struck camp and marched in a southerly direction. I wished to reach a hill called Molindoko, but as our guides do not know this country I was thrown back on my own resources. After leaving the Embo cultivation we toiled along a narrow forest path, the advance guard clearing the way with knives and bayonets. Most of the brush to be cut was one form or another of rubber vine, and the whole column was covered with the sticky juice which poured out of the cut stems. My hair and shirt were in an appalling state when I got out of the forest, everything having a thick coating of raw rubber. It seems to me that these forests must be valuable if they are so rich in rubber.

Wild rubber

We finally reached the Ruppingazi River where it tumbles over rocks in the densest part of the forest. Here we lunched and halted for about an hour and a half to enable us to get the captured stock across in safety. It is on such occasions when an attack is most likely, and we took full precautions against such an eventuality.

We surprise the enemy and take their stock

After cutting our way through the forest for another mile or so we emerged on to some grassy plains intersected by numerous ravines. My advance guard halted at the edge of the forest and reported the country alive with stock. Now no people were supposed to live here, so I presumed all these herds were those of the Waembo which had been taken here for safety, thinking we should never find a way through this dense forest. I therefore closed up on the head of the column, quickly assembled some patrols, and burst like an avalanche on the herds of grazing cattle and goats. These herds were accompanied by a few small parties of Waembo warriors, who fought us in the open. They tried to concentrate for a fight against one of my patrols, but we were too quick for them, and I threw my small reserve, which I personally commanded, into the fight, and we picked up 47 of the enemy in no time. We lost 7 levies killed and 8 wounded, while one of my men got killed and I had 3 slightly wounded by arrows, including my colour sergeant. We also captured 410 head of cattle and over 1000 sheep and goats. It was a grand day.

I now found that we were some 4 miles west of Molindoko Hill and that the Ruppingazi River flows still further east. Having reformed the column and got out our advance, flank and rear guards, I decided to move west, as I thought we must be somewhere near the River Namindi. We struck it after going some 3 miles, and camped on its left bank at 5.30 p.m.

13 . III . 1904. *Embo Expedition*

We accidentally shoot two porters

At 2 a.m. last night two porters left camp and stupidly squatted down on their haunches. They were challenged by a sentry but failed to reply, and a shot was fired at them. The whole camp at once stood to arms, and we then found that one of these unfortunates had been hit, but it was a superficial wound through both cheeks of his buttocks. There were thus 4 holes, 2 in each cheek—a most remarkable wound.

Today we moved camp in a southerly direction, following down the River Namindi. We have so much captured stock with us that I am not too anxious to have another fight for the present.

15 . III . 1904. *Embo Expedition*

A rest

The Waembo fight the Irryeni

As we are now out of the enemy's country I gave all ranks a rest yesterday morning and in the afternoon sent a strong patrol to Gutu's village on the Ziba River, as I had received information that a lot of Waembo had appeared among the Irryeni and fighting was in progress. If the Waembo succeeded in breaking through Irryeni country they might try to intercept me on my return journey, and I wished to take the initiative against them before they make up their minds. The patrol returned today, reporting that the Irryeni had beaten back the people of Embo, who had retired disconsolate to their own country, so all is well.

We cross the Namindi River

We crossed the Namindi today by a natural rock bridge. The plains between the Namindi and the Ziba are covered with haartebeeste, warthog and guinea-fowl. We killed a haartebeeste and a warthog for food.

16 . III . 1904. *Tana Ford*

To Tana Ford

We marched to the Tana ford today and camped. Humphery went straight in to Fort Hall. In the evening I killed a brace of sandgrouse and an Egyptian goose.

17 . III . 1904. *Fort Hall*

End of the Embo expedition

Marched into Fort Hall, and the Embo expedition comes to an end. To my mind the people of Embo have not been sufficiently hammered, and I should like to go back at once and have another go at them. During the first phase of the expedition against the Irryeni we killed about 796 niggers, and during the second phase against the Embo we killed about 250.

Casualties

Captured stock

We took from the Irryeni 782 cattle and 2150 sheep and goats, and from the Waembo 498 cattle and 1500 sheep and goats.

18 . III . 1904. *Fort Hall*

The Kikuyu

I am sorry to leave the Kikuyu, for I like them. They are the most intelligent of the African tribes I have met; therefore they will be the most progressive under European guidance and will be more susceptible to subversive activities. They will be one of the first tribes to demand freedom from European influence and in the end cause a lot of trouble. And if white settlement really takes hold in this country it is bound to do so at the expense of the Kikuyu, who own the best land, and I can foresee much trouble.

20 . III . 1904. *Punde Milia*

To Nairobi

My tour of duty at Fort Hall being regretfully finished, I started off with my company for Nairobi, camping this evening on the Thara River at Punde Milia.

I am indeed sorry to leave the Kikuyu, for I have many friends among them. Their great assets are cheerfulness even in adversity, and they bear no grudge after punishment; I was always pleased when local people called on me with small presents—sweet potatoes, honey, the skin of some animal—which I always paid back in money compensation, which they appreciated. I found them honest and truthful, but behaving quite differently to some of the European administrators, who treated them as "bloody niggers." The same cheerful young men or girls who visited me would become unscrupulous, dishonest and treacherous to the man who behaved badly to them. Even among themselves their behaviour is good, young people respecting the old, and children seldom being scolded. Frequently when out in their country I would see young people running across their fields to greet me and bring me some small present. Yes, I definitely like and admire the Kikuyu: they are intelligent, and I can see that with education they will turn out to be a great asset to East Africa provided we do not let them brood over grievances.

24 . III . 1904. *Nairobi*

To Nairobi

On the 21st I marched to the Thika River. Soon after leaving Punde Milia a large herd of giraffe came into view and kept alongside the caravan for some time, eventually moving towards the Ithanga hills.

On the 22nd I reached the Ruiru River and on the 23rd the Nairobi River, where I met two sportsmen from home called Lumsden and Murray. On the plains near the Nairobi River I saw a large herd of eland which were very wild.

Today I marched into Nairobi, where I again met Col. Harrison, Pope Hennessey our second-in-command, and Carey of the Grenadier Guards.

Facts concerning a giant forest pig

I may as well note down what I know of the huge forest pig which I found on 11 March in the Kenya forests. Up till now I have seen but one, a sow, and she after she had been killed. All I have of this beast is a small piece of skin. I asked all my Masai levies whether they knew the animal and they all said they did but that it lived in thick forest and was called *elguia* by them. They make their shields of its tough skin, and I actually purchased a shield which purports to be made from the forest pig. Its owner told me he bought the skin from a Dorobo hunter who had killed it on the Mau escarpment, which shows the animal has a wide range.

Towards the end of the expedition my men found several large pieces of skin in villages. One piece in particular is enormous and could never have been taken off an animal much smaller than a donkey. The hair is long and black, measuring some 10 inches on the crest.

On returning to Fort Hall I enquired from the Wakikuyu concerning the pig and found they all knew it well, calling it *numirra*. I have offered a cow to the first man who can get me a complete skin with the skull.

I have sent all the skin I have, together with the above information, to Ray Lankester at the British Museum. I think there can be no doubt that the animal is new to science. It is exasperating not to have got a skull, but I live in hopes and shall hunt for him in forest when I get the chance.

I am convinced that the pig I saw in the Aberdares near Karurie's was this forest pig and that the red antelope I saw was a bongo.

7 . IV . 1904. *Nairobi*

Ostrich and rhino

On the 6th I killed my eighth lion on the Athi River. Today I spied a rhino feeding among thorn scrub. I stalked to within about 60 yards, when a hen ostrich with some chicks came over a rise not 100 yards from me. I watched them for about half an hour, when the rhino lay down and went to sleep. Taking a steady shot for the shoulder I fired at him. He at once rose, snorted, and making a wild rush for mother ostrich did his best to toss her, thinking her responsible. The hen ostrich, in defence of her chicks, did a lot of sparring with the rhino, which astonished me. I never knew an ostrich could be so active. She waltzed round the huge pachyderm, constantly striking at him with her feet. His efforts to chase her and to turn his clumsy carcass quickly to prevent his getting a kick on the rump made me scream with laughter. But the rhino was sick unto death and collapsed after about two minutes. I am sure the hen ostrich took all credit for his collapse, but when I suddenly rose to my feet within 40 yards of her she must have changed her mind, for she decamped quickly with her family. Why she did not clear out when I shot I cannot understand. I suspect the rhino's sudden onslaught put everything out of her head except the protection of her chicks.

10 . IV . 1904. *Nairobi*

Pig-sticking

Our fellows have been doing a good bit of pig-sticking on the plains round Nairobi. I was out today on Natalie and enjoyed a good run. The warthog took me through fairly rough ground at first, when I was unable to gain on him, but eventually I got him into the open, and then soon caught him up. But he turned all over the place, and Natalie was not over-anxious to face him. I never got my lance really home. He finally went to ground, which was a ridiculous performance. I noticed that he was most anxious to head for a certain spot, which was where his earth lay. On arrival at the entrance he stopped dead, turned round and went in backwards. The hole only just fitted him, and at one time I thought he was going to stick. Natalie unfortunately would not go near him.

14 . IV . 1904. *Donyo Sabuk, near Nairobi*

After buffalo on Donyo Sabuk

Yesterday I came out to Donyo Sabuk, a hill near Nairobi, to try for buffalo. My camp was at the base of the hill, and this morning I arrived at the top just before daylight. As dawn approached I spied a solitary bull buffalo, a troop of apes, two bushbuck and a rhino, all within a mile of me. I at once slipped off after the buffalo. I had no difficulty in getting to within some 500 yards of him, but he was feeding into the forest and would have got my wind if I had approached closer. This involved a wide detour. When I got to within 200 yards of him I found to my dismay that he was accompanied by 4 cows and a calf. Getting to some 120 yards of him, I fired at his shoulder. I heard the bullet strike, but he and his family lumbered off into the forest, much to my disgust. I dived in after them, following a good blood spoor, and seeing what I took to be my bull making off about 400 yards from me I fired and rolled him over. On examining him I found to my surprise that he was not the animal at which I had first fired, so I returned to the first blood spoor and undertook a systematic tracking. I soon realised from the froth on the blood which stained the grass and leaves that my beast must be badly wounded in the lungs. He was obviously bleeding copiously from the wounds and the nostrils. After an arduous two hours I came up again with the first bull, which had wandered round the hill and was now standing not 300 yards from my second dead bull. He looked terribly sick and had his head hung low. A shot in the neck at not over 30 yards killed him. At the moment of my firing the shot he spotted me, but my bullet must have killed him at that very moment. Neither of these bulls had a really good head, and as I only had a special licence to kill one I have to pay a fine of Rs.75 for the second, which I much grudge.

18 . IV . 1904. *Nairobi*

Blaney Percival

I have made great friends with Blaney Percival, the game ranger. He is not only very knowledgeable about big game but is madly keen on birds and has a large collection. I like him. In view of the likelihood of a vast invasion by European settlers it seems that the larger game must disappear. One cannot have farms and game, and I have suggested to Blaney that he puts up a scheme for a very large area in country unsuitable for white settlement where game can remain for ever. This area would need to be vested in trustees based on London and be completely divorced from local government, the trustees being responsible only to the British Parliament.

I suggest a game reserve

There must be no risk of interference from an East African administration which cares nothing for game. I think the area might be some three or four thousand square miles and possibly in Masai country. The Masai are good game preservers but are very wasteful of grazing land. Moreover, both game and Masai cattle can co-exist. Blaney has promised to formulate a scheme.

19 . IV . 1904. *Nairobi*

Charles Eliot

Charles Eliot asked me to dine with him this evening. He is a great admirer of Aunt Bo [Beatrice Webb]; I said I thought she was doing a great deal of harm, aiming at a dictatorship of the lower classes headed by trade unions, and that I thought Marxian socialism a foul infectious disease. Eliot snapped at me and quickly changed the subject to East Africa. He tells me he is having a terrific row with the Foreign Office over white settlement and their ridiculous attitude over grants of land in the Kikuyu country, which they regard as an infringement of native rights. Eliot hopes to attract thousands of Europeans to East Africa and does not appear to accept the fact that natives have any "rights." I suggested that East Africa belonged to Africans and that we had no right to occupy any land which is tribal land. We should develop East Africa for the African and not for strangers.

I like Eliot, but after tonight I doubt if he likes me. But I was pleased when on parting he said I must come and see him again.

Oh yes: I spoke to him about the game and its preservation for posterity; he was not interested and said that farming and big game did not mix and that sentiment must not stand in the way of progress! He asked me to write him a note on the subject, which I shall do, for I like the African and I like the game and wish to preserve both.

20 . IV . 1904. *Nairobi*

To Muhoroni

We have a company at Muhoroni to guard the railway, as the Nandi have been giving trouble lately. It is in the charge of Leveson Gower, who has now been detailed for escort duty to the Anglo-German Boundary

Commission, so I am going up to relieve him. I shall probably be there some 3 months, and then I hope to get 6 months' leave home to England. I leave tonight.

21 . IV . 1904. *Muhoroni*

Arrive Muhoroni

Arrived Muhoroni today. The place lies in the Nyando valley, is very hot and unhealthy, and Leveson Gower tells me it has rained here every day for the last 6 weeks. It certainly poured this afternoon.

Gailey of the Railway

Met two railway engineers, Gailey and Roberts. The former has been out here since the railway started and has built most of the bridges between Nairobi and Muhoroni. He tells me he is fed up and is going into partnership with Roberts. They will import all sorts of hardware, electrical goods and machinery. He is hoping to get a special concession from the railway authorities for reduction in freight from Mombasa. I like Gailey. We dined together this evening in his private railway carriage.

Frederick Jackson and Geoffrey Archer

I travelled up as far as Naivasha with Frederick Jackson, a man who has immense personal charm. At Naivasha I met his nephew Geoffrey Archer [Sir Geoffrey Archer, later Governor of Somaliland, Uganda and the Sudan], an enormous lad and mad keen on birds. He had just discovered the nest and eggs of the African wryneck and was most excited. He hopes to get a post in the Administration.

23 . IV . 1904. *Muhoroni*

The Commissioner's attitude towards my report on the Irryeni and Embo Expeditions

When I returned to Nairobi from Fort Hall I began to compile a report on the recent operations in the Irryeni and Embo country. I naturally stated facts as they occurred and did not attempt to hide anything. The report was handed in to Harrison on the 17th instant.

Today I had a letter from Pope Hennessey telling me that the Commissioner took exception to many of the statements in the report, especially the list of enemy casualties. In order to shield Hinde, and I suppose the Commissioner, these are being reduced. I really cannot see how a tribe is going to be punished without fighting them.

30 . IV . 1904. *Muhoroni*

Trouble among the Nandi at Kaimosi

This afternoon I received a wire from Mr. Hobley at Kisumu telling me that the Nandi were giving trouble at an American mission station called Kaimosi, some distance north of Kisumu, that one of their American staff was missing and that he wanted me to move up there at once with my detachment.

There is no time to refer the matter to Nairobi, so I went to the station, ordered a special train to be ready at dawn tomorrow to take us to Kisumu, and spent the rest of the evening packing up and issuing ammunition.

It is good to be on the move again.

1 . V . 1904. *Kisumu*

Arrive Kisumu

As I have no porters here, my men were on fatigue throughout most of the night getting the baggage to the station. Our train pulled in at 7 a.m., and we got on board at once and steamed off for Kisumu. Never have I been so glad to leave a place. The quarters are most uncomfortable, the climate is depressing and unhealthy, and it is impossible to leave camp owing to the high matted grass and the treacherous natives, who are said to be on the look-out for a victim whenever the chance comes their way. I left 4 of my men behind as a guard to the heavy baggage, which I am sending back to Nairobi.

We arrived at Kisumu at 11 a.m., where I was met by J. W. T. McClellan, the acting Sub-commissioner, who is kindly putting me up for the night. I also met Major Bright of the Rifle Brigade, who is one of the commissioners on the Anglo-German Boundary Commission, which starts from here in a week's time.

My first view of the Victoria Nyanza

Kisumu is the terminus of the Uganda Railway and lies at the head of a gulf known as the Kavirondo Gulf of the Victoria Nyanza. I was thrilled at seeing this wonderful lake for the first time. It came over very stormy in the afternoon and poured with rain.

In the evening I strolled down to the small port and saw the S.S. *Winifred*, which had just come in from Entebbe on the Uganda side. I also again met Dr. Mann, whom I had not seen since he accompanied me on the expedition against the people of Tetu last year. Murray and Lumsden were also on the *Winifred*, having returned from a trip on the lake. I had met them before at Nairobi.

I have now completed my arrangements to reach Kaimosi tomorrow. No further developments have come to hand, but the American has not yet turned up and it is feared that the Nandi have killed him. If so, there is a good chance of my having a lively time up there.

2 . V . 1904. *Kaimosi*

To Kaimosi

At dawn I started off for Kaimosi with my detachment. Late yesterday evening we heard that the American missionary, Dr. Wenthe, had been found dead, having been speared and badly cut about by the Nandi. A native policeman who had accompanied him had also been murdered.

The road to Kaimosi ascends the Nandi escarpment soon after leaving Kisumu, and then passes over an undulating plateau which is densely cultivated. The country gradually rises towards Kaimosi. When I had been on the road for some three hours a messenger from McClellan at Kisumu overtook me with a message stating that he (McClellan) was following me, as he had received orders "to co-operate with the military column and meet Mr. Mayes." Mayes is the administrative officer at Nandi Boma. Such a message is ambiguous and really tells me nothing. It emanated from Hobley, who is always ambiguous in his letters and boasts of it. He prides himself in never "letting himself in." The result is that his subordinates find it most difficult to work on his orders, and they have to assume the responsibility which he shirks.

I dine with Mr. Hole

I reached Kaimosi about 4.30 p.m., having done the 23 miles in 8½ hours. I dined with Mr. Hole, one of the missionaries, who gave me an excellent dinner, but only tea to drink. After my march today I could have managed something different, as I had a bad thirst.

All is apparently quiet now at Kaimosi.

The country through which we passed today is cultivated by the hill section of the Kavirondo, who struck me as being a rotten race of savages. Both sexes go stark naked. They are poor porters and seem to be a poor type of Bantu nigger. The country I saw today is well watered. Its most characteristic feature is the profusion of huge boulders which lie about in every direction. The Kavirondo seem fond of sitting on these in small groups, and in some districts nearly every boulder had a man perched on its top watching my caravan. True to custom, it rained heavily from about 3 p.m. until midnight.

3 . V . 1904. *Kaimosi*

My lack of observation

I breakfasted with Hole, and to my amazement he told me his wife gave birth to a child early this morning. I had never noticed Mrs. Hole's condition last night!

Detail of the murder of Dr. Wenthe

Today I got all the details of the murder of Dr. Wenthe. There are altogether in Kaimosi three American missionaries, Messrs. Hole, Blackburne and Chilson, the two former being married and having their wives with them. About a fortnight ago Dr. Wenthe arrived to join them. He introduced himself as an American Quaker and sponged on the mission for everything. The mission was getting rather tired of him, and hoped he was not going to stop much longer, when he was killed.

About a week ago, Mayes from Nandi Boma visited the Kabwuren section of the Nandi, who live near Kaimosi, with the idea of forcing them to give up two rifles which they were said to possess. Mayes apparently indulged in some irresponsible shooting against this section of the Nandi and remained in their country for 3 days, during which desultory fighting, showing no result on either side, took place. Mayes raided a certain amount of stock, which appears to have been entirely illegal. They heard this fighting going on from the mission, and Wenthe announced his intention of going out and watching it. He was warned that it would be a dangerous thing to do. However, this did not deter him, so on the third day of the fighting he strolled out with one policeman into the forest, and the Nandi, thinking they were at war with all Europeans, soon discovered him and killed both him and his policeman. He had been speared through and through, and all his clothes had been stripped off him. The policeman's rifle had also been taken.

It was also unfortunate for Wenthe that on the morning he was killed one of the missionaries had heard cattle in the forest near the mission and took upon himself the responsibility of going out with two policemen to round them up, thinking he would be helping the Government. It is small wonder, then, that the Nandi should have retaliated on Wenthe.

The first error was that Mayes should have got into collision with the Nandi so near a mission. Having done so, he should have afforded the mission adequate protection and advice. He did neither, but left the country with a perfect hornets' nest of natives round the mission. It is a wonder that the Nandi did not completely wipe out all the Americans at the mission. The second error was the mission taking a part in the raiding of cattle, and the third error was Wenthe going out to view the fighting. As a matter of fact the Nandi had complete confidence in the neutrality of the mission and drove their cattle to its neighbourhood for protection, only to find that the mission was prepared to take an active part in the fighting.

Primarily I blame Mayes, and then I blame the indiscretion of the mission and thirdly the stupidity of Wenthe. I do not blame the Nandi, who acted under the severest provocation. I have drafted a letter in this sense to the authorities, recommending that Wenthe's belongings and the policeman's rifle must be returned, and that no proceedings be taken against the Nandi. Meanwhile the Nandi suspect we shall revenge ourselves on them, and my presence up here confirms their views. They are most repentant, and I have already promised them that if they keep quiet they will not be severely punished.

McClellan arrived at noon. He has agreed with my view of the case.

3 . V . 1904. *Kaimosi*

We visit the spot where Wenthe was killed

McClellan and I with a small escort visited the spot in the forest where Wenthe's body was found, which was in a small clearing. The poor fellow must have been mad to wander about under those conditions with only one policeman as escort.

We found the natives very shy, but after a lot of trouble we got an old man to come and talk to us. He said his people were terrified of what was going to happen and that they were sincerely sorry for what had been done. McClellan told him that before any decision could be reached, Wenthe's clothing and the policeman's rifle must be surrendered.

4 . V . 1904. *Kaimosi*

We embark in a futile attempt to get into touch with the Nandi

McClellan and I spent all day trying to get natives to come into Kaimosi and talk the matter over, but without success. We saw a few men, but they would not come near us. They have moved all their women and cattle out of the district, which means they expect trouble.

5 . V . 1904. *Kaimosi*

Mayes arrives

Mayes arrived here today from Nandi Boma. I have seldom taken such a dislike to a man at first sight. He started life as a common seaman from Glasgow, was discharged or deserted his ship in Madagascar, and took to gold digging in that island and failed. He then drifted to the Seychelles, where he married a Creole, whom he at once deserted. He then, some 10 years ago, came to Mombasa and was employed in the Uganda Mutiny as a transport man; he did well, and received as reward a post in the Civil Administration.

Hobley the ambiguous

McClellan received a message from Hobley today which curtly said, "Murderers must be punished." He obviously has not appreciated the facts of the case, and how are we to catch the murderers when we cannot even get into touch with the tribe? If he means that I am to start punitive operations against these people he is mistaken, for I shall do no such thing without very definite orders from Nairobi. So we are in rather a fix to know what to do and have restated the facts and asked for further instructions. Meanwhile we are trying by every peaceful means to get into touch with the local people.

I told Mayes this evening that I regarded him as mainly responsible for this unfortunate business.

11 . V . 1904. *Kaimosi*

The authorities vacillate

We have all been wasting our time up here for the last 10 days, as the Commissioner is unable to make up his mind as to what must be done. Perhaps he has referred the matter to the Foreign Office. Today comes news that Hobley has been told to go to Nandi Boma, where he and Mayes are "to enquire into the murder of the American." So Mayes left here this morning. How they intend to enquire into the matter some 50 miles from the spot is not explained.

14 . V . 1904. *Kaimosi*

Death of Dr. Mann at Kisumu

News came from Kisumu today that Dr. Mann had died of blackwater fever. The medical officer's house at Kisumu was a broken-down shanty and not fit for a pig. It was most unfair to expect men to live under such conditions in one of the worst climates of Africa. This economic policy of the Foreign Office is responsible for the lives of many good fellows out here. They refuse to give us decent accommodation.

15 . V . 1904. *Kaimosi*

McClellan ill

McClellan has been ill with a bad throat and returned to Kisumu today. I am surprised that more of us are not ill, for it has poured with rain ever since we have been here and mosquitoes are bad. Our tents, bedding, etc., are sodden with wet, and our food is bad and, of course, miserably cooked.

Negotiations opened with the Nandi

Hobley and Mayes have moved into the Kabwuren country, where I hear thay have at last got into touch with the Kabwuren section who killed Wenthe, and that things are going well.

20 . V . 1904. *Hamisi's, near Kaimosi*

I join Hobley and Mayes at Hamisi's

Hobley and Mayes arrived at Kaimosi today on their way through to Hamisi's, which is some 7 miles from Kaimosi on the Kisumu road. I struck camp and joined them at Hamisi's, but got drenched through, together with all my bedding. I left a small guard at Kaimosi. Hobley tells me he has settled matters with the Kabwuren. They are to be fined 48 head of cattle (which, by the way, Mayes had taken from them before they killed Wenthe), and they are to be put on their best behaviour for 3 months, during which time my detachment is to live in their country. It is a curious compromise but I think just.

I heard this evening that Col. Harrison is coming to Kisumu, and as I must see him on several matters I shall accompany Hobley tomorrow to meet him.

Hobley

I like Hobley, always known as Hobley Bobbley. By profession he is a trained surveyor and geologist, and though rather a rough diamond and with all the faults of rough diamonds, he is both intelligent and well mannered. At his work he cannot come to quick decisions and is unable to assume responsibility; he has no sense of humour and will never get very high up the official ladder.

21 . V . 1904. *Kisumu. Victoria Nyanga*

To Kisumu

Arrived at Kisumu this morning. Lunched with my old friend Collyer. As Harrison is now at Nakuru I have decided to go there and meet him, his visit to Kisumu having been abandoned.

23 . V . 1904. *Nakuru*

To Nakuru

Delme-Radcliffe, Grogan and McClure

I left Kisumu at 8 a.m. by train and arrived at Nakuru at 9 p.m. I travelled down with Major Delme-Radcliffe, who is returning home from Uganda, and at Londiani I met E. S. Grogan (of Cape to Cairo fame). At Fort Ternan I met McClure, who crossed me on his way up to Kisumu. I met Harrison immediately on my arrival at Nakuru and settled many matters of detail. I am putting up with "High" Church of the Uganda Railway, who has a bungalow near the station.

Grogan

On meeting Grogan I was immediately attracted to him; he has great charm, a brain as clear as crystal and a strong character. He not only means what he says but says what he thinks. He knows Uncle Ernie well. On parting he said he had heard the most flattering things about me and he hoped we would meet again. He is a great man and will be even greater some day.

[Uncle Ernie refers to my uncle, Sir Ernest Meinertzhagen. "High" Church refers to the taller of the two Churches; the smaller Church was known as "Low" Church; both were engineers on the Uganda Railway. Col. E. S. Grogan worked with me in the Intelligence Department of the East African Expeditionary Force during the First World War: his ability and courage, both moral and physical, placed him very high in my estimation. Since then he has risen to great distinction in Kenya, where his clear brain has made him pre-eminent in the Colony. He is a most lovable man.]

25 . V . 1904. *Nakuru*

I go shooting at Nakuru

As there is no train back to Kisumu till this evening I have had to remain here two whole days. Mr. Costello of the Railway kindly lent me 4 porters to carry game, and off I went.

Yesterday afternoon I found a herd of Jackson's haartebeeste between the station and the lake. I made a successful stalk to within 80 yards of the herd, and killing what I took to be the largest bull was disgusted to find it was a cow. In the evening I went down to the lake to watch the flamingo, and also saw a flock of 7 great bustard (*Otis kori*). I saw plenty of duck on the lake, but they were all far out and mostly unrecognisable. Waders were practically non-existent, all the northern birds having passed to their breeding grounds in northern Europe and Asia. There were a few stilts, two common sandpipers and one marsh sandpiper.

Today I was out on the grassy plains north of the line but saw only a few herds of Thomson's and Grant's gazelle. I was disgusted at seeing so little, which is probably due to the dry state of the country, when a male and female bohor reedbuck jumped up almost at my feet. The male made off to the right and the female to the left. I fired at the male and heard the thud of my bullet. My second shot missed him. I marked him for about a mile, when he looked very sick and could scarcely move. However, he disappeared over a small kopje and I followed as quickly as I could. On cautiously looking over the kopje I spied him standing in a slight hollow some 60 yards from me. I at once fired and dropped him dead. This is the first bohor reedbuck I have shot. After measuring and weighing him, I returned home well pleased with my day.

I leave for Kisumu tonight.

26 . V . 1904. *Kisumu*

To Kisumu

My train left Nakuru at 1.30 a.m. last night and we reached Kisumu about 3 this afternoon. On my way through Muhoroni I picked up the men I had left there last month.

Vincent, McClure and Collyer

Tonight I dined with Vincent, the Town Magistrate of Kisumu, where I again met McClure and Collyer. The former tells me he has come up to build a bridge over the Nzoia River near Mumias.

30 . V . 1904. *Kabwuren. Nandi*

To Kaimosi and Kabwuren

I left Kisumu on the 28th and camped at Hamisi's that evening, having again got drenched to the skin. On the 29th I camped at Kaimosi. Hearing that Mayes was in Kabwuren I joined him with my detachment, and was not at all pleased to find that Mr. and Mrs. Cary were with him. Cary commands our detachment at Nandi Boma. Rained all day, and we were all drenched to the skin by the evening. [Cary was Master of Falkland, Grenadier Guards.]

Mayes and the Carys

1 . VI . 1904. *Kabwuren. Nandi*

The new military camp in Kabwuren

Yesterday I spent selecting a site for the new military camp and in clearing a site. Mayes and the Carys left for Nandi Boma early this morning and I was glad to see the last of them. I dislike and mistrust Mayes and have no use for an English lady under these conditions.

I more or less completed my camp today. The spot is now cleared of bush for some 200 yards round the perimeter and the camp itself is strengthened by some huge granite boulders. The Nandi seem quite friendly now, and several came in to see me bearing presents of fruit, beans, sweet potatoes and a sheep. *Timeo Danaos et dona ferentes.*

I should say our altitude here is some 5500 feet. It is quite cold at night and rains every afternoon, but is quite hot by day. I suspect I shall get bored here, as there is nothing to do except watch the grey parrots.

6 . VI . 1904. *Kabwuren. Nandi*

McClure joins me

I am happy to say that McClure, who finds that the material for his bridge is not yet ready, has come up here to join me. He is a cheery lad, and I shall not feel a bit bored with him in camp.

7 . VI . 1904. *Kabwuren. Nandi*

I start a stock farm

For lack of something better to do I have started a cattle and sheep farm. A few days ago I got McClellan to buy a bull, two bullocks and three cows for me in Kisumu for which I paid Rs.375, or £25. Today I augmented this by purchasing 5 sheep from a local savage for Rs.25, or £1 13s. 4d. Today a native brought me 3 large sheep which he wished to exchange for one of my bullocks. I told him I must have 4 sheep, and he agreed to this. On producing the sheep and the bargain having been concluded, he told me that he would have given me 8 sheep for the bullock if I had insisted. So I was badly done.

But I now have 5 cattle and 9 sheep.

16 . VI . 1904. *Kaimosi. Nandi*

I am granted leave to England

I heard today from Nairobi that my leave home has been granted and that I can catch the French mail steamer leaving Zanzibar about 27 July, so that's good. We have been having nothing here but rain, which is most depressing.

Mount Elgon

Every morning is beautifully clear, and then we get good views of Mount Elgon to the north and some 75 miles distant. McClure unfortunately has to go back to Mumias tomorrow to build his bridge. I am very sorry he cannot stay longer.

McClure goes

22 . VI . 1904. *Kabwuren. Nandi*

Ever since I have been up here I have been enquiring from the natives about the forest pig I found on Mount Kenya early this year. Through the kindness of Blackburne of the Kaimosi Mission I got a skull from a native, and it proves to be very distinct from the skull of a warthog.

The forest hog

But today I had even better luck. I had seen the tracks of pig in the forest and have often been out after them. It was only today when I was successful. I came on her in some thick stuff and killed her at about 40 yards. She is a young sow, and I was able to preserve the complete skull and skin, which I shall send to the British Museum. This is probably the first of her kind to be killed by a European.

I kill a forest hog

25 . VI . 1904. *Kabwuren. Nandi*

Received an English mail today. Mother tells me that the Commissioner has resigned and that my first battalion has been ordered on the Tibet expedition. I also heard from Mackay, our adjutant, that the battalion was for Tibet. Just my luck! I at once wired down to Col. Harrison, asking him if I might apply to rejoin it in India. If he replies in the affirmative I may yet get to India in time. It will not be my fault if I do not.

Sir Charles Eliot resigns and my regiment goes to Tibet

30 . VI . 1904. *Kabwuren. Nandi*

I received a wire from Col. Harrison today saying he had no objection to my wiring to my battalion in India to try to join them there for the Tibet expedition. I therefore cabled to Col. Cooper as follows: "If I come to India on leave may I join battalion for Tibet. Authorities here sanction. Reply Nairobi." [I received no reply.]

I wire to my battalion in India, asking if I can join them

9 . VII . 1904. *Kabwuren. Nandi*

Wilson of the Connaught Rangers arrived here today to take over my company and allow me to get away on leave. I had not seen him since we served together as subalterns in the 3rd West York Militia in 1898. I handed over this afternoon.

My relief arrives

10 . VII . 1904. *Kisumu*

To Kisumu

Left Kabwuren camp at dawn and am heartily glad to see the last of the place. The incessant rain, the lack of anything to do and being absolutely by myself would have forced me to some vice or other if I had remained there much longer. My last remembrance of Kabwuren is of an old grey parrot sitting on the topmost branch of a tall tree in the grey dawn, chattering to himself in satisfaction that yet another day had dawned.

32 miles in 8 hours

I passed through Kaimosi Mission at 7 a.m. and said adieu to my friends the missionaries. I lunched at Hamisi's and reached Kisumu at 3.30 p.m., having done the 32 miles in 9½ hours, which included halts of 1½ hours.

Stephen Bagge

Isaac, Malony, Haran, Donald and Lawson

At Kisumu I met Stephen Bagge, the Sub-commissioner, who kindly put me up for the night. I also met Isaac, who was the first to find the bongo in the Nandi forests and who is a District Officer. Also Toncks (a local lawyer), Haran, Donald, Malony and Lawson, the latter having been recently transferred from Fort Hall.

The luxury of getting back once more to comparative civilisation combined with the thought of going home and the result of the 32-mile walk today gave an impetus to my appetite which astonished my friends. There is no doubt that mental satisfaction and anticipation affect the appetite as much as physical exertion. When these two causes are combined, the result sometimes leads to disaster.

13 . VII . 1904. *Lake Elmentaita*

Leave Kisumu

I did not leave Kisumu until yesterday, as there was no train. Before leaving I met Lieut. Bahrens, R.E., a member of the Anglo-German Boundary Commission.

Gilgil

I travelled from Kisumu with Malony of the Railway, who kindly let me share his private carriage. As the train was "goods" I should otherwise have had to travel in a goods van. Near Kibigori I saw a Cobus kob, the first antelope of its kind I have seen. I arrived at Gilgil station at 5.30 p.m. today, where I intend to stop and shoot for a couple of days. From Gilgil I marched to Lake Elmentaita, which took me about 2 hours. The country is dry and covered with Masai and their herds. There is consequently little game about. On the lake there are masses of geese and duck, but they are unapproachable. It has been bitter cold all day with a violent wind.

14 . VII . 1904. *Gilgil*

I returned to Gilgil this afternoon, killing a fine bustard on the way. In the evening I strolled round, but only saw some doe Thomson's gazelle, some zebra and two hen ostrich. Shot a Thomson's gazelle for food.

To Gilgil

I have heard many people say they do not like the flat-topped or umbrella acacia trees which grow so well round the Rift Valley lakes. I think they are most attractive and picturesque; they are nature's picture of democracy—formless, with an utter lack of distinction; nature's attempt at equality and of terrible strength. If I ever lived in Kenya I should like to have one magnificent specimen just in front of my house as a frame for some distant view.

Umbrella acacia

15 . VII . 1904. *Nairobi*

I boarded a train at 5.30 a.m. and reached Nairobi about noon. Col. Eric Smith joined my carriage at Naivasha. Our 3rd Battalion has moved out into camp at Ingong, as a battalion of Yaos is arriving from Nyasaland. Major Osborn, our second-in-command, arrives here on the 16th.

To Nairobi

18 . VII . 1904. *Nairobi*

I lost my poor little dog Baby yesterday under the most revolting circumstances. It has been a great blow to me, as she had been my companion for so long and we so thoroughly understood each other.

Baby killed by baboon

Yesterday afternoon I walked out towards the Athi River, without gun or weapon of any sort. Baby accompanied me as usual. On approaching the Athi River I sat down and spied through my glasses. I saw a large mob of baboon close to the river, and Baby and I decided to stalk them and give them a good fright. We did it most successfully, and getting to within about 60 yards of them we jumped up with a shout and chased them into the river. Baby, of course, ran in front and was catching them up when I called to her. Normally she would have returned, but there was a strong head wind and I suppose she did not hear me. On she went, for she feared nothing. Suddenly the whole mob turned on her. Undismayed she went straight for the nearest baboon, but the contest was hopeless from the first. Then, not 150 yards from me and in full view, they caught her, and with diabolical yelling and grunting they tore her to bits in a second. I ran up, yelling as I went, to try to save poor Baby, but it was no use. I saw the disgusting creatures making off with her limbs. Never did I long so much for a rifle.

I get even with those baboon

When my first horror was over I sat down and contemplated how I could teach those baboon a lesson. I noticed that when I chased them they made off into a rocky cliff on the right bank of the Athi, where they were unassailable except by long shots from a rifle from the opposite bank. It was getting dusk, and it was clear that the whole mob would roost in that cliff. Therefore, if I could get out to their roosting place before light, surround it with men and then open fire from the front, I should most certainly stampede them and kill the bulk of the brutes. As I returned sadly that evening I had murder in my heart.

On arriving back I went off to the Sergeant-major and told him I wanted 30 men at 3 a.m. tomorrow with rifles, bayonets and 100 rounds each. No questions were asked, and at 3.15 a.m. today we set out across the plains for the baboons' stronghold. We arrived well before daylight; we halted, and I explained to the men exactly what my plan was: 25 of them were to surround the place on the right bank while 5 of us kept up a fire from in front to dislodge the brutes. The baboon were to be shot down without mercy. They thoroughly enjoyed the prospect of the assault. Quietly, in the dark, I posted the men and then returned to the left bank to await the dawn. As the first rosy flush of the new day appeared over the eastern horizon I heard the mournful note of a scops owl down by the river and a jackal began to howl on the plains. As it got lighter some small bustard rose from the grass near me and flew off with their melodious call. The crested crane flew off to their feeding grounds and nature awoke. But no sound came from the cliffs where I felt sure the baboon must still be. There was no chatter, nor the grunting usually inseparable from any concourse of simians.

It was now light enough to shoot, and I gazed at the 200 yards of cliff through my glasses. I could see nothing, so I fired a shot. At once there was a hubbub, with much chattering and grunting. The face of the cliff seemed alive with baboon. They looked at me and at once moved off, hopping along the ledges, contemplating an escape upstream. They were led by an old female, and when she found her advance was barred she barked loudly and turned back to the rocks. We now began to fire freely at them from in front, which panicked them, and racing across the face of the cliff they tried to escape downstream. Several showed themselves over the top and were at once shot down. The mob then returned to the cliff, when we in front again opened a rapid fire on them. They then made up the face of the cliff, and, gaining the top with wonderful agility, bolted into the open. They must have realised then that they had to run the gauntlet in some direction, for they suddenly became quite silent and charged through my men, who killed a number of them. A few turned back to the cliff and attempted to hide, and among these were two old males whose blood I was determined to spill before the sun went down. Having marked them down, I stopped the firing and closed the men in to the edge of the cliff, telling them to kill only these two old males. I then from the top threw down huge boulders, which soon dislodged them, and out they came upstream, where I killed one and one of my men shot the second. We collected altogether 25 baboon, only some 15 or so escaping. We killed every full-grown male, and I was pleased.

We returned to Nairobi before noon, and in the evening I rode out to the Nairobi River and shot an impala and a haartebeeste for the men who had assisted me in avenging Baby.

19 . VII . 1904. *Nairobi*

Abel Chapman

Abel Chapman has come out here for a shoot and I had a long talk with him this evening in the Club. He is a much older man than I suspected and seemed rather dry and bitter about the world in general. He was disinclined to talk about birds, being temporarily obsessed by the fever of larger game.

20 . VII . 1904. *Nairobi*

Game census

I took Abel Chapman out the whole day and found him charming, though I fear he was tired out at the end. We saw every variety of game between Nairobi and the Athi River south of Nairobi in an area of about 16 square miles. It amounted to:

3 rhinoceros	1267 wildebeeste
18 giraffe	1654 haartebeeste
42 ostrich	432 Grant's gazelle
31 warthog	234 Thomson's gazelle
42 eland	66 impala
568 zebra	11 wild hog
8 great bustard	1 cheetah
34 baboon	9 lion

We shot nothing.

How lion hunt

The highlight of the day was watching a pride of lion hunting, a scene I had always hoped to see. It was about 4.30 p.m. in thin bush, over which we were able to have a good view from a slight eminence. The whole procedure was most deliberate. When we first saw the pride they comprised 2 lion, 4 lionesses and 3 half-grown cubs, and they were all more or less in a bunch and looking in all directions. About 500 yards from them and upwind was a herd of 15 zebra. From the stealthy movement of all the lion it was clear that they were on the hunt and that they had spotted the zebra; the two lion with two lionesses and the three cubs then made a wide detour, using every possible fold in the ground and bushes to keep hidden from the zebra, with the clear intention of getting round them and stampeding them by giving them their wind. The two lionesses left behind separated and took up crouching positions some 100 yards apart, both intently watching the zebra. Meanwhile the main body of lion had reached a position where the zebra should have got their wind. Suddenly up went the zebras' heads in alarm and they stampeded downwind, while the lions with cubs lay flat with only their heads erect. The herd of zebra passed between the two crouching lionesses but only some 20 yards from one of them; she lay very flat in a ready-to-spring attitude; it was most exciting. As the herd of zebra got more or less level with the lionesses they suddenly stopped and looked back. At that moment the nearest lioness launched her attack at full gallop and sprang at her victim. It was all over in a moment. She leaped at the zebra, knocked it over, and quick as lightning got a hold on the throat; the zebra scarcely struggled. The herd, now thoroughly alarmed, dashed away in panic towards the second lioness, who launched her attack as they passed her at about 30 yards; she apparently had no difficulty in overtaking one, sprang on it and, like the first lioness, seemed to grip the throat all in one movement—spring and catch hold. The rest of the pride now came up at a trot, the two lion and one lioness joining one kill and the other lioness and the cubs joining the other kill.

The whole hunt was beautifully timed and executed. I doubt if Abel Chapman followed the whole thing or realised what was happening. We were about 10 yards apart and not within speaking distance.

I have spoken to several people who have seen lions hunting and they have all told me the same thing—it is the lioness who kills; the rest of the pride drive or wait patiently until there is a kill.

21 . VII . 1904. *Nairobi*

The Nairobi Races took place today amid much gaiety. Harrison won the K.A.R. cup and the Machako's Cup with his Arab horse Sheikh.

Nairobi Races

23 . VII . 1904. *Mombasa*

I left Nairobi yesterday and arrived in Mombasa today. I saw masses of game on the way down from the railway, including rhinoceros and giraffe. The latter I saw near

To Mombasa en route for Zanzibar and home

Sultan Hamoud Station. They were not in the least alarmed by the train and stood some 70 yards from us among thorn trees as we passed.

A rebel Dutchman

At Voi an old Boer got into my carriage. He told me he had come out here to settle. In talking of the South African War he volunteered the statement that we had fought with the women and not the men, that we had captured over 20,000 of the former, placed them in concentration camps, had starved them and allowed our soldiers to outrage them. I told him that we had placed the women in safety while we dealt with the rebels still in the field, and that as regards the outraging of the Dutch women, their morals were so loose that "outrage" was not the correct term to apply to them. If there had been any immorality it was undoubtedly done by consent. I told him that I thought the Dutch women had probably seduced many innocent British soldiers and had passed on to them their disgusting diseases. I added that Dutch women were so notoriously ugly that no self-respecting Englishman would touch one with the end of a barge pole.

This sort of poison has been spread among the Dutch by such people as the Courtneys, Emily Hobhouse and others. This old man told me that he thought Kitchener was our worst general and that Buller was our best. He finished up his tirade by saying that the English, not content with enslaving the Boers, were now enslaving the Chinese and transporting them to South Africa. This is more poison started by our politicians Campbell Bannerman and Lloyd George and is, of course, designed to catch votes.

Bowring puts me up

C. C. Bowring is kindly putting me up in Mombasa. Breading, recently returned from Somaliland, is also here. After lunch today we adjourned to the rocky foreshore with forks and axes, accompanied by lemons and bread and butter, in order to feast on the oysters which can be easily obtained at low tide.

Sooty falcons

I was delighted to see the little grey falcon this evening when they come out from the old fort with the bats which they catch on the wing; there were three of them this evening. I think they must be *Falco concolor*.

24 . VII . 1904. *S.S. "Juba," Mombasa*

After a merry send-off from Bowring I embarked on the little coasting steamer *Juba* for Zanzibar.

I leave Mombasa for Zanzibar

Bowring has great charm and is one of the most intelligent men in the Administration. He is the Protectorate Treasurer and first-rate at his job. He is both hospitable and kind, especially to newcomers like myself. He should go far if given the chance.

C. C. Bowring

25 . VII . 1904. *Zanzibar*

Arrived here this morning. I am stopping at the Afrika Hotel but am feeding with the Meades. Mrs. Meade is a great friend of mine. Zanzibar is purely Oriental, most of the European quarter being within the old Arab town. The streets are narrow and the climate is hot and damp. I long for a grey English sky and a strong north-east wind.

Arrive at Zanzibar

26 . VII . 1904. *Zanzibar*

Lunched on H.M.S. *Forte*. In the afternoon I went shopping in the native bazaar and picked up some old Arab coffee pots, afterwards going for a drive with the Meades among the vanilla and clove plantations. I am told that seven-eighths of the world's production of cloves comes from Zanzibar and its neighbour Pemba. The clove bushes I saw were mostly about 12 inches high, with leaves like a bay leaf. The clove is a pink waxy bud, which becomes black when dried. Besides cloves, I saw quantities of mango, coconut, pineapple and other exotic fruit trees. The vanilla is a vine which grows to some height.

H.M.S. "Forte"

Cloves

The French mail steamer *Djemnah*, of the Messageries Maritimes, arrived in harbour this afternoon, so I went aboard and am sleeping there tonight. We sail first thing tomorrow morning.

I embark for home

27 . VII . 1904. *S.S. "Djemnah," Indian Ocean*

We left Zanzibar early this morning. The only other Englishman on board is a fellow called Elwell, a naval officer from H.M.S. *Forte*. He also is proceeding home

Leave Zanzibar

on leave. All the other passengers are French officers and their wives. A pretty moth-eaten lot they are too. They all come from Madagascar and they all look broken down either with fever, drink or some form of vice.

[And that ended my first tour in East Africa.]

On reading through the first part of this record I am shocked by the account of taking human life and the constant slaughter of big game. I do not pretend to excuse it, but perhaps I may explain it. I have no belief in the sanctity of human life or in the dignity of the human race. Human life has never been sacred; nor has man, except in a few exceptional cases, been dignified. Moreover, in Kenya fifty years ago, when stationed with 100 soldiers amid an African population of some 300,000, in cases of emergency where local government was threatened we had to act, and act quickly. To do nothing in an emergency is to do something definitely wrong, and talking comes under the category of "nothing." There was no telegraph or telephone, no motor cars or wireless, and action was imperative for safety. Thank God there was no time or opportunity for talks, conferences and discussions.

I also regarded discipline in my company as paramount, more important when dealing with coloured troops than with one's own countrymen. What may appear to have been outrageous and cruel conduct on my part was an insistence on strict discipline—the obedience of orders. I have seen so many coloured troops rendered useless by inefficient discipline.

For the amount of big game I shot during my first tour in Kenya I have no excuse. I am not proud of it, neither am I ashamed of it. When I arrived in the country I was obsessed by an unashamed blood-lust. Hunting is man's primitive instinct, and I indulged it and enjoyed it to the full. In Kenya's early days fresh meat was not easy to obtain. The African was loath to part with his stock and there was no European settler in the country who could provide meat. Also, when travelling with from 20 to 200 healthy Africans, all doing hard work, meat becomes almost an essential, and more than three-quarters of the animals I shot went to provide meat for hungry and deserving mouths.

I do not believe that the shooting of big game for sport or for food has done much harm. The commercialisation of game, such as killing for hides, killing crocodiles for their skins, elephants for their ivory, and rhinoceros for their horns, and indiscriminate poaching in reserved areas—these do definite harm and have done so in the past. Also I wholeheartedly disapprove of the catching up of wild animals for zoological gardens and condemning them to solitary confinement for life amid squalid surroundings; I have seen a good deal of this in the "catching-up" stage and can vouch for the high rate of mortality, for the shooting of mothers to obtain the young, for deaths in transit and for the cold-blooded nature of the catchers-up. But the main factor in destroying the enormous numbers of game which existed fifty years ago is the deplorable fact that farming and big game cannot thrive side by side, though fifty years ago, when the Masai did not molest wild game, vast herds of Masai cattle roamed the Athi Plains side by side with vast herds of game.

The hunting of big game gave me good healthy exercise when many of my brother officers were drinking rot-gut or running about with somebody else's wife; it taught me bushcraft and how to shoot straight. After all, the hunting of men—war—is but a form of hunting wild animals, and on many occasions during the First World War I thanked my God that I had learned several tricks of my trade when hunting wild and dangerous game.

PART II

SECOND TOUR IN EAST AFRICA: NANDI

17 . III . 1905. *Mombasa*

We arrived at Mombasa this morning just as the sun rose. *Arrive Mombasa*

Vincent has asked me to stop with him while I am in Mombasa, and I have gladly accepted. My old friends *Old friends* McClure and Mrs. Mackay met me on the quay and told me all the news. I made all my fellow passengers honorary members of the Club for the day and they gave me an excellent lunch before they re-embarked. Met my old friends Bowring, Bell, Barnes, Neligan, Henderson, Brandt and many others. In the afternoon I was forced into a picnic on the mainland and in the evening I was enticed into attending St. Patrick's Dinner at the Club. Towards midnight the dinner resolved itself into a drunken orgy and I slipped away and got to bed.

Once I had landed in Mombasa I almost felt as though I had never left the country. I have had a good leave in England, but I feel that my ties with my family and my home are even looser than before. I prefer Africa and the savage to England and the over-civilised society which lives there.

18 . III . 1905. *Mombasa*

I hear I am promoted to be Company Commander and *Promotion* am to proceed direct to Nandi Fort to take over Cary's company. Spent most of the day buying stores and engaging servants. I succeeded in getting a good Goanese cook at Rs.45 a month and a personal servant at Rs.20.

I met Wardle and Hart (son of General Hart, V.C.), who arrived from Jubaland today in the S.S. *Juba*.

Wardle has proved himself a failure and goes home for good, while Hart is off on leave.

19 . III . 1905. *Mombasa*

"Cocktail parade" at Bowring's

Bowring's Sunday morning "cocktail parade" has become an institution in Mombasa. Its object is to mix and drink as many of these poisonous drinks as possible, then have a gigantic lunch and a sleep afterwards. After a well-attended parade today, McClure, Barnes and I stopped to lunch.

I find that my old servant, the Masai boy called Kaninge, has taken on under McClure. I tried to get him to come back to me, but having once tasted the fleshpots of Mombasa and Nairobi he is loath to return to the wilds of Nandi. I am sorry to lose him, as he is such a good skinner of both birds and mammals.

22 . III . 1905. *Kibigori*

I leave Mombasa

On the 20th I left Mombasa by the Uganda Railway on my way up to the Nandi country, whither I shall march from Kibigori Station on the Uganda Railway. I travelled from Mombasa to Nairobi with Mrs. Mackay, Mr. W. Touch, Inspector of the National Bank of India, and Mr. F. A. Pape, an American settler who has a fibre concession at Voi.

Nairobi

At daylight on the 21st I found myself near Machako's Road, where I saw lion and the usual amount of haartebeeste and gazelle. Owing to the recent heavy rains there had been a "wash-out" on the Kapiti Plains which delayed us. We arrived at Nairobi about 2 p.m.; Mackay, Barlow, Barrett and Sharpe came down to the station to see me and have lunch. I dined last night at Nakuru with R. Church of the Uganda Railway.

Game census on the Athi Plains

I counted the various big game I saw from my carriage between Stony Athi Station and Nairobi, all on the south side of the railway. It amounted to

2 rhinoceros	11 giraffe
7 eland	876 wildebeeste
543 Coke's haartebeeste	169 Grant's gazelle
174 Thomson's gazelle	98 impala

19 warthog	974 zebra
42 ostrich	1 hyaena

I arrived at Kibigori Station at 1.30 p.m. There I found porters and escort awaiting me, having been sent down for me from Nandi Fort by Cary. It was pouring with rain, so I have decided to delay my departure for Nandi until tomorrow.

Kibigori

I sent for the local Kavirondo chief and asked him what news he had of elephant in the neighbourhood. He told me that there were none about at present, but that he would send me news to Nandi if any came into his district; meanwhile he would very much like to have some fresh meat and incidentally see how I shot. So I reluctantly sallied forth in the rain in search of game and soon came across a large herd of Jackson's haartebeeste, with one solitary topi antelope. This latter beast I stalked, and coming to 200 yards of him I hit him. He ran some way and lay down, when I again approached him and killed him. The Kavirondo rushed in and secured the meat, the chief being delighted. He promised me solemnly that he would now let me know at once if elephant came to his part. But I am convinced the old villain will never trouble to do so. Returned to camp as the sun set over a gorgeous evening after the rain.

Elephant

23 . III . 1905. *Nandi Fort*

I marched up to Nandi Fort from Kibigori. The only British inhabitants of the station are Mr. and Mrs. Cary and Walter Mayes.

I arrive at Nandi Fort

After dining with the Carys I became violently ill and retired to bed. Nandi lies some 3000 feet above sea level and a sudden rise in altitude always affects me like this; after 24 hours I am all right again.

24 . III . 1905. *Nandi Fort*

I do not think much of Cary as a company officer. When General Manning inspected the company only a few months back he ordered it to be disbanded next August. Meanwhile I have to get it into a decent shape, and I hope

The rotten state of Cary's company

that when it is next inspected the disbandment order will be suspended.

I refuse to take over

The state of the men's clothing, the numerous deficiencies from the company stores and the appalling state of the men's rifles have induced me to send a full report down to Nairobi, in which I have refused to take over the company or be responsible for their stores or rifles.

I can see that I am going to have a difficult job getting the company together. The first thing to do is to get some discipline into them, which will mean some fairly drastic action.

Cary and his wife leave, I am thankful to say, for Nairobi tomorrow.

30 . III . 1905. *Nandi Fort*

Mayes' curious methods of administration

I give below two examples of the way in which Mayes administers the local natives. The other day some natives stole two head of cattle from Mayes' cattle *boma*. At 2 a.m. yesterday morning Mayes with his police surrounded their village, shot one man and captured the other, who was later shot while trying to escape. He also recovered his own cattle and lifted 10 more as a fine. These have been absorbed into Mayes' herd.

This is the second instance. Mayes got word yesterday that a section of the Nandi had gone raiding some of the Elgon people, so last night he made a march into the culprits' country, lifted 82 head of cattle and 200 sheep and goats. These rough-and-ready methods may be successful in keeping a tribe down by brute force, but they savour too much of Congo atrocities. But what is much worse is that Mayes, when he steals these cattle from the natives, feathers his own nest with the proceeds and does not credit the Government. Neither does he report his actions to his superiors. I know this from having seen the entries in Mayes' accounts, where he credits the Government with but a tenth part of what he takes.

I certainly do not intend to stand by and see the Government cheated in this way, and, moreover, it is not the way to administer a backward African tribe.

1 . IV . 1905. *Nandi Fort*

A deadly snake

While clearing some ground near the lines my men killed a black mamba, one of the most poisonous of African snakes.

I warn Mayes

I told Mayes today that I considered his administrative methods brutal, and that in the interests of the safety of the station I must insist that in future reports of all police patrols which involve the killing of men or capture of animals shall be submitted to the Sub-commissioner. He practically admitted his dishonesty by begging me not to be too hard on him, as he depended on his job for his bread and butter. I told him that if he would play the game there would be no trouble.

13 . IV . 1905. *Nandi Fort*

Boer settlers

The only European settlers in the whole of the Nandi country are two Boer families called Garvie and Steyn. They have recently come from the Transvaal and are related to the ex-President of the Orange Free State. They all seemed terrified of the Nandi and have been applying for a guard of my men. Yesterday I went over to them to have a look at their camp, which is some four miles distant. They had, of course, taken no steps to guard against attack, in spite of the fact that they were told that they could only remain at their own risk. The two families were living in filthy grass huts without any attempt to make them either comfortable, sanitary or weatherproof. There is no excuse for this, as grass is plentiful and the men are not badly off. It is simply the Boer standard of life. They told me that if I would send a small guard over they would give them any room I wished. I chose the only suitable one and promised them 10 men tomorrow morning, but they clamoured for a guard at once, so this morning I sent them 10 men.

After the guard had started Garvie came to see me and told me I could not now have the room I had chosen but could have another one, which was not suitable. I told him he must abide by my first choice or not have the guard. He said he would sooner have the guard, so I did not recall it. But this afternoon the guard returned with the report that the room had been changed and that they had been put in with the pigs. So I withdrew the guard. These Boers are indeed slippery customers.

It is absurd that settlers should be allowed in Nandi at present, as the country is by no means safe. Not only that, it is very bad for my men to be away from me and the strength of my company will not stand many such detachments. I have reported the whole affair to Nairobi for confirmation. These Boers came up here without anyone's permission and are squatting on Nandi-owned land for which they pay no rent. I asked Mayes if they had any right to be there; he said no and that they squatted at their own risk. Seems to me a pretty poor arrangement.

15 . IV . 1905. *Muhoroni Plains*

Shooting

Yesterday I came down the Nandi Escarpment to the Muhoroni Plains for a day's shooting. I had to march for about 11 miles along an abominable road before I sighted game. I then stalked and shot a bull Jackson's haartebeeste and camped close to the carcass. I was feeling very tired at the time and, foolishly, at once went out to search for roan antelope. The grass was over 4 feet high, the heat was intense and the ground was rough. I soon became so exhausted that I could scarcely get back to camp. I have never before been so completely done up, and I cannot account for it, as I have not really had a hard day.

Exhaustion

Feeling quite fit again this morning, I was out at dawn after roan. After killing another Jackson's haartebeeste I spied two small roan lying down. I approached them to some 40 yards, but they were too small to shoot, so I left them. Later on I came on a large herd of some 49 roan, but they had been disturbed by haartebeeste and were unapproachable. I eventually drove them into some good stalking country and let them rest. They lay down, and when they were quite settled I began to stalk them; this would have been an easy job, as the wind and ground were both favourable, but when I was some 400 yards from them I disturbed a small herd of haartebeeste which had been lying down unnoticed in the long grass. These troublesome beasts first went off to my left and stood staring at me. The roan could not see them, so all was well, and I continued my approach, but when I was some 300 yards from my goal these miserable haartebeeste wheeled round and galloped direct for the herd of roan, which instantly took alarm and made off out of sight. This was a most unfriendly act on the part of the haartebeeste, but there was nothing for it but to return disgusted to camp. But to my joy I spied a solitary haartebeeste standing on an ant-heap. Approaching to 200 yards, I fired and hit him. At my shot a whole herd of haartebeeste, accompanied by 7 fine bull roan, jumped out of the long grass and made off. I rushed off in pursuit, but it was no good and I never came up with them. I returned to my wounded haartebeeste, but the porters foolishly jumped it in their eagerness to cut its throat; making off over a rise I failed to locate him and lost him, though we searched for nearly an hour.

I was surprised to see so many roan, which are very local and by no means plentiful in British East Africa. I must have toiled over some 24 miles today and was glad to get back to camp, tired and thirsty.

I shall return to Nandi Fort tomorrow.

24 . IV . 1905. *Nandi*

Mayes and I go to Ravine Station

Mayes has to go to the Ravine and asked me for an escort, so I decided to accompany him myself. Today we camped about 10 miles out in a north-easterly direction and on the edge of the cultivation where it joins the Mau forest. The famous old Nandi chief called Terurie visited the camp this evening. I am taking the opportunity to survey the country, which is comparatively easy, as prominent features are frequent and the country is open.

25 . IV . 1905. *Kongoni Camp, Sclater's Road*

To the edge of the Mau Plateau

We struck camp at 5.39 a.m., and marching in a northerly direction we got on to the old caravan route to Uganda known as Sclater's Road, which was always used before the railway was open. We camped at Kongoni Camp. I saw many oribi, reedbuck and bushbuck in the evening. We are now at over 6000 feet and it is mighty cold at night.

The Mau Plateau We had a long march today over the Mau Plateau, starting at 5 a.m. and reaching camp at 4 p.m. We must have covered some 28 miles. We traversed the most gorgeous country, open downland and primeval forest, all lying between 7500 and 8500 feet. The air was exhilarating and crisp, which made fast going a pleasure. I was surprised to have seen no four-foot game at all, though we saw fairly fresh spoor of buffalo and elephant, and in one piece of thick forest I saw what must have been bongo spoor. It was that of an antelope nearly the size of an eland, and could have been nothing else. I saw signs of my pig (*Hylochaeros*).

Flora The downs were carpeted with wild flowers in full bloom, which included masses of gladioli, forget-me-nots, broom, blackberries, clover, red-hot pokers and many others which I did not know. Two of these latter particularly interested me. One is a blue variety of a small plant which I found two years ago on the Markham Downs and is not unlike a small petunia. I dug up several roots and obtained some seed. The other plant is a small ground creeper which was growing and flowering in profusion. It has brilliant orange flowers. I also secured roots of this. Both these latter I have pictured. Water was plentiful, and in every gully grow masses of maidenhair fern. Wherever I found the true maidenhair I also found another plant which is not unlike it. I have called it the bastard maidenhair and am pressing two sprigs of each.

African snipe In the evening I wandered down to a swamp near camp and put a snipe off its nest. It contained 4 eggs, which looked like those of our common snipe. The bird is undoubtedly the African snipe (*nigripennis*), as I flushed several of them later round the swamp, and their call is unmistakable. I did not hear one drumming, though I was on the look-out for it. I also, on this same swamp, killed a brace of duck which are the red macoa duck. I had intended to skin them, but unfortunately the cook got to them and plucked them both before I could rescue them, for which he received a good flow of abuse.

A record distance view

On emerging from my tent just before the sun rose I was surprised to see a crystal-clear day after a cloudy, misty night. The whole of the Laikipia and Elgeyo (Kamasia) escarpments were visible, and also Mount Kenya, looming up black over the Aberdare Mountains. I could not believe my eyes when I saw an amazing optical illusion. Balanced upside down on the top of Mount Kenya was a complete reproduction of the mountain, as black as the mountain itself, reflected in the sky. The sun was below the horizon. It lasted about ten minutes and slowly faded away as the sun rose. To make sure I was not seeing ghosts I called Mayes, and he could not account for it. To the north-west Mount Elgon stood out to advantage, looking like what it is, a huge volcano. Kenya is about 150 miles distant and Elgon some 80 miles. Mounts Elgon and Kenya are 230 miles apart as far as I can judge. To see clearly over such distances gives one an idea of the magnificence of the scenery, for there was no mist or blurred outlines, the two huge hill masses standing out clear-cut in the morning air.

Such distances, when reduced to a scale which we can appreciate at home, would be as follows: if I had been standing in the middle of Hampshire I should have seen Calais and the top of Exmoor at the same time; or again, if I had been on Westminster Bridge I should have seen the Channel Islands and Dunkirk.

Timber

A large part of our journey today took us through forest containing fine timber. I believe that Grogan and a Mr. Lingham have obtained a concession for cutting it, but I doubt if any money is to be made out of it unless a branch railway is built or freights on the Uganda Railway are reduced. In any case I trust that whoever cuts timber up here is compelled to plant 10 trees for every one cut.

The Ravine Station

We arrived at 11 a.m. at the Ravine Station, where we lunched with Jack Foaker and his wife, both of whom I had met before. He is the Administrative Officer in charge. From the house we could look right up the Rift Valley and in the dim distance we could see Lake Baringo some 50 miles distant.

I spent the afternoon collecting and skinning a few birds, shaving, bathing, washing my clothes, cleaning my guns, drying my blankets and plotting the various bearings I had taken during the trip.

28 . IV . 1905. *Mau Plateau*

Return journey to Nandi Fort

Mayes having completed his business, we left the Ravine today on our return journey to Nandi, camping at Mianzini (bamboo) Camp some 12 miles distant. Saw large numbers of both grey and green parrots near camp, many hornbills, green pigeon, the small African peregrine (*minor*) and several common sandpipers on a stream. They looked like breeding and indeed were in full breeding plumage.

Mayes ill

Mayes is suffering from a bad throat and went to bed on reaching camp. As he has difficulty in swallowing I made him some excellent broth out of grey parrots and dried vegetables, which should do him good.

29 . IV . 1905. *Mau Plateau*

Mayes is better today. We started off at 6.30 a.m. and camped at 12.15 p.m. but saw no game the whole day. I spent the day collecting birds, ferns and seeds of various flowering plants in the hopes of getting them home. The belladonna lilies are in full bloom now, mostly striped magenta and white. I collected many bulbs.

30 . IV . 1905. *Kongoni Camp. Uasin Gishu*

Shooting

We marched to Kongoni Camp, where we pitched our tents. As the men are rather short of food I went out to try to get some game. I got a reedbuck, an oribi and two Jackson's haartebeeste. I unfortunately wounded a third haartebeeste which I failed to recover. I was shooting with solid bullets, having run short of others, and after putting 6 consecutive shots into this beast he made off over a rise and I failed to locate him. Haartebeeste are notoriously tough, but I never knew they could stand such treatment.

I also shot a couple of snipe (*nigripennis*), which must breed in these parts, as the female had an almost fully developed egg in the ovaries.

Snipe

When we arrived in camp we were visited by the local chiefs, who told us they thought we had all been massacred by the Kamalilo, a troublesome section of the Nandi. They seemed quite surprised and somewhat annoyed that the rumour was not true.

Our reported massacre

1 . v . 1905. *Nandi*

We got back into the Nandi country today and camped in cultivation. Mayes shot a female oribi in the evening; it is rather an interesting specimen, being much darker than others I have seen, with a brown frontal patch like one sometimes sees in steinbock. I am keeping the skin and skull for the British Museum.

Back to the Nandi country

As my men have either eaten or dried all the meat which I got for them yesterday, I purchased some sheep from the local natives. My men being mostly non-Mohammedan Manyema, they did not trouble to cut their throats but got the natives to kill them. This the Nandi did by simply squeezing the noses of the poor sheep until they died of suffocation. The process so disgusted me that I have forbidden it for the future.

Nandi method of killing sheep

2 . v . 1905. *Nandi Fort*

We got back to Nandi Fort.

Back to Nandi Fort

Having travelled with Mayes during the past 10 days or so I have got to know him and his character rather well, and I have not altered my opinion. His ideas are those of an uneducated man. He is frankly out to make what he can out of his job and has been in the habit of robbing the Government at every opportunity. I have told him that I do not mean to stand by and do nothing.

Walter Mayes

4 . v . 1905. *Nandi Fort*

The Boer squatters came in to see me, complaining bitterly about thefts of stock by Nandi. I told them they were lucky to be allowed to squat on Nandi land without

The Boer squatters

paying any rent; to my surprise they told me they paid Mayes Rs.60 a month rent, and in return for that they demanded protection. They have complained to Mayes, but he has refused to see them; worse still, he has threatened to turn them out if they do not pay their rent regularly.

Mayes' wife arrives

Mayes' first appearance in East Africa was during the Uganda Mutiny, when he was a Distressed British Seaman in Zanzibar. The Administration raked in every person they could, and Mayes was taken on as Transport Officer and did very well. At the end of the Mutiny he was given a job in the Administration.

This evening he rushed into my house, hair dishevelled and in frantic excitement; he had run all the way from his own house. He screamed out: "A terrible thing has happened; my wife has arrived and upset everything! For Gawd's sake give me a bottle of whisky." I said I would come over and see her. She was a dirty-looking slut of a woman and was weeping. I am not too good on these occasions. She called Mayes Wally and said she was bloody well going to stop here. Apparently Mayes deserted her in Mauritius—she is a Mauritian Creole—and she finally found out where he was and suddenly appeared. It is all a bit difficult, as Mayes has half a dozen Nandi concubines in the house. I left them to fight it out among themselves.

5 . V . 1905. *Nandi Fort*

Sleeping sickness

A case of sleeping sickness has occurred here. The patient is a boy who doubtless contracted the disease down by the Victoria Nyanza, as he has been there recently. Whenever he is left to himself he falls asleep. His eyes are very bright when he is awake. He is becoming weaker and weaker every day and has probably had the disease on him for some time, for he is now suffering from the last stages of the sickness. There is apparently no cure. I am sending him down to Kisumu, where he can get medical attention and a certain amount of nursing. I have no accommodation for such cases. I have, however, been giving him slight doses of arsenic and gradually increasing

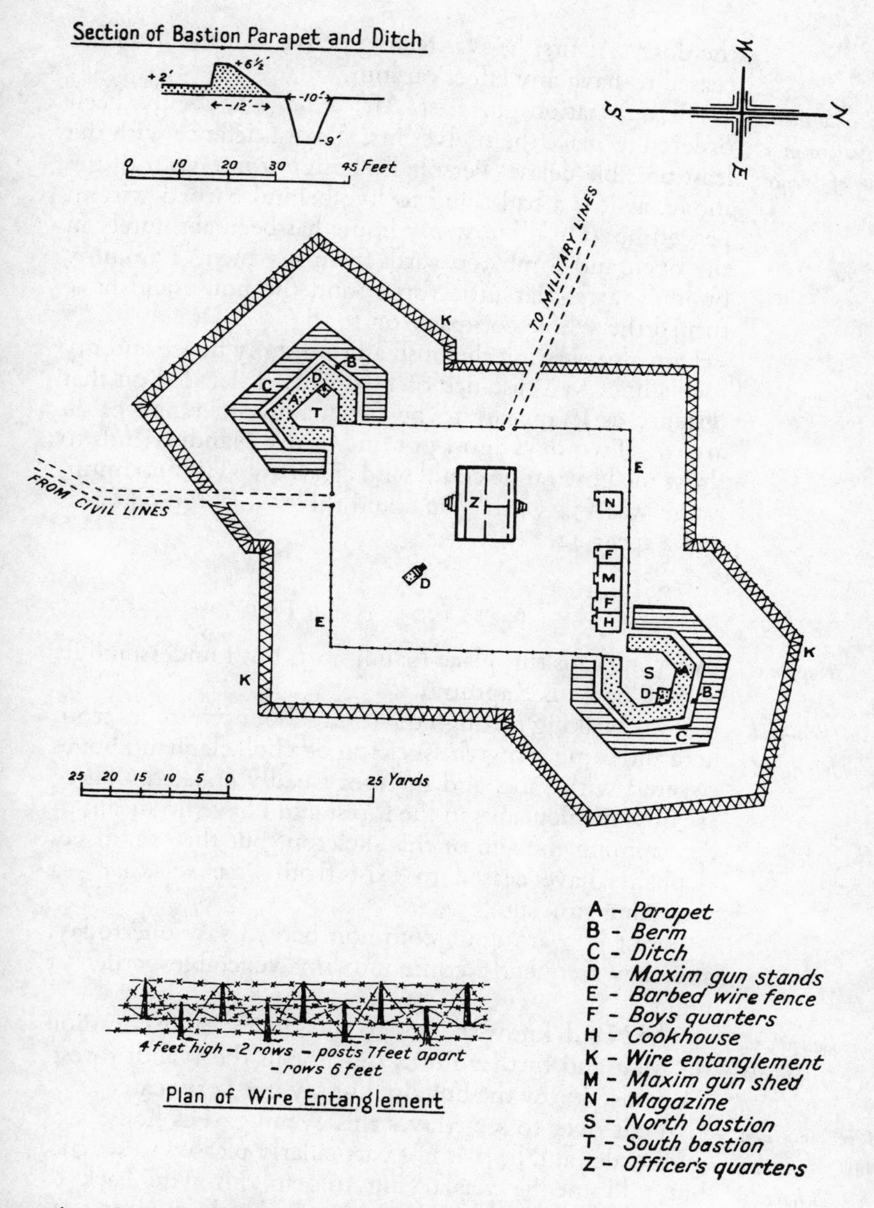

Plan of military defences at Nandi, commenced 2 May, completed 1 June 1905

the dose. At first he was feeling better, but the drug has ceased to have any effect on him.

Orders to place stations in a state of defence

All out-stations in East Africa have suddenly been ordered to place themselves in a state of defence with the least possible delay. Personally I am not in favour of the move, as it is a bad thing to live behind barbed wire in peacetime. Up till now my house has been absolutely in the open and some 300 yards from my men. I am now building a regular little fort round the house and have turned the whole company on to dig.

I am also clearing the bush all round my house and my men's lines to a distance of 150 yards; I decided on that distance as it appears to be the maximum range of an arrow. Two days ago I got one of my Nandi friends to show me how far he could send an arrow. His maximum range was 134 yards. He could throw a rungu 68 yards and a spear 42.

6 . v . 1905. *Nandi Fort*

Kaptumo

Everyone calls this place Nandi Fort, but I understand its correct name is Kaptumo.

Elephant and forest hog

I was walking through the forest about two miles from here and came across the skeleton of a bull elephant, bones covered with moss and the ivory badly cracked. There are now no elephants in the forest and I have no means of determining the age of this skeleton, but the Nandi say elephants have ceased to exist from "*zamani sana*"—a very long time ago.

Forest hog are quite common here; I saw one today, and they frequently come into my vegetable garden at night.

Bongo and buffalo

The Nandi know the bongo and say it is quite common on Mau and further north but not in the Nandi forest. They also know the buffalo, but say it is very scarce.

Mayes' wife and further dishonesty

Went over to see Mayes this evening. His house was in disorder and he was not particularly pleased to see me, but told me he was trying to send his wife back to Mauritius and had written to Bagge on the subject.

I told Mayes that the Boers had informed me that they pay rent for their land and that this is at variance with what he had told me before. His reply was, "You bloody well mind your own business!" I explained that it was my business, as I had to find men to protect them and that if they were paying rent they had a right to assistance. To whom was the rent paid? Did Bagge know about it? I said I should apply to have them removed, as there was too much unrest among the Nandi, and the question of rent was bound to arise. Then Mayes broke down and asked me not to be too hard on him; he was a poor man.

So I told him plainly that if he would run straight and not try to rob the Government he served we would remain friends, but if he found he could not do so it would be my duty to send a report in to Bagge at Kisumu. Mayes muttered something about "You bloody interfering soldiers," and I left. I fear he is a hopeless case and quite unfitted for his very responsible post.

7 . V . 1905. *Nandi Fort*

Blue buck and leopard

I was in the forest early this morning catching butterflies and was lucky in shooting one of those delightful little blue buck. On my return for breakfast I saw a nice leopard cross my path only some 40 yards from me but without giving me a chance of a shot, so this evening I tied up a small goat in a clearing in the forest and sat up over it. As dusk approached, sure enough the unsuspecting leopard showed itself not 15 yards from me. It sprang at the goat and was in the act of dragging him into the bush when I killed it with a shot which broke both shoulders. It proved to be a female.

8 . V . 1905. *Nandi Fort*

The discipline in my company

So far I have not had much trouble with my company. I have had two cases of insubordination, which I dropped on very severely. But last Thursday my Colour-sergeant got drunk, threatened to shoot a native officer and refused to obey an order. He was up before me this morning and I reduced him to the ranks and discharged him with ignominy. I am extremely sorry about it, as he is a first-class man with a clean sheet after 11 years' service. I entirely blame my predecessor for allowing him and the company to get out of hand. Apparently, when under Cary, he used frequently to get drunk, but no notice was taken of it.

The company was watching to see how I would deal with such a case, and I could not afford to let the man off more lightly than I did. The poor little man feels it dreadfully, having been the "big man" for so long. He is a Zanzibar Arab, and I have probably ruined his chances of further employment in any decent capacity. Though it is small consolation to him, it will I hope have a salutary effect on the company. I sent him to Nairobi this afternoon under escort, and then gave the company a lecture on discipline. I explained to them that if I had any more of this drunkenness and insubordination I should punish offenders more severely.

I report Mayes

I have had so many complaints from natives about the way in which Mayes is robbing them of their cattle, sheep, goats, and even girls, that I have embodied them all in a report to Bagge, the Sub-commissioner at Kisumu, asking him to send someone up here to verify what I suspect. At the same time I have sent a copy of the report to Nairobi and to Mayes for his information. Mayes has not acknowledged the copy, but I hear from his police lines that he is very angry and has abused me to his police, which has made my men rather annoyed. Mayes has a Nandi interpreter, whom he has told to tour the neighbouring Nandi and instruct them not to supply me with meat, eggs, milk, vegetables or anything else. In other words, he is trying to boycott me. But that form of reprisal does not worry me, as my friends among the Nandi will give me anything I want in spite of Mayes.

14 . V . 1905. *Nandi Fort*

Mayes recalled

Mayes received orders from Bagge to return to Kisumu last night, as he is being transferred to another station. Isaac, whom I have met before, takes his place and arrived here today. Bagge has obviously told him of the contents of my report and Isaac has been instructed to find out what has been going on up here. Isaac lunched with me today.

I recently saw an article and map in the *Journal of the Royal Geographical Society* by Hobley, one of our Sub-commissioners. He comments on country with which I am well acquainted and incidentally copies my map. He asked me for a copy some time back, but I had no idea that it was his intention to publish it as his own work. I have sent an original of my map to the *Journal* and asked them to publish it with a few notes.

Hobley copies my survey work

My article deals mostly with the watershed of the Aberdare Range, which has always interested me.

[This map was published in the *Journal of the Royal Geographical Society*, 1905.]

15 . V . 1905. *Nandi Fort*

I have been busy lately starting an intelligence service to find out exactly where the Laibon Koitelal lives, what are his intentions, and what might be his plans if the Government launched an expedition. Most of my agents are Masai from the small kraal near my house. They can wander freely among the Nandi.

I commence an intelligence service

17 . V . 1905. *Uasin Gishu Plateau*

Yesterday I left the *boma* and camped at Kilibwan, a few miles north of Kibturi. My object in this trip is partly to survey the country and partly to find out where the Nandi graze their cattle. The people seem very friendly, and a broad grin came over their faces when I told them that Isaac had replaced Mayes. They gave me lots of information about water and grazing and did not appear to be in the least suspicious. They brought me welcome presents of sheep and milk, for which, as is the custom, I gave them presents of equal value in rupees.

A trip to the Uasin Gishu Plateau

Today I marched on to the Uasin Gishu Plateau. I crossed several marshes where snipe were in abundance and breeding, but as I was not carrying a shotgun I denied myself the pleasure of snipe for breakfast. I killed three Jackson's haartebeeste for the men and saw a topi antelope among a herd of the former.

Just before I left Nandi I received a present of two huge pineapples from Barrett in Nairobi. I ate one today, demolishing the whole thing at one sitting, and to-morrow I intend to eat the second. They are particularly luscious, and to eat a pineapple with one's fingers and a hunting knife, sitting on the soft crisp grass of Uasin Gishu, is a joy.

18 . V . 1905. *Uasin Gishu Plateau*

Samburi swamp

Today I marched to the Samburi swamp, which was fringed with all kinds of flowering and aquatic plants, including masses of belladonna lilies and another with foliage rather like a blue hydrangea. Owing to the heavy dew in these parts I got drenched through in the long grass. The sun does not appear to have much drying power before 9 o'clock.

Wandorobo

After my tents were pitched I discovered a small en-campment of the Wandorobo quite close. But they had made tracks as soon as they saw we were camping, and no amount of coaxing would bring these shy hunters back again.

Game

Abyssinian oribi, bohor reedbuck and Jackson's haarte-beeste are plentiful, and I flushed numerous snipe, francolin, quail and duck. I also saw two solitary bull topi antelope, both of which I stalked and shot. These ante-lope never seem to run more than three or four hundred yards when alarmed, which is quite contrary to the habits of the rest of their genus, haartebeeste going miles when badly scared. I shot a bohor reedbuck with my ·450 cordite rifle, which is the first time I have used it. I am bound to say I prefer my ·256 Mannlicher with the Schonauer magazine, which has never yet failed me.

19 . V . 1905. *Uasin Gishu Plateau*

Oribi and reedbuck

Today I marched back to the camp of the day before yesterday, having completed that part of my survey which I set out to do.

I have noticed that the Abyssinian oribi do not have such a shrill whistle as the Kenya oribi. It is a hoarser whistle and more like a cough or bark.

I have also noticed on this trip that the bohor reedbuck (especially the old bucks) usually lie out in the open plains during the daytime, generally in some hollow. The immature buck frequent the marshes and reeds. Early yesterday morning I must have seen over 20 round the Samburi swamp, and they were all young buck or does with young. In the middle of the day all these had retired to the reeds and only old buck remained out on the plains.

20 . V . 1905. *Nandi Fort*

Ordered to join the coming Sotik Expedition

I returned to Nandi today and found a wire awaiting me, ordering me to place myself in readiness to join the forthcoming Sotik Expedition. I am awfully pleased with myself, having had no idea that I had a chance of getting on this expedition. It gives me much virtuous satisfaction to think that I never even tried to join it.

I believe the expedition is taking place, as about a month ago the people of Sotik raided the Naivasha Masai and carried off a lot of their cattle. On being asked to return them they refused, and sent insulting messages to the Government. I believe the expedition starts about 2 June.

21 . V . 1905. *Nandi Fort*

My orders regarding the Sotik Expedition are cancelled

With the greatest disappointment I received a wire cancelling my joining the Sotik Expedition. I have written to Nairobi and asked the reasons.

7 . VI . 1905. *Nandi Fort*

Visit to old slave mart at Quitale

I returned today from a most interesting visit to the old slave emporium at Quitale, about 70 miles due north from Nandi Fort. I was induced to go there for two reasons: I wished to complete my survey in that direction and I was most interested in seeing the old slave mart where the Arabs collected their slaves before their final march down to the coast at Bagomoyo. I was originally put on to this by an old Sudanese called Mbarak who served under Tippoo Tib as a soldier and spent many weeks at Quitale. He came with me, but we could do only about 10 miles a day because of his old legs. We left here on 22 May and reached Quitale on the 28th. We left Quitale on 1 June. It was easy going all the way. Nandi settlement reaches almost to Sclater's Road, and from there to Quitale there was no sign of human habitation. I had expected to find Masai north of Sclater's Road but found none.

Big game

After leaving the plateau, which is mainly open grass, and crossing the Nzoia River 20 miles south of Quitale we ran into fairly thick bush with patches of forest and some open glades. I have never seen so much game, especially giraffe; in fact, on the last two days we were never out of sight of these strange and fascinating animals. They seemed to be near the Baringo race, but the old bulls varied a great deal, many being brilliantly reticulated and others slightly less so. Other game which abounded was topi, Jackson's haartebeeste, waterbuck, oribi, bushbuck in incredible numbers and a few zebra. I saw no sign of the Uganda kob on the Nzoia River. Every afternoon, as soon as camp was pitched, I sent Simba Manyema out to shoot meat; of course, he always wanted to kill a giraffe, but I only allowed him to kill topi or haartebeeste. I was too busy surveying to shoot.

On reaching Quitale I was delighted to find the remains of the double stockade which encircled the slave market, an area of about 4 acres on a slight rise, with open ground for about 200 yards on all sides and a glorious view of Elgon to the west and of the Cherangani hills to the east. Old Mbarak became quite excited when he found himself back in his old haunts and took me round the stockade, explaining what went on in every corner of the camp. The main gate was on the south of the stockade, the latter being made of solid wooden uprights woven together with thorn and smaller branches. Much of it had decayed or had been burned, but several reaches were in almost perfect condition. Mbarak showed me where the Arabs slept, near the entrance, where the girls were kept, where the boys were kept and where they were castrated, and where the men were kept constantly shackled in eights to a heavy log by iron chains. I shuddered to think of the cruelty which must have gone on here; young children raped, boys castrated and left to recover without antiseptics, and the men bundled down to the coast under cruel conditions and simply shot if exhausted. Human suffering for greed, and it continued for centuries, a disgrace to so-called civilisation.

[I again visited this place, now Kitale, in 1956; so far as I can recollect, the present club is on the site of the old slave mart, but all traces of it have disappeared.]

Game census

On the march back from Quitale I counted 124 giraffe, 232 topi, 167 Jackson's haartebeeste, 17 bushbuck, 85 waterbuck, 24 oribi, 4 rhino, 7 warthog, 62 Chapman's zebra, 27 ostrich, 14 kori bustard and 4 lion in a little over 10 miles.

8 . VI . 1905. *Nandi Fort*

Description of my new forest pi[g] in the P.Z.S.

I received by today's mail the description and figure of the skull of my new forest pig. Though the beast occurs in the forest all round my house up here, my efforts to obtain specimens have so far proved fruitless; yet the natives know the beast well. I have offered a handsome reward for a specimen in the flesh, but I suppose they cannot conceive that anyone can be so mad as to want a pig and merely regard my whim as a form of insanity.

Mbarak on the slave market

Old Mbarak came round to my house this evening after supper. I gave him a sheep, for which he was most thankful. I tried to get more information from him about the Quitale slave market. I tried to find out how the slaves were taken to the coast, their casualties and the route taken, but he remembered very little. The only definite statements he made were that the castrated boys were best looked after as they were the most valuable but that over 50 per cent. died before reaching the coast; the girls were not shackled but went free and were raped both at night and all through the day whenever the caravan halted. About 10 per cent. of the men died from fatigue and undernourishment; if a man showed fatigue he was shot and left. Mbarak had originally worked under Emin Pasha but deserted with his rifle and joined up with the slave raiders under Arab leadership; he had never met Tippoo but had heard of him. Slave caravans went down to the coast, always avoiding the Masai. I asked him what route they took from Quitale and he was very vague; he thought Lamu or Bagomoyo did most of the export trade in Zanzibar.

I asked him if he enjoyed it all. He said: "Plenty food, plenty women; very lovely."

11 . VI . 1905. *Nandi Fort*

An earthquake

At 4.50 this morning I was suddenly wakened by a loud rattling noise as though somebody was hammering on every sheet of tin on the roof. I soon realised that the house was shaking violently and that I could not keep still in bed. Assuming that an earthquake was responsible for all this, I jumped out of bed and got out of the house before it fell to pieces, but the shocks subsided as I left the house. The whole affair lasted but a minute and a half but was most unpleasant.

This is my first experience of an earthquake, and it was uncanny. To feel the whole earth heaving under foot and see everything swaying about and rattling was most weird. I found the sentry outside my house in a great state of excitement, not quite knowing what was going to happen next. He at once attributed it to some devil which the Nandi had conjured up against me. The night was cold and cloudless and without a breath of wind. Isaac had also bundled out of his house, expecting it to tumble to pieces any moment. Except for the crumbling of a wattle and daub outhouse, no damage appears to have been done.

Earthquakes cannot be rare in these parts, for the Nandi know all about them, calling then "aika." The Swahilis call them "ku-temeka inchi" or "shaking the world."

I have written a full account of this one to Greenwich Observatory and to Professor John Milne of Newport in the Isle of Wight, asking them if it was recorded on the seismographs in England.

14 . VI . 1905. *Nandi Fort*

Unrest among the Nandi

There have been signs lately that the Nandi are becoming restless. I hear that the Laibon, the chief medicine man of all the Nandi, is busy making medicine against the

Government and that various meetings take place regularly among the elders to discuss a means by which they can rid themselves of British rule.

The first act

I was therefore not surprised last night when my quarter guard sounded the alarm at 1.30 a.m. The company turned out in quick time and I bundled out in my pyjamas with a rifle. It transpired that several small parties of Nandi had been prowling around the lines, one party attacking the Masai camp and stealing some cattle. The Masai were out at once and pursued the thieves with their usual war-cries in the moonlight. One Masai was killed and two Nandi, one of the latter also being captured. This led to a regular stampede and shouting on all sides, which induced my native officer to get the men out. After sending a patrol over to the civil lines to see that all was well I dismissed the company.

There is little doubt that the Nandi are brewing up for trouble and are daily becoming more daring. I have several good friends among those who live near my house and they give me excellent information about the situation.

Murders and raids are being reported from every part of the district and the country is undoubtedly in a most disturbed state, which I attribute entirely to Mayes' misrule and dishonesty.

17 . VI . 1905. *Nandi Fort*

Hyaena and jackal

The hyaena and jackal have recently been taking a heavy toll of the fruit and vegetables in my garden. The jackal seem particularly fond of tomatoes and the hyaena do not scruple to tear my cabbages to pieces. Both pests also keep up a hideous din at night. I have therefore resolved to try to shoot some of them.

Last night I sat up over some meat. There was nearly a full moon and one of my men had slaughtered an ox nearby, which added to the bait. At about 8.45 I became aware that a hyaena was approaching the bait, which lay some 18 yards from me. I could dimly see his huge figure some 25 yards distant. The moon at the moment had disappeared behind a cloud and the light was not good. However, he came on silently and apparently unsuspicious of my presence. I was using my 12 bore Paradox with ball, and by the aid of night sights I drew a bead on him and fired as he turned broadside on when he reached the bait. He rushed off some 10 yards and fell over dead. I waited on in the hope of bagging another, and at 11 p.m., just as I was thinking about turning in, a jackal rushed up to the bait and began to worry it. I killed him instantly with some heavy shot from my left barrel.

Both these animals are males in good condition. The hyaena weighs 121 lb. I was gratified to see some of my tomatoes in the jackal's stomach, which makes one thief the less.

18 . VI . 1905. *Nandi Fort*

More hyaena and jackal

Last night I sat up over the carcass of the hyaena I shot on the previous night. Two hyaena came near it, but neither relished a meal off a comrade. But two jackal who were not so particular came up to the carcass and I killed them both. They were both bitches.

20 . VI . 1905. *Nandi Fort*

I kill a serval cat

Last night I sat up over some meat and killed a serval cat. He came up close to the meat, but saw me and bolted off. I killed him running at about 25 yards with buckshot. I am glad to have got him, as I suspect him to be guilty of stealing my men's chickens.

23 . VI . 1905. *Nandi Fort*

Animals raiding my kitchen garden

When I came out here last March I brought with me a one guinea box of Sutton's seeds, mainly vegetable. I now have most English vegetables growing and they are now being raided by jackal, small antelope and forest pig. I sat up last night and saw a forest duiker and two forest pig, one an enormous boar, calmly rooting up my potatoes and tomatoes while the duiker was helping himself to my lettuce. I shot the duiker, of a species unknown to me, and gave a severe fright to the pig, who crashed

J. W. Barth. C. F. Hickie. H. Bromley. F. W. Isaac. R. M. The Court of Enquiry on Mayes just before it left Nandi

My company descending the Nandi Escarpment on the Kibigori Road where I was unsuccessfully ambushed

off with loud grunts of anger. Some day I shall pepper those pig or put a bullet into one.

24 . VI . 1905. *Nandi Fort*

To Muhoroni

Bagge, the Sub-commissioner at Kisumu, asked me to meet him at Muhoroni today, so I started off at dawn. After discussing Mayes and his doings he told me he had asked for a court of enquiry to be held at Nandi, in order to find out exactly what had been happening under Mayes' administration.

Wild dog

We finished our talk by 11 a.m., so I indulged in a shoot before returning to Nandi. I killed a topi antelope and a waterbuck for meat for my men, and as I was on the point of returning I disturbed 7 wild dog resting in a *nala*. They made off leisurely and I had 3 shots at them, killing a fine dog with my third at about 130 yards.

I got back to Nandi about 8 p.m., having walked some 32 miles during the day. I start back for Muhoroni again tomorrow to see Col. Harrison about my company. I hate sleeping in the place as it is such a trap for malaria, and it is a long distance to travel, 24 miles there and back, for five minutes' conversation.

12 . VII . 1905. *Nandi Fort*

Court of enquiry on Mayes

Last Sunday Barth, the Crown Advocate, Hickie of the Treasury and Bromley of the Audit Department arrived here to sit on a court of enquiry convened by the Commissioner to enquire into certain allegations against Mayes, namely certain alleged defalcations in the accounts, certain acts of illegal raiding and cruelty to natives, and his methods of administration.

For the last two days the court has been sitting and taking evidence from Isaac, myself and certain natives. The whole business has been most disagreeable, and though responsible for initiating the enquiry I cannot help feeling sorry for Mayes. I wish to goodness he had profited from my first warning. The real fault was placing a man of his calibre in a position of trust. His code of honour could never resist the temptation of making a small fortune by dishonest means.

Grave charges against anyone are unpleasant, but when preferred against a brother official the unpleasantness is accentuated a hundredfold. But I have hardened my heart, determined to tell the court everything I know. When I think what an unscrupulous little blackguard the man has been, I think I have been right in bringing his misconduct to light. If I had failed to do so I should have neglected an unpleasant duty.

The court has as yet come to no decision and left here this morning for Kisumu. Isaac and I accompanied them as far as the escarpment, where we all breakfasted before parting. [I never heard the decision of the court.]

The Nandi bear

Barth asked me what I knew about the Nandi bear. All the Nandi I have questioned about it say it is very hairy and sometimes stands on two legs; they do not think it still exists in the forest, but when they first came here many hundreds of years ago it was common. I imagine it was some sort of anthropoid ape now extinct on account of decreased rainfall. This is confirmed by a curious coincidence. When King Edward was crowned, 5 men of the King's African Rifles were sent home for the celebrations. One of these was my native officer, Massud Effendi. He speaks good English and told me that one of the 5 men was a Nandi; on being taken to the Zoo they were introduced to a chimpanzee, when the Nandi shouted with delight: "There is the Nandi bear." Whenever I have asked a Nandi to trace the outline of this "bear" it is always shown in an erect position.

16 . VII . 1905. *Nandi Fort*

One of my men is murdered by Nandi

The day before yesterday one of my men asked leave to go to Kibigori to purchase a Kavirondo girl whom he wished to marry. I told him he could not do the journey by himself as it was not safe but that he could come down with the company next week, when I intended to go there myself. He was apparently in too great a hurry, broke out of barracks and went down by himself with his rifle and 10 rounds of ammunition. While making his way down the narrow path on the escarpment he was waylaid and murdered by Nandi, his rifle and ammunition being stolen.

As Bagge was coming up here yesterday from Kisumu I went out to meet him with my company to see that he was not attacked. On my way down the hill I found considerable bodies of armed natives in the neighbourhood, so I halted the company and tried to get them to talk. Negotiations were commenced across a gully, but they soon assumed the nature of a brawl. To put an end to this I abruptly asked them whether they would like to fight it out then and there, to which they said they did not wish to fight. However, I took the precaution of mounting the machine gun. We were 87 rifles and they were some 300 spearmen. So I told them to disperse in 10 minutes or I should open fire. At the end of 10 minutes they had gone, so I resumed my journey down the escarpment. On approaching a part of the road which passes through dense bush, my advance guard reported an ambush in the bushes on either side of the road. I again halted and expostulated. I refrained from firing, as it would have brought on a general rising at a moment of considerable embarrassment to the Government and I doubt if I could have extricated the company without the risk of serious losses. On the other hand, I had a tempting target for my machine gun and would most certainly have taught them a lesson. As it was, seeing they were discovered, they got up from the bushes and slunk away, shouting rude threats to me and my men. When the coast was clear I continued the journey and reported the whole episode by wire to Nairobi.

An abortive ambush

Leveson Gower arrived here today with No. 7 company, which I used to have at Fort Hall and Nyeri. My present company, No. 10, goes back to Nairobi to be disbanded. These are Manning's orders, but when they see No. 10 in Nairobi they will realise that its state is as good as or better than most of the others. I flatter myself that I have improved it both in discipline and in musketry. I have written down pointing this out and asking that disbandment be cancelled. After all the trouble I have taken it seems a pity to carry it out. If I were allowed to keep them for another 3 months I would guarantee they could hold their own with any other company in the

My company go to Nairobi and I take over No. 7

battalion. [Manning was Inspector-General of the King's African Rifles. The company was not disbanded and later did well on the Nandi Expedition.]

20 . VII . 1905. *Nandi Boma*

The Commissioner meets the Nandi chiefs and tries to settle the trouble

Yesterday the Commissioner came to Muhoroni as the result of my man being murdered. All the chiefs were called to the conference, but the Head Laibon refused to come, pleading illness. The murderer's name was divulged and the stolen rifle restored. The reason for the murder was given as follows by the man's relations:

The culprit had been making love to a young Nandi girl and eventually quarrelled with her and beat her. The girl's mother remonstrated with the young man, which so annoyed him that he needs must relieve his feelings by killing someone. He therefore lay by the escarpment path, and my man, being the first to come along, was speared. The story is a lie, as there was a party of over 20 men present when my man was murdered; the deed was done for political reasons, and incidentally to get the rifle.

At the meeting with the Commissioner the Nandi were warned that if they persisted in their behaviour the Government would be compelled to force them to live further from the railway line, where their lawless habits would be less obnoxious. The chiefs complained that they could not hold back the young hotheads in their tribes who were clamouring for war, also that the Laibon or chief medicine man was preaching war against the Government and teaching his people all sorts of nonsense, persuading them that our bullets turn to water when fired at a Nandi, that we dare not fight them, etc.

The meeting broke up without any satisfactory results. The Commissioner seems to think that a large military expedition will be necessary, and he is probably right. I should dearly like to take on the young men of Nandi and smash them up, as they are becoming too full of themselves, but the old men and the girls who live round me at Nandi are the most charming type of savage I have met and I should be sorry to molest them.

21 . VII . 1905. *Nandi Fort*

Leveson Gower and my old company leave for Nairobi

Leveson Gower with No. 10 Company left here today for Kibigori en route for Nairobi, leaving me with No. 7 Company. They appear to be disorganised and their equipment is filthy. The fact is that they have recently been under so many apathetic officers, such as Cary, Sharpe, etc., so that their condition is not very surprising. I am getting rather tired of knocking into shape material which others have allowed to deteriorate, and find it most heart-breaking work. It is like constantly moving into a house without a garden, making an attractive garden, and then moving on to another house without a garden and doing the same thing.

31 . VII . 1905. *Kibigori*

To Kibigori

I left Nandi Fort at dawn this morning for Kibigori, where I arrived just before noon. On the way down the escarpment I noticed several of those lovely trees—spathodia—in full bloom. Their masses of huge scarlet flowers are most effective. The seeds are large and winged. I collected a large number and shall send them home in the hope that they may be induced to grow. By judicious root pruning they might be kept within the limits of a hot-house.

Spathodia in full bloom

About half-way down the escarpment and right on the path is a magnificent tree with bright yellow flowers instead of the usual flame colour. I always sit under that tree and rest for a few minutes on the way up. I sent seeds of it to the Forest Department, but they are not interested in beautiful trees, only in those which they can cut down for timber—wattle and euphorbia. I have also sent seeds to Uncle Ernie and asked him to give them to Kew.

Maycock and Leveson Gower

At Kibigori I found Maycock and Leveson Gower, both very tired of life and grumbling like bears with sore heads. Neither of them is fit and they both suffer from liver. But what can they expect from the life they lead? They both do themselves too well, retire late to bed and rise late, and never take any exercise. I should soon be ill if I followed their example. This Nyando valley is no place to tempt ill-health.

1 . VIII . 1905. *Kisumu*

To Kisumu

The nude Kavirondo

I spent the morning trying to get some photographs of the Kavirondo. Though stark naked they are not a bit bashful, but are rather nervous of the camera, which they regard as an "evil eye." They cannot take their eyes off the lens. The Kavirondo are all inveterate smokers of tobacco, which they grow themselves. Their pipes, which are made of a black earthenware, usually polished and ornamented, have iron stems and must be most uncomfortable. I tried their tobacco, which I found unpalatable. Both men and women smoke, and the pipe and tobacco pouch are sometimes the only articles of apparel.

I discuss with Bagge the merits of an expedition against the Nandi

In the afternoon I got into Kisumu by train. Bagge met me at the station. I am stopping with Dr. F. L. Henderson. I dined with Bagge this evening and we had a long talk about the Nandi situation and the advisability of an expedition. Personally I doubt if we have exhausted our last resources in negotiation and told Bagge that I thought our political officers might still stave off an expensive expedition if they had their heart in it. I know most of the soldiers are moving heaven and earth for an expedition, as it will mean a medal, and I fear that the political side are not doing their best to avert it. I like the Nandi and shall be sorry if they are beaten up for the sins of a few hotheads.

2 . VIII . 1905. *Kisumu*

Bagge gives me his views on the Nandi situation

I took a long walk with Bagge this morning and he told me he had been thinking a lot over what I said last night. His views were as follows:

The very name Nandi stinks in his nostrils. The constant trouble they have given him has taken up all his time and has prevented him from paying much attention to the Kavirondo, who comprise by far the larger part of his province. Scarcely a week passes without some complaint against the Nandi. They are like a troublesome schoolboy, and must be whipped. The Government's inaction is interpreted by them as a weakness, of which they are only too quick to take advantage. Other natives

Kavirondo group at Kibigori

A Kavirondo woman at Kibigori

are also attributing our inaction to fear and have been asking why we continue to tolerate such affronts from the Nandi.

But Bagge is still averse to a large military expedition on account of expense, and because sufficient troops are not yet available. But he realises that delay in punishing the Nandi only aggravates the situation, and that at any moment we may have our hand forced by some extra special stupidity on the part of the Nandi. We both agree that the root of the trouble is the action of the Laibon, who continues preaching the eviction of the Government by force.

The fact is, Bagge cannot make up his mind and hates the idea of an expedition. He regards it as inevitable but prefers to wait until it is forced on him by circumstances. I told him I thought this was a dangerous and weak policy. The Nandi should in my opinion be given a definite ultimatum, setting forth their past offences, and calling on them to stop these by a certain date, and give guarantees in the shape of some 500 head of cattle for their good behaviour for a year. The Laibon should at the same time be compelled to come in and be given a good talking to by the Commissioner. Any hesitation on his part should be met by his instant arrest. That is a job I would esaily undertake with success. But I suspect the Administration are afraid of his power and the consequences of his arrest.

He is the spiritual head of the Nandi, or supreme witch doctor, but he is rapidly assuming political power and becoming a dictator in the worst sense, for he will weld the Nandi into a formidable fighting force which in a few years might challenge our position in East Africa and constitute a deplorable example to other tribes.

Kisumu

Kisumu has grown considerably since I was last here. A large market has been built by a trader called Clarke, new Government offices have been built, and houses of all descriptions are springing up.

Game census

I went along the south coast of the gulf for 4 miles this afternoon. I counted 7 schools of hippo, numbering 39 beasts in all, and 105 crocodiles slithering off the bank into the water. Quite close to the houses in Kisumu is a large herd of impala, very tame and unmolested. Bagge is trying to encourage them and allows no shooting. Splendid!

This evening I again dined with Bagge. Church of the Railways, Judge Hamilton, Barth and Morrison, Henderson of the Medical Department, Hickie of the Treasury and Sidney Couper were also present. We had a first-rate dinner and played bridge afterwards.

3 . VIII . 1905. *Kisumu*

Dry dock at Kisumu

This morning Bagge took me down to inspect the new dry dock, which is nearing completion. Port Florence is rapidly developing into a port of some consqueence, having wharves in the making and a small lighthouse.

Hippopotami

Early this morning from the veranda of Henderson's house I watched a school of hippopotami disporting themselves in the Victoria Nyanza only some 600 yards distant. It was a delightfully clear morning and the view across the waters was most pleasing. At night these hippo come ashore and raid the vegetable gardens, doing great damage if they are not scared off by natives.

4 . VIII . 1905. *Kibigori*

The S.S. "Sybil"

McClure

I was down at the pier early this morning to see the *Sybil* come in from Entebbe. In the afternoon I returned to Kibigori, where I met McClure on his way through to Kisumu. Near Kibos I saw a herd of topi and some impala.

5 . VIII . 1905. *Kibigori*

I try to get porters

I spent the day trying to get porters, as I have to transport some 200 loads of food to Nandi. I did not succeed in getting one single man.

I found Maycock still grumbling and growling. I must admit that Kibigori is no place for an inveterate grumbler. There is nothing to do, the climate is hot, damp and fever-stricken, flies pester one all day and mosquitoes all night, and one never sees a fellow creature except on the passing trains. The naked Kavirondo are the only bright spot.

F. W. Isaac. Maj. Pope Hennessey. Col. Gorges at Nandi. Sept. 1905

The Government Interpreter at Nandi. He was an agent of the Laibon and was shot when the latter was killed

6 . VIII . 1905. *Nandi Fort*

Return to Nandi

Having got what porters I required overnight, I left Kibigori early this morning with a strong escort. Those rascally Nandi again tried to catch me. Their ambush was badly placed and ill concealed. My men noticed two spearheads sticking up out of the grass, and, halting, drew my attention to them when they were not more than 80 yards distant. I put a bullet over their heads, at which some 30 men jumped up and bolted, but, unfortunately for them, one or two of them could not resist the temptation of firing a few arrows at us. I at once told my men to open fire, which they did, and successfully dropped two of the rascals, one being killed outright and the other being hit in the shoulder, though merely a flesh wound. I am taking this rascal along with me and shall hand him over to the Civil when he recovers.

It is too childish to see the way the Nandi try to catch me. I could tell them a much better way which would probably succeed.

My native name

I have two hen ostrich feathers festooned round my pith helmet and find they make splendid camouflage. On this account I understand my native name among the Nandi is *Kipkororor* (meaning "ostrich feather").

The native station master and the lion

I heard an amusing yarn at Kisumu about an Indian stationmaster at a station on the Kapiti Plains below Nairobi. Apparently every night lion used to come and roar around the station, which somewhat unnerved him, and he at last persuaded the traffic manager to give him 3 policemen with rifles, who were told to scare the lion away by rifle fire. The policemen arrived and the following evening the traffic manager received the telegraphic message: "Now in the time of roaring soldiers not so brave." The policemen disliked lion as much as did the stationmaster and had flatly refused to move from the station as soon as the lion appeared.

12 . VIII . 1905. *Nandi Fort*

Hooliganism

These last three nights stones, rungus and arrows have been aimed at my house, which has necessitated boarding up my windows. Moreover, these missiles make a great noise on my tin roof. So last night I got 10 of my men and we lay in wait for the young hooligans; we caught 5 boys and one girl, all red-handed. I locked them up in the guard room and gave them bananas and a blanket each. I had them up this morning, marched in before me under escort. They were shaking with fright, thinking they would be killed. As I suspected, they had been told to do it by agents of Koitalel. I got my colour-sergeant to give each boy 7 hard smacks on the bottom, while I made the girl dig in my garden the whole of today. The boys had to carry water to my garden. This evening I dismissed them all with a rupee each and then they smiled. I warned them that any more stone or arrow shooting at my house would be met by rifle fire.

13 . VIII . 1905. *Nandi Fort*

An ultimatum to the Nandi

The Commissioner has now issued an ultimatum to the Nandi and their Laibon. He imposes on them a fine of 300 head of cattle which are to be delivered up within 3 weeks. In default they are threatened with a military expedition to punish them for their past sins. I am convinced that the Nandi will roar with laughter at such a proposal now that matters have been allowed to go so far. I am sorry for them, as they are going to suffer serious loss with a military expedition touring their country.

2 . IX . 1905. *Nandi Fort*

Verreaux's eagle takes a young pig

About 4 miles from here is a huge rock on which Verreaux's eagles often sit; they also use the rock for feeding. I often walk out and watch them. Yesterday morning as I watched, a sounder of warthog passed by at about 400 yards, the old sow and 6 porkers. The sow entered an ant-bear hole while the little fellows played about outside. The eagle watched them intensely, bobbing her head up and down, and finally launched herself in a rapid and magnificent swoop; with flexed wings and without apparently checking her speed she landed with terrific force on one of the little pigs. The rest scuttled back into the hole in such haste that there was a traffic jam at the entrance to the hole. The eagle sat for about a minute on the pig, which did not appear to have struggled at all, and then flew back to her rock without effort. The other eagle soon arrived and both birds fed together. Later on I visited the rock and examined the remains of the little pig. The eagle's talons had pierced the spine in two places and the neck was lacerated. I also waited outside the ant-bear's hole and finally shot a little pig which should be excellent eating. It weighed 8 lb.

4 . IX . 1905. *Nandi Fort*

Preparations for the Nandi Expedition

Last Saturday Col. Gorges and Major Pope Hennessey came up here from Nairobi to make preliminary arrangements for an expedition which seems inevitable, as the Nandi show no signs of paying the fine or of repenting their misdeeds. Gorges and Pope Hennessey left here for Kibigori today. The Commissioner, Sir Donald Stewart, is still not satisfied that an expedition will be necessary, but expense will soon force his hand, as in addition to my company, which is the normal garrison of Nandi, there are 4 other companies doing patrol and escort work in the district and the situation is intolerable. The Nandi are now completely out of hand, and the longer the expedition is delayed the more prolonged and expensive will it be. It looks as though the Commissioner will wait until there is a small massacre or some regrettable incident before he acts, and he will then be forced to fight at a moment which might be extremely inconvenient. Meanwhile the military situation in Nandi is expensive, exhausting and demoralising to us all. I do wish they would let Gorges and me talk to the Laibon.

10 . IX . 1905. *Nandi Fort*

Weak Government policy on the Nandi question

The situation has not improved these last few days, though actual acts of violence on the part of the Nandi have temporarily abated owing to the presence of so many troops in the district. But this temporary remedy is in fact but an irritant. The question is most serious, for if troops were now withdrawn the Nandi would be up and active at once, destroying all communications and necessitating our withdrawal or an expedition.

In my opinion the wisdom of bringing two companies to Muhoroni is doubtful, as it commits the Government to some form of action, which is apparently not their policy. It is a pity that the Government policy of humouring the Nandi and of peace at any price is so inconsistent with their actions, which are more likely to bring about collisions than bring success to their policy.

If the Government really cannot face an expedition they should send Mayes back here and give him a free hand in raiding and murder. The proof of the cake is in its eating, and certainly Mayes kept the Nandi quiet but at a price which we could never afford to pay. I for one should refuse to remain in Nandi for a moment if Mayes were sent back, as I could never agree to his demoralising and cruel methods of administration. And, moreover, such a drastic remedy would be but a half-measure, as in the end an expedition would be necessary. The Nandi would at first be cowed through fear, but this would soon be replaced by sulkiness, exasperation, hatred, treachery and revenge. At present the Nandi are free from these vices, and their only fault is a great desire to fight someone and let out some of the pent-up spirit of adventure. A small well-organised force could now successfully compete with the trouble, and neither side need suffer too much. If the expedition is delayed, it may mean a war of hatred and extermination in which both sides would suffer severely but in which we would eventually prevail. And I should indeed be sorry to see the Nandi decimated by war and their gorgeous country despoiled.

I am told that the Commissioner is determined that there shall be no expedition. Why then does he act in the one way which makes such an expedition inevitable? I do not understand his attitude. Meanwhile I have organised an intelligence system and collected all information which might be useful to an expedition.

A slight accident on the rifle range

I had a bit of a fright today while I was putting my men through musketry. The danger flag went up at the butts, so I sounded the cease-fire and the markers shouted out that a man had been killed by a bullet. I at once went down the range to the butts, expecting to find a corpse, but instead I found one of my men hopping about like an active monkey, holding his stomach with both hands and shouting out that he was a dead man. I seized hold of him and threw him to the ground, when my men helped to strip him. I found that a bullet had hit the edge of the iron target and that a small splinter of the target had hit the man in the stomach but had not penetrated. After administering a severe reprimand I made him continue his work and raised a small banquette to prevent any further accidents.

14 . IX . 1905. *Nandi Fort*

Patrol work

As the Nandi–Kibigori road is no longer safe without a strong escort I patrol it with my company every Thursday to receive mails and food, and close it to all traffic on other days. Cuffe of the Marines, who has recently joined the K.A.R., has a detachment at the base of the escarpment and meets me half-way. Isaac, who is going to Kisumu today, accompanied me.

15 . IX . 1905. *Nandi Fort*

Moral and physical depression

The feeling of slowly becoming a prey to one's own mind has taken possession of me, and I have been experiencing much difficulty in constantly finding some distracting work. In daylight I can usually find sufficient to occupy my mind, but in the evenings time hangs heavily on my hands, and except when I write or endeavour to use my paint box, needs must I brood and worry over things which will not leave my mind. I think it is a family fault inherited from the Potters. But climatic influences have a good deal to do with mental depression and tend to accentuate any feelings of morbid dissatisfaction with life in general. I have been trying to analyse my mind and find that what worries me most is disappointment and bitterness that my own family seems to regard me as a black sheep.

Local conditions in Nandi only accentuate these feelings. Living isolated in a savage country, rarely speaking my own language, and surrounded by a population whose civilisation is on a much lower plane than my own are conditions to which I have indeed grown accustomed, but which do not improve on acquaintance unless one lowers one's own plane to that of the savage, when perhaps one might be contented. Isolation from my family, whose formative effect has been considerable on my character, is dreary and might of itself account for unwholesome ideas and gloomy thoughts. I seem to have received a heavy sowing of unhappiness and depression, which seems to thrive in the isolated conditions which I now experience at Nandi.

Effect of climate and surroundings on mental efficiency

Normally I am healthy-minded, but the worries and conditions of the past few months have been too much for me. All men are not affected in the same way. Others with greater strength of character than myself might suffer little from moral and intellectual starvation. To others, natural history or some object of unceasing pursuit is an effective barrier against complete isolation. But my experience shows me that it is but a small percentage of white men whose characters do not in one way or another undergo a subtle process of deterioration when they are compelled to live for any length of time among savage races and under such conditions as exist in tropical climates. It is hard to resist the savagery of Africa when one falls under its spell. One soon reverts to one's ancestral character, both mind and temperament becoming brutalised. I have seen so much of it out here and I have myself felt the magnetic power of the African climate drawing me lower and lower to the level of a savage. This is a condition which is accentuated by worry or mental depression, and which has to be combated with all the force in one's power. My love of home and my family, the dread of being eventually overcome by savage Africa, the horror of losing one's veneer of western civilisation and cutting adrift from all one holds good—these are the forces which help me to fight the temptation to drift down to the temporary luxury of the civilisation of the savage.

The curse of Africa is her climate. As surely as it lowers morale and character in a weak-minded person, so surely must it not be accepted as an excuse for brutality or dishonour. A slight deterioration in mental and moral tone is inevitable to anyone in close grips with savage Africa, but the Government does not help in the least or even consider the dangerous conditions of isolation. Short periods of isolation, good accommodation, and a stricter choice of personnel would go far to ameliorate the evil. An Englishman's character in Africa should be irreproachable. The Government has yearly examples of moral and intellectual death among some of its best servants, but takes no steps to remedy conditions.

Africa's climate is her curse

Such are my ideas, and it does me good to commit them to paper. The process of deterioration is slow and creeps on one like old age. It is only by frequently reviewing my own acts and by recognising the dangerous influences which constantly beset me that I am able to realise in time how far I have sunk and how fast is the process. It enables me once again to set myself up on the pedestal of English tradition before it is too late.

The safety valve of committing one's thoughts to paper

Life in Africa is healthy enough provided one's mind and tastes are healthy. Worry or hard work reduces one's resisting powers. I am always surprised that I keep so fit on the small amount I eat. I often scarcely touch anything for days, until I discover some appetising dish and make a meal off it. It has shown me how little a healthy man really requires, and how considerably we over-eat in England. Society is, of course, conducive to over-eating and over-drinking; at least it is so in my own case. Normally I am a small eater, but in company, especially when congenial I eat more than do most men.

Food and health

But to eat too little is as bad as eating too much, and I am beginning to feel the effect of little and poor food, especially after severe physical exertion. I do not seem to have that reserve of strength which never used to fail me in times gone by. Sometimes after a tiring day I can scarcely force myself to eat. Of course, I realise that better spirits would soon revive my appetite, but for the moment I am steadily using up the reserve strength which is so vital to any man in these wild parts.

17 . IX . 1905. *Nandi Fort*

A day in the Nandi Forest

Today being Sunday, I spent the day in the forest with my gun and butterfly net. The skipper family are the best represented, then come the shade-loving *Ypthima* and *Precis*. The Lycoenidae are poorly represented, not only here but throughout East Africa. There were numbers of large butterflies feeding on the tree-tops, but I was able neither to catch nor to identify them. In the course of my wanderings today I got several nice birds, and I saw a large chestnut-coloured squirrel about the size of a rabbit. He had a grey tail and was most active.

21 . IX . 1905. *Nandi Fort*

I meet Cuffe and Barrett on the escarpment

Today being Thursday I marched down to the escarpment, where I met Cuffe. He was rather late, and when he arrived he was accompanied by Barrett, who commands the Sudanese company. A settler from Lumbwa called Bishop was also with him. I persuaded Barrett to accompany me back to Nandi for a night. Bishop has apparently purchased the pigs and poultry belonging to Garvie. I promised to try to get them for him by next Thursday and bring them down with me.

Peace between Japan and Russia

Barrett brings news of peace between Russia and Japan. It seems that though Japan has been successful throughout the war, she was rapidly approaching exhaustion and was compelled to sign a peace which is out of all proportion to her sacrifices. But she has attained her object and gained Port Arthur, Southern Manchuria, besides destroying Russia as a naval power in the Far East.

Nandi Expedition

It now looks as though there is going to be an expedition against the Nandi. The Commissioner has sent for Bagge and Pope Hennessey to consult with them on the subject.

An orchid growing out of an eagle's nest

While waiting for Cuffe on the escarpment I hunted about for birds and found the nest of a bateleur eagle, off which I flushed the old bird. A large red and white orchid was in full flower and apparently well rooted in the side of the nest. I made a rough sketch of it.

A snake hunt

I also disturbed a snake some 9 feet long which I took to be a rock python from its very beautiful reticulated markings. I could easily have shot him in the body, but as I wanted his skin I tried to locate his head. He eventually got in among some boulders and I lost him, much to my disappointment.

26 . IX . 1905. *Nandi Fort*

I have some 60 porters attached to my company, and in view of the approaching expedition I have been teaching them to shoot. None of them had previously fired a rifle, and their grimaces and gestures were most comical. On the whole they are shooting a great deal better than I expected. They have been using single-loading Martinis. These terrified some of them at the start, but when they found the bullets were actually hitting the object aimed at their delight was immense, and they have become quite keen. To give them confidence I started them off firing at 50 yards at kerosene tins filled with water, which goes up in a spout when hit. They can now all hit a tin at 100 yards when standing, which is a high average for 60 savages. But when it comes to using their rifles in action I am sure they will fire wildly, eager to make as much noise as possible, regardless of hitting anything. This is bound to be, as I cannot spare them any N.C.O.s to control them.

I put my porters through musketry

I heard today that the Commissioner has received permission from home for an expedition against the Nandi and that preparations are to commence forthwith. We start business towards the end of next month. I expect to hear details soon, but I trust the concentration will not take place in full view of the Nandi. If it does, it will lengthen the life and heighten the cost of the expedition. But I fear the importance of striking quickly and silently is not appreciated at Headquarters. During the recent Sotik Expedition the enemy had sufficient warning to enable them to drive the bulk of their stock off before troops even entered their country.

The Commissioner decides on an expedition against the Nandi

I received news today that the Laibon has just convened a large representative meeting of the whole Nandi tribe, at which it was decided that the British Government was afraid of the Nandi, that no expedition would take place, and that therefore the Nandi must renew their aggressive

The Laibon

tactics and drive all Government officials and troops from the district. Uproarious scenes took place, and it was further decided that both Isaac and I must be murdered.

I am threatened with murder

The situation now resolves itself into a personal quarrel between me and the Laibon, and I will bet a small sum that he falls first. I strongly object to anyone wishing to kill me, and they will not do it except in fair fight. I do not know why I should be so honoured by their selection, except that I am considered to be the most dangerous person in the district and therefore the most eligible for murder. When 25,000 people are trying to kill one European in their midst it sounds as though it would be an easy job, but in reality it is going to be difficult. Their methods will be crude and simple, and I do not expect any difficulty in beating them at their own game, but I must not run stupid risks.

My intelligence service

Ever since I came here I have been organising an intelligence service. The men I have employed are taken from a small colony of Uasin Gishu Masai who live not far from my house. They hate the Nandi but can pass to and fro unmolested. I have them scattered about the country, a few living in some capacity with the Laibon and most of the larger chiefs. By this means I hear about everything which is going on in the district. But the Laibon himself has not neglected to play the same game on me, his agent being the official interpreter at the civil lines. This glib-tongued fellow is a member of the Laibon's family and keeps this wicked medicine man supplied with all the latest information about me and our doings in Nandi Fort. I find his presence convenient, as it gives me an excellent means of conveying false information to the Laibon. But before the expedition starts I shall have to put him away somehow.

28 . IX . 1905. *Nandi Fort*

I hear of the Laibon's activities

My intelligence service is working well, most of my men being Masai from the local Mynyatta or young Nandi living near my house whom I feel I can trust. There is no doubt now that I have become the focus of the Laibon's hatred and that he is anxious to meet me, lay an ambush and kill me. His name is Koitalel and he is a man of about 40 or so. He has told his warriors that the white man's bullets will be quite harmless if only he can get bits of my anatomy for his medicine, especially my brains, heart, liver, palms of the hands and eyes. He would mix all these with certain plants, bring the whole to a boil, and sprinkle his warriors with the broth; then nothing would harm them. He is going to pose as a peace-maker, entice me out to an ambush and secure the necessary parts of my anatomy. As he shakes hands with me, he will pull me over towards him and a man near him will spear me. He will have many warriors in the bush nearby and these will fall on my party and annihilate them. Koitalel's father had apparently, many years ago, brewed a broth which he claimed would turn bullets, but it proved useless and his fighting men killed him. Koitalel has promised that this will not happen again. He is, according to my agents, fearful of assassination by his own people and always has, day and night, an armed guard near him.

Koitalel is a wicked old man and at the root of all our trouble. He is a dictator, and as such must show successes in order to retain power. He is therefore in favour of fighting the British. Many of his hot-heads support him, but the bulk of the Nandi I have met are a peaceful and lovable lot, enjoying jokes. I have many friends among them; they trust me and I trust them. I can, or could until quite recently, walk about their country unarmed; they would not touch me but might not think twice about killing my men, just for fun.

My main reason for trying to kill or capture the Laibon is that, if I remove him, this expedition will not be necessary and the Nandi will be spared all the horrors of military operations. But both the civil and military authorities in Nairobi are intent on a punitive expedition. The military are keen to gain a new glory and a medal and the civil people want the Nandi country for the new proposal of the White Highlands—just brigandage.

I am to be poisoned

One rather amusing story comes from a Masai agent who came to my house after dark. Apparently a very beautiful young virgin is to be sent to me as a present from the Laibon and she carries with her some deadly poison which she will place in my food. Should this young lady arrive she will be searched, and if the poison is found on her she will get 25 of the best on her bottom with my hand.

I go beetle-shooting

I have often noticed in the forest near my house many large beetles flying around the treetops, so this evening I went beetle-shooting with my shotgun, and using dust shot I bagged 5 huge insects, the largest being slightly over 5 inches from front horn to tip of abdomen. I have sent them all to the Natural History Museum.

2 . X . 1905. *Nandi Fort*

The Nandi Expedition takes shape

At last the Nandi Expedition, which has been talked about and threatened for the last 10 years—in fact, ever since Europeans first came to this country—has taken definite shape, and I received mobilisation orders today.

Mobilisation

Col. Harrison commands and Pope Hennessey is his chief staff officer. Four columns are employed, commanded respectively by Col. Gorges of the 1st K.A.R., Hookey Walker of my regiment and the 2nd K.A.R., and Captain Maycock and Barrett, both of the 3rd K.A.R.

I am with Barrett's column, which is styled No. 4, my appointment being staff officer to the column. No. 1 column operates from Ravine Station, No. 2 from Lumbwa Station, No. 3 from Muhoroni and No. 4 from Nandi Fort.

The whole field force is composed of:

540 men 1st King's African Rifles
780 men 3rd King's African Rifles
260 armed police
10 machine guns
2 armoured trains on the Uganda Railway
1000 Masai levies
100 Somali levies
500 armed porters
3460 unarmed porters

The above does not include some 80 British officers, numerous medical personnel, and veterinary and various other non-combatant services.

3 . x . 1905. *Nandi Fort*

The Commissioner dies

News has just come in reporting that Sir Donald Stewart died yesterday. *De mortuis nil nisi bonum.* But I trust his death will be an example to many other good men, who have only themselves to blame for an untimely end. It is a nuisance that the Commissioner should die just at a moment when quick decisions have to be made, but it is not going to interfere with the expedition.

Supply services

I am now busy filling up the station with food, ammunition and stores of all sorts. I am bringing up some 380 loads a day from Kibigori, these being carefully secreted in my lines. In order not to attract too much attention it is all carried by night, and of course a large escort must be found for every party. So far the Nandi are unsuspicious, but the stack of stuff in my lines is growing to such huge proportions that they are bound to suspect something soon.

5 . x . 1905. *Nandi Fort*

Preparing for the Nandi Expedition

The plot rapidly thickens, and preparations for the expedition are being hastened forward. Letters and wires reach me at all hours of the day and night, each marked more urgent than the other. Even the most ordinary routine message is now deeply scored in red ink, with the cryptic words "secret" and "urgent." I believe the telegraph clerks are almost worked off their heads, which is entirely due to the harmful practice of not only sending telegrams of 100 words when 20 would suffice, but of sending a telegram when a letter would have done. The expedition seems to have sent some of our Headquarters officers temporarily off their heads.

As we have not been issued with a cipher or even code, I have been sending my telegrams in French, which seems to be understood. It is as well that a short telegraphic language hides many grammatical errors and lack of accents.

Today I received the "standing orders" of the Nandi Field Force. I am glad to see that in most cases these comprise suggestions. The document is in parts amusing, and whoever compiled it must have a mighty poor opinion of column commanders.

Poisoned arrows and the antidote

Some remarks by the Medical Officer on the subject of poisoned arrow wounds are interesting, but on one point he is not clear. He recommends an injection of strychnine for a wound by a poisoned arrow, But how is one to know whether the arrow was poisoned or not? If the arrow was not poisoned the antidote of strychnine would surely kill the patient. Being killed by a poisoned arrow is all in the day's work, but to be killed by a dose of strychnine is quite another matter. It reminds me of the youngster who some years ago at Mombasa was bitten in the finger by a snake and chopped the finger off, thinking the snake was poisonous; he might as well not have done so, as the snake proved to be harmless.

8 . x . 1905. *Nandi Fort*

Martial law having been proclaimed in Nandi, quite illegally, I have sent all the three traders down to Kibigori, their presence here being a source of embarrassment to me. Some of them—they were all Indians—being reluctant to obey my orders, I had to resort to gentle methods of persuasion. I also sent an order to the two Boers insisting that they come into Nandi Fort with all their stock and belongings. They have 47 head of cattle but their personal belongings amount to nothing, and they have no women or children with them.

Capt. McLeod

A fellow called McLeod arrived here today to be attached to my company. He belongs to the 1st K.A.R. and recently received his commission through the ranks. He is a typical sergeant-major and I do not much like the look of the fellow, but he may turn out all right. Isaac dined with us tonight and we broached a bottle of champagne to the success of the Nandi Field Force.

9 . x . 1905. *Kibigori*

To Kibigori to see Col. Harrison and Capt. Barrett

As Col. Harrison wishes to see me about the coming expedition I came down today to Kibigori. I am stopping with Barrett, who is at Mark's Boma with his Sudanese company. Lieut. S. S. Butler of the Warwicks has just joined the K.A.R. and is attached to our column. I like the look of him. He seems keen and the right sort. His home is at Hambledon, so we had a good deal in common. [A distinguished officer who reached the rank of Major-General. I saw a good deal of him at G.H.Q. France at the end of the First World War.]

Isaac came down with me, as he must join No. 1 column, which operates from the Ravine. I am told that Mayes has been appointed political officer to Maycock's column, which operates from Muhoroni. I should have thought that Mayes' record in Nandi would have prevented this; Isaac is furious and thinks he will make trouble; it will certainly do no good.

10 . x . 1905. *Lumbwa*

I divulge a plan to kill or capture the Laibon

I came into Kibigori early today and met Harrison and Pope Hennessey. I travelled with them to Lumbwa and settled many details. I told them of a plan I had in my mind to try to kill or capture the Laibon on the first day of operations. I am convinced that if we can remove this gentleman and break up his headquarters at the start we shall have an easier nut to crack during the operations. They eventually agreed that it was a good plan and allowed me to proceed with it, promising to consider it fully and wire me their assent when they reached Nairobi. I have begged them to give me a free hand as regards the detail.

McClure, Walker and officers of the 1st K.A.R.

McClure was on my train and got out with me at Lumbwa. Here I met Hookey Walker of my regiment who commands the 1st K.A.R., also Capt. J. Rosborough and R. S. Hart of the Sherwood Foresters.

11 . x . 1905. *Kibigori*

To Kibigori

I returned to Kibigori today in drenching rain. At Muhoroni I met Cuffe, Wilson and R. P. Lewis of the Devons, who is Brigade Signaller. I am stopping this evening with Barrett at Mark's Boma at the foot of the escarpment. Between Kibigori and Mark's Boma I saw a small sounder of pig.

Discipline in Barrett's Sudanese company

While Barrett's company was standing at Kibigori Station today a Somali trader, who knew the men well, shook hands with several of them. The men were standing easy at the time, but Barrett told them not to shake hands when in the ranks. But a man in the rear rank, who may or may not have heard Barrett, shook hands with the Somali. Barrett took his name and later punished him with 25 lashes and 42 days' imprisonment for refusing to obey an order. The man pleaded that he never heard the order, which is quite possible, as there was naturally a certain amount of noise on the platform when the train came in. It is also in the man's favour that being a Sudanese, whose natural tongue is Arabic, he would not understand Barrett's very bad Swahili. The man was flogged on arrival at Mark's Boma and Barrett ordered that his term of imprisonment should be done in Nairobi. Nevertheless he was allowed to remain in a grass hut by himself, where he seized a bayonet and threatened to kill himself or any person who came near him. As none of the company volunteered to go in and bring him out, Barrett himself pluckily went in and remonstrated with him. After three-quarters of an hour the man was induced to give up the bayonet. He was again left to himself but soon managed to get his rifle, and marching out of the camp again announced his intention of shooting himself. Barrett again went after him, argued with him and eventually remitted the imprisonment, ending up by shaking hands with the man.

Such methods of maintaining discipline are open to grave criticism. In the first place the punishment was grossly unjust and unnecessarily severe. But once having given it, and the man having committed a further and graver offence, the punishment should have been carried out. There was no excuse for the fact that the man was not confined to the guard tent from the moment the punishment was given. Again, after 4 years with a Sudanese company Barrett should be able to talk to his men in Arabic.

I am not surprised that this company behaved so badly on the Sotik Expedition. I trust it will not let us down on the Nandi Expedition.

12 . x . 1905. *Nandi Fort*

The Nandi still unsuspicious

I returned to Nandi today and find through my agents that the Nandi are still unsuspicious of the blow which will shortly fall on them. When I left Nandi for Kibigori the other day they were a bit restless and showed signs of breaking into open hostilities almost at once. They appear to hold me solely responsible for any evil which may befall them, and apparently they think I am safer in Nandi, where I can be watched, than away, where I might be planning their destruction.

Meanwhile I hear that the Laibon has given out that he has killed the Commissioner by his medicine, and this is implicitly believed by the tribe.

The Laibon

Today I received a wire in French from Pope Hennessey which allows me to try to kill or capture the Laibon on the 19th instant. So like Pope Hennessey: "if I am sure of my plans," thereby shifting the responsibility from him to me, so that if anything goes wrong he can blame me. My men are quite good enough for me and I shall certainly not ask Barrett for any of his ill-disciplined Sudanese. My plans for this coup are well advanced. My spies tell me that he is now living about 9 miles from here at a place called Kaidparak, and if the old gentleman only remains there a few more days I shall most certainly bag him. I am receiving all the latest information about his movements, his daily habits and his bodyguard, which is said to consist of some 300 trusty spearmen.

I receive permission to try to remove the Laibon

The wire reads: "Si vous est sure de vos renseignments et du fait que votre attantat n'empecherat pas la quatrieme colonne de marcher vers son but le matin du vingt premier vous avez permission d'essayer d'attrapes le veillard le dixneuf avec un detachment stop le detachment pur ce service speciale comptera au moins quatre vingt hommes bien choisis sous votre commandement stop demandez au capitaine Barrett de vous preter des hommes fermes."

I still possess this remarkable document and its abominable French. The Goanese telegraphist who brought me the message was smiling all over. I asked him what it was that amused him. He said, "French is my native language and of course I understand this message, which can only refer to the Nandi Laibon." I said, "All right, my friend, if you divulge the contents of this message to anyone I shall convene a field general court-martial, of which I shall be president and court. You will be convicted of treachery and sentenced to be shot, and I shall shoot you with my own hands." He smiled and said he understood.

The Nandi desire my head

I heard today that the head of my man who was murdered some months ago adorns a stake outside the Laibon's hut; dances are held round it amid great rejoicings, and there is going to be a huge orgy when my head rests by its side. I have at any rate the satisfaction of knowing that my head will be an object of amusement and interest to the Nandi and that it will be the centre of a native orgy if I fall into their hands. Worse things might happen to one's skull.

A damsel sent me with poison on her

My agents told me some time back that the Laibon was sending me a young damsel as a peace offering but that her real motive was to poison me. The poor girl arrived this evening, very bashful, very young and quite attractive. She had nothing on except a small leather flap in front and behind to cover her private parts. I told my boy to strip her, and sure enough behind the rear piece of leather was a small packet of dark powder. I submitted it to one of my Masai agents and he pronounced poison; then the poor child broke down, fell flat on the ground, seized my feet and howled for mercy. I had not the heart to punish her, so sent her back with a message to the Laibon recommending him to take the stuff himself.

15 . x . 1905. *Nandi Fort*

The Laibon

I received news today, together with quite an accurate plan of the Laibon's village. It consists of 20 huts, and he sleeps in a different one every night in case the place is raided. The roads approaching his village are closely guarded by his men, and it seems that surprise would be out of the question. But he is apparently considering the plan of inviting me out to meet him, ostensibly to repent on the eve of the expedition, which he now suspects, and to ambush and destroy me and my party. Forewarned is forearmed and I should most certainly accept such an invitation, as it would give me the chance I seek.

The wicked old gentleman has just sent a deputation of warriors to the Lumbwa asking their assistance in case of

Scraggie, Baggie and Maggy, the three Nandi sisters whose father brought them to me, asking me to look after them during the expedition

Masai method of attacking in the open, reminiscent of the Roman testudo

attack, but I understand the Lumbwa have refused to become embroiled.

I have now established visual communication both by lamp and by heliograph with Muhoroni, which is roughly 20 miles distant.

Communication with Muhoroni

16 . X . 1905. *Nandi Fort*

Lieut. R. P. Lewis of the Devons, who is Brigade Signalling Officer, arrived here yesterday. He was up at Oxford with Dan and Bernard Drake and knows Hornby and Phillips. On his way up the escarpment he had rather a fright, several small bodies of Nandi threatening to attack him. But he drank half a gallon of fresh milk on his arrival at my house, which restored him to his usual self. He returned to Kibigori today.

R. P. Lewis

As I received instruction some time back that my porters were to be trained in the use of rifles, they have been steadily drilled for the last few weeks. Their role is to act as garrison troops for bases and supply depots, and I think they will do this well. I have christened them the "New Army." They are rather an undisciplined rabble, but can shoot quite well and are keen as mustard.

My "New Army"

About a fortnight ago a neighbouring Nandi came to see me to ask a great favour. He is an old friend of mine who lives quite close to my house, and he had been in the habit of supplying me with milk and eggs, and also providing casual labour in my garden. His wife died some time ago, leaving him three girls. These girls have frequently been to my house with eggs, milk and vegetables, and I have often employed them on odd jobs such as bringing water up from my drinking spring. I have thus become rather a friend of theirs. But today their father asked me to look after his daughters as he suspected there was going to be fighting in Nandi, and otherwise they would have to hide in the forest, where they would probably die. Would I, therefore, look after them until the expedition was over? In return they would work for me and do whatever I wished. I agreed to do it and the girls have been working for me ever since, one as my butler, one as my gardener and the other doing odd jobs.

Three Nandi girls left in my charge

The first thing they asked for was clothes but this I refused, and they do their work in their native kit. In order to make sure they do not get into trouble with my men I make them sleep in the house.

Their presence has occasioned some surprise among my numerous visitors, and I must admit that to see them at work in the house in their native kit is a bit astonishing. The eldest I have christened Maggie, the second Baggie and the youngest Scraggie. They are cheerful souls and I could not wish for better servants. Maggie is the butler, Baggie the gardener and Scraggie the maid of all work. When I complain to one of them about the plates not being hot or a meal being late, they each blame the other and usually all appear together shouting loudly that it was not their fault. It usually ends in their all receiving a sound smack, when they return cheerfully to work.

When they first arrived I insisted on their having a bath every day, which they do in the stream. The smell of native was more than I could bear in the house, but they are now quite sanitary. Their father paid them a visit today and asked me if they were being well-behaved. He reminded me that beating was the only punishment they understood, but was somewhat surprised when I told him that Europeans did not beat women. He then said that no woman could keep out of mischief if she was not soundly beaten every few days.

18 . x . 1905. *Nandi Fort*

My plan to kill or capture the Laibon

My plans are now complete for the undoing of the Laibon. It has been clear for some time past that to surprise the Laibon in his village was out of the question, as the roads are too well watched; also, he changed his village only two days ago and I could not make certain of locating his new abode. So I thought that if I could arrange an interview with him tomorrow I should then know where to find him the following night. The Laibon had already suggested such a meeting, and I sent him word by the Government interpreter that I should be with him on the morning of the 19th to explain certain matters to him. He jumped at the suggestion but asked me to come with only 5 men. My agents meanwhile confirm me in my suspicion that the interpreter is a spy of the Laibon's, for they have heard him conspiring to destroy us when we meet tomorrow. But native plans often fail, and I expect I shall meet the Laibon tomorrow and capture him the following night. If he attacks me at our meeting I know how to defend myself. However, come what will, I meet him tomorrow, and during the next 24 hours I suspect that either he or I will have said goodbye to this world; I do not really very much care which of us it is.

19 . x . 1905. *Nandi Fort*

The Laibon dies

Only half an hour ago I returned from the scene of my meeting with the Laibon, and both he and his retinue lie dead where we met. We left Nandi at 5 a.m. and have covered 24 miles. The risk and excitement of the whole business have tired me considerably, so I shall only record the main facts, leaving the detail for an official report. I took with me Sammy Butler and 80 men with a machine gun. Leaving Sammy with 75 men and the machine gun, I advanced to meet the Laibon with 5 men. As I suspected, he ambushed me as soon as I shook hands with him; but we were ready, and he, the interpreter and several others, some 23 in all, were left dead. I had my clothes torn by both spear and arrow and one of my men was slightly scratched by a spear. Before going down to meet the Laibon I had warned Butler to open fire at once if he saw us being overwhelmed. He mounted the machine gun and covered the place of meeting. As soon as the affair was over, we trekked for home as fast as our legs would carry us. The swiftness and suddenness of the blow momentarily stunned the Nandi, who had been gathered about in large numbers to see our discomfiture, but when the tables were turned they did nothing. But they soon recovered and were hard at our heels for the last 8 miles of our homeward journey. I was really glad to get back again to my little fort, as our ammunition was almost exhausted when we met a welcome patrol which had been sent out on my instructions to cover our retreat.

So may all the King's enemies perish. The Nandi Laibon deserves some obituary notice, as he was a man of some consequence. He was both spiritual and temporal chief of all the Nandi, his office being hereditary. As both he and all his successors male were gathered today, I much regret that the dynasty must stop from today. The only people I am sorry for are his wives, for they most certainly will be buried with him as is the custom. It is their own choice to be interred dead or alive.

I have sent a brief wire to Headquarters announcing my success. The long-expected Nandi Expedition has now commenced, and I am entirely satisfied with the first day of operations.

[I revisited Nandi in 1956 and on returning to my old quarters found them occupied by a local chief called Elijah, a Christian, decked out in immaculate shirt, bow tie and flannel suit. I had known him as a small boy. A few days later I was asked to be present at a parish council at Kapsabet, my friend Elijah being chairman. There were some 25 Africans present, all immaculately dressed in European clothes. I was introduced to each in turn with some appropriate remark:

"This is the gentleman whose house I now live in."

"This is the gentleman who lived in Nandi before you were born."

"This is the gentleman who knew Bwana Mayes."

"This is the gentleman known as Kipkororor."

When we arrived at the final chief, a young and extremely good-looking young man, Elijah to my horror said: "This is the gentleman who shot your grandfather."

This was greeted with much clapping. Not knowing what to say, I muttered, "I hope you will forgive an act of war," at which there was renewed applause.]

20 . x . 1905. *Nandi Fort*

My official report on the death of the Laibon

I have today addressed the following official report to Col. Harrison regarding the events of yesterday. The whole episode has been considered in quite a different light from what I had expected, for I have already had wires of congratulation from Frederick Jackson, the acting Commissioner, Col. Harrison, Hookey Walker and several others. Barrett, MacLeod and Butler have also sent in a strong recommendation that I be awarded the Victoria Cross. This is the limit, and is making too much of so small an affair.

I am recommended for the V.C.

Acting under instructions from the Chief Staff Officer contained in his cipher wire of the 11th instant authorising me to attempt the seizure of the Laibon on the 19th instant, I have the honour to report that yesterday a patrol under my command came into collision with a party of the enemy with whom was the Laibon and his family, and both he and his suite were killed.

The report

The following is the detail of this affair.

On the evening of the 18th instant in order that my intentions should not be divulged, I ordered a simple route march for the following morning of the following forces:

Capt. Meinertzhagen and Lieut. Butler.
80 rifles and a machine gun.

The column was to fall in at 5 a.m. on the 19th and it was my intention to march direct for Kaidparak Hill, where it had been arranged that the Laibon would meet me.

My original plan for the capture of the Laibon was to make a night march to his village and arrest him by dark in his hut. My information showed that not only were the roads approaching his village carefully guarded day and night, but he never slept in the same hut two nights running, and indeed he recently changed his village from one I knew to one I did not know. This plan had to be abandoned, as its chances of success were remote.

The plan I adopted was as follows. I had been informed that the Laibon intended to invite me to a meeting where I and my party were to be destroyed. As no definite invitation arrived and as time was getting short I let the Laibon know that I was anxious to see him on the 19th. I thought thereby to get sufficient knowledge of the location of his village to enable me to arrest him the following night. The Laibon agreed to the meeting, stipulating that I must only be accompanied by 5 men.

At the same time my intelligence agents warned me that the Laibon intended to make an attempt on my life at the meeting and that he would have a considerable body of men around him in hiding, though he too had promised to come to the meeting with but 5 men. I also learned at the same time that the Government interpreter at Nandi was acting clandestinely for the Laibon and was himself to strike the first blow. I employed this spy as my go-between throughout my negotiations with the Laibon.

I had no qualms about walking into a trap as I had little confidence in such plans being successful when carried out by natives. And if they did attack me I was confident that, being forewarned, I should not come away without having accounted for the Laibon. It was, therefore, an opportunity not to be missed, for I should either gain the knowledge I required or I should achieve my object by killing the Laibon if he molested me.

The Government interpreter, who was employed by me on the 17th in taking the final message to the Laibon, was ordered to return to Nandi on the 18th in order to act as guide to Kaidparak Hill. This he did not do, but I only met him again on the morning of the 19th when I was close to Kaidparak. At the same time one of my Masai agents informed me that the trap to catch me was complete and that the Laibon had some 300 spearmen secreted in the bush near the meeting place.

On the evening of the 18th Lieut. Butler and 40 men of No. 3 Company arrived at Nandi from Kibigori with an order from Capt. Barrett that I was not to make the attempt on the Laibon unless I thought success assured. In view of my instructions from Headquarters I disregarded this order.

(Really, this shifting of responsibility is shocking. How can I assure success with a very delicate operation? What Barrett means is that if I fail he, at any rate, is not to blame.)

The column as outlined above left Nandi Fort at 5 a.m. on the 19th, and on approaching Kaidparak we met several of the Laibon's fully armed warriors, who seemed quite friendly. The Government interpreter also joined the column and informed me that the Laibon had now decided that he would come with only 3 armed men and would I do the same. I told him that I could not change my plans and would come with 5 men as arranged. He also asked that my main body should halt on top of Kaidparak Hill. To this I agreed.

We arrived at Kaidparak Hill at 8.47 and I halted on the summit of the hill. I sent the interpreter off to find out whether the Laibon had arrived and then explained to Butler and my men the reason of the march and exactly what was to be done under all eventualities. If we were not attacked the column was to await my return, but if we were attacked, the machine gun was at once to try to cover our retreat, while 50 rifles were to double down to our assistance, the remainder of the column covering our eventual retreat. If we were overwhelmed and killed, no attempt was to be made to remove our bodies, but rifles and ammunition must be recovered and Butler would have to extricate the column as best as he could.

While waiting for the interpreter to return Lieut. Butler and I were busy with our glasses and we located considerable numbers of Nandi in the bush on the opposite hillside. At about 10.30 the Laibon was seen approaching with an escort of 22 warriors, which was entirely contrary to our agreement. Our column was meanwhile halted in a hollow and was invisible from down below where the Laibon was, and Lieut. Butler and I were well concealed behind bushes.

It was now abundantly clear to me that the Laibon intended to practise treachery. I had asked that the meeting should take place within full view of my column, but when the interpreter returned it was clear that the meeting would take place in a hollow and out of view of the column, so I ordered Lieut. Butler to move the machine gun and men into a better position as soon as I approached the Laibon or got out of sight.

At 11.15 I left the column accompanied by a native officer, Mbaruk Effendi, Corporal Simba Manyema and 3 men. We approached with rifles at full cock and loaded, also with bayonets fixed. I told my men to fire the moment treachery was apparent, but that I hoped to have a peaceful meeting.

On advancing into full view of the Laibon it was clear that he had some 50 armed men around him. One man standing on the Laibon's right even had an arrow placed in his bow. The bush all round bristled with spears and shields. I halted my small party within four paces of the Laibon and asked him to come forward and shake hands. He replied that the sun was too hot, which, of course, was a ridiculous statement from a native. I also considered it wrong that a white man should have to make advances to a native, so I replied, "Very well, we will conduct our conversation at this distance. Shall we sit down?"

No sooner was this interpreted than the Laibon made a quick sign with his spear and an arrow pierced the sleeve of my shirt. The interpreter wheeled round on me, making as if to strike me with his spear, but was instantly shot by my corporal. I seized the Laibon and dragged him forward, getting scratched by his spear, and an arrow knocked off my helmet. The Laibon wrenched himself free, but by dragging him towards me I had prevented having spears thrown at me, as they would most certainly have hit him. Both I and my party at once opened fire. I am unable to state with certainty what followed. The Laibon was shot simultaneously by myself and my native officer, and several dead were left at the meeting place, including several of the Laibon's near relations. I took 2 stone-headed knobkerries from the Laibon's belt.

Lieut. Butler now joined me with 50 rifles and we soon extricated ourselves and formed up on the Kaidparak Hill. The return journey to Nandi was conducted as rapidly as possible. At 7 miles from Nandi Boma we were compelled to conduct a running fight with small parties of the enemy till we met a patrol from Nandi, whose presence compelled the enemy to withdraw.

So ends my official report.

No. 4 column

No. 4 column is now assembled at Nandi with Barrett in command, the Hon. K. Dundas as Political Officer and Capt. Darley of the Yorkshire Artillery Militia acting as Transport Officer. 240 Masai levies have also arrived from Kibigori. At 5 a.m. tomorrow we start out against the Nandi and I have been mighty busy all day arranging it all.

Young Dundas is a very charming boy but without any experience of Africa or knowledge of his duties.

My agents tell me that the death of the Laibon has completely knocked the stuffing out of the Nandi and has left them without a head. They have lost their organisation and their confidence. From all accounts there will not be much serious resistance now that there is nobody left to control the Nandi. From stinking in the nostrils of the Nandi they now appear to have some respect for us and never dreamed of so sudden and so severe a blow. So on the whole I am feeling rather pleased with myself.

The effect of the Laibon's death on the Nandi

20 . x . 1905. *Nandi Fort*

Information shows that the death of the Laibon has completely disorganised and demoralised the Nandi. The plans they had for hiding their cattle have been abandoned and there is no organising head for resistance. They must all now shift for themselves, which will mean a stampede in every direction. A large mob of cattle appear to be still in the vicinity of Old Nandi Boma and Kongoni Camp. It seems that they are generally disheartened and resistance to our columns will not be great.

Disorganisation caused by the Laibon's death

We completed our arrangements today for the column to start tomorrow in a northerly direction.

21 . x . 1905. *Nandi Expedition*

Our column left Nandi Fort before dawn this morning and met with great success, capturing 1150 head of cattle and about 4000 sheep and goats. A large number of these were captured in open country and entailed but little fighting. Few warriors were encountered during the day and resistance was negligible. Both huts and *shambas* had been hurriedly evacuated without any attempt to remove household property or food.

The column leaves Nandi Fort

We captured some 50 prisoners, who all say that resistance is now futile, since the Laibon is dead, and that the warriors have fled into the forest of Kabwuren, leaving old men and women to look after the stock. This is borne out by the events of today.

22 . x . 1905. *Nandi Expedition*

Captured stock is returned to Nandi

Owing to the large amount of stock captured yesterday, Barrett decided to return it to Nandi Fort under an escort commanded by Butler. If we had taken it on with us it would have paralysed our mobility and we could not have hoped to defend it if attacked in force. From information given by women prisoners yesterday, two raiding parties were sent out today, one in a north-easterly direction and another towards Tobolwa's Stone. The former party started at 5 a.m. and returned at 4 p.m. They found no cattle but brought back a fine flock of some 900 sheep and 17 old men and women. These latter tell me that on the day on which the Laibon was killed large numbers of cattle were driven into the Kabwuren Forest. Neither of the patrols met with any serious resistance, and both reported mobs of cattle having been driven north towards Suringai.

Today we established signalling communication with No. 1 (Col. Gorges') column, which is halted at Kongoni Camp, on the edge of the Mau Forest. Butler should be back late this evening.

23 . x . 1905. *Nandi Expedition*

We cross the Kapte River

Butler returned with the escort before dawn this morning, having made a night march from Nandi Fort. The column moved again at 5.30 a.m. and crossed the Kapte River at 9.30 a.m. At 2 p.m. we camped in Sangalo.

We have conflicting information about the amount of cattle said to have been driven to Seringai. Tracks leading into the Kabwuren Forest are both fresh and numerous, but I think there is still a lot of stock at or near Seringai. Unfortunately we captured no prisoners today, so got little information. But we hear there are several parties of warriors near our camp, and this is borne out by one or two collisions which occurred this afternoon between them and our patrols. The enemy lost two killed and we lost one man slightly wounded.

A night attack

Last night at 9.15 p.m. a considerable body of Nandi warriors crept unobserved to within arrow-shot of our camp and delivered a hail of poisoned arrows for about a minute. The alarm was at once sounded and the camp stood to arms. We blazed away with rifles and machine guns for about two minutes. One of the men at a machine gun was hit and fell over, so I took the gun and was at once hit in the hand by an arrow. When all the excitement was over we found that one porter and 7 goats had been killed, 7 men wounded and most of the porters severely frightened. Over 270 arrows were picked up in camp this morning.

I am slightly wounded

The arrow which hit me went through the fleshy part of my thumb. I quickly fastened my whistle cord round my wrist as a tourniquet to prevent the poison running up my arm. My hand went black in about 10 minutes but has calmed down this morning, though I cannot yet use it.

Strychnine

We had been issued with strychnine for injections if hit by a poisoned arrow. Mine was definitely poisoned, so I gave myself an injection. These arrows are barbed, and if one is hit in the leg or arm one must push it through; if in the neck or body, one must cut it out. Rather painful whichever happens. However, among the 7 wounded men I could only push 3 arrowheads through; the rest I had to cut out. I gave them all an injection of strychnine and two died within an hour, whether of strychnine or arrow poison I shall never know. Dundas was a great help but Barrett and Darley were quite useless, not even offering to help. I think Darley was scared stiff and Barrett utterly apathetic and perhaps suffering from shock at such a sudden onslaught in the dark.

To Sangalo Hill

We left camp at dawn and marched to Sangalo Hill, where we camped in drenching rain at 3.45 p.m. Our progress was slow today owing to the many swollen rivers we had to cross, the slippery paths and the numerous barricades and pits the enemy had constructed to impede our progress.

We now have definite information from prisoners captured today that the bulk of the cattle have gone into

Kabwuren Forest, but that a large lot have gone north to Seringai.

We have not done much in the stock line today but one of our patrols had a pretty little fight in the bush, losing 2 killed and 4 wounded by spears and arrows. The enemy's losses are unknown. One of my corporals came in beaming with delight, having 3 arrows stuck in his helmet.

25 . x . 1905. *Nandi Expedition*

We raid to the north and get into touch with No. 1 column

Information seems to point to large numbers of cattle having been driven towards Kabras. Our patrols to the north got into touch with No. 1 column. We have had no information about any cattle having broken back, and I believe the bulk are in the Kabwuren Forest.

A little fighting

We sent out 3 strong patrols today who all got on to the same lot of cattle, and it was just as well they did so, for they found them being escorted by some 150 warriors. After a short fight they got the cattle and were closely followed on their return journey by the enemy, who had meanwhile been reinforced. They had a running fight back to camp, and when 3 miles from us I sallied out with every man I could collect and we completely routed the enemy, who lost 17 killed in about 15 minutes. We got the cattle into camp just as it was getting dark, and no sooner were they safe behind our barbed wire than a sentry reported natives some 400 yards from camp. Collecting some 80 men I went up against them, and we had a short fight in the failing light. I had two men hit and I do not know what were the enemy's casualties. But they must have been discomfited, as they drew off and never came near the camp again.

Cannibalism

I have a corporal in my company who is a Manyema, and this tribe practise cannibalism in so far as they eat their enemies, thereby gaining the enemy's strength. When this man returned from patrol yesterday he shouldered arms with his left hand level with his belt and to my amazement I saw 5 other black hands stuck in his belt. I asked him the reason and he said they were for his supper, explaining that fingers are the tenderest part of a man. I made him bury the hands and told him I would talk to him today. He obviously did not think he had done anything wrong. I searched the Army Act in vain for any offence of that nature.

This morning I had him up and told him he must not in future mutilitate his enemies. I then asked him about cannibalism; he tells me that fingers are most succulent, adding: "But the best of all is the buttocks of a young girl."

26 . x . 1905. *Nandi Expedition*

A raid towards Kabras

The main column remained in camp today while I went out with a strong patrol towards Kabras at dawn. We must have covered some 28 miles and returned with 48 head of cattle, 460 sheep and goats and 4 men prisoners. Unfortunately one of my men was accidentally killed in the thick bush by our shots. We only came up with the enemy once when passing through thick thorn scrub. They tried to ambush us but failed to get near us. I saw 3 of them drop to my shots. In the scrimmage 4 prisoners escaped, or rather attempted to escape, for they were at once shot down by my men. Altogether I was quite pleased with the shooting and discipline of my men.

The prisoners give me the following information. No cattle have gone to Kabras or into the Kavirondo country. All the enemy's remaining cattle are collected in the Kabwuren Forest not far from Kiptoya Hill. One of the prisoners is a brother of Kabellas, a local chief, and absolutely refused to speak, for which I admire him.

Headquarters are convinced that a lot of cattle have been driven into the Kavirondo country and have ordered us to move there tomorrow. As the only way there is via Seringai, we proceed there tomorrow.

My hand is now much better, though I cannot yet use it comfortably.

27 . x . 1905. *Nandi Expedition*

Move to Seringai

Today the column moved to Seringai, reaching camp at 11.45 a.m. Our two flanking parties captured 406 head of cattle and in the afternoon our patrols caught another 106 head.

Bad weather for visual signalling

Today is the first occasion on which we have been able to use our heliographs. We tried to call up Nandi Fort, Kaidparak Hill and No. 1 column but received no replies.

The enemy appear to have retired into the Kabwuren Forest with their stock, and we shall have a job to come up with them. But they cannot last long in there and will have to come out sooner or later to graze their cattle.

Attitude of the Kavirondo

Headquarters seem obsessed with the idea that the Kavirondo are unfriendly to us; they wish us to enter their country and, if they prove hostile, commence operations against them. I do not believe the Kavirondo are anything but friendly to us, and I am sure Headquarters is solely prompted by a desire to grab their cattle under some pretext or other. So far all information goes to show that the Kavirondo are observing strict neutrality.

Darley sleeps when on night duty

It is a nightly custom that one of us remains up all night in camp to ensure that the sentries do their duty in a proper manner. Darley, who is attached to us for duty, slept last night. I got out of bed at 3 a.m. last night and found him fast asleep. I placed him under close arrest and took the rest of the night watch myself. This morning I reported the matter to Barrett, who released Darley with a warning. I strongly advocated that Darley should be returned to Headquarters under arrest. A private soldier would have been court-martialled and is liable to be shot. Why should an officer escape punishment? I told Darley that if I had been in command of the column he would have been tried for his life. But I fear he is an incorrigible but amusing rogue, though he comes from a distinguished Yorkshire family.

28 . x . 1905. *Nandi Expedition*

The enemy in Kabwuren Forest

I am now convinced that all the remaining enemy stock has been driven into the Kabwuren Forest, and that only small isolated parties remain outside. No resistance was offered today, and no enemy party larger than 12 was encountered. It looks as though they were beat. I further doubt whether any Nandi cattle have entered

One of our Masai warriors with captured stock

Sammy Butler and myself in camp on Nov. 20, 1905

Kavirondo country, all tracks showing a precipitate flight into the forest. Among the stock which our parties caught today are the fine herd belonging to the local chief Kabellas. Most of them were tightly muzzled to prevent them lowing and giving away their position.

29 . X . 1905. *Nandi Expedition*

Camp in Kavirondo country near Tobolwa's Stone

Today the column moved west into Kavirondo country and camped at the bottom of an escarpment due west of Tobolwa's Stone. From the top of the escarpment we had a good view of the Kavirondo country and Mount Elgon, but the strong wind made plane-table work none too easy. Tobolwa's Stone is a huge boulder on the edge of the escarpment and is a fine landmark.

At the base of the escarpment we crossed a stream which only required a few trout and the call of a cock grouse to complete its likeness to many a Scottish burn. The water was nice and brown, obviously having come from some peaty soil. The bed of the stream was a mass of glistening talc and quartz.

The day passed without incident, and we could not find the tracks of any cattle having come this way.

30 . X . 1905. *Nandi Expedition. Kaimosi*

Dundas and I go in advance to Kaimosi

The column moved into Kabras today. They experienced great difficulty with the cattle and sheep, as the Kavirondo were employing every artifice to steal them on the line of march, one of the favourite ones being to drive a small herd of their own across us and just lifting a cow or two during the proceeding.

Dundas and I came straight on to Kaimosi Mission Station to arrange for the camp, food, etc., of the column on arrival. After an arduous march of 37 miles Dundas and I with 30 rifles and 25 Masai reached Kaimosi at 7.30 p.m. As each of us carried a day's food, a rifle and 200 rounds, it was no mean performance. At Kaimosi, which was supposed to be a fortified post on the lines of communication under Lieut. Olivier, we found the whole place asleep, and just walked in through the open door in the barbed wire fence. I did not compliment Olivier on his watchfulness.

Kakamega and Kabras. Lucosi River

We passed through Kabras and Kakamega today, which is inhabited by the Tiriki tribe of the Kavirondo. They were fearfully excited by our sudden appearance in their midst, mainly on account of the truculent attitude of the Masai, who roared with laughter at them. Hundreds of Tiriki assembled on the path to stare and yell at us, and at one time I had to use all the influence I could bring to bear to prevent the Masai teaching the people of Tiriki a little lesson, which would have meant the slaying of some dozen or so of their young men. At one spot there were some 300 fully armed Tiriki across our path, assuming a most threatening attitude in their war-paint. On my advancing against them with my camera they fled, but one young hot-head stupidly fired an arrow at me. I told the Masai to catch him, which they did, and he then received as good a thrashing as my sergeant could administer, in full view of the rest of his people.

We crossed the Lucosi River today by one of the best native suspension bridges I have seen.

31 . x . 1905. *Nandi Expedition. Hamisi's Hill*

To Hamisi's Hill

Dundas and I moved on to Hamisi's Hill, where we have commenced to build the thorn *boma* for the cattle and to store sufficient food for the next phase of operations.

The column is still far behind us in Kakamega. Progress is slow owing to the elaborate precautions which Barrett has had to make to prevent thefts by the Kavirondo.

The Nyangori

The Nyangori who live round Hamisi's Hill are said to have secretly thrown in their lot with the Nandi, and I received evidence today that they are harbouring cattle driven here from the Kabwuren Forest. Several of them put in an appearance in my camp late this evening on the pretext of selling us food, but I have detained them all as spies.

Difficulties of getting food from the Kavirondo

I have been having great difficulty in getting grain, flour, eggs, milk and quail from the local Kavirondo. They have plenty of it, but will not part for fear of incurring the anger of the Nyangori. So this afternoon I seized 5 of their headmen and told them they would stop in my camp until food was brought in. By 9 o'clock this evening I got as much as I wanted, including about 5 gallons of milk, many dozens of eggs and some 100 fat quail. As all this has to be paid for in cash, I have scarce a farthing left. The quail are excellent eating and are all caught locally. The Kavirondo use decoy birds and catch the birds in small cages in the quail runs in the long grass. Each bird is kept in a small cage and they are then strung on long poles in the fields to attract yet more, sometimes as many as 30 cages being on one pole, arranged one above the other.

Quail

1 . XI . 1905. *Nandi Expedition*

The column arrived this afternoon at Hamisi's Hill, having had a hard time since we left them. In spite of their vigilance they lost some 50 cattle stolen by the Kavirondo.

The column arrives at Hamisi's Hill

Dundas left this evening for Kisumu to carry despatches and buy us some small delicacies in the food line. Just at the moment we crave for sweet stuff, especially jam. For the last 5 days we have subsisted on beans and bacon, which is sufficiently nourishing, but too much of it at breakfast, lunch and dinner makes one curse the name of Heinz and all his 57 tinned products.

2 . XI . 1905. *Nandi Expedition. Hamisi's Hill*

It is confirmed that the Nyangori are definitely hostile to us and that they are harbouring lots of Nandi cattle.

Hostile surroundings

Some of my agents brought in rumours of a Nandi concentration near camp, saying that it is their intention to attack us tonight and rescue their cattle, assisted by the Nyangori. If it is true it should be a good fight. We are taking every precaution for the safety of the camp. Our patrols have not seen anything of a formed body of natives, though great excitement prevails in the neighbourhood.

4 . XI . 1905. *Nandi Expedition. Hamisi's Hill*

No attack materialised on the evening of the 2nd.

Yesterday was spent refitting and washing. As no orders have been received regarding the disposal of our vast herds of captured stock, and as it is a source of embarrassment and weakness to us, Barrett has decided to leave it all at Kaimosi Mission, whither we move this evening.

Enemy stock at Tobolwa's Stone

A reliable report that large herds of cattle have recently moved from the Kabwuren Forest north via Tobolwa's Stone is confirmed. They are apparently making for the Nzoia Valley of Mount Elgon.

Enemy observation on our column

Ever since we left Nandi country and entered Kavirondo country we have been closely watched by the enemy. Their agents are everywhere among the Kavirondo, and it now appears that they have an observation station north-east of Kaimosi. With strong glasses we could see numerous small groups of natives sitting on the rocks on the escarpment. Olivier, who is in charge at Kaimosi, noticed the same thing on the day we entered Kavirondo country.

5 . XI . 1905. *Nandi Expedition*

We move north from Kaimosi Mission

The column moved north from Kaimosi today and camped at Kivini, about 12 miles out on the old Uganda or Sclater's Road. Our object is to march right through the heart of the Kabwuren Forest in order to verify our information about stock being collected therein. It is a somewhat risky undertaking, but I think we shall get through all right provided we do not fall into a well-laid ambush.

6 . XI . 1905. *Nandi Expedition. Kabwuren*

We enter the Kabwuren Forest

We made slow progress today along the old Uganda Road, which is now completely overgrown. We met with no serious opposition, though we were sniped by arrows at three points, which was a bit uncomfortable. Nobody was hit. One of the enemy was caught and speared by our advance guard. We pitched camp on the Kesowin River just before dark.

7 . XI . 1905. *Nandi Expedition. Kiptoya Hill*

We join Headquarters and No. 2 Column

We continued our march and emerging from the Kabwuren Forest made for Kiptoya Hill, where we camped alongside Headquarters and No. 2 Column under

Maycock. We saw a good many cattle tracks in the Kabwuren Forest, but they all seemed fairly old. I suspect that most of them have now gone north to the Nzoia River.

I heard today for the first time that somebody is spreading rumours that the methods employed by me which culminated in the death of the Nandi Laibon were of a disgraceful nature. They say that I invited the Laibon to a friendly conference and shot him as he was shaking hands with me, and that afterwards I shot the Government interpreter to keep his mouth shut. Headquarters and my many friends naturally do not believe it. But among the heterogeneous crowd on the expedition there are many who are only too willing to listen to scandals when framed against the "brutal" soldiery. I have asked Headquarters to find out who originated these rumours and to give me an opportunity to challenge them. I suspect my old enemy Mayes, who feels he has a good deal to get back on me. If the rumours persist I shall ask for a military court of enquiry to enable me to clear myself.

Someone is spreading ugly rumours about the way in which the Laibon was killed

The Nandi appear to have had a pretty good dusting during the last three weeks. They have lost some 10,000 head of cattle and about 500 warriors killed, besides some 70,000 sheep and goats. They now profess to be suing for peace at any price. Our only terms to the rascals should be unconditional surrender, with insistence on their moving completely from the neighbourhood of the Uganda Railway. Sufficient stock should be returned to them to enable them to carry on.

End of first phase of the expedition

I am gratified to hear that our column captured more stock than any other. They also incurred more casualties. I put this down to the activity of our patrols. In the whole force the casualties have amounted to 97 killed and wounded.

The first phase of the expedition being now over, columns are being broken up.

Accompanied by Butler, I am to go to the Tinderet country to complete my map of the Nandi country, and we leave for Nandi Fort tomorrow. If the Nandi do not accept unconditional surrender we are to have a huge drive from the railway towards the Uasin Gishu Plateau. In the meanwhile we are still at war with the Nandi, and an effort is to be made to get all chiefs assembled at Muhoroni for a conference as soon as possible.

8 . XI . 1905. *Nandi Fort*

Return to my house at Nandi

I returned to Nandi Fort today with Barrett, Butler and D. Macleod, the latter of the Indian Contingent. On our way in we shot three of the enemy scouts. One of them was hiding by the path in the forest and was killed by our guide within a few feet of me as he jumped up behind a bush with an arrow in his bow. Another was shot as he bolted across a clearing in the forest.

I found my three girl servants delighted to see me. They have lost all trace of their father, who is hiding in the forest. I trust he will come back to them after the expedition, as I do not wish to be saddled with his three daughters for the rest of my life, though they all three have expressed their intention of sticking to me. These three girls have caused considerable amusement among my brother officers, and I am glad to say my motives in looking after them have not been misunderstood. I admit that I run the risk of being misunderstood. Those who know me will understand; I do not value the opinion of those who do not know me.

Unwin

There is a man called Unwin up here, a regular soldier, who has thought fit to suggest that I was keeping these girls for my own purposes. In addition to this he has calmly established himself in my house during my absence, and to add to the insult not only slept in my bed but made immoral advances to my three servants. When I returned today he showed some disinclination to move from my bedroom, so I gave him 10 minutes to clear out of the house or be pushed out. He chose the former, so I have one enemy more.

Unwin is of the type whom I despise. He has sat in Nandi while we have been out under the greatest discomfort, and when ordered out to join a column he went sick. I have absolutely no use for the man.

9 . XI . 1905. *Nandi Fort*

Barrett and Macleod left here for Alagabiet on the Uasin Gishu Plateau, where they are to establish a small post.

11 . XI . 1905. *Kosoigwa Hill, Nandi*

Butler and I set out on a mapping tour

Butler and I set out from Nandi Fort today to map the country round Tinderet. We took two cows with us to supply us with fresh milk, which is a great luxury. We camped at Kosoigwa Hill.

An armistice

Meanwhile we are enjoying an armistice, the terms of which are:

1. All murderers to be given up.
2. All stolen Government and private property to be returned.
3. The Nandi to move into a reserve away from the Uganda Railway within a month from today.

We met several Nandi today, who came up to greet us with smiles on their faces. About 40 warriors appeared in camp this evening and surrendered their weapons.

12 . XI . 1905. *Silie Hill, Nandi*

We meet Withers and Stephens of the 1st K.A.R.

We marched to Silie Hill, where we found a post of the 1st K.A.R. under Capts. Withers and Stephens.

The Nandi seem most friendly but rather sore at having lost so much of their stock. They brought me a lot of presents, which I refused to accept.

A lunar rainbow

I went to the top of Silie Hill after supper. It was full moon at the time with a fairly heavy mist. I witnessed for the first time a lunar rainbow, which was very beautiful though somewhat weird.

13 . XI . 1905. *Ison Point. Nandi*

We move down the escarpment

We descended the Nandi Escarpment today and camped near Ison Point. The actual site of our camp is near a small stream with lots of dwarf doum palms on its banks. It is a most peaceful place and full of charm. I was busy with my plane table all day but spoke to many Nandi, who appeared very subdued and said they were anxious to do anything the Government wished. The rascals!

They will behave themselves only so long as it suits them, and I am convinced that when it comes to moving them into a reserve we shall meet with lots of obstruction.

14 . XI . 1905. *Kabaret Hill, Nandi*

We marched to Kabaret Hill on the western slope of Tinderet. Here we had a gorgeous view right down the Nyando Valley, the Victoria Nyanza showing as a silver streak in the far distance. I was able to do much useful survey work from here, but I noticed that any magnetic instrument was perfectly useless, owing to the amount of ironstone in the neighbourhood.

Snakes

I killed a small snake with legs (a skink?) on the top of Romoru Hill, and a puff adder in camp.

15 . XI . 1905. *Old Soba, Nandi*

To Soba

Today we marched to the now deserted Government Station of Soba, whence we sent a small party into Muhoroni for rations.

We passed a perfect little gem of a waterfall today, festooned with maidenhair fern. We had another gorgeous view right down the Valley of Death, as I call the Nyando valley. We could see the whole length of the railway from Muhoroni to Kisumu.

In the deserted Soba vegetable garden we found masses of ripe tomatoes and canna lilies in full flower. We feasted on the former and Butler decorated our humble table with the latter, which went well with the bunches of maidenhair fern from the waterfall.

16 . XI . 1905. *Soba, Nandi*

Sunset over the Victoria Nyanza

The party which I sent to Muhoroni yesterday for rations returned today.

The evening sun setting over the Victoria Nyanza surpassed itself today. The lake itself is some 2000 feet below us and 30 miles distant. Homa Hill, at the mouth of the Kavirondo Gulf, was lit up by an exquisite pink glare. The flashes of gold and silver light on the lake itself and in the evening sky were beyond description in their excellence.

17 . XI . 1905. *Savoy Valley, Nandi*

We marched round the southern slopes of Tinderet and camped in a valley known to the natives as Savoy, a peculiar name for this part of Africa.

The Savoy valley

I got into heliographic communication this afternoon with Muhoroni, and they tell me that General Manning, the Inspector-General of the K.A.R., is shortly coming up to Nandi.

General Manning is expected in Nandi

Owing to grass fires and a thunderstorm in the Nyando valley we were deprived of our evening sunset.

18 . XI . 1905. *Kamasia, Nandi*

Today we moved in a north-easterly direction and eventually camped at a spot called Kamasia—quite a different place from the Kamasia north of the ravine. The country now becomes more open, with fairly short grass and small clumps of trees dotted about as in an English park. It looks superb grazing country and will soon be overrun by settlers. We also found a spot which I carefully marked on my map, where a blue stone was abundant and which looked uncommonly like the famous Kimberley blue clay in which diamonds are found. Near this spot we found some silica or lead ore, a piece of which I am sending down to Nairobi for assaying together with a parcel of blue clay.

To Kamasia

The country through which we passed today is thinly inhabited, and we scarcely met a soul.

There is a small Nandi village near our camp, and on my arrival here I sent word that all arms were to be brought into my camp. Late in the afternoon the young men of the village duly appeared with numerous spears and arrows. I asked for the village chief and was told that his name was Arabteno and that he was one of the irreconcilable group and refused to give up his arms. He had oppressed the village, preached against the Government and brought untold misery on both men and women. So I sent for him, but he bolted into the bush. The villagers begged me to set fire to his hut and then they would arrest him when he returned and bring him to me. Even his wife implored me to remove him from the

Mr. Arabteno has his hut burned

village. So I went down to the village and was shown children whom he had mutilated and young girls whom he had violated. So I burned his hut and all his goods amid the rejoicings of his people.

Late this evening we heard a disturbance in the village, and thinking the villagers had caught Mr. Arabteno I sent two men down to enquire. Apparently Mr. Arabteno had returned soon after dark and, finding his hut burned down, commenced to beat his wife and children. But a young man just knocked him on the head, and Mr. Arabteno now lies a corpse outside his village. The whole village is now in an uproar of joy at his demise. I presume they had never dared to do it before, but the presence of our camp so close to them had given them courage.

Butler changes his blankets for skin rugs

Butler today exchanged his good English blankets for two smelly monkey-skin rugs. They are certainly warm enough but simply reek of natives. I do not envy him his nights in bed.

19 . XI . 1905. *Segedete Hill, Nandi*

Segedete Hill

We marched east to Segedete Hill and camped at its base. After lunch Butler and I ascended the hill, passing a salt-lick on the way, where we saw a considerable amount of rhinoceros spoor but none of elephant or buffalo. From the top I managed to get some useful observations. On our way down we spied a small herd of Jackson's haartebeeste, which we failed to approach. We are probably the first Europeans to make the ascent of Segedete.

The eastern limit of the Nandi country

Nandi country just about ends here. The occupant of the last hut we saw did a deal with my cook, exchanging two fowls for the cook's loincloth—a filthy old rag. Both parties seemed thoroughly satisfied.

In the evening an enveloping Scotch mist came down on us from the Mau Plateau. A few black duck started to flight down a small stream near camp, which afforded me much pleasure, reminding me of Mottisfont.

20 . XI . 1905. *Saini, Nandi*

Move towards Tinderet

Today we commenced our return march and camped on the edge of the forest at a place called Saini on the south-east slopes of Tinderet. The burned villages marked the track of No. 2 (Walker's) Column during the recent operations.

All the streams we passed today were fringed by a red-leafed shrub and a small flowering bush with white jasmine-like flowers. They both gave off a most pleasant smell not unlike that of the tuberose. *Aromatic shrubs*

Near one stream we passed a salt-lick where the Nandi had placed huge troughs hewn out of massive tree trunks. They were about 2½ feet off the ground, supported on tripods and some 4 feet long. In these troughs salt was placed for cattle and goats. These are the first of their sort I have seen in the Nandi country. *A Nandi salt-lick*

21 . XI . 1905. *Kipyour, Nandi*

Today we marched over Tinderet by the northern track through the forest. The more southern track passses near the gap in the centre of Tinderet (which I have named Walker's Gap, after Major Walker of my regiment, his column having passed through it during the recent operations). No other track passes through Tinderet Forest as far as I can ascertain. *We pass over Tinderet* *Walker's Gap*

Tinderet is a long ridge, entirely forest-clad, and is in reality a projection from the Mau Plateau. There are six peaks to the ridge, the northernmost one being capped by an open space which is called Kaburen. The rest is fairly free of creepers and undergrowth compared with a typical African forest. It is very damp, and maidenhair fern is able to thrive far from water. There are several kinds of rubber vines in the forest, but they are not too common. One of the commonest woods is that from which the Nandi and Wandorobo make their bows. In the forest we saw fresh tracks of leopard and forest pig. This latter beast the Nandi call *tonda*. *Tinderet* *Forest pig*

We debouched from the forest on the western slope of the ridge and camped at a spot called Kipyour.

22 . XI . 1905. *Chabtavatch, Nandi*

Marched west and camped in the valley between Chabtavatch and Kabaret Hill.

Nandi greed for meat

The Nandi, having had most of their stock taken from them, are a bit short of meat. Today I killed some goats for my men and the Nandi gathered round like a flock of vultures, trying to barter flour and sweet potatoes for fids of flesh. I was particularly attracted by an old woman who was ogling my men to let her have meat for nothing. She was entirely unsuccessful, so I presented her with a goat's head, at which she was delighted. Trade was brisk, and a general sense of satisfaction was writ on every countenance.

23 . XI . 1905. *Kibigori River*

Out in the Muhoroni Plain

We marched in a westerly direction and camped in the Muhoroni Plains on the Kibigori River between Jemelil and Songorrh Hills. I shot a buck oribi just before entering camp.

Butler and I go shooting

In the afternoon Butler and I went out to get some meat for the men, as we had seen lots of game tracks near camp. We stalked a reed-buck, which was successfully shot by Butler, but we were not so successful with a large herd of topi and haartebeeste. We had crept up to within about 100 yards of them when an old cow haartebeeste saw us, and off they went as wild as hawks. On our way home we got drenched to the skin in a heavy rainstorm, which has brought on a slight touch of fever for poor Butler.

I ask for a court of enquiry on the death of the Laibon

On returning to camp I found a letter from Pope Hennessey awaiting me which has been following me about since the 18th. He tells me that rumours are still rife concerning the way in which the Laibon met his death, so in order once and for all to clear the air and myself I have asked for a court of enquiry, when the whole matter can be sifted and witnesses called.

24 . XI . 1905. *Nandi*

We ascend the escarpment

Today we ascended the escarpment and camped at the top. Just at the top of the escarpment we found a small fig tree covered with small scarlet figs in clusters of 10 and 20. They proved excellent eating, and we stripped the tree in no time. It rained nearly all day, which made survey work impossible.

25 . XI . 1905. *Koyo Hill, Nandi*

To Koyo Hill

Today we marched in a westerly direction towards Koyo Hill, where we camped near the sacred grove on its summit. This grove is apparently a burial place, so I would not let my men enter it. I entered the grove myself but found little of interest. A large flock of guinea-fowl inhabited it, but they would not leave the trees, and as I did not wish to fire off my gun within the grove we had to do without guinea-fowl for dinner, which was disappointing.

I heliographed into Nandi Fort, telling them that we should be in tomorrow.

28 . XI . 1905. *Nandi Fort*

Return to Nandi

Sending Butler on ahead with the safari, I remained behind to do a little survey work from the top of Koyo. On my way into Nandi Boma I had to wade a river which came over my waist. The water was icy cold, and it was far from pleasant.

Manning

General Manning arrived in Nandi yesterday but left again today for Uganda. I have now completed the survey of all Nandi country east of the Fort, at which I am rather pleased.

1 . XII . 1905. *Nandi Fort*

Court of enquiry on the death of the Laibon

The court of enquiry which I had demanded took place today under the presidency of Col. Gorges. The opinion of the court is as follows and speaks for itself: "The court is of the opinion that the Laibon Koitelal was killed by a native officer of the 3rd King's African Rifles during a fight, which was the result of treacherous conduct on the Laibon's part, at a meeting which had previously been arranged between him and Capt. Meinertzhagen."

I only wish they had allowed natives to give evidence, and I should also have liked to cross-question Mayes in front of the court. The men in my company are furious that any accusations should have been made and more than one of them has asked to be allowed to get even with Mayes.

I am ordered to the Nzoia River

As it is intended to place the Nandi in a reserve astride of the Nzoia River, I have been ordered to proceed there and make a rapid reconnaissance of the river from the Broderick Falls upstream. I start on the day after tomorrow.

2 . XII . 1905. *Nandi Fort*

A dance by my three girls

This evening I entertained Gorges, Hookey Walker and several others to dinner, and afterwards showed them a cabaret, the main feature being a dance by Maggie, Scraggie and Baggie, my three Nandi girls, now fully trained to housework. I got them to dress up as Nandi warriors, complete with spears, bows and arrows, stark naked and painted with white and red colour. They were splendid, and my guests were delighted.

4 . XII . 1905. *Alagabiet Hill, Nandi*

I leave Nandi for Alagabiet

I left Nandi Fort yesterday for this place and camped in Barrett's *boma*. I found Sergeant Milton of the Grenadier Guards in charge. He has recently been sent out to assist in reorganising the Protectorate Police but is attached to the military for the expedition. Yesterday I camped a few miles north of Kabsikak Hill and came on to Alagabiet today. Barrett and Butler also arrived today from Nandi Fort. I spent today building a cairn on Alagabiet Hill, which should come in useful later on for survey work.

5 . XII . 1905. *Surungai, Nandi*

Over Surungai

Today I marched over Surungai. I left Alagabiet at 6 a.m. and camped at 2 p.m., having covered 22 miles. The site of my camp is at the headwaters of the Lol Burgoti stream and overlooking Ketosh. In the stream I saw plenty of land crabs and a few gudgeon-like fish. I found a few Nandi living in the neighbourhood, but they do not seem to undertake any cultivation. From the number of game traps I found I should imagine their main food is game meat. Haartebeeste, oribi and francolin are common. I saw a few hares, one of which my men caught under a rock. It proved excellent eating. I shot a very old female oribi, which had a great deal of white about her face and back, though her general colour was a great deal darker than that of the typical Abyssinian oribi.

6 . XII . 1905. *Nzoia River*

The Broderick Falls on the Nzoia River

I marched down the Lol Burgoti stream to its junction with the Nzoia River at Geribot Hill. I saw and photographed the Broderick Falls, which are in fact a series of cascades and not so fine as I had expected.

I cross the Nzoia

I met two natives of Ketosh, who showed me a ford over the Nzoia River, and I crossed to the right bank. The water was 4 feet deep at the ford, which was 220 feet broad. I pitched camp near the ford and spent the evening measuring the current and depth of the Nzoia. Its average breadth here is 165 feet and its waters travel 3¼ miles per hour.

Absence of game

I saw practically no game; this was easily accounted for by the network of game pits dug in all directions by the people of Ketosh. Some of these lines of pits are several hundred yards long and at right angles to the river. They are so well concealed that I floundered into a pit myself, but escaped with no more than a bruise.

A scarlet ground fruit

I came across a peculiar scarlet ground fruit which my men ate greedily. It comes out of the ground like a fungus and has no leaves. It is of the size and shape of a large fig, smells like an apple and tastes like an unripe orange.

7 . XII . 1905. *Nzoia River*

Hippopotami

I marched up the right bank of the Nzoia, surveying as I went, and finally camped at its junction with the Guasa Masa. I saw a huge crocodile and many hippopotami, one of which I shot at in the river. I hit him through the lungs, which, of course, made him come out on to land to prevent water pouring into his lungs. As he mounted the bank I finished him with a bullet through the brain. On returning to camp I ran into a second hippo wandering about on dry land and in the open about 100 yards from the river. A single shot in the brain killed him. My shot evidently disturbed yet another old hippo who was taking a walk on dry land. He scampered off to the river, passing within a few feet of where I was standing, but I did not molest him. The bush here swarms with hares. It looked most out of place to see them scurrying about among the huge pachyderms. No sooner had I begun to cut these hippo up than crowds of hungry Ketosh arrived, apparently from nowhere, and in an hour's time every vestige of meat and bone was gone.

Hares and hippo

8 . XII . 1905. *Nzoia River*

I follow up the Nzoia River

Today I recrossed to the left bank of the Nzoia, and finding the going very bad along the bank I struck inland with the intention of again making the river higher up, which I did some 5 miles farther on. The river had now changed its character and contained a considerably smaller volume of water, due evidently to some large tributary from Elgon which joins it on its right bank and whose junction with the Nzoia I had missed during my detour. The country also changed to water meadows instead of bush, which was delightful. The waters of the Nzoia are now clear instead of muddy; it is a typical Welsh stream, running over boulders, with nice squashy grassy banks, pools and rapids.

Uganda Cob (Cobus thomasi)

This water meadow land was covered with small herds of the Uganda cob, a delightful antelope, which I at first mistook for impala. The first I saw was resting in the grass. I killed him with one shot and was delighted to find what I had shot. I killed my second one on the opposite bank of the river and in trying to ford across to it was carried off my legs by the current and had to swim. As I had a stick in my left hand and my rifle in my right it was no easy task. The current was so fast and I was being so rapidly taken downstream to some nasty rapids that I decided to drop my rifle. I was on the point of doing so when I was carried past a flat rock in midstream, where I hastily deposited my rifle and then struck out for the opposite bank. My men found a ford lower down and crossed, afterwards helping me to bring the meat into camp. Later on I swam back and recovered my rifle.

In the evening I tried my hand at fishing with a bent pin at the end of some string. I caught three barbel of about 2 lb. each, and one of my men landed 7 similar fish. I tried them for supper this evening, but their bones defeated me.

Fishing

9 . XII . 1905. *Nzoia River*

Today I continued following up the left bank of the Nzoia, meeting large quantities of Uganda cob. Solitary bucks were lying out in the open meadows and were continually jumping up and scampering off as I disturbed them. Two of these I bowled over, also a fine old bush-buck. The latter I came on quite unexpectedly and could see only his head and horns in the long grass. I hit him at the base of the left horn, killing him dead. His horn was blown away and I picked it up some 25 yards from the body. He was a particularly brightly marked buck.

More cob on the Nzoia River

I found a huge crocodile basking in the sun on a small shingle bank. He saw me first and glided into the stream, exposing only his head. I fired and hit him, and though I never recovered him, I have the satisfaction of knowing the brute is dead. These large reptiles are certainly the most evil-looking objects and should be killed without mercy whenever they give a chance. They are so silent and ugly and yet so quick and dangerous. An attractive deep pool may look an ideal spot for bathing, and God help the poor man who falls a victim to the crocodile, who will drag him under water without any warning, drown him and pull him to pieces. I am thankful I was not attacked when swimming the Nzoia yesterday. As a matter of fact the presence of crocodiles never occurred to me, so keen was I to get across the river. If any beast can represent death it is fully personified in the crocodile, lying motionless and showing only his nose and eyes above water like some half-submerged rock.

Crocodiles

In the evening I came across a large herd of sing-sing waterbuck, and I shot my third cob.

As I have carried my reconnaissance from the Broderick Falls to a hill known as Esoyo Sambo, I shall tomorrow return to Muhoroni via Alagabiet.

Reconnaissance completed

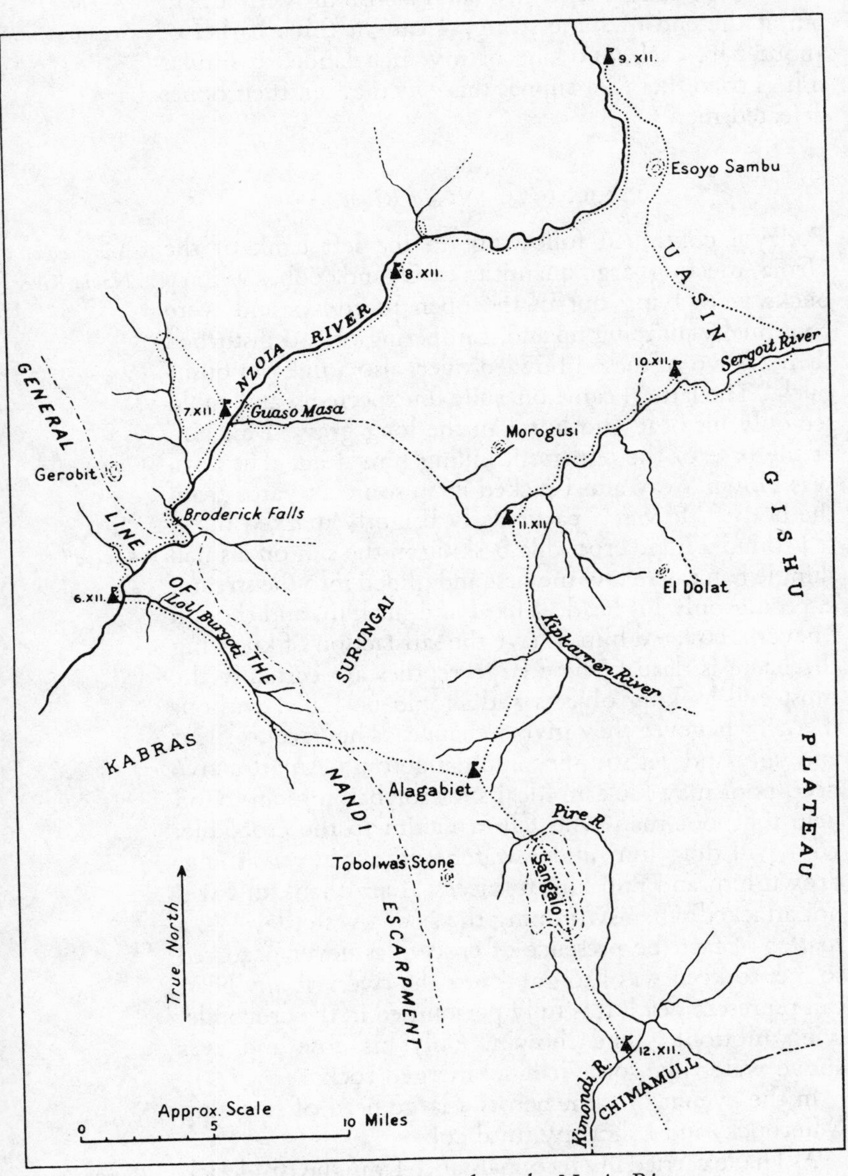

Rough sketch of my route along the Nzoia River

10 . XII . 1905. *Uasin Gishu Plateau*

This morning I struck south towards Alagabiet and camped on the Sergoit River about 8 miles due north of El Dolat Hill. I am now on the Uasin Gishu Plateau, a delightful rolling grass country. From my camp Esoyo Sambo Hill stands out above a sea of mist. Its curious outline is most weird.

I move south towards Alagabiet

Uasin Gishu

I shot an old sing-sing waterbuck soon after leaving camp and a Jackson's haartebeeste in the evening. I saw a rhinoceros, who deliberately went and hid himself in some long grass when he heard our safari, so I went and routed him out, just for the fun of seeing him scamper over the plains. I saw several of that small blue duiker (*aequatorialis*), some zebra, topi and a fine warthog.

11 . XII . 1905. *Kipkarren River, Uasin Gishu*

Sergoit River

I followed down the right bank of the Sergoit River to its junction with the Kipkarren, and crossing to the south bank of the latter camped about half-way between Morogusi and El Dolat Hills. I shot a brace of oribi, a young warthog, a green pigeon and 5 francolin. The latter were very numerous in the grass and were constantly being flushed in large coveys. They are about the size of the English partridge, and as soon as they get well on the wing they begin to scream just like a yelling baby, which is most alarming when a large covey makes off. The screaming only becomes worse if one fires at them. I missed a good many of them through laughing at them.

Screaming partridges

Hyaena by day

While crossing the Kipkarren River 3 hyaena slunk away from some reeds. It is not often one sees these ungainly creatures in broad daylight.

Game census

During 10 miles on the plateau I counted 2 rhino, 2 hyaena, 1 cheetah, 28 oribi, 7 bohor reedbuck, 5 giraffe, 27 warthog, 244 Jackson's haartebeeste, 86 Grant's gazelle and 410 zebra.

12 . XII . 1905. *Chimamull, Uasin Gishu*

To Alagabiet

Marching south, I arrived at Alagabiet for lunch with Barrett and Butler. In the afternoon I came on and camped at 6 p.m. on the Kimonde River in the Chimamull District, having successfully joined up my survey at Alagabiet. I shall arrive at Nandi Fort tomorrow and go direct to Muhoroni on the 14th.

14 . XII . 1905. *Muhoroni*

To Muhoroni

Leaving Nandi Fort soon after dawn, I marched into Muhoroni at 4 p.m. Dr. F. L. Henderson accompanied me from Nandi. The place fairly hums with people of importance, including Hayes-Sadler, the new Commissioner, F. Jackson, his deputy, Hobley, Harrison, Bagge, Gorges, Pope Hennessey, Mackay, and numerous small fry such as myself. The reason for this plethora of brain is a meeting with the Nandi chiefs, who are also collected here. A chief called Kabellas, whose ivory and stock I captured last month, has been appointed the new Laibon and paramount chief of all the Nandi.

Kabellas, the new Nandi Laibon

Dinner with Leveson Gower

Henderson and I dined with Leveson Gower. As usual, he is tired of life and wants to get home.

15 . XII . 1905. *Muhoroni*

Conference with Nandi chiefs

General Manning arrived here today from Uganda and a conference with the Nandi chiefs was held in the afternoon. After what I considered a weak and disconnected harangue by Hayes-Sadler, who neither knew what he wished to say nor could speak coherently, the terms were delivered in phrases of doubt and vacillation. They are as follows:

Peace terms to the Nandi

1. By 15 January 1906 the Nandi tribe must be concentrated in a reserve. This reserve will be an area bounded on the south by the Nandi Escarpment, on the west by the Nyangori and the Elburgoloti Escarpment, on the north by the Nollo Segelli and Guaso Masa Rivers, and on the east by a line drawn from where the Nandi–Muhoroni road cuts the crest of the escarpment to Kipchomba or Alagabiet Hill and thence to the Nollo Segelli.
2. That after 15 January 1906 force will be employed by us to compel all sections of the Nandi to move into the above reserve.

3. Meanwhile all murderers are to be surrendered.

As I framed this reserve myself I naturally consider it a fair one, but I have serious doubts about it being strictly adhered to. Unless we are very firm and put a first-class man in charge we shall only have a repetition of violence from the Nandi. It turns out they have not suffered so severely as we thought. We have taken some 10,000 cattle from their total stock of 18,000, and very few of their fighting men have been killed or captured. It is a pity that operations were stopped just as we were going to take them on in the Kabwuren Forest. I understand that Mayes was responsible for stopping operations and advised Harrison and Manning that the Nandi would do as they were told. It remains to be seen whether Mayes' judgment is sound or whether he was influenced by the squeals of his friends among the Nandi. Personally I doubt whether the Nandi have been sufficiently punished to persuade them to move quietly into the reserve.

My comments

There are two officers here called Cuffe and Wilson who have written a most insubordinate letter to headquarters, complaining that native evidence was suppressed at the court of enquiry, that they are not satisfied with the finding of the court, and that they demand a second court which will sift all evidence and allow Mayes to state his case. Manning is dealing with Cuffe and Wilson from a disciplinary aspect. Meanwhile I have told Manning that I should welcome as many courts of enquiry as he considered necessary, as I had nothing to hide and nothing of which I feel ashamed. Manning himself is entirely satisfied with my conduct and was most sympathetic.

I see Manning about the death of the Laibon

16 . XII . 1905. *Muhoroni*

General Manning, accompanied by Headquarters staff, left here today on a tour of inspection. He will visit Soba, Silie Hill, Kongoni Camp, Alagabiet and Nandi Fort. I spent the day tracing my map of the Nzoia River so that it can be printed for future operations if necessary.

Manning goes on inspection

Meanwhile I am detailed to demarcate the eastern boundary of the new Nandi reserve. As I made the map

I am detailed to mark out the eastern boundary of the Nandi reserve

and suggested the limits of this reserve I suppose they think me a fit and proper person to mark the boundary on the ground. My bare instructions are to demarcate the eastern boundary. I asked what form of marking was required—wire fence, palisade, trench, poles or pillars. Headquarters had no ideas on the subject except that it was not to cost any money. So I am at my wits' end to know what to do.

The reserve they contemplate is much too small and does not allow for expansion; I fear it is all based on requirements for white settlement and not on the welfare of the Nandi. This is a very short-sighted policy and must lead to grievances; after all, it is African land, not ours to dispose of.

18 . XII . 1905. *Nandi Fort*

To Nandi Fort

Isaac and I came up to Nandi Fort today via Kibigori, where we spent last night.

21 . XII . 1905. *Kapsikak Hill, Nandi*

To Kapsikak

I spent yesterday in Nandi cleaning my instruments and collecting my boundary party. I left Nandi today and camped at Kapsikak Hill, where I start laying out the boundary tomorrow. Dr. Henderson accompanied me but goes on to Alagabiet tomorrow.

22 . XII . 1905. *Kapsikak Hill, Nandi*

I start laying out the boundary of the reserve

I have brought about 50 axes with me from Nandi and I shall lay the boundary out with stripped poles, which can be connected by wire later if necessary. The poles are some 20 yards apart in bush and 100 yards apart in the open. Bush is cleared for some 25 yards on either side of the line. Today we completed only about 2 miles, the thick bush taking a long time to clear, stack and burn. But I have 140 men at work, and tomorrow I should do much more. When I get into the open we shall go faster, but I shall have to carry the poles farther. Meanwhile I have asked for another 100 men, which should enable me to complete the work in 3 weeks.

Kabellas, the new Nandi Laibon, visited me in camp today. I asked him to come into my tent and he sat down. He was silent for a long time, just staring at me. Then he asked me if I was the person who shot Koitelal. I told him I was. Another long silence. He then said that Koitelal was a bad man and he was pleased I had shot him. He said he thought the Nandi had been too severely punished and he did not like the idea of a reserve with movement restricted. They must be a free people with a much larger reserve and he would guarantee their good behaviour.

A visit from Kabellas

Before he left I photographed him. I have sent in a report about our conversation.

25 . XII . 1905. *Rungi River, Nandi*

I met Pope Hennessey at Headquarters today on the Rungi River, where I camped, dining with Harrison, Hennessey and Mackay. Archer of the 4th K.A.R. was also there. In the morning I killed a small francolin, which is a poor substitute for a turkey, and this evening Harrison and I killed some pigeon.

Christmas with Headquarters

As the Commissioner has changed his mind about the alignment of the boundary and has referred the matter to London, I am to stop work for the present. I am returning to Nandi Fort for the moment, and shall hope to resume work next week.

Boundary work suspended

I hear that Cuffe and Wilson were persuaded by Mayes to bring accusations against me regarding the killing of the Laibon. After the first court of enquiry they were told to withdraw their accusations. I had a letter of apology from Wilson, but Cuffe refused to withdraw his complaints and has been ordered home.

31 . XII . 1905. *Kimondi River, Kabwuren Forest*

On the 28th a second court of enquiry on the death of the Laibon was held at Nandi, when native evidence was heard. The result was the same as that of the first enquiry.

Second court of enquiry

I left Nandi Fort today to sketch a route through the Kabwuren Forest. This evening I am camped on the Kimondi River where it enters the forest.

Survey in the Kabwuren Forest

The African honey guide

I had the most delightful experience today with a small bird known as the honey guide (*Indicator*). While working in the forest I became aware that a small bird was endeavouring to attract my attention by chattering at me from only a few feet away, evidently in a great state of excitement and often flying away into the forest but always in the same direction.

He was so persistent that I decided to follow him. His excitement then increased and he would keep some 20 yards ahead of me, usually fairly high up in a tree, but he never for a moment lost sight of me. After some 150 yards he was joined by two others, and their united chorus left me in no doubt as to the direction they wished me to take. The three birds finally came to rest in a smallish tree, and as they refused to leave it I was convinced that the honey they required was near at hand. A short inspection found the bees' nest under a strip of rotten bark, and my men soon laid it bare and spread the comb, rich with golden honey, on the ground.

As soon as it was clear to the birds that we had discovered the honey they sat fairly still in the tree within a few feet of us with very obvious feelings of satisfaction. Their little breasts were puffed out, and they would constantly throw their heads back and utter a low churning sound. But their greed was not untempered with jealousy, for with an angry call one would lift his head-feathers and make a dash at one of the others. Then would ensue a regular scurry through the surrounding trees, but the three birds would soon return to watch anxiously our operations. Having spread the comb out on a bare piece of ground we sat and watched from a distance of some 25 yards. The birds came down at once but did not feed on the ground. They each took a large bit of comb and flew off with it out of sight, and as soon as they had finished that bit they returned for more. I tried to follow one to see it feed, but could not locate it in the thick trees.

There is no doubt that these birds deliberately attracted my attention in order that I should follow their guidance to the bees which they had already located.

Kabellas: the new Nandi Laibon

A caricature by my friend McClure, depicting Isaac and myself as Two Bloody Jews, an epithet applied to us by Mayes

I imagine that man is but seldom used as the means by which these birds obtain their food. Such animals as squirrels, monkeys, etc., and perhaps the honey badger (*Mellivora*), are probably the usual media, though I know of no observations on the subject. There is, however, no doubt that the bird knows his job exceedingly well and is almost human in his guidance.

Natives tell me that if, after finding the honey, none is left for the birds, they will guide one next time to a snake or some noxious beast. But I fancy this is pure imagination, for none of them can quote an instance.

1.1.1906. *Kiptoya Hill, Nandi*

I meet Hookey Walker at Kiptoya Hill

Marched to Kiptoya Hill, where I found Hookey Walker. We camped together and had a long chat about recent events and the future of the Nandi.

2.1.1906. *Kabwuren Rock, Kaimosi*

Orders cancelled

I commenced at daylight building a good-sized stone cairn on Kiptoya Hill for future use when surveying, but at 8 a.m. I received an urgent letter from Headquarters telling me I was to stop the work I was on and proceed at once to Aldai to investigate certain rumours which have been received about the disloyalty of the Kamalilo tribe. The Kamalilo are a section of the Nandi and are said to have moved into Aldai, partly to escape moving into the reserve and partly to recoup themselves for their recent losses in cattle. The people of Aldai are not Nandi but a section of the Kavirondo, who could never stand up against the Nandi. I am to warn the elders of Aldai that, if the rumour is true, the Kamalilo must be instantly turned out, failing which the Government will despatch troops to evict them, and that under these circumstances it will be difficult for us to discriminate between the Aldai and Kamalilo.

I make a rapid march through the Kabwuren Forest

So I packed up hurriedly and got started by noon. At 5 p.m. I camped at the Kabwuren Rock, within 100 yards of my old camp there in June 1904 when I was protecting the Kaimosi Mission. As Headquarters want me back in Nandi on the 4th for a conference on future operations I have not much time to waste.

3 . 1 . 1906. *Aldai, North Escarpment*

To Aldai

Marching through the western extremity of the Kabwuren Forest I reached Aldai, where I camped. I was constantly coming across natives fully armed in the forest. Most of them bolted on coming into view, but I caught three, all of whom are Kamalilo, and they confessed to me that they had come into Aldai to avoid moving into the reserve and to raid the unfortunate people of Aldai.

My meeting with the Aldai elders

I camped at 10 a.m. and at once sent my men out to summon the chiefs. They had all assembled by 4 p.m. I had profitably spent the time in watching the grey parrots feeding in the treetops and in collecting a few nice birds. I delivered my message, when they one and all denied all knowledge of the presence of the Kamalilo in their midst. I told them they were lying and, delivering my ultimatum, broke up the conference by warning them that the responsibility was theirs. At this they became rather truculent, so I turned them all out of the camp. As I may have trouble from them tonight I have taken all precautions for the safety of my party.

4 . 1 . 1906. *Nandi Fort*

To Nandi

Nothing untoward occurred last night, and I left camp in Aldai soon after dawn and marched into Nandi Fort about 2 p.m.

I decide to go up for the Staff College

I have recently been considering the advisability of presenting myself at an examination for the Staff College. While walking through the forest today I determined to have a try some time in 1912, which is the last year my age permits for entrance. So as soon as this expedition is over I shall begin to work for it. My idea is to get as much regimental experience as possible before going to the Staff College, as I feel sure that once one has passed out one never again gets the chance of regimental soldiering, which is far and away the most attractive side of my profession.

Mrs. Burke

There is a sturdy young fellow called Ulick Burke who has been attached to my company for duty. But he is not fit enough to travel at the pace I go, neither would he be of much assistance, as he is ignorant of the rudiments of survey work, cannot talk to natives, and has little or no knowledge of soldiering. I have therefore left him behind on all occasions, and recently sent him to command a small detachment I have at Kapsikak.

When I returned to Nandi today I went straight to my office to write my report on the Aldai. Suddenly I heard a noise behind my safe. On looking up, to my astonishment, from behind the safe crept a most unkempt figure of an unattractive white woman dressed in men's clothes. "And who the devil are you?" I asked, to which the reply came, "I want my husband. I am just thirsting for my husband." So I said, "I'm not your husband. Who do you want?" She then said she was Mrs. Burke and that she had smuggled herself up to Nandi. Not wishing to have this desperate woman in my house, I had a tent pitched for her and sent the following helio message to Burke: "A woman in men's clothes who says she is your wife has emerged from behind my office safe. Come here at once and identify her or deny her allegation by helio message."

Burke arrived late this evening, identified his wife and then asked me what to do. I told him I would send her back under his escort to Kibigori tomorrow. Apparently poor Burke is terrified of the woman and she leads him a dog's life. She had the effrontery to tell me in front of her husband that if she was sent away she would go off with the first man who would take her. I told her she ought to be ashamed of herself for making such a statement to her husband, when she knew perfectly well that he was on active service. I also told her that her conduct in following her husband to Nandi was most unfair to all of us, but that her future plans were no real concern of mine. I then told Burke in front of his wife that he would be well advised to get rid of such a pestilential woman, and the sooner the better. Poor Burke is very upset and annoyed about the whole thing and I am extremely sorry for him. What a curse it must be to be tied to such a woman.

[Burke took his wife to Kibigori and sent her back to Nairobi to await the end of the expedition. But the woman went as far as Naivasha, where she misbehaved herself with a local innkeeper. Burke died very shortly afterwards of kidney trouble.]

I walk 926 miles in 73 days

During the last 73 days I have been on the march for 62, during which time I have covered 926 miles, my longest march being 38 miles. The result is that I am feeling rather tired but thoroughly fit and well.

6.1.1906. *Kibigori*

I ask for a third court of enquiry

As I hear Mayes is still talking about my conduct in regard to the death of the Laibon, I have asked Manning for a third court of enquiry and have insisted that I should be given an opportunity of cross-questioning Mayes. I consider it most unfair that the authorities should still allow Mayes to talk as he does. They should stop him themselves and not leave all their dirty work for me to do. But I shall now have no mercy on him.

We camped at Mark's Boma, Walker and I going into Kibigori in the afternoon, where we met Isaac, Col. Gorges, Olivier of the D.C.L.I., and Capt. J. Harrington of the Rifle Brigade. Tomorrow we all go into Muhoroni by special train.

11.1.1906. *Muhoroni*

Hundreds of marabout storks

All the captured cattle from the Nandi expedition have been concentrated at Muhoroni, where two Englishmen called Duder and Dick have got the contract for looking after them and moving them to Nairobi and other centres. Naturally there have been many deaths among 10,000 head of cattle, and this seems to have attracted all the carrion-eating birds in Kavirondo. I have never seen such a congregation of kites, crows (both *scapulatus* and *albicollis*), vultures and marabout storks. Kites, crows and vultures were in hundreds, and I counted over 350 marabout storks sitting on the surrounding trees. These birds have handsome under tail-coverts, and I shot a couple with my rifle.

My third court of enquiry which has been sitting here, in the station waiting room, since the 9th instant completed its work today and recorded a finding very much in my favour. It is a great weight off my mind, as I now feel that all evidence has been thoroughly sifted and no more points can possibly crop up.

My third court of enquiry

The main enquiry has been on a letter which Mayes sent to Bagge on 2 November last year, setting out certain complaints reflecting on my character. My object has been to show that Mayes wrote this letter out of personal animus, that he had no just cause for such animus, that his statements were falsehoods, and that Mayes himself should not be believed.

There was really no excuse for Mayes' conduct. He made untrue accusations against me because I had been instrumental in bringing to light certain acts of fraud and misappropriation of Government property. For this he was very lightly punished on account of his past good services. Mayes has pleaded that he wrote the letter from purely public motives. This was not borne out by the evidence. I proved to the hilt that Mayes wrote the letter with a view to having his revenge.

In the midst of the enquiry Mayes offered to withdraw his charges and make a full apology. This I flatly refused to consider.

It might be useful to record a short summary of the events which led to my three courts of enquiry.

Résumé of events which led to my three courts of enquiry

10 *July* 1905. I had to give evidence before a court of enquiry at Nandi to verify certain charges of dishonesty brought by the auditor against Mayes, as a result of which Mayes was removed from Nandi and reduced in rank.

19 *October* 1905. While meeting the Laibon I was ambushed and the Laibon was killed. Received congratulatory telegrams from Col. Harrison and others.

29 *October* 1905. Mayes was brought back to Nandi as an Assistant Political Officer owing to his knowledge of the country. When his column was camped near Ketparak Hill some Nandi prisoners whom he was

interrogating complained that the Laibon had been treacherously killed by me. This complaint he embodied in a report to Bagge on 2 November, and told his friends that he intended to pay me out for giving evidence against him at his court of enquiry.

4 *November* 1905. While at Kaimosi Mission I heard from Col. Harrison that certain rumours were afloat regarding the manner in which the Laibon was killed and which were prejudicial to my character. I denied these rumours by return letter.

7 *November* 1905. Saw Col. Harrison and Major Pope Hennessey at Kiptoya Hill and they furnished me with details of the above rumours. Hennessey took a more serious view of them than did Harrison or myself. I was informed that they emanated from Capt. D. Macleod.

9 *November* 1905. Met Macleod at Nandi and taxed him with these rumours. He denied starting them, and said that they emanated from Mayes.

23 *November* 1905. While camped at Jemelil Hill I received a private letter from Hennessey telling me that rumours about my conduct were spreading. I at once asked for a court of enquiry to clear my character.

1 *December* 1905. My first court of enquiry was held at Nandi Fort, native evidence being disallowed by the president. The finding of the court was embodied that evening in Field Force Order No. 99, which was issued as a special order.

(Field Force Order No. 99 reads: "The Officer Commanding congratulates Capt. R. Meinertzhagen, 3rd K.A.R., on the results which have attended the affair at Kaidparak Hill on the 19th Oct. The death of the Laibon Koitelal, who was there killed whilst ambuscading Capt. Meinertzhagen, has to a great extent contributed to breaking up the resistance of the Nandi.")

4 *December* 1905. While at Alagabiet I was told by Barrett that Capt. Cuffe and Lieut. Wilson, for reasons which I shall never be able to understand, had announced their intention of resigning from the K.A.R. if native evidence was not heard at a court of enquiry

and if another court was not immediately held. Both these officers also wrote private letters to me, but they threw no light on their attitude. As I also had asked that native evidence be heard I did not pay much attention to the request of these officers, but I strongly resented the insubordinate and dictatory tone of the letters.

15 *December* 1905. Saw General Manning at Muhoroni about Cuffe's letter and placed the matter in his hands. As a result Cuffe was asked to resign from the K.A.R. and is already on his way home. Wilson withdrew his letter and sent me an apology, which I accepted.

28 *December* 1905. Manning granted me a second court of enquiry at Nandi. All native evidence was heard and I was again exculpated from all blame. But I had particularly asked that Mayes might be present, and he was not. I definitely asked to be allowed to cross-question him before a court. Manning provisionally promised me a third court of enquiry at which Mayes would be present.

11 *January* 1906. My third court of enquiry at Muhoroni. Mayes was there and produced native evidence to try to show that his story was correct, but it did no more than prove its own untrustworthiness and brought out the fact that it had all been put into the mouths of the natives by Mayes. This was admitted by two witnesses.

I proved Mayes to be a liar, his evidence to be a concoction of lies, and himself a man whose code of honour is of the lowest order.

The court, in summing up, considered that Mayes' accusations were unfounded and that the whole report was written out of personal hatred for me. They recommended his removal from Government service.

Mayes evinced the utmost uneasiness as I brought witness after witness and put question after question, bringing out his true character and exposing all his past misdeeds. At one time he wept, at the next moment he was offering an apology and a withdrawal of his accusations. But I had no mercy on him, till finally Mayes broke down and refused to take any further part in the proceedings.

[Mayes was transferred to a small post on the coast. He resigned soon afterwards and took up land near Vanga. In November 1914, when I was forming my Intelligence Department during the First Great War, I heard that Mayes was almost destitute, so I offered him a job, which he accepted, but within a month I had to remove him as he was embezzling Secret Service funds. He returned to his plantation and died soon afterwards.]

14.1.1906. *Fort Ternan*

To Fort Ternan

My company having joined me yesterday evening, I left Muhoroni today and marched to Fort Ternan, where I found Ward and Maycock and their companies.

Future operations

As it now seems certain that the Nandi will not move into the reserve without force being used, we are to take part in a huge drive in a north-westerly direction, starting operations on the 19th. All crops are to be destroyed, all huts burned, and the country generally laid waste. It is not a pleasant job but most necessary if we are to get security from the Nandi in future. The driving line is divided into two wings, Gorges commanding the right wing and Hookey Walker the left. My company is the inside company of the left wing. The whole line is some 40 miles long and some 1100 men are employed, split up into 11 small columns.

15.1.1906. *Savoy, Nandi*

Move towards Tinderet

I left Fort Ternan today and, marching towards Tinderet Ridge, camped in the district known as Savoy. Both Walker and Ward arrived in my camp during the day but left later for Fort Ternan.

19.1.1906. *Savoy, Nandi*

Second phase of the Nandi Expedition commences

Operations commenced today. At 3 a.m. I sallied forth and climbed up Kokwet Hill, both to get a good view of surrounding country and to get into helio communication with other columns. I reached the summit as the first grey streaks of dawn were approaching in the east, and found one of the enemy's sentries perched on a small rock and not 500 yards from us. It was some few moments before we made each other out in the dim light. Then I fired at him and he dived into the forests of Tinderet. I had my breakfast on Kokwet Hill and got into heliographic communication with other columns at Ketparak Hill, Muhoroni, Soba and Segedete Hill, and with Capt. Ward, one of whose patrols passed close to my position.

My company was split up into several small patrols today but scarcely got into touch with the Nandi. We captured three prisoners, who will be useful as guides. We burned some 140 huts and caught a few cattle and goats.

Nandi obstinacy

The Nandi are showing great reluctance to move into their reserve. They have now had 6 weeks' grace in which to comply with our terms, and in many cases whole villages have ignored our warnings. They are now having to move at our convenience instead of at their own leisure, and I am sorry for the women and children. I shall help them as much as possible, as I think it is great hard luck on them, but they have got to go into the reserve.

20.1.1906. *Near Soba, Nandi*

Today I moved camp slightly nearer Soba in order to correct my position between Nelson's company at that place and Ward's at Kokwet. There was but little contact with the Nandi today. We simply kept a gentle pressure on them to make them move. Several small parties who tried to break back were headed off in a north-westerly direction. I am thankful to say that no shot was fired today by my men.

21.1.1906. *Near Soba, Nandi*

A patrol attacked

I ascended Chabtavatch Hill today and built a stone cairn on its summit for future survey work. I was also in signalling communication with Muhoroni, Soba and Ketparak throughout the day. One of my patrols was attacked by some 40 warriors today; 18 of the enemy were killed before they withdrew. We had two men slightly wounded and one killed.

22 . 1 . 1906. *Near Soba, Nandi*

The drive hangs fire

The drive appears to be hanging fire for some reason or other. I think it is probably because we all hate this class of work. Evicting families and burning villages is not part of a soldier's work.

On the 24th I moved camp slightly nearer to Tinderet. Hookey Walker visited me during the day. Yesterday I visited Ward's camp at Kokwet and today I went into Soba to meet Nelson and arrange details before entering Tinderet Forest. At Soba I met Lieut. Craigie Halkett.

27 . 1 . 1906. *Tinderet, Nandi*

A conflict of abuse

While one of my parties was cutting crops under a wooded precipice today they were sniped by a few arrows from an unseen enemy. A couple of volleys into the bush failed to stop it, so my men withdrew out of range. At this moment I arrived on the scene. Then followed the most terrible curses and epithets of abuse directed at us by an unseen enemy. After attacking all our relations they explained in the most graphic terms what our death would be if we were caught. Every part of our anatomy was carefully accounted for, and every possible relation was consigned to some form of treatment. As almost every epithet was proclaimed by an arrow or two, followed by a shot at the bushes whence we judged the arrows were coming, it was rather comic.

28 . 1 . 1906. *Tinderet, Nandi*

Headquarters go to Nairobi for the races

Hookey Walker paid me a visit today. It appears that the whole of Headquarters, while supposed to be conducting operations, have adjourned to Nairobi for the races, giving out that they must confer with the Commissioner about the situation up here. Manning has not only consented to this but has adjourned himself. Such extraordinary conduct on the part of a responsible military headquarters is inexplicable, especially at a period when the proper co-ordination of our columns is of primary importance. It does not inspire me with much confidence in Headquarters, nor can I judge very highly of their definition of duty. It has created a most unfortunate impression among us junior officers. Meanwhile we are completely without orders and are just doing nothing.

However, I celebrated the occasion by taking a patrol into the Tinderet Forest, where I collected butterflies and chased guinea-fowl till it was almost dark. I found it more entertaining than burning harmless villages and evicting families from their homes.

29 . I . 1906. *Tinderet, Nandi*

Patrolling in the Tinderet Forest

I accompanied a patrol into the Tinderet Forest today. It is exciting work, as one never knows when a volley of arrows is coming. We actually saw no enemy, though other patrols came into contact with small parties. But we heard the Nandi. While crossing a small stream in the heart of the forest a Nandi suddenly cried out that he hoped our legs were as rotten as twigs and would break just as easily. I thought this rather a poor opening to a fight, but my men replied in equally spirited terms, which gave away his position, and a few shots silenced him, though I shall never know if he was hit.

The flowers of the forest

I was much struck by the beauty and profusion of flowering creepers and trees in the forest. From the floral aspect it is finer than the forests of either Kenya, Kinangop, Mau or Kabwuren. One blue-flowering creeper in particular attracted my attention, but I could not get any seeds.

31 . I . 1906. *Tinderet, Nandi*

Formation of a new driving line

I received orders today to move to Jemelil Hill on the west of Soba in order to form the left of a new driving line.

I . II . 1906. *Jemelil Hill, Nandi*

Reggie Hart and V. C. de Crespigny

I passed through Soba on my way to Jemelil. At the former place I met Hookey Walker, Reggie Hart and V. C. de Crespigny—all three old friends and quite first-class.

On arrival at Jemelil I received fresh orders to move back to my old camp under Tinderet. Apparently Headquarters, having taken a week's leave in Nairobi to be present at the races, have now returned, and finding themselves completely out of touch with operations and anxious once more to get back to Nairobi are determined to hurry things on. Since they returned they have issued various contradictory orders direct to columns instead of to the two wing commanders. I can only imagine that they are anxious to show their renewed zeal after a week's leave. The result is that the whole drive has been disorganised and many Nandi will have taken advantage of the muddle to slip back. It will certainly be small credit to Headquarters if the drive succeeds. They have done their level best to make it a failure.

I shall return to my old camp first thing tomorrow morning.

2 . II . 1906. *Tinderet, Nandi*

I find the enemy in my old camp

I returned to my old camp under Tinderet today. On approaching its site my advance guard reported that there were several Nandi walking about the site. I ordered them not to fire, but to try to surround them and make them prisoners. My men began to creep round through the bush but were spotted, and the Nandi bolted. I then ordered fire to be opened and one Nandi dropped. He was a full-blown warrior, wearing a new short sword or *seme* in a red leather sheath.

4 . II . 1906. *Tinderet, Nandi*

I am poisoned

Yesterday, as I was returning to camp after an uneventful patrol in the forest, I was met by two Nandi girls who professed to have come from behind us and to wish to go north to the reserve. I commended them for their righteous desire and let them pass, but before leaving camp they expressed a wish to present me with some choice honey. They then left camp with a pass from me. I was very hungry at the time and ate most of the honey.

Some 10 minutes later I broke out into a profuse perspiration and felt giddy and sick. Most fortunately it flashed across my mind that I might have been poisoned, so I quickly mixed some salt and water and vomited hard; in fact I vomited for nearly an hour until my stomach was fairly clean. During the last half-hour I was almost unconscious. I then took huge doses of castor oil and chlorodyne at intervals and suffered severe pain throughout the night in my intestines. My men were upset at my state and told me that I would certainly die, which was not encouraging, though I thought they were right at one period, when only by great effort of will could I prevent myself from falling off into a stupor. This morning I am feeling better, though completely prostrated with exhaustion. I should like to catch those two girls. They would shout "*peccavi*" all right.

An interrupted carouse

During the afternoon I sent patrols out into the forest. One of the parties, hearing laughter and singing coming from the depths of the forests, followed it up and came on a hut where they found 7 Nandi in a merry condition. They were summoned to surrender but snatched up their arms and were shot down at once.

Tomorrow we are all making a combined effort to tackle Tinderet Forest, which still harbours a good many Nandi who are loath to leave their homes. We shall not have much success, but it is a final effort, and we shall not waste more time on it. Headquarters appear to have now completely recovered from their week's leave to Nairobi and are now functioning in a normal manner.

5 . II . 1906. *Tinderet, Nandi*

I move camp

I moved through the Tinderet Forest today and camped on the north-west slopes of the ridge. In the heart of the forest, in a deep dark gully, I found an exquisite ground orchid in full flower. The petals were of the size of those of a large sweet pea and of a delicate salmon-pink colour with deep orange centre. I tried hard to preserve it, but it perished at once on my exposing it to strong light, and by the time I got into camp I was unable even to press it, so completely had it withered.

A wonderful ground orchid

6 . II . 1906. *Near Soba, Nandi*

I move nearer to Soba

I moved camp to a high ridge about 4 miles north-west of Soba. I found Wilson and Olivier camped on the same ridge and only a mile distant. Ward and his company came through Tinderet Forest also and joined Olivier's camp. We all rather lost our bearings while coming through that forest.

The red tape of our Inspector General

Just as I was moving out of camp this morning Nelson put in an appearance and told me that General Manning has ordered Walker and Stevens down to Nairobi to check the stores of their battalion. To withdraw two senior officers from active service so that they can count blankets in their battalion store is a most uncalled-for act of interference on the part of the Inspector General, more especially when the drive is passing through a delicate stage. To allow such side issues to influence military operations stamps the man as small-minded and festooned in red tape.

I have also been considerably annoyed by a message I received today ordering all companies to send a patrol into Muhoroni to draw soap, as the Inspector General wishes to see all men clean when he next inspects. I have no intention of doing so. Either we are on active service or we are not. If we are, I shall not employ troops in carrying soap or in washing their clothes. Cleanliness is a most important part of discipline in peacetime, but I decline to make my men turn out here in Tinderet Forest as they would on parade in Nairobi. The idea is too absurd. I have replied that my men are sufficiently clean and require no soap.

8 . II . 1906. *Songorrh Hill, Nandi*

I move into the hot plains

I moved camp today into the hot fetid plains of Muhoroni and camped on the slopes of Songorrh Hill. Nelson accompanied me. I think we have now almost completed our task in this part of Nandi, and there cannot be many of the enemy left in and around Tinderet Forest.

Our achievements

Since this second phase of the expedition began my company has burned 917 huts, 239 granaries and 46 stock enclosures, captured 8 prisoners, killed 51 of the enemy and captured 54 head of cattle and 399 sheep and goats. We have also destroyed some 145 acres of standing crops, mostly millet. I doubt if a single hut or square yard of cultivation has been left behind the driving line, though a few of the more obstinate Nandi are doubtless still hiding in Tinderet, living an uncomfortable and precarious existence.

9 . II . 1906. *Songorrh Hill, Nandi*

New phase

Our part of the driving line is now formed into a subsidiary or second line to catch any of the enemy who break through the first line. The main line now has its left about Jemelil Hill and its right near Alagabiet and is semicircular in formation. There still appear to be many of the enemy ahead of us. The way into the reserve is still open, and many families are availing themselves of this line of escape at the last moment. I was out with a patrol all day between Songorrh and Jemelil Hills and saw no sign of the enemy.

An unusual sight

I saw an unusual sight today. I was sitting on a low ant-hill when I suddenly heard a small shrill squeak quite close to me. On looking up I saw a grass snake about 4 feet long, with its forepart erected and holding a small mouse in its jaws. I had heard the last squeal of the poor mouse, and he was now limp and lifeless. The snake, after looking around, coiled himself up on the ground and proceeded to swallow his prey head first. When he had finished I dealt him a blow on the head with a stick. I always kill snakes at sight.

I shot a nice male waterbuck near camp in the evening, which rejoiced the hearts of my hungry men.

11 . II . 1906. *Songorrh Hill, Nandi*

My annual plum pudding arrives

Today is chiefly famous for the arrival of an English mail which included my plum pudding, which Mother sent from Brockwood. It is somewhat belated, but that did not prevent my making a very large hole in it this evening. Such excellent and well-cooked food is indeed a treat in these wild parts.

We had 4 patrols out today in a north-western and north-eastern direction, but saw no recent signs of the enemy. One of the patrols reports smoke seen from the higher slopes of Tinderet, so I suppose I must go and investigate tomorrow.

14 . II . 1906. *Kapteldon, Nandi*

Back to Tinderet

As there are still some Nandi in Tinderet I moved my camp back to Kapteldon, a spur of Tinderet, so as to be nearer the forest. The whole afternoon I had patrols out in the forest, but they did not get into touch with any of the enemy. I found Ward and his company camped below me on the Ainomaton River.

15 . II . 1906. *Kapteldon, Nandi*

A man-hunt

As my men were busy cutting high millet this morning, one of the enemy, fully armed, broke cover and fled across the open. The whole company gave chase in full view of my camp. It was more like a pack of hounds after a fox than warfare. I am glad to say they did not use their rifles, but pulled him down in the open and brought him back to camp. I have sent him off to the reserve under escort.

Ward came up and camped near me this evening. He moves back through the forest tomorrow.

17 . II . 1906. *Kapteldon, Nandi*

A storm

Last night I was completely defeated by the elements. About midnight it came on to rain and blow, so I had all the tent ropes tightened. But it was no good. A really vicious gust carried all the tents away and flattened out the camp. The rest of the night we spent trying to put things together, but as we were all drenched to the skin and the darkness was intense we did not meet with much success. This morning we got straight again and moved camp down the slope to a hollow, where we are more sheltered.

Photo of myself taken by Princess Patricia of Connaught

H. R. McClure at my house at Nandi

18 . II . 1906. *Kapteldon, Nandi*

Duke of Connaught

As Nelson has to go to Nairobi to command the guard of honour for the Duke of Connaught, who is expected shortly, he has handed over the command of the troops in Kamalilo to me from today.

A leopard

As it was getting dark this evening one of my sentries shouted out that he had that moment seen a leopard enter some bush not 100 yards from camp. I at once ran out with my rifle and saw the beast calmly walking about in the open some 80 yards off. I fired at once, hitting him in the shoulder, and he fell over. After struggling for a short time he died. As I fired I heard cheering in the distance and saw some Nandi on the edge of the forest, who had been watching me from about 900 yards distance. So I put a bullet among them which sent them headlong back into the forest. Really these Nandi have the cheek of the Devil.

19 . II . 1906. *Kapteldon, Nandi*

A wild cat

While cutting crops today I saw a wild cat break back, so I made the men form line for a drive. To my astonishment two Nandi warriors broke cover at the same moment as the cat. I made rather a good shot at the cat as he bounded across the open some 50 yards from me. The Nandi, thinking I was shooting at them, threw themselves on the ground and were caught by my men. I shall send them on the reserve tomorrow.

As I have been ordered to take permanent post at Ketparak Hill, I move there tomorrow.

20 . II . 1906. *Ketparak Hill*

To Ketparak Hill

Marched to Ketparak Hill, where I found R. P. Lewis, the Brigade Signaller, and Capts. Harrington and Olivier. I shall move into Nandi first thing tomorrow to see Harrison and collect my men and my baggage.

21 . II . 1906. *Nandi Fort*

To Nandi

I arrived in Nandi Fort soon after breakfast, and saw Harrison, Gorges, Pope Hennessey and Burke. I learn that the Nandi are moving fast into the reserve and that pressure is to be slightly relaxed. But a ring of posts is being established round the reserve, and Nandi found outside it are to be shot at sight. I and my company are posted at Ketparak. Apparently Manning's desire to get home has hastened matters, and in spite of local advice he has determined to stop further operations just as the fruits of our complicated drives are within reach. However, I fancy that most of the Nandi have moved.

Close of the expedition

The reserve boundaries have still not been fixed, which is unsatisfactory. The result is that many of the Nandi simply treat the reserve as a sanctuary into which they retire when hard pressed and then come out again when the spirit moves them.

My three girl servants rejoin their father

The father of Maggie, Baggie and Scraggie paid me a visit today, and after being most profuse in his thanks for harbouring his children took them off. They were not a bit keen to go, and wished to come to Ketparak with me. But I am rather glad to have done with the responsibility of looking after them. On their departure I presented them with a sheep each and 10 rupees. They presented me with some rather nice beadwork which they had made and have asked me to send them each a small looking-glass— so typically feminine. My little glass was a source of endless amusement to them, and they would laugh by the hour when playing with it. Of course it is the first time they have ever seen themselves. It speaks well for the honesty of these three girls that during the last 5 months I have lost nothing from my house.

22 . II . 1906. *Ketparak Hill, Nandi*

To Ketparak

I returned to Ketparak Hill today, meeting Sammy Butler, who was on his way into Nandi. I was walking in front of my party with my orderly when coming round a corner I suddenly met 7 armed Nandi. They were out of the reserve and, knowing their guilt, at once fled. I could easily have shot a couple of them, but I chased them instead, shouting to them to stop, but they refused to. I shot one and caught another. Sending my orderly off to round up some dozen sheep they had with

I capture a Nandi and run a foolish risk

them, I looked after the prisoner. He sat down and refused to move. As I wished to get along, and was unable to convince him that so long as he behaved himself he would suffer no harm, I told him that he could carry my rifle and must walk in front of me. We proceeded in this fashion until he suddenly threw the rifle into the bush and bolted in the opposite direction. I rushed for my rifle and just picked it up in time to bowl him over at about 30 yards. I was very angry with him, first for throwing my pet rifle into the wet bushes and secondly for having bolted when I was putting such trust in him. On thinking the matter over, I was a perfect ass for trusting Providence in this way. He could easily have shot me if he had wished. Never again do I trust a nigger.

23 . II . 1906. *Ketparak Hill, Nandi*

R. P. Lewis and I visited the spot where I killed the Laibon last year. The place has a peculiar and not altogether pleasant attraction for me. I still consider I was right in what I did, and should do it again if asked to.

I visit and photograph the spot where I killed the Nandi Laibon

24 . II . 1906. *Ketparak Hill, Nandi*

I heard today that Maycock has gone sick at Alagabiet and is invalided to Nairobi. I have therefore had to send Burke up there from Nandi, and I shall have to try to run this place and Nandi Fort. It also means that a great deal of work must be neglected, such as issuing rations not only to the Nandi but to 4 or 5 out-stations, patrolling the country around Ketparak and making up my company accounts for the past 6 months. It would be a physical impossibility to do this latter task single-handed, and I am writing to Nairobi to tell them that they must either send me a clerk or do without the accounts. As they require everything in triplicate, and as I have no intention of satisfying their requirements, the matter is solved. But it is good to have plenty of work in this country. I could not live without it.

Maycock ill

25 . II . 1906. *Nandi Fort*

To Nandi Fort

I came in to Nandi Fort, where I found Maycock ill in bed suffering from severe malaria. I packed Burke off to Alagabiet at once.

26 . II . 1906. *Nandi Fort*

The end of the Nandi Expedition

Manning, having now assumed charge of the Nandi Expedition, has ordered the demobilisation of the Nandi Field Force from today. Five posts are left outside the reserve to see that the Nandi do not come out. Though the Government have achieved their purpose in punishing the Nandi and confining them to a reserve, I am not so sure that it has finally disposed of the Nandi question. To my mind it depends on the man who is placed in charge over the Nandi. If he is first-class we may have no more trouble, but if they send up men of the calibre of Mayes the Nandi will be as truculent and difficult in two years' time as they were last year.

Partington

The Commissioner has appointed a man called Partington to be District Officer at Nandi. He has recently given up charge of the Lumbwa. In my opinion he is not at all the right sort, being rude, ill-mannered and ill-educated. He appears to be a most disagreeable fellow.

28 . II . 1906. *Muhoroni*

Duke of Connaught

The Duke of Connaught, accompanied by Princess Patricia, arrived here today on his way through to Uganda. As the Duke wished to be introduced to all officers on the Nandi Expedition I have been dragged down from Nandi to this fever-stricken spot to meet him. I am rather ashamed of myself, as my only clothes are a pair of ragged shorts and a khaki shirt. However, he seemed rather amused at my kit and even asked me to lunch in his railway carriage. After lunch I found

Princess Pat

Princess Patricia struggling with her camera, which she was trying to use on some Kavirondo women who were stark naked. So I asked her if I could help her and she was delighted. I took her off to a Kavirondo village, where we took many photos together. I thought her a particularly nice girl, with no frills and full of fun. She thanked me profusely and has promised to send me the result of her photos when she gets home. She took one of me with my camera. When we got back to the carriage I found we had kept the royal train waiting, and poor Princess Pat came in for a scowl from her father, but when I told him what we had been doing he was amused. As the train steamed out of the station I waved my hand to Princess Pat and she waved back.

2 . III . 1906. *Nandi Fort*

Return to Nandi

Hookey Walker

I came up to Nandi from the plains yesterday and am grateful to get out of the heat. Hookey Walker, who is left here in charge of the troops, arrived this morning.

3 . III . 1906. *Ketparak Hill*

Parties of Nandi break out of the reserve

I moved to Ketparak Hill this morning with every available man, leaving but a small post in Nandi Fort. I received information today that parties of Nandi have broken out of the reserve and have collected near Chebarus Hill, not far from Ketparak. They are said to have taken up their abode in some caves. I have therefore ordered Wilson to bring his company to Ketparak this afternoon, and tomorrow we shall have at the rascals. Hookey Walker came out to Ketparak in the evening and we all dined with R. P. Lewis.

Today is my 28th birthday.

6 . III . 1906. *Ketparak Hill, Nandi*

The brilliant affair of Chebarus

We have been most successful against those Nandi who broke out of the reserve and came to Chebarus. We left Ketparak at 3.30 a.m. in two columns. My column of a machine gun and 58 men moved on the caves about 4 miles east of the hill. The caves could not be found, but numerous deep fissures and craggy cliffs were found among which the Nandi were hiding. R. P. Lewis accompanied Wilson as signalling officer.

At 5.45, when it was just light enough to shoot, we surprised a party of Nandi in a hollow not more than 40 yards from us. I at once ordered rapid fire and the whole party of 13 were shot down. Now that the alarm was given I hurried a section of men into a pass leading to Chemalil Hill in order to block the road, and then, sending out 4 patrols, we drove the country in an easterly direction towards Wilson's column. By this time Wilson had reached the vicinity of the supposed caves and the enemy was completely surrounded. They lost 32 killed. I took up my position on Chebarus Hill, whence I could overlook the operations.

Chanler's reedbuck

While on Chebarus Hill I saw a small herd of Chanler's reedbuck, out of which I killed a couple of beasts. I was surprised to find these small antelope on the Nandi Escarpment, as they have not previously been reported west of the Mau Escarpment.

I hope that our operations today will convince the Nandi of the futility of breaking out of their reserve. I also heard today that there are other small parties hovering about the reserve boundary and so far unwilling to enter. I shall make up their minds for them tomorrow morning.

I got Wilson to co-operate with his company. Lewis accompanied us. We left Ketparak at 3 a.m. on a bright starlit night, but the path was hard to see owing to the absence of the moon. We reached our destination at 5.30 a.m. and parked our haversacks and all heavy kit by the side of the path under the charge of Lewis and a small guard, thus leaving us free with only rifles and ammunition. I attacked the enemy north of the path and Wilson went south. We effected a complete surprise, finding many of the enemy still in their huts. We killed 19 Nandi and captured 34. We also bagged 542 sheep and goats. We had two men wounded. When natives are surprised like this they have little heart for opposition, especially when they find themselves surrounded. Neither yesterday nor today did the Nandi show much fight.

Having taught these Nandi their lesson we came on to Nandi Fort in the evening, where we found Hookey Walker.

6 . III . 1906. *Nandi Fort*

Many years ago there used to be a section of the Masai on the Uasin Gishu Plateau. Some 15 years ago they were exterminated by the Nandi, but a tiny colony of them were enslaved and settled near where the present Nandi Fort stands. It has been decided to send this colony to the ravine under escort, and they commenced their journey today under Lewis and 30 of my men. It was an interesting procession as they filed north. The children herded the stock, small boys led blind old men and women, then came the old men, closely followed by the old women. Then came the young girls, closely followed by the warriors, who swaggered along carrying nothing but their spears and shields. The women carried all the baggage. The move reminded me of those stories of patriarchal times in Biblical days. There were among those Masai many Abrahams, Esaus and Jacobs, not to mention many representatives of the wives of Lot.

Migration of Masai from Nandi

7 . III . 1906. *Nandi Fort*

Now that the Nandi have been driven out of their country it has been thrown open to European settlement. I often wonder whether it was this idea which lurked at the back of the minds of the Colonial Office and the civil authorities out here when they not only sanctioned the Nandi Expedition but defined the reserve. If this is the case, it was a most immoral excuse for dispossessing the Nandi.

Prospective settlers begin to arrive in Nandi

Two prospective settlers, called Clarke and Hurst, arrived here yesterday to have a look round. Clarke comes from New Zealand and asked if I had relations out there. On telling him that I had, he said he knew Waimarima well and that it was one of the most neglected estates in the colony and also one of the best. He told me he could easily make £10,000 a year out of it. He, of course, knew Donelly and his Maori wife. He had left New Zealand because the Government forced him to sell his estate, which had been in the possession of his family since the colony was founded. This so disgusted

Arrival of Clarke and Hurst

him that he decided to come and settle in East Africa. But he thinks he has jumped out of the frying pan into the fire, for he finds the East African Government just as hidebound and unsympathetic as the New Zealand Government. He likes this country and the climate. He thinks the Land Office is incapable, as they cannot tell him when or where he can have land. It must be disheartening to prospective settlers when they have to wait months and months, eating up all their capital during their idleness and not even getting a word of encouragement from the Administration. Many settlers, unable to get satisfaction, have gone home disgusted, and yet matters are as bad and inefficient in Nairobi as they were two years ago.

10 . III . 1906. *Nandi Fort*

McClure

My old friend McClure arrived here today on a visit from Kerungu. He came via Kisumu and Nyangori.

The Nandi still active

During the last week two soldiers have been murdered by the Nandi. I regard this as due to the premature closing down of the expedition. The Nandi regard the end of the expedition as a sign of weakness and have now given out that we stopped because we were too weak to continue operations.

11 . III . 1906. *Ketparak Hill, Nandi*

To Ketparak

McClure and I visited Ketparak, where I had to go to inspect my detachment at that place.

Unwin

C. H. Unwin, whom I had to turn out of my room at Nandi some time ago, is to be invalided home. McClure tells me that he was so annoyed at my turning him out of my room that he spread all sorts of rumours about me, saying that I drank, that I falsified my returns, etc.

Unwin was also in the habit of pointing to the defences which I had been ordered to construct round my house at Nandi and saying that I had made them owing to my fear of the Nandi. Yet Unwin was only too willing to avail himself of the shelter of my barbed wire during the expedition and whenever his turn came to go out on column, he used to go sick; in fact, he never left Nandi

Fort throughout the expedition. He spent his time drinking and amusing himself with native women, with the result that he is now going home with a ruined constitution.

17 . III . 1906. *Ketparak Hill, Nandi*

Came out to Ketparak Hill again to inspect my detachment. McClure leaves for Alagabiet tomorrow. At Ketparak I found R. P. Lewis, who has just returned from escorting the Uasin Gishu Masai to the Ravine.

To Ketparak

I am beginning to think I have had enough of this country. I have had a certain amount of active service and have gained invaluable experience. I doubt whether a prolonged stay in East Africa will do me much good from a professional or from a health point of view. My 5 years are up this year, and I must decide whether or not to revert to my regiment. I think I had better go back, for if I were to remain out here much longer I should get less and less anxious ever to go back to my British regiment, and that I know I would in the end regret. But I admit I am a bit tired of this sort of life. It is too solitary for any length of time. Niggers are rather getting on my nerves, the climate is making me feel depressed, and altogether I feel I want a change. I want to be more with my own folk than with these savages.

My desire to get out of Africa

19 . III . 1906. *Nandi Fort*

Owing to scarcity of troops on the railway line I have been ordered to send my armed porters down to assist in protecting it and to escort the numerous gangs of Indian workmen. So last night I paid them all up to date. Many of them distinguished themselves by at once getting drunk. They purchase the liquor from the civil police lines. When Isaac was here he and I combined to stop this traffic, and we were successful. I have approached Partington on the subject, but he declines to take any action against his men for supplying my men with liquor. So I have told him that I have placed the police lines out of bounds for my men and at the same time I have

My "new army" of porters goes down to protect the railway

ordered the arrest of any policeman found in my lines. Partington is now furious.

Settling down again in Nandi fort

Now that the expedition is over I am beginning to settle down here again. After all, I have now been here a year and the place seems quite homely. In spite of many drawbacks the place and the work have many attractions, though I can never reconcile myself entirely to the solitary life.

Birds

The joy of my life here is the birds. Several pairs of the African pied wagtail are resident round my house. They have become absurdly tame and will feed at my breakfast table on the veranda. They have an exquisite song, though small and subdued. Then there is a pair of giant swallow (*senegalensis*) which bred in my bedroom last year. At dawn from my bed I hear the black ibis leaving their roosting place in the forest and going forth on their daily search for food. In the evening they return just as the sun goes down. Their call, though ugly in itself, is familiar, and therefore pleasant. Guinea-fowl and green pigeon live in the forest close by and can be heard and seen on most days. To shoot them would be to deprive me of one of my chief pleasures up here. Then there are the three species of crows: the huge massive-billed *Corvultur*, a pair of which breed somewhere in the neighbourhood, the piebald *Corvus scapulatus* which occurs in flocks, and the African Rook (*capensis*) which very occasionally turn up in small parties for a day or two. They do not breed in the neighbourhood. The brilliant bee-eaters and orioles are exceedingly common in the forest, and the small emerald cuckoo is always to be found in a huge tree close to my house. The bateleur eagle and the crested hawk turn up at intervals. Then there is a delightful small bird which always skulks in thorn bush. The cock screams out, "Did you see him do it?" and the hen replies at once, "No, I didn't see him do it."

European migrants

But it is the migrants from the north which have interested me more than the African birds. The willow wren is common from October, though I have never seen a chiffchaff for certain. The European oriole comes in small numbers from the end of September. The cuckoo I have seen only in February and March. Blackcaps simply swarm for some days in October, and I have seen a few common wheatear on the Uasin Gishu Plateau in November. Common, green and wood sandpiper, marsh sandpiper, little stint and the Caspian plover arrive in October, the latter in large flocks. The African representatives of the moorhen and dabchick are to be found wherever there is sufficient water.

My vegetable garden

I have made an effort to reopen my garden. For the last 6 months I have been unable to attend to it, with the result that there is little in it but parsley and arrowroot. I fear my brother officers raided it rather ruthlessly for potatoes and other vegetables and allowed their servants to pull the place about. Whole rows of peas and beans have been pulled up by the roots and bushes of tomatoes have been taken bodily away. Not a potato remains in the garden, some three sackfuls having been stolen. So I am now busy getting the place in order again, though it is rather disheartening.

I have also planted some 50 baby blue gum trees, the seed for which I got from Mumia's. I have also saved a few geranium cuttings, but it will take a long time to get the wilderness straight again and revive the glories of my old garden.

[When I revisited Nandi in 1956 I found my gum trees had grown into giants and now form a conspicuous landmark. One trunk measured 16 feet in circumference, 6 feet from the ground.]

20 . III . 1906. *Nandi Fort*

More Nandi atrocities

I heard today that two of our men were killed in a skirmish near Soba. The Nandi die hard. This is the result of stopping the expedition before we had sufficiently punished the Nandi.

Lewis wired me today that he has news of a Nandi concentration with cattle and asks permission to attack them. I am only too delighted that he should do so, and I wish I could get away to assist him. But at present I am completely tied to my office and can scarcely find time to get out to see my men at Ketparak.

More trouble with the Nandi

I have recently had suspicions that the Nandi have been breaking out of the reserve and have resorted to a spot some 8 miles from here called Kabsimotwa. I therefore sallied out today on a reconnaissance to verify the news. I left my house an hour before dawn and took 45 men with me. Sure enough, I found large parties of the Nandi outside the reserve. I attacked them at once, killed 14 and captured 28 goats. They were so taken by surprise that they offered but little resistance and I had only one casualty. They had apparently come to stay, as they had even built new huts for themselves. These I burned. The thatch of the huts was drenched wet, which produced volumes of white smoke. It was a magnificent sight, if such miserable destruction can be so honoured. I think even Nero might have been impressed by it.

We caught 4 Nandi girls today wandering about in the bush. They could not account for their presence outside the reserve and professed complete ignorance of the illegality of their peregrinations. I packed them off under escort to the reserve.

A deputation

When I got back to Nandi Fort I found a small deputation of friendly Nandi awaiting my arrival. They bore with them honey and a sheep as presents, which I refused. After the usual flattering and friendly remarks they said they were delighted that I had caught some of their friends outside the reserve—the old hypocrites! I expect some of them were in my drive today. Their real object in visiting me is difficult to arrive at. It was probably prompted by the desire for news and by fear lest I should be angry at finding Nandi out of the reserve and should wreak my vengeance on them.

The native mind

Natives are queer creatures and hold still queerer ideas. No European can fully understand the working of the black mind. Their morals, ideals and principles are all based on quite different models from ours, and it frequently happens that some trivial and unnoticed incident gives them an impression which the European would never discern.

It is hard to put oneself in their place, as I try to do.

A white man is so essentially different in every respect, and unless one is master of their language, manners and customs, only attainable after many years' residence in their country, it is a risky boast to imagine that one understands them. By doing so one arrives at wrong conclusions, which is worse than having an empty mind on the subject. I imagine Mayes understands the Nandi better than most men. But then he has been out here so long that he has sunk to the nigger mode of thinking. His morals are no better than those of a savage.

Burke's idea of a "marching out state"

My subaltern, Ulick Burke, who is a member of the Volunteers and therefore not expected to be the complete soldier, amused me today with his idea of a "marching out state." He is now in charge of No. 6 Company at Alagabiet, and on its recent move I told him to let me have a marching out state. This document is supposed to show the strength of the company when it moves. He replied today: "Please tell me what you mean by a marching out state. The state of the company as it marched out is dammed disgraceful, as few of the men have any trousers and their jerseys are all in rags. Is this the sort of thing you require?"

29 . III . 1906. *Nandi Fort*

To Ketparak

R. P. Lewis

Yesterday I went out to Ketparak to inspect my detachment, returning to Nandi Fort today. Lewis was there in a very unsettled state of mind, and as usual worrying about the Staff College. I doubt whether his vacillating indecision will ever allow him to go up for the examination, and he is much too nervous to pass in successfully. But he is frantically keen about it and is working hard. I also doubt whether he has either the brains or application to pass in by examination.

Boiled claret

Bacon arrived at Ketparak in the evening and dined with us. He brought two bottles of claret—a great luxury in these parts. One bottle was corked and the other proved to be sour, but that did not deter us from thoroughly enjoying it. We told the cook to warm it, but the wretch went and boiled it and produced it bubbling over in a saucepan. But it was quite good when it had cooled down a bit.

30 . III . 1906. *Nandi Fort*

Burke and the Masai company

Burke arrived here today with the ragged remnants of the Masai company. They have been such a failure during the expedition that they are going to be disbanded. I expect I shall have to take them down to Nairobi. The Masai have not proved themselves suitable material for soldiers. They are constitutionally delicate and cannot stand hard work. They are also an undisciplined rabble, but that is probably the fault of Maycock, their commander.

1 . IV . 1906. *Kibigori*

I take the Masai company to Kibigori

I am ordered to Voi to make a reconnaissance into German East Africa

Today I took the Masai company down to Kibigori and met Col. Harrison, The company gave me a lot of trouble, grumbling the whole way in. I am thankful to say that I shall not have to take them to Nairobi, as Harrison wants me to go to Voi and make a reconnaissance of the Voi–Taveta–Moshi road and find out what the Germans are doing at Moshi. I shall therefore return to Nandi tomorrow to collect my kit. I am delighted with the idea of getting away from Nandi for a spell, and the idea of smelling out the fat of the land in German East Africa appeals to me. Sooner or later we are sure to have a war with the Germans, and what I do now may be of great value to any force of ours advancing from Voi towards Kilimanjaro.

2 . IV . 1906. *Nandi Fort*

To Nandi

Noises at Kibigori

I returned to Nandi Fort today to collect my kit for Voi. I got very little sleep last night, owing to the howling of the pariah dogs. Apparently there are elephants in the neighbourhood, and on such occasions the natives sit up all night to scare them off the crops. I never heard such a din as went on last night from sunset to dawn. Niggers howling, drums beating, women shrieking, dogs barking; and all this accompanied by the continuous hum of myriads of mosquitoes. As though this were not sufficient, some railway coolies sleeping near me kept up an intermittent but gorgeous chorus of snoring such as would awaken the dead. I am glad not to have to spend two nights at Kibigori.

On my way up to Nandi I found a small tent by the side of the road with an obvious servant standing outside. Thinking it curious that the white man was not yet out of bed, I entered the tent and found a white man whose name I do not yet know. He was lying on a broken-down camp bed, apparently unconscious. He had a raging fever on him and his servant told me he was putting up the telephone line from Nandi to Kibigori. I packed him up in blankets and had him carried on a rough stretcher into Nandi. His pulse was so weak I thought he was dying.

A dying white man

I have seldom seen a degree of discomfort and filth such as this poor fellow was suffering. His tent had not been ventilated for days, there were stinking antelope skins hanging all round him, stale food was on the floor, flies were buzzing all over and inside the tent, and the bed was bug-infested. If men will travel like this, what can they expect? How can they expect to keep healthy when they do not give themselves a chance? Such cases are nearly always due to a desire to save money and travel on the cheap. It always ends in disaster. This man would get Rs.5 a day when travelling, and there is no excuse for not spending it. It is a liberal allowance, but few of them spend it, thereby selling their health for a few shillings.

On arrival at Nandi I explained to Partington that I had brought a sick man in and asked him to look after him, as I had to return to Kibigori tomorrow. He replied that as I had brought him in I could look after him. I at once telegraphed to Kisumu asking that Partington be instructed to do his job in a gentlemanly and Christian-like manner. So Partington got a nice rap over the knuckles for his churlishness and my sick friend is now in bed in Partington's house. I went over this evening to see that he was being cared for and told Partington what I thought of him. If looks could kill I should now be doubly dead, but I fancy Partington will not now dare to neglect this poor fellow.

Partington's churlishness

[I heard later that the man was called Bruce and was employed by the Public Works. He died on the day after I left.]

I meet Bagge

I also met Bagge, the Sub-commissioner of Kisumu Province, on his way down the Nandi Escarpment to Kibigori. He told me he had not much faith in military plans, which were vague and vacillating. I rather resented the criticism. He has no opportunity of knowing the conditions which may lead to the countermanding of orders, and he is not conversant with the facts which prompt military orders; even if he were, he has not the military knowledge to appreciate them; and even if he had that knowledge, it is no business of his. He forgets that the military problem in East Africa is applicable to the whole protectorate and not only to the Nandi or the Kisumu Province. The Nandi Expedition is but an incident in the military life of the military forces in the colony, and we do not exist solely and entirely for quelling the Nandi. He is now very sore that we soldiers are not doing work which his police are doing. I told him that we were not here to do police work, and that if his police were better trained he would get better work out of them. The Nandi Expedition was the direct result of bad administration and of the failure of the civil police to deal with the situation.

Civil versus military

But I like Stephen Bagge; he is one of the oldest administrative officers out here, having been with Lugard in Uganda 15 years ago. Of course, he knows the country and the people much better than I do, but he does not resent criticism and usually encourages it. One of my great faults is blurting out what I think, often regretting it a moment later, and often giving advice to people who know much more about the facts than I do; but there it is, I cannot help my nature. I think Bagge is sufficiently broad-minded to forgive my impetuousness; in any case we always part friends.

3 . IV . 1906. *Nakuru, Uganda Railway*

I leave Nandi for Nairobi

I left Nandi Fort at 4 a.m. and arrived at 8.30 a.m. at Kibigori, where I met Bacon of the 1st K.A.R. Before leaving Nandi I met Hart, who had been sent up to take over from me. On the train I met Harrison, Bagge, Isaac, Hookey Walker, Sidney Couper and Weeks.

We lunched at Muhoroni and dined at Nakuru. Lord and Lady Hindlip joined the train at Njoro. He made a terrible noise on joining the train and generally got on everybody's nerves. She seemed equally anxious to proclaim her presence and was most suitably dressed, with a revolver in her belt and a *sjambok* in her hand. They both of them looked exactly what they are.

Lord Hindlip and his wife

I heard Harrison and Gorges discussing Pope Hennessey. Gorges described him as a charlatan and Harrison does not trust him and despises him. Pope Hennessey is an exceedingly able man with much academic knowledge, but lacks both character and personality. His ambition dominates everything, and he is always thinking how this or that may affect his military career; he is rude to his subordinates and craven to his superiors; he is intellectually dishonest. He is certainly not my cup of tea.

Pope Hennessey

4 . IV . 1906. *Nairobi*

Arrived at Nairobi this morning. I naturally expected to find great changes in the place, but was much surprised to see such a transformation scene as I witnessed today. The town has trebled itself in size. Trees have sprung up everywhere, hotels exist where zebras once roamed, private bungalows in all their ugliness now mar the landscape where I used to hunt the waterbuck, impala and duiker. The place is full of strange faces and I felt quite lost. Two years ago I knew every soul of the 20 or 30 Europeans. There are now over 1200 Europeans in the town.

Nairobi

I visited my miserable little 10 acres, now bereft of duiker and guinea-fowl. I was much amused when I was told that the new Government house was going to be built on my property; nobody has asked my permission, and I shall certainly not broach the subject. I can see a most amusing tangle developing.

5 . IV . 1906. *Nairobi*

When the Duke of Connaught was here he went out shooting on the Athi Plains and wounded a wildebeeste which was not recovered. Harrison, who accompanied

The Duke of Connaught's wildebeeste

him, told him that it could easily be recovered the next day. The Duke was apparently very keen on securing the head, and as he left Nairobi the next day he asked Harrison to wire whether it had been recovered. Harrison, of course, wired to say that it had been found dead and that its head had been brought in. As a matter of fact no trace of the ducal wildebeeste could be found, and Harrison had to kill another, which is being sent to Clarence House as the ducal wildebeeste.

7 . IV . 1906. *Uganda Railway*

I leave Nairobi for Voi

I started today on my trip to Moshi. I take the train to Voi and then walk across the Serengeti Plains. I saw a good deal of game from the train. My fellow passenger, Mr. Shaw Kennedy, saw some giraffe, but I was not so lucky.

Census of game on Athi Plains

From the train between Stony Athi and Nairobi and on the north side of the railway I saw 2 lion, 27 ostriches, 1644 zebra, 702 Coke's haartebeeste, 186 wildebeeste, 734 Grant's gazelle, 167 Thomson's gazelle, 16 impala, 8 kori bustard and 1 rhinoceros.

8 . IV . 1906. *Mwatate, Taita Hills*

I am mistaken for a doctor

I arrived at Voi at 2 a.m. in pouring rain. I went to the Dak Bungalow but found all three rooms occupied, so slept on the veranda. At dawn I awoke and found the three rooms were occupied by a party who were also on their way to Moshi. They were a mixed lot, comprising a German Count, an Irishman and a young Boer. The German told me that the young Dutchman was ill in bed, so I asked if I could be of any use. They asked me to see the boy, which I did. I found him in bed and obviously recovering from a slight attack of malaria. His pulse and temperature were normal. It amused me to go through all the usual doctor's formulas, such as looking at his tongue, etc. I prescribed some medicine from my box and told him he would be all right by noon. The Irishman burst in with, "So you see, my boy, what the doctor says. Pull yourself together and we'll cancel your coffin!" I was quite sorry for the lad, having to travel with these two obvious rogues. The German had the effrontery to ask me what was my fee, and when I said it was usually Rs.25 but that I would only charge him 10 he gave me a 20 rupee note and told me to keep the change, which I did.

I leave Voi

I had collected my porters by 10 a.m., when I started off along the Taveta road, reaching Mwatate at 4 p.m. As soon as I crossed the Voi River it began to pour with rain, which drenched me to the skin and made the road too slippery to be pleasant. At Mwatate I found my old friend McClellan in bed with fever, but he kindly insisted on my being his guest.

9 . IV . 1906. *Mwatate, Taita Hills*

Sketching at Mwatate

I remained here for the day in order to sketch the surrounding country. There are several good positions covering the water, but the country is so densely wooded that it would be an easy matter for attacking troops to work round the flanks unseen. The secret of holding Mwatate is to hold a position as far forward as possible with the water behind one. The Germans must have as much waterless desert as possible to cross before they attack, so that when defeated they perish in the wilderness. It is a gorgeous country for ambushes.

10 . IV . 1906. *Bura River*

Jolly the Maltese trader

I came on today to the Bura River, some 5 miles from Mwatate. I met a Maltese trader called Jolly. He gave me a lot of information about the Voi–Taveta road. He tells me there are 2500 irreconcilable Boers settled on the slopes of Kilimanjaro who would take up arms against us in the event of an Anglo-German war. This might be a serious proposition, and I shall have to sift this evidence carefully.

Mongooses and butterflies

While sketching today I was much struck by the number and variety of the butterflies and mongooses. I must have seen hundreds of the latter today.

11 . IV . 1906. *Maktau, Serengeti Plains*

Partridges and plover

I left camp at dawn and am now camped on the path opposite Maktau Hill. Mongooses and butterflies gave place today to partridges and plover. Of the former there are two species, a large and a small. If I had had the appetite I might have killed 50 brace, but I contented myself with one bird. There are always two or three plover running ahead of me on the sandy path, but I did not molest them.

Game

I saw a small herd of zebra and haartebeeste and two female Peter's gazelle (a race of Grant's gazelle). I killed one of the latter for my men. I also saw some vulturine guinea-fowl, which I was unable to come up with.

Maktau Hill

I paid a visit to the Maktau water-hole on Maktau Hill. It lies some 1½ miles from the road in an N.N.E. direction. The water-holes consist of two large rock pools, the larger of which is about 21 feet long and 5 feet broad, and shelves back to 4 feet deep. In this water I was surprised to find numbers of what I at first took to be small fish but which are no doubt the larvae of some mosquito. They were about an inch and a half long, with huge protruding eyes and a vermilion tail. Several antelope bones round the water showed that lion are in the habit of visiting it.

12 . IV . 1906. *Mbuyuni, Serengeti Plains*

I kill a bull giraffe

I left Maktau before dawn and camped at Mbuyuni. About half-way between the two places I saw 3 giraffe standing close to the road ahead of me. The party consisted of a bull, a cow and a three-parts grown youngster. I stalked them to within 50 yards and fired at the bull. I was using my Mannlicher with solid bullets. The beast ran about 100 yards and fell over dead. I found that he was hit behind the shoulder and that the bullet had passed right through him, coming out as solid as it had gone in. Though richly marked he is not a very large specimen, measuring 8 feet at the withers and weighing about half a ton. His skull is a most interesting study. He belongs to the three-horned variety—if a large bump on the forehead can be strictly termed a horn. My men were delighted at the prospect of so much meat, and I am looking forward to a good meal this evening off giraffe marrow bones and roast partridge. I am salting his prehensile tongue for some future occasion.

There must be a good many giraffe about here, as the soft ground is a mass of their spoor. I also saw a good deal of fresh lion spoor.

Game census

As I write lion are roaring from two directions, which means there is much game about. I saw the following from the road between Maktau and Mbuyuni: 18 *Oryx collotis*, 14 gerenuk, 2 lesser kudu, 37 zebra and 123 Grant's gazelle, 3 rhino and 25 ostrich.

Two German soldiers

No sooner had I pitched my tent than two German soldiers from Moshi arrived from Taveta. I was rather astonished to see them with arms and ammunition, so I asked to see their papers. They had been instructed by their commandant to take letters into Voi. I told them that they had no business in British territory with their arms and that they would have to leave them with me. They were at first a bit reluctant to part, but I told them quite frankly that if they showed any resistance their arms and equipment would be taken by force. They thereupon surrendered and I gave them a note to their commandant explaining why I had disarmed them. They then proceeded on their way with their letters. Apparently it is a regular custom for the Germans to send their mails to Voi. But I suspect it is also a means of getting their men accustomed to the Serengeti Plains and acquainted with the shortest route by which British East Africa can be invaded. It is a custom I must stop. Meanwhile I have a good opportunity of closely scrutinising German rifles and ammunition.

13 . IV . 1906. *Taveta, Serengeti Plains*

Taveta

I left Mbuyuni at dawn and came through to Taveta. It was raining when I left camp and never stopped till I reached Taveta. The road was soft and muddy, closely resembling a ploughed field with a clay soil. Several species of francolin were abundant on the roadside, but the only four-legged animal I saw was an *Oryx collotis*. I tried a half-hearted stalk, but he was wide awake and

Game

made off. His fringed ears were quite conspicuous even at 300 yards.

Collyer

On arrival at the Lumi River, which runs quite close to the old Government bungalow, I found that my old friend Collyer was living a mile further on, the new Government quarters being built on a small rise nearer the German frontier and not far from the Mission Station. Collyer is kindly putting me up.

Military considerations regarding Taveta

I spent the day with my plane table. The ridge on which the Mission Station stands offers a good position for a small force covering the crossing of the Lumi River, but it is beset with many grave disadvantages. In the first place the whole of the Taveta position is untenable so long as Chala, a hill and crater lake north of Taveta, is in enemy hands. The Taveta position is really of no importance, and one must look further afield for the correct method of checking German invasion on this line.

The only real way of holding the Taveta salient is to base one's right on Chala and one's left on the Taveta Forest. It would require at least a brigade to hold this against anything the Germans could bring against us. Salaita Hill to one's rear offers a good small position for a rearguard, but it is devoid of water. But the great objection is that one has 80 miles of waterless country behind. I should therefore never advocate holding the Taveta position unless as a bridgehead which was awaiting strong reinforcements from Voi.

If, therefore, war breaks out between England and Germany we must either defend this line against German invasion or attack them with 80 miles of waterless desert behind us. To make the former successful an Indian expeditionary force of at least two brigades should be hurried over while a battalion of K.A.R. held on to Taveta. This plan would require such preparations at Taveta as would preclude the chance of secrecy, and it could not succeed.

We must therefore adopt the other alternative and, based on Voi, concentrate for a determined and slow advance across the Serengeti Plains, which means a railway. Such a railway presents no difficulties and it should be comparatively immune from raids. On the other hand, we need fear no attack on Voi in strength. So long as we keep command of the seas the Germans could never organise a serious attack across that desert while we had a battalion or two at Bura with outposts at Maktau. I regard the deserts of Serengeti and Kapiti as the best defences of British East Africa, but on the other hand they make any British invasion of German East Africa a task out of all proportion to its importance, and scarcely worth undertaking if one accepts the principle that the real decision in any Anglo-German war will be arrived at in Europe and not in Africa. If that is so, the only real problem in British East Africa is its immediate defence, which is simplified by geographical conditions.

Taveta Forest and the natives of Taveta

In the evening I paid a visit to Taveta Forest to measure a spring. The forest is exotic and dense, with a few huge timber trees, but it consists mainly of matted creepers and impenetrable undergrowth. I came across a few of the remnants of the Taveta tribe, who are fast disappearing under the influences of their climate and of drink. They were formerly a tribe which lived all along the Lumi, but they have been raided and decimated by the Wachagga from Kilimanjaro and the Masai from the plains. They are now a miserable community of a few hundred souls and their fate is sealed. They and their unique language will be dead in half a century.

Taveta Mission

I had tea at the Taveta Mission, where I was entertained by Miss Mayor and Miss Austen, both nice English girls without any of that evangelical pretentiousness which usually stamps such people. I have a great admiration for English girls who come out here and do the work of these two women. Both were very happy. They gave Collyer and me an excellent tea, and I came away with a strong taste of home in my mouth.

Collyer

I notice that Collyer could walk only at a snail's pace. He was so done up after our walk to the Mission that I thought he was going to collapse. I fear he has bad consumption on him. He is naturally an athletic man, and his inability to take exercise has sent his weight up to 15 stone. His racking cough made me feel so sorry for him, but he is in excellent spirits.

Insects at Taveta

As I write now the lamp is a mass of moths and other

noxious insects. They crawl all over one's hands, neck and face, and it is quite an effort to think under their annoying interruption. They consist of mantises, beetles of all colours and sizes, moths from the tiniest micro-lepidoptera to the gaudiest fluffy things the size of small birds, flying ants and, of course, the inevitable hosts of mosquitoes. Outside it is close, damp and sultry, with a babel of night noises—owls, nightjars, cicadas, crickets and the continuous buzz of myriads of mosquitoes.

15 . IV . 1906. *Taveta*

Lake Jipe

Before dawn I was out on a trip towards Lake Jipe to the south-east of Taveta. I was sketching most of the time but took the opportunity to stalk a fine fringe-eared oryx. Reaching to within 120 yards of him, I bowled him over with one shot. On my way home I killed a haartebeeste and a steinbock.

I kill an oryx

Kilimanjaro

Early this morning I had a perfect view of Kilimanjaro. The clouds lifted for a few minutes and disclosed those fascinating snow-clad slopes. Through my glasses I could distinctly see the glaciers and the open country above the forest. But by 8 a.m. dense cloud had again descended and one could see no sign of a hill. There must have been a heavy fall of snow recently, as it was still lying across the main plateau from the big peak to the northern spur known as Mawenzi.

Woman bitten by a snake

This evening a native woman was brought in who had just been bitten by a snake. She was on the point of collapse, so we poured whisky down her throat, lanced the wound and poured ammonia into the fang marks. Meanwhile we set two sturdy policemen to keep her on the move at a brisk trot. She pulled round in about an hour and was then conducted to her hut, roaring drunk but out of danger.

16 . IV . 1906. *Mbuyuni, German E. Africa*

I cross the border into German East Africa

I left Taveta this morning and soon crossed the boundary between British East and German East, which is marked by a typically German red, white and black post.* On our

* In 1916 when we invaded German East Africa I removed this post, which is now in my house.

side of the boundary the road was good, but on entering German East it became bad and had obviously not been lately repaired. About noon I reached a spot called Mbuyuni, called after a magnificent example of the baobab tree. Mbuyuni is on the right bank of the Shalo River, and there are some splendid examples of the baobab tree in the neighbourhood. The finest of these was 94 feet in circumference 4 feet from the ground. At Mbuyuni I camped close to the tent of a German trader who was already there. As soon as he knew I was English he volunteered that he had fought against us during the Boer War and that he now regretted it, as he had since found out the true character of the South African Dutchman. Nothing in the world would induce him to help them again. He described them as lying, thieving, filthy, lazy scoundrels. I expect he describes us in much the same way to his Boer friends. As he was so communicative, I enquired about the Boers who had settled in German East Africa. He assured me there were some 400 souls, most of them were near Arusha, and that they were most unsatisfactory settlers. There were no Boer families on the slopes of Kilimanjaro. He also assured me that the Boer was so independent that he would probably leave German East for British East shortly, as he was most dissatisfied with existing conditions.

A German trader

At a small store kept here by a Somali trader I purchased 30 bananas of good quality for one heller or an eighth of a penny. Other food was correspondingly cheap, eggs being 8 for a penny.

Cheap bananas

17 . IV . 1906. *Moshi*

I marched up the lower slopes of Kilimanjaro and entered Moshi Fort this morning, where Oberleutnant Abel, whom I had previously met at Nairobi, is in command. He very kindly put me up. The other Germans living in the fort comprise a doctor, a lieutenant, a paymaster and three non-commissioned officers.

I enter Moshi

The whole of this afternoon I was bombarded with questions about our army, its customs, organisation, strength, etc. During dinner and till near midnight the bombardment continued. I fancy it was all intentional,

I am bombarded with questions

so that I should not have an opportunity of asking them questions. But I have very few to ask and can find out all I want by seeing and hearing. Our officers' mess system was a conundrum to them all. They could not understand how a colonel could sit down and eat at the same table with subalterns or how a major could play cards with a second lieutenant. Such a thing would be impossible in their army. Such a disgrace as an officer playing games with his men has never been heard of in the German army.

They were most anxious to hear about the Nandi Expedition, about which they had heard many tales. When I told them that I had killed the Laibon they were delighted, as they had heard all about it from some English traders who were through here lately.

The Boers

Abel tells me that a good many Boer families have recently come to German East Africa and have not acquitted themselves well. They are inveterate thieves, treat the natives abominably and will not pay any attention to regulations. Many of these families have not been able to stand the discipline of German rule and have already migrated to British territory. Abel told me that the Germans are now beginning to understand our motives in the recent South African War and the injustice of the severe criticism levelled at our heads by the Continental press during that war.

Military considerations at Moshi

In the evening, while the Germans were playing tennis, I had a stroll round and noted many things, such as the water supply, the best means of attacking Moshi and the obvious methods of defending it. I was also able to form a pretty good idea of the country lying between here and Arusha, and between here and the Pangani River. It all lay outstretched before me on a brilliantly clear day. But I do not attach much importance to the building. It is on the road to nowhere, and the Germans would not attempt to defend it if we invaded their country. They would fight us in and around Taveta and if beaten retire towards Arusha.

I came across the three German N.C.O.s out for a walk and went some way with them. I told them I was stopping with their officers. I think they must have thought I was a Boer, but I got a lot of useful information out of them which their officers would never have given me. They told me a lot about the different tribes enlisted, how they took to discipline, the fighting qualities of the various races, and the strength and distribution of companies. I learned that there was no reserve in the country but that one was to be formed fairly shortly. There are some 140 Europeans in the country who have done their term in the German army and who would join the companies in the event of war. I found these fellows most communicative, and from one or two things they said I am convinced they think I hail from the kopjes and veldt of South Africa.

18 . IV . 1906. *Moshi*

I inspect a German company on parade

I never thought I should be allowed to inspect a German company on parade, but I did so this morning, walking solemnly round the ranks. The company afterwards marched past me and Abel insisted on my taking the salute. After breakfast I witnessed some musketry practice at 150 and 300 yards. They do not train their men to fire beyond that range. The fire discipline was excellent but the marksmanship vile. I also witnessed the shooting of the small 37 mm. guns. The range was roughly 800 yards but the shooting was abominable. Out of 24 shells fired, 6 were misfires and only one hit the target, which was 12 feet by 8. But I expect they have better and more reliable ammunition in their magazine.

I was much impressed by the discipline and drill of the men under their N.C.O.s. It was perfect. I do not doubt that the Germans have created as fine a military machine out here as they have done at home, and it must be reckoned with in case of war. They are every bit as good as our K.A.R. but lack the ties which exist between officer and man. In the K.A.R. it is a bond of genuine friendship. Among these Germans it is the tie of an iron discipline. War alone can prove which is the most effective.

European politics

After dinner conversation drifted to the European situation. Abel expressed the greatest confidence in again being able to smash France. He said that in numbers alone they were superior. The German army was also infinitely superior in command, discipline and morale. It was a perfect machine, while the French army was rotten to the core. He went so far as to say that he thought it would be to the benefit of the world if Germany were to crush this rotten race. Abel is a Prussian and has studied Frederick the Great. Abel spoke with confidence, and I believe with truth, when he said that the German army would be thundering at the gates of Paris before France was completely mobilised. I believe that is true. I told him that it was common knowledge that in any invasion of France Belgian neutrality would be violated. He agreed, and added, "And what would Belgium do beyond protest?" I hinted that there was such a thing as respect for a weaker neighbour, at which he got excited and said that where national existence was at stake nothing else mattered. Germany must crush France or France would crush her, and when the time came Germany would know how to defend herself, or how to attack.

I nearly added, "My friend, you have not taken into account the attitude of England. The growth of your navy is a direct challenge to us, and when the time comes we shall not stand by and see France crushed by Germany. It will be our opportunity to settle matters once and for all with our great naval antagonist."

German opinion of the Russian army

I asked Abel his opinion of the Russian army. He said it was too slow and would never mobilise in time. It was also rotten and corrupt to the core. He said that if Germany had had Russia's problem in the Far East she would have finished Japan off in a year. The Russians were brave and came from good fighting stock, but they were badly led, and the higher command was hopeless.

War in British and German colonies

Abel asked me what was my opinion of the chance of a European war spreading to our African colonies. I told him I had never heard it discussed but that it would be a pity if Europeans should fight with black men in Africa when no real decision could be arrived at. He agreed and hoped that our Governments would arrange that in the event of an Anglo-German conflict the African colonies would remain neutral. Of course, that would be the ideal course, but sooner or later they would fight it out among themselves in spite of previous agreements. If it came to a fight we should have the whip hand of Germany, as she would at once lose command of the sea and could get no more reinforcements in either personnel or material. We could easily defend British East until we were prepared to send an expeditionary force from India to conquer the country. Abel realised that. I explained to him that any agreement on the lines he suggested would be to the advantage of Germany. What I did not tell him was that I thought such a conflict between his and my country inevitable, and equally inevitable our eventual victory and our acquisition of German East Africa. With that in my mind I could not help feeling satisfaction over the development schemes the Germans are now undertaking out here, for they will all some day revert to us.

German railways

I asked Abel about railway development in the colony. He tells me the line which will link up the Kilimanjaro area with the coast is well advanced, as also the railway which they are building from Dar-es-Salaam to Lake Tanganyika. They also intend to take the Kilimanjaro railway to Arusha, Magadi and the Victoria Nyanza, with a view to tapping our Uganda trade, which will all come down the Uganda railway, But they will be a bit late.

19 . IV . 1906. *Kilema, Kilimanjaro*

I leave Moshi

Today I left Moshi for Taveta but am taking the top road in order to visit Lake Chala. Owing to dense mist I never saw farther than a few feet from me the whole day, which was most annoying. After marching along a slippery mountain track for 5 hours I fetched up at a Roman Catholic mission called Kilema, where I was given a bed and a meal, for which I was most grateful. Altogether I cannot have come more than 12 miles today. It is most annoying not to have seen the summit of Kilimanjaro at close quarters.

I found the missionaries most communicative. They also thought I was a South African and told me a lot about the Wachagga, the tribe which lives in these parts. Some years ago they gave the Germans a great deal of trouble, but they are now completely subdued. He did not think they would ever again give any trouble, but they did not like their masters and preferred the English. I asked why, and was told that German rule is too severe and too full of restrictions. British rule is more elastic and takes the native character into account. German regulations are based on Western ideas and ride roughshod over native prejudices and customs.

20 . IV . 1906. *Lake Chala, Kilimanjaro*

Lake Chala

Leaving my kind hosts soon after dawn I marched to Lake Chala, which I reached just as it was getting dark. I camped in the old Boundary Commission huts, which still exist in a tumbledown fashion on the west side of the lake. Having marched in pouring rain the whole day, everything was sodden. A fluffy green mould was growing on my remaining bread but the inside was excellent. I dined off a tin of caviar and a tin of pears.

Slugs and bananas

The whole of today I marched through banana plantations and slugs. I appear to have seen little else. There was a dense mist which obscured all view. Both slugs and huge snails littered the path. The slugs were of all colours and sizes. Some were opaque blue, others pink, some green, some white and green, and others a dirty grey. They ranged from some 5 inches long to tiny creatures scarcely visible.

Mariali, the chief of the Wachagga

Today I passed the house of Mariali, the chief of the Wachagga tribe. His house was a two-storied stone structure, well built and well furnished. Mariali was once banished from German East Africa by the Germans and fled to Nairobi. The Germans quite recently enticed him back with the promise of restoring to him his cattle which had been confiscated. He returned, and though the Germans have done a lot to make life comfortable he has not yet got his cattle back, which has made him bitter against them. He complained to me about the treatment afforded him by the Germans, and asked me openly why we did not come and throw them out. He said his tribe would assist. As I did not wish to be dragged into expressing myself on this subject, I said I did not understand, so he expressed himself on the same lines, elaborating his wish, but in different language. Again I said I did not understand, and then I think he appreciated my point of view. If I had given him any favourable opening he would have jumped at it. He is credited with having great influence with his people, and should the occasion arise I shall not forget what he said.

21 . IV . 1906. *Taveta*

Mosquitoes

I was glad when daylight came and silenced the hosts of devouring mosquitoes. It also gave us all a chance to get dry.

Lake Chala

Lake Chala is a crater lake of great charm. It lies at the bottom of a deep crater, with steep cliffs on all sides. There is only one path down to its waters, and this I descended. From below it was indeed weird. The slightest noise was echoed over its silent black waters. No wonder the natives have all sorts of legends about it. A fish eagle (*vocifer*) was circling over the waters, screeching hard. The lake is said to be full of crocodiles, but I saw no sign of them. On gaining the top again I found some haartebeeste near camp, so I killed one for the men. I had previously seen a rhino some distance off but had no intention of molesting him. On my firing at the haartebeeste he trotted off to a patch of bush lying directly across my path, in which he concealed himself. As I did not wish my porters to make a detour, I told them to follow the path into Taveta, and said that I should watch to see the rhino did not molest them. I hurried on and posted myself near the patch of bush into which the rhino had gone. No sooner had I sat down than there was a snort and out he came with tail erect. He was looking at my caravan and standing some 100 yards from me. In order to divert his attention and perhaps make him move away I put two shots just under his tail, but this made him frantic with excitement and he began to stamp the ground, showing an inclination to move towards my caravan, so I put a bullet in his neck

I am compelled to kill an excited rhinoceros

and toppled him over. I was sorry to have to do it, but I could not risk having my party charged.

A curious corncrake

After cutting up the rhino I searched for some partridge which had been calling in the grass. I flushed a curious-looking corncrake with barred underparts. I have never heard of such a bird before, and I shall most certainly keep his skin. The corncrake was actually flushed in German East Africa but fell in British East Africa. Which colony claims him?

I reached Taveta at 1 p.m. and lunched with my friend Collyer.

22 . IV . 1906. *Mbuyuni, Serengeti Plains*

Game

Today I commenced my return journey to Voi. I saw a fine bull giraffe near the road at Salaita Hill and another small herd of the same animals at Lanjoro watercourse. They were absurdly tame and kept on the path till I was within 80 yards of them. Even then they merely walked off. There was a good deal of game about, including two lots of Waller's gazelle, lesser kudu and *Oryx collotis*.

Lion kills giraffe

I was fortunate today in seeing a single lion kill a half-grown giraffe. What astonished me was the ease with which he did it and the stupidity of the giraffe. I first saw the lion standing up in full view, his tail slowly twitching; he was intently watching a herd of three adults and one half-grown youngster. He was about 300 yards from the giraffe and they were looking in his direction. The ground was quite flat, without bushes or cover of any sort. Then the lion began to walk towards the giraffe. At 200 yards from them he broke into a trot, the giraffe remaining stationary and watching him. There was no effort to conceal his attack. It seemed to me that the giraffe never appreciated the danger until it was too late. When about 100 yards from the giraffe the lion broke into a canter and the giraffe then lumbered off, the last in the procession being the unfortunate calf. The lion's canter became a rush and he soon overtook the calf and sprang on it, the two tumbling in a heap with the lion firmly fixed on the throat of the calf. He remained thus for about two minutes, then stood up, regaining breath, and did not begin to feed for fully 5 minutes. Meanwhile the giraffe had made no attempt to protect the calf but stood watching the lion from about 300 yards. It was all so easy but rather horrible. I might have stalked the lion while he fed but I thought that would be a breach of good manners, and after all he had afforded me a most interesting spectacle.

Birds

All the birds have begun to nest. I never saw such a scrimmage for nesting sites and such a fuss. I found many nests, including those of a small bustard, many nightjar nests and countless numbers in the small bushes. What interested me was a huge colony of hundreds of a weaver bird, all nesting in a mass on a tree. Their babble could be heard several hundred yards away. In the morning I killed a great bustard for my dinner.

23 . IV . 1906. *Mbuyuni, Serengeti Plains*

I enjoy a record day's sport

Last night lion roared almost continuously, so I decided to stop here the day and try for them. I must also plead guilty to having shot more today than my party could eat. I have no excuse except a hunter's love of the chase.

A brace of cock ostrich

Just as it was getting light my orderly came in and said there were ostrich near camp. I leaped out of bed and found a dense mist enveloping the whole country. Through this and only some 150 yards from my tent I saw two cock ostrich feeding. I crept out in pyjamas, and working round to some bushes approached to within 50 yards of them. They were both feeding, so selecting the largest I hit him through the thighs, and down he went. I finished him off with a stick. The second bird ran some 200 yards and stood. I hit him, and down he went. Returning for breakfast, I dressed and again sallied forth.

Waller's gazelle

I soon came across a buck and two doe Waller's gazelle. They spotted me and made off, but at 200 yards I put a bullet through the buck's heart and picked him up dead some 20 yards farther on. These peculiar long-necked antelopes seem to be not uncommon in the district. When they make off they hold their heads straight in front of them and trot off in a quaint skulking attitude.

Peter's gazelle

About half an hour after this I found a large herd of

eland in a clearing together with a solitary buck Peter's gazelle. The eland gradually fed away from me, leaving the gazelle unapproachable, but he soon solved the problem by lying down. I was then able to creep up to within 100 yards of him and killed him with a bullet behind the shoulder. I then made my way back to camp and out of a thicket bounded a fine lesser kudu, at which I fired when some 60 yards distant. I heard the bullet strike, but he kept on and was soon lost to sight. There was a slight blood trail, which I followed for some distance but soon had to abandon it. This is most annoying, as he was a really fine buck and I thought I was shooting straight.

Lesser kudu

A brace of Coke's haartebeeste

Haartebeeste had been giving me a great deal of trouble today in their efforts to spoil my sport and generally disturb the whole countryside. They persistently alarmed game when I was trying to approach unseen, and I was considerably annoyed with haartebeeste in general. A pair of these ungainly and abominable beasts had even so much forgotten themselves as deliberately to dog my footsteps for over an hour. But eventually I managed to throw them off and then stalk them from an unexpected quarter. Coming to within 100 yards of them I dropped them both with a bullet each before they knew what was happening.

Bustard's eggs

Quite close to camp I found two nests of some small bustard and a nest of some stone plover (*Oedicnemus*). I took all the eggs and enjoyed them for supper this evening, along with ostrich liver and the tongue of the Waller's gazelle.

Game census

I counted the game I saw from the road between Mbuyuni and Maktau. It amounted to 18 giraffe, 7 rhinoceros, 34 ostrich, 7 gerenuk, 3 lesser kudu, 46 *Oryx collotis*, 18 eland, 68 Coke's haartebeeste, 36 Grant's gazelle, 17 impala, 8 warthog, 9 wild dog and 1 cheetah.

Wild dog and oryx

I was most interested to see the tactics of a small herd of oryx when attacked by a pack of 9 wild dog. I first saw the dogs galloping towards the oryx; as they approached they separated and went into the attack from three sides. The oryx closed ranks, faced outwards and kept their heads down. The dogs kept on charging up to them but kept out of range of their sharp horns. I think the dogs were after two calves which sheltered more or less in the centre of the group. After much charging almost up to the oryx in the hope of stampeding them, the dogs drew off. The oryx maintained their close formation for about a quarter of an hour after the dogs left them. I was glad to see that these wild dogs do not always have it all their own way.

24 . IV . 1906. *Maktau, Serengeti Plains*

Butterflies

I moved to Maktau today. After the rain it was a still balmy day, and clusters of butterflies collected on the path in search of moisture. Some of these clusters were nearly 3 feet across.

Lion

As I moved out of camp this morning there was a thick mist and the still air reverberated with the majestic roar of a lion. Though he must have been a mile off it sounded loud and clear in the silence of very early dawn. I became conscious of the majesty of the wild lion, which can only be appreciated by those who have heard him. A lion is probably at his best when he roars. A lion skulking away is neither inspiring nor majestic. But when he roars or charges he is a different animal, though a good roar is finer than the snarling grunt which is emitted when he is angry. A charging lion, with bristles erect and tail going like a flywheel, is an inspiring sight. He personifies temper, anger and rage.

I have never seen a lion roar. Perhaps he looks silly when he roars; but that makes the roar no less fine.

I intercept an interesting letter

While some of my men were up at the Maktau water-hole this evening a native turned up bearing a letter addressed to "Count Cudenhove" at Bura. The man was brought into my camp and owned that he was a German soldier in disguise, which I had suspected from his general demeanour. He also told my men that his instructions from Herr Leutnant Abel were to avoid my camp and deliver the letter personally to Cudenhove. I told the man he had better sleep in my camp tonight for fear of lion and he could proceed tomorrow. I also told two of my men to wait till he was asleep and then

Cudenhove

extract from him that letter, the contents of which I wished to see. Who was Cudenhove, what was he doing, and why was the man told to avoid my camp? Also, why should Abel send his men disguised as porters to a German, obviously up to some mischief in British territory?

At 10.30 p.m. one of my men brought me the German soldier's letter, which was sealed up. When I carefully cut round the seal with a sharp knife, it came off with the paper to which it was attached. Then I steamed open the letter, which read as follows in German:

My dear friend,

A British officer called Meinertzhagen has recently been staying here and it is thought he may have been sketching the country and making notes of military value. As he returns to Voi through Bura you should endeavour to ascertain from him or his men what has been the actual nature of his visit to German East Africa, and if it is possible try to secure any maps or notes he has made. I leave matter of detail with confidence in your hands. The bearer of this letter has been instructed to proceed to your camp via Chala and Maktau without attracting attention. You may keep him with you if you wish. Hoping to hear from you shortly and that your work has been a success,

With kind wishes from us all,

(Signed) A. Abel

Moshi, 20 *April* Oberleutnant

I carefully stuck up the letter again, replaced the seal and, running the edge round with a hot pin, spread the wax over the cut paper in such a way that nobody could suspect that it had been tampered with. I then told my man to replace the letter where it had been.

The letter is illuminating and has kept me thinking far into the night. So Mr. Cudenhove is playing precisely the same game as I am, and I fancy I can beat him at it. I shall hatch a plan of operations on my way in to Bura tomorrow, and shall send the German soldier well ahead of my party so that Cudenhove can have plenty of time to prepare for my coming.

I recorded the speed of a black mamba at Mbuyuni. They are reported to travel as fast as a trotting horse. This one, when chasing one of my men, only did 7 m.p.h., timed with stop-watch over 47 yards distance. I think the snake was going all out, as we had baited it and it was very angry. It eventually chased one of my men, but as the latter tripped up I had to shoot the snake. It measured 5 feet 7 inches.

Speed of mamba

Before leaving my camp at Mbuyuni this morning I made a final search for my wounded kudu. One of my men, seeing vultures in a tree, approached the spot and found his picked carcass. The horns were undamaged.

I recover my lesser kudu

25 . IV . 1906. *Bura, Serengeti Plains*

At dawn this morning the German soldier left my camp with his letter for Cudenhove at Bura. After giving him a start of two hours I proceeded to Bura, where I camped. Here I met one Pattison, a local planter. Pattison tells me that Cudenhove moved his camp yesterday to Mwataate. I made enquiries of Pattison about Cudenhove, and there can be little doubt that the man is simply surveying the country and clandestinely gleaning all the information he can about the Voi–Taveta route and its possibilities as a line of invasion of British East Africa. I am quite clear in my mind that it is my duty to prevent him from acquiring this information and I must use every means in my power to that end.

To Bura

Pattison

Pattison employs three Europeans on his estate—an Italian, a German, and an Englishman called Edgell. This latter fellow has just got into trouble with the German authorities over the border and is now on bail from Moshi. They treated him badly, for he was arrested by black soldiers and marched with handcuffs through native villages. His offence was that he had omitted to pay land tax. Edgell therefore hates the Germans. It was obvious that he could and would help me in defeating Cudenhove. I asked Pattison for the loan of his services for two days, and also asked Pattison if he would invite Cudenhove over to his camp on the day after tomorrow. He said he would. Cudenhove has a retinue of 7 persons,

Pattison's men

all natives: his personal servant, his cook, the German soldier who must have joined him today, and 4 others. He poses as a geologist and prospective settler, but Pattison tells me that he is neither, simply a German official on rather doubtful business. Cudenhove says he is an Austrian subject, but unfortunately he is on the books of the German East African Administration as an engineer officer. This evening Edgell and I hatched a plan which is quite simple. While Cudenhove is with Pattison I will get McClellan to order his servants up to the Government station, which is within a stone's throw of Cudenhove's camp. Edgell and I will then go through Cudenhove's papers, take what we want and burn the camp. It should look like a careless accident.

Tattersall, one of Pattison's partners

Pattison has been unlucky in losing one of his partners, a man called Tattersall. He recently went off his head, a common occurrence due to the climate, shot two policemen and tried to shoot Collyer's servant. He is now lodged in Mombasa gaol awaiting trial.

As I do not wish to encounter Cudenhove for the moment I shall stop tomorrow night at the French Roman Catholic Mission Station in the Taita Hills, where my property will be safer than in camp at Mwataate, for these French priests hate the Germans.

26 . IV . 1906. *Bura Mission*

Bura Mission

I came up to the French Roman Catholic Mission in the Bura Hills and asked if they would take me in as a paying guest. Father Lutz, an Alsatian, was in charge, the Mother Superior being in Mombasa. After handing over my notes and maps to the safe custody of Father Lutz, Edgell and I proceeded to make a reconnaissance of Cudenhove's camp, which took us the whole afternoon. I also saw McClellen at Mwataate. As Cudenhove's servants are not yet registered, he will send for them at 3 p.m. and keep them busy till 4 p.m. That should give Edgell and me all the time we require to go through his papers and burn his camp.

We reconnoitre Cudenhove's camp

The Mission gardens

I spent an enjoyable evening in the peace and quiet of the Mission gardens. The place has now been running for 8 years and the orange trees are well grown and bearing a good crop of luscious fruit. These French missionaries do themselves well. I had for lunch a most excellent non-intoxicating drink made from honey, together with a home-made cream cheese which could not be beaten by our Devonshire ones.

27 . IV . 1906. *Mwataate*

The defeat of Mr. Cudenhove

I spent the morning sifting the notes I had made in German East Africa, and after lunch, having said goodbye to my kind hosts, moved down to Mwataate. I passed McClellan's office at 2 p.m. and learned that Cudenhove had already gone to Pattison's camp about two hours before. I pitched my camp about 800 yards from Cudenhove's. At 2.30 I saw a policeman come to Cudenhove's camp and march the whole of Cudenhove's retinue up to the Government office. Edgell and I, who were in the thick bush near the camp, at once entered the camp, quickly removed two despatch cases and some maps from a small tin box under Cudenhove's bed, sprinkled the place with paraffin and put a match to it. Up it all went, and in 10 minutes Cudenhove's tent and grass hut, and those of his men, were but heaps of black ashes. As soon as the flames were spotted from the Government station all hands rushed down to try to rescue Cudenhove's belongings, but too late. My own men also ran down to help, but it was no good. Grass huts burn very quickly. Cudenhove's retinue were in a terrible state of alarm, dreading the rage of Cudenhove. Meanwhile, pending Cudenhove's return, I told my men to build him a grass hut near mine, saying that I would feed him tonight. I also fed his men and allowed them to sleep in my camp. Cudenhove's belongings are safely stowed under my bed.

Cudenhove's return

About 5.30 p.m. Cudenhove, some of whose men had gone along the road to meet him and apprise him of the disaster, arrived in my camp. I introduced myself and saw his look of astonishment when he heard my name. He spoke English perfectly, and I expressed my regret that his camp had been burned down. We visited the ashes of his tent, but there was nothing recognisable except the few twisted tin cases of instruments and the skeleton of his camp bed. He appeared to be much upset at his loss but was grateful for my hospitality.

During the course of the evening he asked me if I had had a pleasant visit to German East Africa, to which I replied that I had. I told him that a messenger for him had passed the night in my camp at Bura, and that I hoped he had received the letter. He said that he had and that it was from the authorities telling him to return. There he lied. He kept asking me questions far into the night about where I had been and what I had done, but he got little but shooting information out of me. Tonight I have a guard on my tent, also a man watching his hut. I suspect that Cudenhove thinks that I was in some way mixed up with the loss of his camp, and I do not intend that he should burn my tent down in the night.

I have not yet dared to examine Cudenhove's maps and papers but I shall do so tomorrow at Voi.

28 . IV . 1906. *Voi*

I meet the Mother Superior of the Bura Mission

Having carefully packed Cudenhove's stuff among my bedding, I left Mwataate for Voi soon after dawn, having breakfasted with Cudenhove. He also leaves at once for Moshi. When I said goodbye, I told him that I hoped we might meet again, I think he knows, and understands.

It was a steaming hot day and on arrival at the Voi River I took my clothes off and bathed just below the ford. I was sitting quite naked on a mossy rock when to my utter dismay and astonishment a very beautiful woman dressed in white nun's clothes appeared at the ford riding a white donkey. The apparition was so lovely that I simply stared. She was riding straddle-legs and, looking straight at me, smiled and wished me good morning in French. I replied in her language, regretting my inability to stand up, but told her that I had recently stopped at her Mission, and that Father Lutz had been most kind to me. Thus we conversed for some time. She told me her name was Cecilia. She looked perfectly heavenly as she sat on her white donkey in midstream, but I was thankful when with a smile she wished me goodbye. I felt rather like a beggar by the wayside when the good Samaritan passed his way.

Pattison's party attacked by lion at Mbuyuni

Soon after I arrived at Voi Pattison turned up and told me that his bullock caravan was attacked by lion at Mbuyuni the night after I was there. Two of his beasts were killed, but the lion escaped untouched.

To Mombasa

I shall go to Mombasa by this evening's train. I found Col. Harrison was travelling up to Nairobi this afternoon, and I saw him and reported progress. He was much amused at my meeting Cudenhove and securing his papers. These I have now cursorily examined. They contain an excellent manuscript map of the Voi–Taveta road across the Serengeti Plains, with detailed maps of Taveta, Salaita, Mbuyuni, Bura, Mwataate and Maktau. His maps are done in much greater detail than mine and he clearly spent much time and trouble on them. They are obviously of a military nature, for he deals throughout for two contingencies, one a patrol of 50 men, and another a force of 500. Taken in conjunction with my work they form a complete military reconnaissance of the route. His notes are most detailed and valuable. His criticisms on the possibilities of invading German East from Voi, and vice versa of invading British East via Taveta, not only agree generally with my conclusions but are most illuminating.

I examine Cudenhove's papers

I am more than glad that I have secured them, as such information in the hands of a potential foe would be dangerous. I shall attach this independent opinion to my report, and it should amuse the War Office, if such a body is capable of a smile.

[This reconnaissance of the Voi–Taveta road was of the greatest value to us in 1916, when Smuts advanced along it; the War Office printed my map and report and it was distributed to troops by my Intelligence Section.]

29 . IV . 1906. *Mombasa*

Mombasa

I reached the coast early this morning, having travelled from Voi with Gorges. Bowring is kindly putting me up. Hartley (formerly of my regiment) and Moon are

G. L. Barlow

passing through on their way upcountry for a shoot. I also met my old friend Barlow, who has just arrived from British Central Africa with a draft for the 1st King's African Rifles.

30 . IV . 1906. *Mombasa*

Dinner party at Bowring's

Bowring gave a dinner party this evening at which were present Mr. and Mrs. Coombe, Mrs. Clutterbuck, Stanley of the railways, my old Fort Hall friend Ronald Humphery, and myself. Mrs. Clutterbuck told me a good story which she declared to be true. Her husband wounded an old bull elephant near Molo on the Mau Plateau but failed to recover him that day. On the following day they found that he had wandered off to a small stream, and in his efforts to get water had sunk down and died actually in the bed of the watercourse. The stream was thus dammed, but instead of the water rising and flowing over the carcass it found for itself a new course underground and now flows for over a mile in this fashion. The carcass has since disappeared, but the stream still persists underground.

The elephant and the river

1 . V . 1906. *Mombasa*

My dinner party

I gave a small dinner party at the Mombasa Club this evening to which I invited Bowring, Gorges, Monson (with whom I was at Aysgarth in 1887) and Humphery.

4 . V . 1906. *Uganda Railway*

Mombasa society

Yesterday I lunched with Gorges at the Club and in the evening attended a dance given by the Turnbulls. I dislike such functions and, soon becoming bored, came home to bed.

To Nairobi

I started back to Nairobi today. Among my fellow passengers is the Duke of the Abbruzzi, who is travelling to Uganda in order to attempt the ascent of Ruwenzori. I had a long talk with him, mainly about his Polar expeditions. I like him. He also spoke to me a good deal about the Italian navy, which he insisted was second best in the world. He complained that Italians were not such

Duke of the Abbruzzi

good sailors or such good marksmen as Englishmen. It was these two characters which prevented the Italian navy equalling ours in excellence.

I saw little game from the train. I managed to photograph a flock of cock ostriches as they bolted over the plains at our approach. Zebra and haartebeeste were plentiful, but the smaller gazelle were conspicuous by their absence. I think the grass is too dry at this time of year and they have all moved elsewhere. I have noted a regular migration among the larger antelope, and mean to publish the results of my notes when I have got more complete data. The springbok of South Africa and the bison of America had distinct periodic migrations, and the movements of these African antelope will be of great interest.

Game

5 . V . 1906. *Nairobi*

I arrived at Nairobi this morning. On my reporting to the orderly room Harrison told me that the Colonial Office have written out stating that they have carefully considered the circumstances relating to the death of the Nandi Laibon, and that while believing in the good faith which prompted me to undertake on my own responsibility to endeavour to seize or kill the Laibon are of the opinion that this action has resulted in the reputation of the British Government for fair dealing and honesty being called in question, and consider it undesirable that I should continue to serve in East Africa.

I am ordered to England

I am therefore to go home as soon as possible.

In the first place, I did not on my own responsibility endeavour to kill or capture the Laibon. I received very definite instructions to do so from Pope Hennessey. In the second place, I have been cleared by a public court of enquiry of all imputations of foul play. Neither Harrison nor I can understand the document. However, one thing is clear, that I must go home at once, where perhaps I shall discover what is meant by this cryptic letter.

Meanwhile I asked Harrison if I could see the Commissioner, Hayes Sadler. After a lot of trouble he consented to see me. It was obvious that he did not wish to face an interview with me. I asked him if I could be

Our Commissioner, Hayes Sadler (he was known in Kenya as Flannelfoot)

given an explanation of the letter from the Colonial Office and if I could see his letter to which this was the reply. He refused even to discuss the subject. I told him that I thought it grossly unfair that I should have things written about me to the Colonial Office and should not have a chance of answering them, that I had been cleared by three courts of enquiry, and that if he was still not satisfied, he should have told me so. He neither looked me in the face nor gave me any coherent reply.

Fred Jackson

I saw Frederick Jackson, the Deputy Commissioner, who told me privately that I should gain nothing by worrying Hayes Sadler; he thought I was being scandalously treated but advised me to go straight home, where I should get justice and sympathy from the War Office. That has cheered me up. I am glad to be going home, but not in this fashion. But it is no use worrying, and I shall dismiss the matter from my mind till I get to London.

Jackson also told me that Harrison had sent in his despatch on the Nandi operations to Hayes Sadler and that I had been recommended for the D.S.O., but that the Governor had insisted that my name be removed. Jackson rather let himself go when he said, "I thought that particularly mean."

7 . v . 1906. *Nairobi*

Wild dogs in coition

How seldom have I seen wild mammals in coition. I have read somewhere an account of wild elephants having been seen; but how many of us have seen the commoner British mammals—badger, fox, weasel, stoat, hedgehog or squirrel? I never have, nor have I ever seen any big game of Africa copulating before today, when I came across two wild dogs, back to back and hopelessly anchored. I approached quite close, when they commenced to whine and whimper but they could not get away. I might easily have shot them both but thought it would be taking an unfair advantage, so left them. This occurred at the south end of the Ngong Hills in the very early morning with a dense ground fog.

And why should dogs be the only mammal to suffer such a disadvantage, for it exposes them to attack when they can neither flee nor protect themselves. I believe it is a muscle in the female which grasps the male organ and prevents withdrawal until complete relaxation occurs.

11 . v . 1906. *Nairobi*

A parting shoot

Mackay, de Crespigny and I enjoyed ourselves today on the Athi Plains. We did not see much game, but we shot several lesser bustard, making some good shooting from our ponies as the birds rose.

12 . v . 1906. *Uganda Railway*

To Nandi

Before leaving the country I must hand over my company to Hart at Nandi, so I left Nairobi today for that place. I must also collect my kit.

Dundas, Collyer and Lawson

At Naivasha, where I dined, I met young Dundas, who was on column with me during the Nandi Expedition, also Collyer, who has recently been transferred from Taveta to Rumeruti, a new station on Laikipia, and Lawson, whom I have not seen since 1904, when we were stationed together at Fort Hall. They were all very disgusted by the treatment meted out to me and showed me every sympathy. They share with me some pretty strong views about Hayes Sadler.

13 . v . 1906. *Nandi Fort*

Back at Nandi

I arrived at Kibigori at 7.30 a.m. and, finding porters and escort awaiting me, came straight on, reaching my old home at noon.

My second-in-command

I found my second-in-command living in the most squalid conditions. He had no cook, his uniform was filthy, he was unshaved, and the house had not been touched since I left some weeks ago. He grumbled that he had nothing to do. Just at the present moment there is an enormous amount of work to be done up here, which he has purposely neglected, thinking he was only to be here temporarily. He has not been near the company and in fact is guilty of gross negligence. If I had the power I should remove him from the country as entirely unfitted to command native troops.

Neither has he taken any interest in my garden, which I took such pains to restore. Everything is again ruined. It has not been that he has not had the time. His fault is that he has no energy. He is hopelessly sapped by his habits. He now says he hates soldiering, and that his one ambition is to avoid anything which may cause his brain to work. What a pity he ever joined the army, and what a pity he does not leave it. Much better for him and the service he disgraces. He has not ceased to grumble since I arrived, and I have told him that I consider him to be a hopeless rotter. He didn't even mind that, so low is his self-respect.

Young trees

I brought with me a number of young eucalyptus trees, which I planted with due ceremony in an avenue on the south side of the Civil Boma. Some day they will be a fine show. I tried to get a better tree, but Nairobi had nothing suitable. It seems they cannot think beyond eucalyptus and wattle.

[These also have grown into huge forest trees; I saw them in 1956.]

17 . V . 1906. *Nandi*

I try to secure photographs of some Nandi girls

As there were lots of gaily dressed Nandi girls in the market place this morning I asked some of them to come up and be photographed. They gladly came and stood in a row in front of my house. Unfortunately one of my officers came out of the house at that instant carrying a huge camera and a stand. Its dimensions were more those of a machine gun than of a camera. The poor ladies panicked and fled in all directions, some crawling under my house, others rushing into the barbed-wire fence and others prostrating themselves at my feet imploring mercy. I soon convinced them that all was well, but had to crawl under my house after one damsel, who insisted on clutching me round the neck, which was embarrassing. They told me that they thought they were going to be killed and eaten.

Nandi girls' superstition that white men eat them

It is a curious fact that most Nandi women think that Europeans eat Nandi girls. I think the idea started when some years ago Dr. Mann of Kisumu, under whose care

One of the gum trees I planted 50 years ago as a small tree 18 inches high

a Nandi girl died, held a post-mortem examination in the mortuary and took some anatomical specimens home with him for diagnosis at his leisure. This was observed by some of the dead girl's friends, who at once jumped to the conclusion that the mortuary was Mann's private larder and that a particularly delicate morsel was being taken home for the evening meal.

When these girls had quite done screaming and had recovered their composure I sent down to the nearest chief and asked him to bring up to my house some of his village beauty to be photographed, in order to show the rest of the girls that we intended no harm. Several girls soon arrived, including my three late servants, and these soon restored confidence. Eventually they allowed me to take what photos I wished.

Packing up

I spent the afternoon packing up, which I always detest. It is always rather sad leaving a place after such a long time, and I have collected lots of rubbish during my stay in Nandi. There are also my natural history collections. My bird skins demanded a lot of care and should now travel well. I also have some small snakes with legs, about which my friends are so sceptical. They are in spirit and I am most anxious to get them home. Then I have a lot of botanical specimens, including a box of giant maidenhair fern, lilies of many kinds, and some small plants of which I do not know the name. The risk and trouble of taking all these fragile things home are great. They are articles which an African native delights in smashing, especially if he knows they are of any interest or value. What with the vagaries of the Uganda railway, the heat and damp of Mombasa, the dishonest and inquisitive stewards on a French ship, French railways, customs houses, and lastly the London cab, I almost despair of getting my collections safely home.

Snakes with legs

18 . v . 1906. *Muhoroni*

I leave Nandi for the last time

I left Nandi Fort for the last time and arrived at Kibigori about noon. I hated saying goodbye to my company. Many of them had tears in their eyes. At Kibigori I found a goods train going to Muhoroni, so I boarded it and

Friends at Muhoroni

came on here, where I met Walker, Wilson, Swire, Mostyn, and two doctors called Chevalier and Connell. Smallpox is now rampant in the district. All my friends expressed their great regret at my leaving, and it was great comfort to me that they should have shown their sympathy.

I leave this evening for Nairobi by a passenger train, travelling with Mr. V. Shaw Kennedy and Capts. Macleod and Rawlings of the Uganda Rifles.

19 . V . 1906. *Nairobi*

My legged snakes

In the course of conversation with Shaw Kennedy I mentioned my snakes with legs. He at once ridiculed the idea, so we had a small wager that if I could produce a snake with legs he would pay for my breakfast at Naivasha. So I unpacked my spirit bottles and produced three specimens. Shaw Kennedy was much surprised and paid for my breakfast to the extent of 8 eggs. We arrived at Nairobi at noon.

23 . V . 1906. *Nairobi*

Am entertained by the King's African Rifles

Last night a terrific dinner was given to me by the officers of the 3rd and 4th K.A.R. Both Gorges and Harrison were there and some 20 other officers, besides several friends of mine from the Administration, police and railways. We sat down 38 to dinner; buckets of champagne and later a rag.

My disagreeable friend Unwin and another rather unpleasant fellow called Younghusband, both in the 4th K.A.R., had given out that they intended to "put me down a peg." Now Unwin weighs at least two stone heavier than I do and Younghusband at least a stone. After dinner we started a rag. Unwin upset my chair, so I collared him by the legs and he went down like a bullock, smashed his nose and left the room bleeding like a pig. Then Younghusband joined in the fray and bent down to tackle my legs, but I lifted my knee full on to his face and he had to retire with a broken nose; everyone roared with laughter. And this morning when I went round to apologise for my roughness I found them both in bed, very surly and disinclined to accept an apology, so I left a note to each giving them a little advice about keeping fit. After all, I was their guest and they had no right to set upon me.

27 . v . 1906. *Mombasa*

Leave Nairobi and arrive Mombasa

Leaving Nairobi for the last time on the 25th I arrived at Mombasa yesterday, and am stopping with Bowring.

I had a most touching send-off from Nairobi and was quite choked with unspoken thanks. All the K.A.R. officers came to the station, except Unwin and Younghusband, many railway officers and my friend Ainsworth; also Frederick Jackson, who whispered to me, "I shall get into trouble for this." And as the train drew out of the station the K.A.R. band did their best with Auld Lang Syne, under their Goanese bandmaster. This all gave me a terrible lump in the throat, and tears came to my eyes as I left behind me so many good friends.

I organise a game drive

Having nothing to do today I hired ten stalwart natives and systematically beat out several patches of bush on the island. There was a good deal of stuff there, but the bush was so thick I could never get a shot at it. I saw altogether 3 bush pig and 2 small antelope. I secured one of the small antelope, which proves to be the Grave Island gazelle, originally described from Zanzibar. The pig is the bush pig.

This will be my last shoot in East Africa.

Game census

I counted game on the south side of the railway between Nairobi and Stony Athi: 14 eland, 5 giraffe, 2 rhino, 486 zebra, 745 Coke's haartebeeste, 456 wildebeeste, 87 impala, 224 Grant's gazelle, 88 Thomson's gazelle, 7 warthog, 36 ostrich, 7 great bustard.

28 . v . 1906. *At sea off Mombasa*

I embark for England

I embarked today on the Messageries Maritimes ship *Natal* bound for Marseilles. We are full to overflowing with women and children from Madagascar.

That finished my second tour in East Africa. I fear it is marked by continuous violence and the slaughter of my fellow men and wild animals. Well, that was our life in those early days. It was a good school for wars to come, and gave me experiences which proved profitable later on; but I am still shocked at the cost.

On arrival in London I drafted a letter to the War Office asking for an interview with the Army Council or Adjutant General, so that I might state my case personally and get an explanation why I was withdrawn from East Africa.

On 17 July I received a letter from the Secretary to the Army Council which ended: "Looking, however, at the measure of doubt as to the exact sequence of events, the Army Council have decided to attribute to Captain Meinertzhagen nothing more than an error of judgement."

I also received a letter from the Adjutant General asking me to report to the War Office on the following day. This I did, and on 18 July I entered in my dairy:

"After lunch I kept an appointment at the War Office. After a brief interview with one of the A.G.'s staff I was ushered into Haldane's room. [Lord Haldane was then Secretary of State for War and a great friend of my uncle Sidney Webb.] I found him most kind and sympathetic. He patiently listened to my story and then told me outright that owing to the Colonial Office having taken such an extraordinary view of my case the War Office had no alternative but to write me their official letter. He congratulated me on my initiative and expressed the greatest sympathy for me. He told me that if it had not been for the Colonial Office's attitude the Army Council would have treated the recommendation for the Victoria Cross with consideration, but to do so now would be a gratuitous insult to the Colonial Office. He added that the Army Council had much appreciated my work in Africa and that a note had been made in my Record of Service that none of this wretched business would count against me as far as the War Office was concerned."

* * * *

After I left the Colony Mayes continued to spread his poison, pointing to my removal as proof of my guilt; even as late as 1956 the killing of the Nandi Laibon by me is still quoted as an act of unpardonable treachery.

I have made every effort to see the despatch which Hayes Sadler sent to the Colonial Office and which led to my withdrawal from East Africa. Though public documents are usually available after fifty years, this particular one has been held up for some reason.

* * * *

On the death of my father in 1910 I found the following two letters among his papers:

Nairobi, 25 . v . 1906

Dear Mr. Meinertzhagen,

Your son is leaving us very suddenly and in a sort of way, under a cloud. I cannot explain the matter to you at length but he has copies of all the papers regarding this unfortunate business; he will explain these to you personally and it only remains for me to assure you that all his brother officers including myself are absolutely satisfied that he acted in good faith and to tell you how sincerely sorry we all are to lose him from the battalion. As a further proof of this I can only add that as Officer Commanding the Nandi Field Force, I mentioned him in despatches and recommended him for reward; also, in his confidential report for the year I reported on him as the best Company Commander in the Battalion. From the above it will show you in what high estimation we hold him and what a loss he will be to us.

Yours sincerely,

Edgar Harrison

Nairobi, 25 . v . 1906

Dear Sir,

I have not the pleasure of your acquaintance though I have the pleasure of knowing your son and therefore trust you may excuse me in writing to you. He will explain to you why he is going home and all the circumstances connected with his case. What I wish to say is that you need have no misgivings concerning your son's conduct which throughout a somewhat trying period has been that of a good soldier and an honourable English Gentleman. He leaves this country regretted by all his brother officers and though I am not his Commanding Officer, he may be sure of my active support should he need it.

I remain,

Yours truly,

E. H. Gorges, Lt. Col.

Commanding 1st Battn. King's Afr. Rifles

APPENDIX I

Some Weights and Measurements of Large Mammals

Accurate weights of larger mammals have for some time been a matter of discussion and speculation. Menagerie animals are scarcely a fair test, and those sportsmen who weigh only their larger beasts give us an entirely false estimate of the average weight. In the following tables it will be seen that weights and measurements fall below those usually given, the reason being that though all my beasts were believed to be fully adult, they were not selected for size and were just weighed and measured as they came. They represent a fair average animal of each species.

All weights were taken in the field, always within a few minutes of death. The machine used was a steelyard specially made for me by Avery and took a single weight of 800 lb. The yard was rigged with block and tackle on to a portable tripod the apex of which was 8½ ft. from the ground. The whole apparatus weighed 58 lb., a complete carrier's load.

A few animals weighed over 800 lb. In that case they were cut into portions and weighed piecemeal, blood and offal being collected in a groundsheet and weighed separately.

Weights taken several hours after death in the tropics or after the viscera have been removed are not reliable. Neither can weights taken with a spring balance be relied on. They have a large and often daily range of error. Rust, heat and cold, previous strain, and rough usage all contribute towards inaccurate results.

Measurements were taken in a straight line between pegs. For length a peg was placed at the nose and another at the tip of the tail, the beast was removed and the distance between pegs taken with a steel tape. The shoulder measurement was taken similarly between pegs placed at the withers and the heel of the foreleg.

Reprinted from the *Proceedings of the Zoological Society of London*, 1938, Vol. 108, part III, by kind permission of the Society.

All the following were shot, weighed and measured by me personally.

Tiger: *Panthera tigris*

Sex	*Locality*	*Length* *ft.*	*in.*	*Shoulder height* *in.*	*Weight* *pounds*
♂	Nilgiri Hills	10	4	41	498
♂	Mysore	9	6	40	454

Leopard: *Panthera pardus*

		ft.	*in.*	*in.*	*pounds*
♀	Nilgiri Hills	7	2	25	129
♂	Mysore	7	4	24	142
♂	Kenya	7	5	25	137
♂	Kenya	6	10	28	131
♀	Kenya	6	5	25½	98
♀	Kenya	6	7	23	129
♂	Kenya	7	10	24	139
♂	Kenya	6	11	26	134
♂	Kenya	6	7	25	144

Lion: *Panthera leo*

		ft.	*in.*	*in.*	*pounds*
♂	Kenya	8	6	36	329
♀	Kenya	7	11	34½	269
♂	Kenya	8	7½	35½	376
♂	Kenya	9	1	38	384
♂	Kenya	9	4	39	379
♀	Kenya	7	11	34	269
♂	Kenya	8	10½	35¾	389
♂	Kenya	9	4	41	406
♂	Kenya	9	4	42	418
♀	Kenya	8	10	39	409
♂	Kenya	9	0	40	396
♂	Kenya	8	6	40	421
♀	Kenya	8	4	40	369
♂	Kenya	8	8	38	346
♂	Kenya	9	3	40	410
♂	Kenya	8	11	39	381
♀	Kenya	8	9	34	349
♂	Kenya	8	1	32	386
♂	Kenya	9	0	34	399

Cheetah: *Acinonyx jubatus*

Sex	*Locality*	*Length* *ft. in.*	*Shoulder height* *in.*	*Weight* *pounds*
♀	Kenya	7 9	33	139
♂	Kenya	7 4	30	136
♂	Kenya	6 7	29	127
♂	Kenya	7 0	32	143
♂	Kenya	6 11	31	129

Serval Cat: *Leptailurus serval*

		in.	*in.*	*pounds*
♂	Kenya	41	19	22
♀	Kenya	40	19	24
♀	Kenya	39	19	23
♂	Kenya	43	20	26
♂	Kenya	44	21	—
♀	Kenya	43	20	27

Rhinoceros: *Diceros bicornis*

		ft. in.	*in.*	*pounds*
♀	Kenya	11 2	61	2812
♂	Kenya	11 4	63½	2896
♀	Kenya	11 0	62	2274
♂	Kenya	11 6	61	2606
♂	Kenya	11 8½	63	2461
♀	Kenya	10 10	58½	2274
♀	Kenya	10 8	60	2199
♂	Kenya	11 2	62½	2364
♂	Kenya	11 7	59	2617
♂	Kenya	11 1	60	2471
♂	Kenya	11 6	63	2382
♂	Kenya	11 8	65	2512
♀	Kenya	11 8	59	2341
♂	Kenya	11 1	62	2672
♂	Kenya	10 11	61	2691
♂	Kenya	11 1	64	2571

Hippopotamus: *Hippopotamus amphibius*

		ft. in.	*in.*	*pounds*
♂	Kenya	13 4	64	5641
♂	Kenya	12 3	61	5461
♂	Kenya	14 6	—	5267
♀	Kenya	12 10	—	4901
♀	Kenya	13 1	58	5174
♂	Kenya	15 4	65½	5872
♀	Kenya	10 11	56	3994

Spotted Hyaena: *Crocuta crocuta*

Sex	*Locality*	*Length* *in.*	*Shoulder height* *in.*	*Weight* *pounds*
♂	Kenya	62	34	148
♂	Kenya	$62\frac{1}{2}$	35	139
♂	Kenya	64	36	161
♂	Kenya	59	33	129
♂	Kenya	61	36	168
♂	Kenya	63	35	141

Indian Wild Pig: *Sus cristatus*

		in.	*in.*	*pounds*
3 ♂♂	Rajputana	67–70	27–30	227, 246, 304

Johnstone's Bush Pig: *Potamochoerus choeropotamus nyasae*

		ft. in. ft. in.	*in.*	*pounds*
2 ♂♂	Nyasaland	4 9 to 4 11	26–27	169, 192

Bush Pig: *Potamochoerus choeropotamus keniae*

		ft. in. ft. in.	*in.*	*pounds*
4 ♂♂	Kenya	4 6 to 4 10	27–29	164–231
1 ♀	Kenya	4 8	26	199

Forest Hog: *Hylochoerus m. meinertzhageni*

		ft. in.	*in.*	*pounds*
♂	Kenya	6 5	$37\frac{3}{4}$	329

Wart Hog: *Phacochoerus aethiopicus*

		ft. in. ft. in.	*in.*	*pounds*
18 ♂♂	Kenya	5 2 to 5 10	29–32	155–234
6 ♀♀	Kenya	4 11 to 5 2	26–31	123–149

Grant's Zebra: *Equus quagga granti*

		ft. in. ft. in.	*in.*	*pounds*
5 ♂♂	Kenya	8 2 to 8 10	44–48	675–713

Giraffe: *Giraffa camelopardalis*

		ft. in.	*ft. in.*	
♂	Kenya	14 6	9 8	—
♂	Kenya	12 7	8 2	—

From the base of horn to forefoot these beasts measured 17 ft. 8 in. and 16 ft. 11 in. respectively.

Indian Bison: *Bibos gaurus*

Sex	*Locality*	*Length*	*Shoulder height*	*Weight*
		ft. in.	*in.*	*pounds*
♂	Mysore	11 7	69	1720
♂	Mysore	12 0	71	1870
♀	Mysore	11 0	62	1546

African Buffalo: *Syncerus caffer*

		ft. in.	*in.*	*pounds*
♂	Kenya	10 0	62	1496
♂	Kenya	10 4	58	1546
♂	Nyasaland	9 7	59	1702
♂	Nyasaland	9 9	66	1668
♂	Kenya	9 11	60	1841
♂	Kenya	10 4	64	1674

Chinkhara: *Gazella bennettii*

		in.	*in.*	*pounds*
8 ♂♂	Rajputana	49–50	24–27	46–52
1 ♀	Rajputana	48	23	41

Thomson's Gazelle: *Gazelle thomsoni*

		in.	*in.*	*pounds*
39 ♂♂	Kenya	45–51	24–28	41–63
1 ♀	Kenya	43	23	41

Blackbuck: *Antilope cervicapra*

		in.	*in.*	*pounds*
21 ♂♂	Rajputana	49–58	29–33	77–94
2 ♀♀	Rajputana	51–54	27–28	71–85

Springbok: *Antidorcas marsupialis*

			in.	
9 ♂♂	Cape Colony	—	29–32	—

Waller's Gazelle: *Lithocranius walleri*

		in.	*in.*	*pounds*
3 ♂♂	Kenya	61–63	38–41	91–115

Grant's Gazelle: *Gazella granti*

		in.	*in.*	*pounds*
20 ♂♂	Kenya	72–75	37–40	162–180
3 ♀♀	Kenya	66–69	35–37	99–134

Peter's Gazelle: G. *granti petersi*

Sex	*Locality*	*Length* *in.*	*Shoulder height* *in.*	*Weight* *pounds*
4 ♂♂	Kenya	59–64	35–36½	128–140
2 ♀♀	Kenya	58	33–34	81–86

Coke's Haartebeeste: *Bubalis cokei*

		in.	*in.*	*pounds*
30 ♂♂	Kenya	83–91	44–50	286–378

Nakuru Haartebeeste: *B. cokei nakurae*

		in.	*in.*	*pounds*
11 ♂♂	Kenya	88–97	45–53	350–399
2 ♀♀	Kenya	87–93	45–46	349–350

Jackson's Haartebeeste: *Bubalis lelwel jacksoni*

		in.	*in.*	*pounds*
14 ♂♂	Kenya	89–96	51–55	431–482
2 ♀♀	Kenya	87–88	47–49	392–402

Lichtenstein's Haartebeeste: *B. lichtensteini*

		in.	*in.*	*pounds*
7 ♂♂	Nyasaland	91–96	51–54	294–310
1 ♀	N.W. Rhodesia	88	49	261

Blesbok: *Damaliscus albifrons*

			in.	*pounds*
2 ♂♂	Orange River Colony	—	41–42	201–219
1 ♀	Orange River Colony	—	40	190

Topi Antelope: *Damaliscus korrigum jimela*

		in.	*in.*	*pounds*
10 ♂♂	Kenya	81–88	45–50	282–334
1 ♀	Kenya	78	44	261

Blue Wildebeeste: *Gorgon taurinus albojubatus*

		in.	*in.*	*pounds*
14 ♂♂	Kenya	90–94	50–55	506–574
1 ♀	Kenya	91	54	588

Nyasaland Wildebeeste: *Gorgon taurinus johnstoni*

Sex	*Locality*	*Length* *in.*	*Shoulder height* *in.*	*Weight* *pounds*
♂	Nyasaland	90	56	602

White-tailed Gnu: *Connochoetes gnu*

Three ♂♂ measured 45, 45, and 46 at the withers.

Sable Antelope: *Hippotragus niger*

		in.	*in.*	*pounds*
♂	N.W. Rhodesia	99	51½	527
♀	N.W. Rhodesia	91	47½	488
♂	Nyasaland	94	50	501
♂	Nyasaland	100	52	524

Roan Antelope: *Hippotragus equinus*

		ft. in.	*in.*	
♂	Kenya	8 8	62	—
♂	Kenya	8 11	63	—
♂	N.W. Rhodesia	8 7½	62	—
♂	N.W. Rhodesia	8 8	61	—
♀	N.W. Rhodesia	8 2	58	—

Eland: *Taurotragus oryx*

		ft. in.	*in.*	*pounds*
♂	Kenya	10 4	61	1604
♂	Kenya	10 2	62	1746
♂	Kenya	10 0	68	—
♂	Nyasaland	10 6	65	2078
♂	Kenya	10 9	64	1969
♂	Kenya	10 8	62	—

Nyala: *Tragelaphus angasi*

			in.	*pounds*
♂	Nyasaland	—	43	252
♂	Nyasaland	—	44	269

Bushbuck: *Tragelaphus scriptus* ? subsp.

		in.	*in.*	*pounds*
14 ♂♂	Kenya	58–64	31–38	139–182
1 ♀	Kenya	55	29	131

Oryx: *Oryx beisa*

Sex	*Locality*	*Length* *in.*	*Shoulder height* *in.*	*Weight* *pounds*
2 ♀♀	Kenya	80–82	46	366, 399

Fringe-eared Oryx: *Oryx beisa callotis*

		in.	*in.*	*pounds*
3 ♀♀	Kenya	87–93	46½–48	419–469
1 ♀	Kenya	84	46	402

Greater Kudu: *Strepsiceras strepsiceras*

			ft. in. ft. in.	*pounds*
3 ♂♂	Nyasaland	—	4 7 to 4 9	584–604

Uganda Kob: *Kobus kob*

		in.	*in.*	*pounds*
5 ♂♂	Kenya	72–80	37–39	229–268

Lechwe: *Kobus leche*

		ft. in.	*in.*	
♂	N.W. Rhodesia	6 8	44	—

Puku: *Kobus vardoni*

		ft. in. ft. in.	*in.*	
4 ♂♂	N.W. Rhodesia	5 8 to 6 2	31–35½	—

Common Waterbuck: *Kobus ellipsiprymnus*

		ft. in. ft. in.	*in.*	*pounds*
24 ♂♂	Kenya	7 5 to 8 2	41–50	475–599

Sing-sing Waterbuck: *Kobus depassa*

		ft. in. ft. in.	*in.*	*pounds*
21 ♂♂	Kenya	7 10 to 8 3	47–58	489–599

Common Reedbuck: *Eleotragus arundinum*

		in.	*in.*	*pounds*
8 ♂♂	Rhodesia, Nyasaland	63–67	36–37	146–171

Bohor Reedbuck: *Redunca redunca* ? subsp.

Sex	*Locality*	*Length*	*Shoulder height*	*Weight*
		in.	*in.*	*pounds*
8 ♂♂	Kenya	55–60	32–35	106–122
1 ♀	Kenya	51	30	—

Chanler's Reedbuck: *Redunca fulvorufula chanleri*

		in.	*in.*	*pounds*
12 ♂♂	Kenya	53–59	29–33	69–78
4 ♀♀	Kenya	49–51	28–29	56–63

Kenya Oribi: *Ourebia kenyae*

		in.	*in.*	*pounds*
11 ♂♂	Kenya	38–44	23–36	36–40
1 ♀	Kenya	38	23	32

Abyssinian Oribi: *Ourebia gallarum*

		in.	*in.*	*pounds*
13 ♂♂	Kenya	39–44	23–24	37–47
1 ♀	Kenya	38	22	44

Klipspringer: *Oreotragus oreotragus*

		in.	*in.*	*pounds*
2 ♂♂	Kenya	38–42	24	36–37
1 ♀	Kenya	38	23	28

Grysbok: *Raphicerus melanotis*

			in.	*pounds*
2 ♂♂	Cape Colony	—	21–22	26–29

Common Duiker: *Sylvicapra grimmi*

		in.	*in.*	*pounds*
20 ♂♂	Kenya	33–40	19–23	24–30
2 ♀♀	Kenya	31–32	19–21	25–27

Steinbuck: *Raphicerus campestris*

		in.	*in.*	*pounds*
23 ♂♂	Kenya, S. Africa	29–35	19–23	24–32
4 ♀♀	Kenya	29–31	19–21	24–28

Cavendish's Dik-dik: *Rhynchotragus cavendishi*

Sex	*Locality*	*Length*	*Shoulder height* in.	*Weight* pounds
1 ♂	Kenya	—	13½	7
2 ♀♀	Kenya	—	13–13½	6–6¾

Livingstone's Antelope: *Neotragus livingstomanus*

		in.	*in.*	*pounds*
2 ♂♂	Nyasaland	27–28	15–15½	7¾–8

APPENDIX II

Speed of some African Animals

Species	*Locality*	*Ground speed m.p.h.*	*Remarks*
African elephant ..	Africa	24	Stop-watch over distance of 120 yards. (Lane, 1940. Field, 16 March.)
African rhinoceros ..	Kenya	28·35	By car speedometer (two counts).
	Kenya	32–35	Speedometer. Charging a car.
	Kenya	27·2	Trotting after a man.
Cheetah	London	44	Chasing an electric hare (three counts).
	Kenya	51	Pressed by car on road over 200 yards.
African wild dog ..	Uganda	38	Chased by car on road.
Giraffe	Kenya	24–26 18–21	Pressed by car. Cantering at ease.
Coke's haartebeeste ..	Kenya	37–38	Speedometer. Pressed by car.
Blue wildebeeste ..	Kenya	34	Speedometer. Pressed by car.
Black mamba ..	Kenya	7	Going full out.

Previously published by

ELAND BOOKS

TRAVELS WITH MYSELF AND ANOTHER

MARTHA GELLHORN

Must surely be ranked as one of the funniest travel books of our time — second only to *A Short Walk in the Hindu Kush* . . . It doesn't matter whether this author is experiencing marrow-freezing misadventures in war-ravaged China, or driving a Landrover through East African game-parks, or conversing with hippies in Israel, or spending a week in a Moscow Intourist Hotel. Martha Gellhorn's reactions are what count and one enjoys equally her blistering scorn of humbug, her hilarious eccentricities, her unsentimental compassion.
Dervla Murphy, Irish Times

Spun with a fine blend of irony and epigram. She is incapable of writing a dull sentence.
The Times

Miss Gellhorn has a novelist's eye, a flair for black comedy and a short fuse...there is not a boring word in her humane and often funny book.
The New York Times

Among the funniest and best written books I have ever read.
Byron Rogers, Evening Standard

THE CHANGING SKY

NORMAN LEWIS

Travels of a Novelist

He really goes in deep like a sharp polished knife. I have never travelled in my armchair so fast, variously and well.
V.S. Pritchett, New Statesman

He has compressed into these always entertaining and sophisticated sketches material that a duller man would have hoarded for half a dozen books.
The Times

A delightful, instructive, serious and funny book. Norman Lewis has the oblique poetry of a Firbank, the eye of a lynx.
Anthony Carson, The Observer

Previously published by

ELAND BOOKS

THE HONOURED SOCIETY

NORMAN LEWIS

The Sicilian Mafia Observed

New epilogue by Marcello Cimino

This book has not a dull moment in it; it is indeed imbued with that quality of *terribilita* which Giuliano himself was said to possess.
The Spectator

Mr Norman Lewis is one of the finest journalists of his time . . . he excels both in finding material and in evaluating it.
The Listener

It is deftly written, and every page is horribly absorbing.
The Times

The Honoured Society is the most penetrating book ever written on the Mafia.
Time Out

If you wish to receive details of forthcoming publications,
please send your address to
Eland Books, 53 Eland Road, London SW11 5JX

Previously published by

ELAND BOOKS

NAPLES '44

NORMAN LEWIS

As unique an experience for the reader as it must have been a unique experience for the writer.
Graham Greene

Uncommonly well written, entertaining despite its depressing content, and quite remarkably evocative.
Philip Toynbee, Observer

His ten novels and five non-fiction works place him in the front rank of contemporary English writers ... here is a book of gripping fascination in its flow of bizarre anecdote and character sketch; and it is much more than that.
J. W. Lambert, Sunday Times

A wonderful book.
Richard West, Spectator

Sensitive, ironic and intelligent.
Paul Fussell, The New Republic

One goes on reading page after page as if eating cherries.
Luigi Barzini, New York Review of Books

This edition is not for sale in the USA

Previously published by

ELAND BOOKS

JOURNEYS OF A GERMAN IN ENGLAND

CARL PHILIP MORITZ

A walking-tour of England in 1782

With a new preface by Reginald Nettel

The extraordinary thing about the book is that the writing is so fresh that you are startled when a stage-coach appears. A young man is addressing himself to you across two centuries. And there is a lovely comedy underlying it.
Byron Rogers, Evening Standard

This account of his travels has a clarity and freshness quite unsurpassed by any contemporary descriptions.
Iain Hamilton, Illustrated London News

A most amusing book...a variety of small scenes which might come out of Hogarth...Moritz in London, dodging the rotten oranges flung about the pit of the Haymarket Theatre, Moritz in the pleasure gardens of Vauxhall and Ranelagh, Moritz in Parliament or roving the London streets is an excellent companion. We note, with sorrow, that nearly two centuries ago, British coffee was already appalling.
Alan Pryce-Jones, New York Herald Tribune

Previously published by

ELAND BOOKS

TRAVELS INTO THE INTERIOR OF AFRICA

MUNGO PARK

With a new preface by Jeremy Swift

Famous triumphs of exploration have rarely engendered outstanding books. *Travels into the Interior of Africa*, which has remained a classic since its first publication in 1799, is a remarkable exception.

It was a wonder that he survived so long, and a still greater one that his diaries could have been preserved . . . what amazing reading they make today!
Roy Kerridge, Tatler

The enthusiasm and understanding which informs Park's writing is irresistible.
Frances Dickenson, Time Out

One of the greatest and most respected explorers the world has known, a man of infinite courage and lofty principles, and one who dearly loved the black African.
E. W. Bovill, the Niger Explored

Told with a charm and naivety in themselves sufficient to captivate the most fastidious reader...modesty and truthfulness peep from every sentence...for actual hardships undergone, for dangers faced, and difficulties overcome, together with an exhibition of virtues which make a man great in the rude battle of life, Mungo Park stands without a rival.
Joseph Thomson, author of Through Masailand